S0-BHR-531

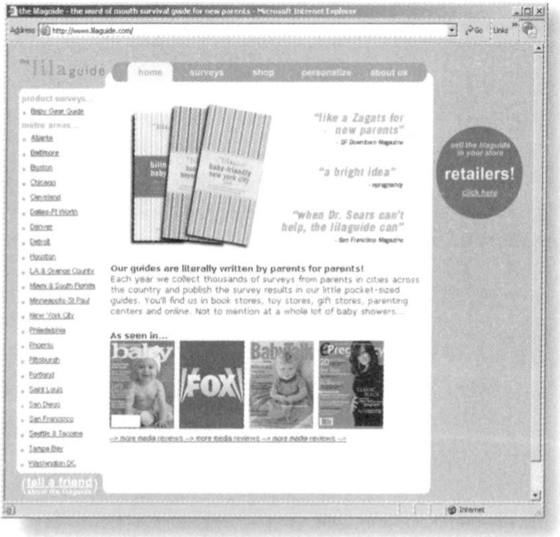

the lila guide

by PARENTS *for* PARENTS

baby-friendly chicago area

NEW PARENT SURVIVAL GUIDE TO SHOPPING, ACTIVITIES, RESTAURANTS AND MORE...

2ND EDITION

LOCAL EDITOR: TRICIA PONICKI

PUBLISHED BY THE LILAGUIDE/OAM SOLUTIONS, INC.
SAN FRANCISCO, CA   WWW.LILAGUIDE.COM

Published by:
OAM Solutions, Inc.
139 Saturn Street
San Francisco, CA 94114, USA
415.252.1300
orders@lilaguide.com
www.lilaguide.com

ISBN. 1-932847-14-6
First Printing: 2005
Printed in the USA

This book is designed to share parents' opinions regarding baby-related products, services and activities. It is sold with the understanding that the information contained in the book does not represent the publisher's opinion or recommendations. The reviews contained in this guide are based on public opinion surveys and are therefore subjective in nature. The publisher shall have neither liability nor responsibility to any person or entity with respect to any loss or damage caused, or alleged to have been caused, directly or indirectly, by the information contained in this book.

If you do not wish to be bound by the above, you may return this book to the publisher for a full refund.

table of contents

07 about the lilaguide
09 thank yous
10 disclaimer
11 how to use this book

Shopping
13 baby basics & accessories
91 maternity clothing

Fun & Entertainment
119 activities & outings
155 parks & playgrounds
167 restaurants

Health & Support
203 doulas & lactation consultants
205 exercise
215 parent education & support
223 pediatricians

Other Necessities
229 breast pump sales & rentals
233 diaper delivery services
235 haircuts
239 nanny & babysitter referrals
243 photographers

indexes
252 alphabetical
257 by city/neighborhood

No, for the last time, the baby does not come with a handbook. And even if there were a handbook, you wouldn't read it. You'd fill out the warranty card, throw out the box, and start playing right away. Until a few hours passed and you were hit with the epiphany of, "Gee whiz honey, what in the wide, wide world of childcare are we doing here?"

Relax. We had that panicked thought when we had our daughter Delilah. And so did **all the parents** we talked to when they had their children. And while we all knew there was no handbook, there was, we found, a whole lot of **word-of-mouth information**. Everyone we talked to had some bit of child rearing advice about what baby gear store is the most helpful. Some **nugget of parenting wisdom** about which restaurant tolerates strained carrots on the floor. It all really seemed to help. Someone, we thought, should write this down.

And that's when, please pardon the pun, the lilaguide was born. The book you're now holding is a guide **written by local parents for local parents**. It's what happens when someone actually does write it down (and organizes it, calculates it, and presents it in an easy-to-use format).

Nearly 5,300 surveys have produced this first edition of **the lilaguide: Baby-Friendly Chicago Area**. It provides a truly unique insider's view of over 1,400 "parent-friendly" stores, activities, restaurants, and service providers that are about to become a very big part of your life. And while this guide won't tell you how to change a diaper or how to get by on little or no sleep (that's what grandparents are for), it will tell you what other **local parents have learned** about the amazing things your city and neighborhood have to offer.

As you peruse these reviews, please remember that this guide is **not intended to be a comprehensive directory** since it does not contain every baby store or activity in the area. Rather, it is intended to provide a short-list of places that your neighbors and friends **deemed exciting and noteworthy**. If a place or business is not listed, it simply means that nobody (or not enough people) rated or submitted information about it to us. **Please let us know** about your favorite parent and baby-friendly businesses and service providers by participating in our online survey at **www.lilaguide.com**. We always want your opinions!

So there you have it. Now go make some phone calls, clean up the house, take a nap, or do something on your list before the baby arrives.

Enjoy!

Oli & Elysa

Oli Mittermaier & Elysa Marco, MD

PS

We love getting feedback (good and bad) so don't be bashful. Email us at **lila@lilaguide.com** with your thoughts, comments and suggestions. We'll be sure to try to include them in next year's edition!

thank yous

We'd like to take a moment to offer a heart-felt thank you to all the **parents who participated in our survey** and took the time to share their thoughts and opinions. Without your participation, we would never have been able to create this unique guide.

Thanks to our extra helpful Chicago area contributors **Jo Ann Haller**, **Ann Johnson**, **Ashley Koerting**, and **Mellissa McCloskey** for going above and beyond in the quest for hip tot spots.

Thanks also to **Lisa Barnes**, **Nora Borowsky**, **Todd Cooper**, **Amy Iannone**, **Katy Jacobson**, **Felicity John Odell**, **Shira Johnson**, **Kasia Kappes**, **Jen Krug**, **Dana Kulvin**, **Deborah Schneider**, **Kevin Schwall**, **April Stewart**, and **Nina Thompson** for their tireless editorial eyes, **Satoko Furuta** and **Paul D. Smith** for their beautiful sense of design, and **Lane Foard** for making the words yell.

Special thanks to **Paul D. Smith**, **Ken Miles**, and **Ali Wing** for their consistent support and overall encouragement in all things lilaguide, and of course **our parents** for their unconditional support in this and all our other endeavors.

And last, but certainly not least, thanks to **little Delilah** for inspiring us to embark on this challenging, yet incredibly fulfilling project.

disclaimer

This book is designed to share parents' opinions regarding baby-related products, services and activities. It is sold with the understanding that the information contained in the book **does not represent the publisher's opinion** or recommendations.

The reviews contained in this guide are based on **public opinion surveys** and are therefore subjective in nature. The publisher shall have neither liability nor responsibility to any person or entity with respect to any loss or damage caused, or alleged to have been caused, directly or indirectly, by the information contained in this book.

ratings

Most listings have stars and numbers as part of their write-up. These symbols mean the following:

❺ / ★★★★★	extraordinary
❹ / ★★★★☆	very good
❸ / ★★★☆☆	good
❷ / ★★☆☆☆	fair
❶ / ★☆☆☆☆	poor
✓	available
✗	not available/relevant

If a ★ is listed instead of ★, it means that the rating is less reliable because a small number of parents surveyed the listing. Furthermore, if a listing has **no stars** or **criteria ratings**, it means that although the listing was rated, the number of surveys submitted was so low that we did not feel it justified an actual rating.

quotes & reviews

The quotes/reviews are taken directly from surveys submitted to us via our website (**www.lilaguide.com**). Other than spelling and minor grammatical changes, they come to you as they came to us. Quotes were selected based on how well they appeared to represent the collective opinions of the surveys submitted.

fact checking

We have contacted all of the businesses listed to verify their address and phone number, as well as to inquire about their hours, class schedules and web site information. Since some of this information may change after this guide has been printed, we appreciate you letting us know of any errors by notifying us via email at **lila@lilaguide.com**.

baby basics & accessories

City of Chicago

"lila picks"

- ★Barney's New York
- ★Galt Toys & Galt Baby
- ★Land of Nod
- ★My Child's Room
- ★Pottery Barn Kids
- ★Psychobaby
- ★The Right Start
- ★The T-Shirt Deli

A J Wright

"...it's like looking through racks of stuff that doesn't even sell at Ross or TJ Maxx... every now and then you will find something... really not all that interesting, a waste of time in my opinion... the prices are great, the clothes are name brand for a fraction of the cost..."

Furniture, Bedding & Decor	✗	$$	Prices
Gear & Equipment	✗	❸	Product availability
Nursing & Feeding	✗	❸	Staff knowledge
Safety & Babycare	✗	❸	Customer service
Clothing, Shoes & Accessories	✓	❷	Decor
Books, Toys & Entertainment	✗		

WWW.AJ-WRIGHT.COM

COLUMET HEIGHTS—1709 E 95TH ST (AT S STONEY ISLAND EXT); 773.731.3360; M-SA 9-9, SU 11-5; PARKING LOT

Active Endeavors

"...adorable clothes for kids and moms too... all the hot kids brands for good prices... especially great for sporty boys and girls... terrific selection of shorts and summer play clothes... sizes can occasionally be tough to find..."

Furniture, Bedding & Decor	✗	$$$	Prices
Gear & Equipment	✗	❹	Product availability
Nursing & Feeding	✗	❹	Staff knowledge
Safety & Babycare	✗	❹	Customer service
Clothing, Shoes & Accessories	✗	❹	Decor
Books, Toys & Entertainment	✗		

WWW.ACTIVEENDEAVORS.COM

CHICAGO—853 W ARMITAGE AVE (AT HALSTED ST); 773.281.8100; M-TH 10-7, F-SA 10-6, SU 12-6

WICKER PARK/UKRANIAN VILLAGE—55 E GRAND AVE (AT WABASH); 312.822.0600; DAILY 10-6; FREE PARKING

Active Endeavors Kids

"...adorable clothes for kids and moms too... all the hot kids brands for good prices... especially great for sporty boys and girls... terrific selection of shorts and summer play clothes... sizes can occasionally be tough to find..."

Furniture, Bedding & Decor .... ✗
Gear & Equipment .... ✗
Nursing & Feeding .... ✗
Safety & Babycare .... ✗
Clothing, Shoes & Accessories....... ✓
Books, Toys & Entertainment .... ✗

$$$$ .... Prices
❸ .... Product availability
❸ .... Staff knowledge
❸ .... Customer service
❸ .... Decor

WWW.ACTIVEENDEAVORS.COM

LINCOLN PARK/DEPAUL/OLD TOWN—838 W ARMITAGE AVE (AT N DAYTON ST); 773.281.2002; M-SA 10-6, SU 12-5

Active Kids

"...lots of high-quality trendy clothing in wee sizes... very stylish... the place for a funky little shirt or outfit... good selection of baby winter and athletic wear... knowledgeable sales staff... get there early for popular items as they run out of sizes... great for girl's clothes, lacking for boys,,, good frequent shopper program... easy to shop with the kids..."

Furniture, Bedding & Decor .... ✗
Gear & Equipment .... ✗
Nursing & Feeding .... ✗
Safety & Babycare .... ✗
Clothing, Shoes & Accessories....... ✓
Books, Toys & Entertainment .... ✗

$$$$ .... Prices
❸ .... Product availability
❸ .... Staff knowledge
❸ .... Customer service
❸ .... Decor

WWW.ACTIVEENDEAVORS.COM

LINCOLN PARK/DEPAUL/OLD TOWN—838 W ARMITAGE AVE (AT N HALSTED ST); 773.755.9371; M-SA 10-6 SU 12-5; PARKING LOT

Alamo Shoes

"...the place to go for shoes for the whole family... I love this store because I can find brand-names I can't find anywhere else... they have a great selection and will order for you too... prices are higher than some department stores, but it's worth it for quality and great service... constantly changing selection of trendy shoes... very accommodating... great with kids..."

Furniture, Bedding & Decor .... ✗
Gear & Equipment .... ✗
Nursing & Feeding .... ✗
Safety & Babycare .... ✗
Clothing, Shoes & Accessories....... ✓
Books, Toys & Entertainment .... ✗

$$$ .... Prices
❹ .... Product availability
❹ .... Staff knowledge
❹ .... Customer service
❸ .... Decor

WWW.ALAMOSHOES.COM

EDGEWATER—5321 N CLARK ST (AT W SUMMERDALE AVE); 773.334.6100; M-F 9-8 SA 9-6 SU 10-6; PARKING LOT

Baby Depot At Burlington Coat Factory

"...a large, 'super store' layout with a ton of baby gear... wide aisles, packed shelves, barely existent customer service and awesome prices... everything from bottles, car seats and strollers to gliders, cribs and clothes... I always find something worth getting... a little disorganized and hard to locate items you're looking for... the staff is not always knowledgeable about their merchandise... return policy is store credit only..."

Furniture, Bedding & Decor .... ✓
Gear & Equipment .... ✓
Nursing & Feeding .... ✓
Safety & Babycare .... ✓
Clothing, Shoes & Accessories....... ✓
Books, Toys & Entertainment .... ✓

$$ .... Prices
❸ .... Product availability
❸ .... Staff knowledge
❸ .... Customer service
❸ .... Decor

WWW.BABYDEPOT.COM

SOUTH SIDE—8320 S CICERO AVE (AT W 83RD ST); 708.636.8300; M-SA 10-9, SU 11-6; PARKING LOT

Baby PhD

"...cozy baby store... does have a small resale section where deals can be found... the staff is super friendly... good selection of distinctive toys... knowledgeable staff that has an eye for what kids like and the kind of stuff parents also want their kids playing with... give the shop a call for direction, can be tricky to find... they also participate in the Hyde Park children's book festival..."

Furniture, Bedding & Decor	✗	$$$	Prices
Gear & Equipment	✓	4	Product availability
Nursing & Feeding	✗	4	Staff knowledge
Safety & Babycare	✗	4	Customer service
Clothing, Shoes & Accessories	✓	4	Decor
Books, Toys & Entertainment	✓		

WWW.BABYPHD.COM

OAKLAND/KENWOOD—5225 S HARPER AVE (AT 52ND ST); 773.684.8920; M-SA 10-6, SU 11-5; STREET PARKING

BabyGap/GapKids

"...colorful baby and toddler clothing in clean, well-lit stores... great return policy... it's the Gap, so you know what you're getting—colorful, cute and well-made clothing... best place for baby hats... prices are reasonable especially since there's always a sale of some sort going on... sales, sales, sales—frequent and fantastic... everything I'm looking for in infant clothing—snap crotches, snaps up the front, all natural fabrics and great styling... fun seasonal selections—a great place to shop for gifts as well as for your own kids... although it can get busy, staff generally seem accommodating and helpful..."

Furniture, Bedding & Decor	✗	$$$	Prices
Gear & Equipment	✗	4	Product availability
Nursing & Feeding	✗	4	Staff knowledge
Safety & Babycare	✗	4	Customer service
Clothing, Shoes & Accessories	✓	4	Decor
Books, Toys & Entertainment	✗		

WWW.GAP.COM

EAST/WEST OLD TOWN GOLD COAST/STREETERVILLE—835 N MICHIGAN AVE (AT E PEARSON AVE); 312.255.8883; M-SA 10-8, SU 11-7; PARKING IN FRONT OF BLDG

LAKEVIEW/WRIGLEYVILLE—3216 N BROADWAY AVE (AT W BELMONT AVE); 773.929.4085; M-SA 10-9, SU 11-7

LINCOLN PARK/DEPAUL/OLD TOWN—1740 N SHEFFIELD AVE (AT N CLYBOURN AVE); 312.944.6792; M-F10-9, SA 10-8, SU 10-7

LINCOLN PARK/DEPAUL/OLD TOWN—2108 N HALSTED ST (AT W DICKENS AVE); 773.549.2065; M-SA 10-8, SU 10-6; PARKING IN FRONT OF BLDG

RIVER NORTH/RIVER WEST—555 N MICHIGAN AVE (AT W GRAND AVE); 312.494.8580; M-SA 9-9, SU 9-8

Barneys New York

"...pretty much what you would expect from Barneys—totally decadent, sensationally cool, big price tags... adorable designer clothes for tots... you can find wonderful little gifts at reasonable prices... a great place for gifts—my friends get so excited when they see the Barneys box... when you're in the mood to impress, Barneys is a sure bet... yes it's pricey, but the experience is so wonderful..."

Furniture, Bedding & Decor	✓	$$$$	Prices
Gear & Equipment	✗	4	Product availability
Nursing & Feeding	✓	4	Staff knowledge
Safety & Babycare	✗	4	Customer service

Clothing, Shoes & Accessories .... ✓
Books, Toys & Entertainment .... ✓
❹ .... Decor

WWW.BARNEYS.COM

CHICAGO—25 E OAK ST (AT STATE ST); 312.587.1700; M-SA 10-7, SU 12-6; PARKING GARAGE

Baron's Shoes

★★★★½

"...they definitely get an 'A plus' for selection... great shoes and very knowledgeable staff... my son wear corrective shoes and I would not trust his feet to anyone else... terrific selection of extra wide shoes... wonderful regular children's shoes as well..."

Furniture, Bedding & Decor	✗	$$	Prices
Gear & Equipment	✗	❺	Product availability
Nursing & Feeding	✗	❺	Staff knowledge
Safety & Babycare	✗	❺	Customer service
Clothing, Shoes & Accessories	✓	❹	Decor
Books, Toys & Entertainment	✗		

MORGAN PARK—3101 W 111TH ST (AT S ALBANY AVE); 773.238.6100; SU-F 10-5:30, SA 9-4:30

Beansprout

★★★½☆

"...a hip store for toddlers... a TV keeps kids entertained while you shop... they have a nice range of prices with lots of cute boy's clothing too... nice place... the owner is super friendly and helpful... cute for little ones..."

Furniture, Bedding & Decor	✗	$$$	Prices
Gear & Equipment	✗	❹	Product availability
Nursing & Feeding	✗	❹	Staff knowledge
Safety & Babycare	✗	❹	Customer service
Clothing, Shoes & Accessories	✓	❹	Decor
Books, Toys & Entertainment	✓		

LAKEVIEW/WRIGLEYVILLE—3732 N SOUTHPORT AVE (AT W WAVELAND AVE); 773.472.4780; T-F 11-7, SA 10-6, SU 11-5; STREET PARKING

Bellini

★★★★☆

"...high-end furniture for a gorgeous nursery... if you're looking for the kind of furniture you see in magazines then this is the place to go... excellent quality... yes, it's pricey, but the quality is impeccable... free delivery and setup... their furniture is built to withstand the abuse my tots dish out... they sell very unique merchandise, ranging from cribs to bedding and even some clothes... our nursery design was inspired by their store decor... I wish they had more frequent sales..."

Furniture, Bedding & Decor	✓	$$$$	Prices
Gear & Equipment	✗	❹	Product availability
Nursing & Feeding	✗	❹	Staff knowledge
Safety & Babycare	✗	❹	Customer service
Clothing, Shoes & Accessories	✗	❹	Decor
Books, Toys & Entertainment	✓		

WWW.BELLINI.COM

LINCOLN PARK/DEPAUL/OLD TOWN—2100 N SOUTHPORT AVE (AT CLYBURN AVE); 773.880.5840; M-SA 10-6, SU 12-5

Bloomingdale's

★★★½☆

"...a wide selection of baby and toddler clothing... they carry all the major brands... some stores have a smaller selection than others so call ahead to double check... well organized racks and good quality merchandise... good for special occasion clothing and gifts... if you shop at the right time you can get some great deals..."

Furniture, Bedding & Decor	✗	$$$	Prices
Gear & Equipment	✗	❹	Product availability

Nursing & Feeding ✗
Safety & Babycare ✗
Clothing, Shoes & Accessories ✓
Books, Toys & Entertainment ✓

❸ Staff knowledge
❹ Customer service
❹ Decor

WWW.BLOOMINGDALES.COM

EAST/WEST OLD TOWN GOLD COAST/STREETERVILLE—900 N MICHIGAN AVE (AT E DELAWARE PL); 312.440.4460; SU 11-7, M-SA 10-8

RIVER NORTH/RIVER WEST—600 N WABASH AVE (AT OHIO ST); 312.324.7500; M-SA 10-9; FREE PARKING

Bombay Kids ★★★★☆

"...the kids section of this furniture store carries out-of-the-ordinary items... whimsical, pastel grandfather clocks... zebra bean bags... perfect for my eclectic taste... I now prefer my daughter's room to my own... clean bathroom with changing area and wipes... they have a little table with crayons and coloring books for the kids... easy and relaxed shopping destination..."

Furniture, Bedding & Decor ✓
Gear & Equipment ✗
Nursing & Feeding ✗
Safety & Babycare ✗
Clothing, Shoes & Accessories ✗
Books, Toys & Entertainment ✗

$$$ Prices
❹ Product availability
❹ Staff knowledge
❹ Customer service
❹ Decor

WWW.BOMBAYKIDS.COM

LINCOLN PARK/DEPAUL/OLD TOWN—1836 N CLYBOURN AVE (OFF RACINE AVE); 312.475.1376; M-F 10-8, SA 10-7, SU 11-6

Carrara Children's Shoes ★★★★☆

"...this family run store is great when it comes to customer service... the store could use a good makeover, but don't let that fool you... free parking... the shoes are well made, attractive and pricey... super cool kids' shoes for $80—hardly necessary, but they are so gorgeous... the best place for kid's shoes... always a positive experience... we love this place..."

Furniture, Bedding & Decor ✗
Gear & Equipment ✗
Nursing & Feeding ✗
Safety & Babycare ✗
Clothing, Shoes & Accessories ✓
Books, Toys & Entertainment ✗

$$$ Prices
❹ Product availability
❹ Staff knowledge
❹ Customer service
❸ Decor

LINCOLN PARK/DEPAUL/OLD TOWN—2506 1/2 N CLARK ST (AT W ST JAMES PL); 773.529.9955; M-SA 10-6, SU 12-5

Carter's ★★★★☆

"...always a great selection of inexpensive baby basics—everything from clothing to linens... I always find something at 'giveaway prices' during one of their frequent sales... busy and crowded—it can be a chaotic shopping experience... 30 to 50 percent less than what you would pay at other boutiques... I bought five pieces of baby clothing for less than $40... durable, adorable and affordable... most stores have a small play area for kids in center of store so you can get your shopping done..."

Furniture, Bedding & Decor ✓
Gear & Equipment ✗
Nursing & Feeding ✗
Safety & Babycare ✗
Clothing, Shoes & Accessories ✓
Books, Toys & Entertainment ✓

$$ Prices
❹ Product availability
❹ Staff knowledge
❹ Customer service
❹ Decor

WWW.CARTERS.COM

LINCOLN PARK/DEPAUL/OLD TOWN—1565 N HALSTED ST (AT LINCOLN PARK CENTRE); 312.482.8603; M-F 10-9, SA 10-7, SU 11-6

Children's Place, The

"...great bargains on cute clothing... shoes, socks, swimsuits, sunglasses and everything in between... lots of '3 for $20' type deals on sleepers, pants and mix-and-match separates... so much more affordable than the other 'big chains'... don't expect the most unique stuff here, but it wears and washes well... cheap clothing for cheap prices... you can leave the store with bags full of clothes without putting a huge dent in your wallet..."

Furniture, Bedding & Decor	✗	$$	Prices
Gear & Equipment	✗	4	Product availability
Nursing & Feeding	✗	4	Staff knowledge
Safety & Babycare	✗	4	Customer service
Clothing, Shoes & Accessories	✓	4	Decor
Books, Toys & Entertainment	✓		

WWW.CHILDRENSPLACE.COM

EAST/WEST OLD TOWN GOLD COAST/STREETERVILLE—1574 N KINGSBURY ST (AT W NORTH AVE); 312.337.3473; M-SA 9:30-7:30, SU 11-6

HUMBOLDT PARK—4855 W N AVE (AT N CICERO AVE); 773.862.7053; M-SA 10-8, SU 11-6

RIVER NORTH/RIVER WEST—520 N MICHIGAN AVE (AT E GRAND AVE); 312.467.0715; M-SA 10-8, SU 11-6

SOUTH SIDE—712 E 87TH ST (AT COTTAGE GROVE); 773.874.1710; M-SA 10-7, SU 11-5

SOUTH SIDE—7601 S CICERO AVE (AT FORD CITY SHOPPING CTR); 773.582.0600; M-SA 10-9, SU 11-7

Costco

"...dependable place for bulk diapers, wipes and formula at discount prices... clothing selection is very hit-or-miss... avoid shopping there during nights and weekends if possible, because parking and checkout lines are brutal... they don't have a huge selection of brands, but the brands they do have are almost always in stock and at a great price... lowest prices around for diapers and formula... kid's clothing tends to be picked through, but it's worth looking for great deals on name-brand items like Carter's..."

Furniture, Bedding & Decor	✓	$$	Prices
Gear & Equipment	✓	3	Product availability
Nursing & Feeding	✓	3	Staff knowledge
Safety & Babycare	✓	3	Customer service
Clothing, Shoes & Accessories	✓	2	Decor
Books, Toys & Entertainment	✓		

WWW.COSTCO.COM

ROSCOE VILLAGE/WEST LAKEVIEW—2746 N CLYBOURN AVE (AT DIVERSEY PKY); 773.360.2053; M-F 10-8:30, SA 9:30-6, SU 10-7

Cut Rate Toys

"...a hidden gem that offers great prices on toys and games... a small store, street parking and at times limited quantities... worth the trip... great deals to be found especially around the holidays... this was the first store I remember my parents taking me to, and now I take my own children too... they have Thomas the Train and other popular brands..."

Furniture, Bedding & Decor	✗	$$	Prices
Gear & Equipment	✗	4	Product availability
Nursing & Feeding	✗	4	Staff knowledge
Safety & Babycare	✗	4	Customer service
Clothing, Shoes & Accessories	✗	3	Decor

Books, Toys & Entertainment........ ✓

WWW.CUTRATETOYS.NET

EDGEBROOK—5409 W DEVON AVE (AT CENTRAL AVE); 773.763.5740; M-TH 9-5:30, F 9-7, SA 9-5:30, SU 11-4; FREE PARKING

Disney Store, The ★★★½☆

"...everything Disney you could possibly want—toys, books, videos, clothes, lithographs and loud Disney music as you shop through the store with your ecstatic tot... giant movie screens show classic Disney movies... perky, friendly staff... can be really busy during weekends and holidays... the best selection of Halloween costumes..."

Furniture, Bedding & Decor	✗	$$$	Prices
Gear & Equipment	✗	❹	Product availability
Nursing & Feeding	✗	❹	Staff knowledge
Safety & Babycare	✗	❹	Customer service
Clothing, Shoes & Accessories	✓	❹	Decor
Books, Toys & Entertainment	✓		

WWW.DISNEYSTORE.COM

CHICAGO—717 N MICHIGAN AVE (AT W CHICAGO AVE); 312.654.9208; M-F 10-8, SA 9-8, SU 10-6

Faded Rose ★★★½☆

"...lovely linens for the nursery... beautiful gift items for a new baby... can be pricey... very French inspired... the owner is kind and helpful... fun to shop for you and your baby at this quaint spot..."

Furniture, Bedding & Decor	✓	$$$	Prices
Gear & Equipment	✗	❸	Product availability
Nursing & Feeding	✗	❹	Staff knowledge
Safety & Babycare	✗	❹	Customer service
Clothing, Shoes & Accessories	✗	❹	Decor
Books, Toys & Entertainment	✗		

WWW.SHOPFADEDROSE.COM

LINCOLN PARK/DEPAUL/OLD TOWN—1017 W ARMITAGE AVE (AT N KENMORE AVE); 773.281.8161; M-F 10-7, SA-SU 10-5

Galt Toys & Galt Baby ★★★★★

"...a wonderful neighborhood shopping destination for new parents... they carry strollers, baby products, and hard-to-find toys... we found things here that can't be found anyplace else... this store has just about everything you'll need for your baby (or they know how/where to get it)... very knowledgeable staff and excellent selection... a must-visit for new Chicago moms and dads..."

Furniture, Bedding & Decor	✗	$$$$	Prices
Gear & Equipment	✓	❹	Product availability
Nursing & Feeding	✓	❹	Staff knowledge
Safety & Babycare	✓	❹	Customer service
Clothing, Shoes & Accessories	✓	❹	Decor
Books, Toys & Entertainment	✓		

WWW.GALTTOYSGALTBABY.COM

LINCOLN PARK/DEPAUL/OLD TOWN—900 N MICHIGAN AVE (AT E DELAWARE PL); 312.440.9550; M-SA 10-7, SU 11-6; GARAGE AT E WALTON ST

Glam To Go ★★★★½

"...beauty essentials for mom and dolls for baby—all with a little bling-bling... they don't have a ton of children's stuff, but what they have is adorable... the owner is awesome—very helpful and nice... you will definitely walk out with a fab gift for a new mom, a new baby, or yourself... so you can't really go wrong ..."

Furniture, Bedding & Decor	✗	$$$	Prices
Gear & Equipment	✗	❹	Product availability

Nursing & Feeding .... ✗
Safety & Babycare .... ✗
Clothing, Shoes & Accessories .... ✗
Books, Toys & Entertainment .... ✓

❹ .... Staff knowledge
❺ .... Customer service
❹ .... Decor

WWW.GLAMTOGO.COM

ROSCOE VILLAGE/WEST LAKEVIEW—2002 W ROSCOE ST (AT N DAMEN AVE); 773.525.7004; M-SA 10-7, SA-SU 11-6

Gymboree

"...beautiful clothing and great quality... colorful and stylish baby and kids wear... lots of fun birthday gift ideas... easy exchange and return policy... items usually go on sale pretty quickly... save money with Gymbucks... many stores have a play area which makes shopping with my kids fun (let alone feasible)..."

Furniture, Bedding & Decor .... ✗
Gear & Equipment .... ✗
Nursing & Feeding .... ✗
Safety & Babycare .... ✗
Clothing, Shoes & Accessories .... ✓
Books, Toys & Entertainment .... ✓

$$$ .... Prices
❹ .... Product availability
❹ .... Staff knowledge
❹ .... Customer service
❹ .... Decor

WWW.GYMBOREE.COM

EAST/WEST OLD TOWN GOLD COAST/STREETERVILLE—835 N MICHIGAN AVE (AT E PEARSON ST); 312.649.9074; M-SA 10-7, SU 12-6

LINCOLN PARK/DEPAUL/OLD TOWN—1845 N CLYBOURN AVE (AT W WILLOW ST); 773.525.2080; M-F 10-8, SA 10-6, SU 11-5

SOUTH SIDE—511 CHICAGO RIDGE MALL (AT CHICAGO RIDGE MALL); 708.229.9763; M-F 10-9, SA 10-7, SU 11-6; MALL PARKING

H & M

"...wonderful prices for trendy baby and toddler clothes... it's the 'Euro' Target... buy for yourself and for your kids... a fun shopping experience as long as your child doesn't mind the bright lights and loud music... decent return policy... incredible sale prices... store can get messy at peak hours... busy and hectic, but their inventory is fun and worth the visit..."

Furniture, Bedding & Decor .... ✗
Gear & Equipment .... ✗
Nursing & Feeding .... ✗
Safety & Babycare .... ✗
Clothing, Shoes & Accessories .... ✓
Books, Toys & Entertainment .... ✓

$$ .... Prices
❸ .... Product availability
❸ .... Staff knowledge
❸ .... Customer service
❸ .... Decor

WWW.HM.COM

EAST/WEST OLD TOWN GOLD COAST/STREETERVILLE—840 N MICHIGAN AVE (OFF CHICAGO AVE); 312.640.0060; M-SA 10-9, SU 10-7; FREE PARKING

LOOP—20 N STATE ST (OFF WASHINGTON ST); 312.263.4436; M-SA 10-9, SU 10-7; FREE PARKING

Jacadi

"...beautiful French clothes, baby bumpers and quilts... elegant and perfect for special occasions... quite expensive, but the clothing is hip and the quality really good... many handmade clothing and bedding items... take advantage of their sales... more of a store to buy gifts than practical, everyday clothes... beautiful, special clothing—especially for newborns and toddlers... velvet pajamas, coordinated nursery items... stores are as pretty as the clothes... they have a huge (half-off everything) sale twice a year that makes it very affordable..."

Furniture, Bedding & Decor .... ✓
Gear & Equipment .... ✗
Nursing & Feeding .... ✗
Safety & Babycare .... ✗

$$$$ .... Prices
❹ .... Product availability
❹ .... Staff knowledge
❹ .... Customer service

Clothing, Shoes & Accessories ...... ✓
Books, Toys & Entertainment .... ✓

❹ .... Decor

WWW.JACADIUSA.COM

EAST/WEST OLD TOWN GOLD COAST/STREETERVILLE—835 N MICHIGAN AVE (AT E PEARSON ST); 312.337.9600; M-SA 10-7, SU 12-6

JCPenney ★★★½☆

"...always a good place to find clothes and other baby basics... the registry process was seamless... staff is generally friendly but the lines always seem long and slow... they don't have the greatest selection of toddler clothes, but their baby section is great... we had some damaged furniture delivered but customer service was easy and accommodating... a pretty limited selection of gear, but what they have is priced right..."

Furniture, Bedding & Decor .... ✓
Gear & Equipment .... ✓
Nursing & Feeding .... ✓
Safety & Babycare .... ✓
Clothing, Shoes & Accessories ...... ✓
Books, Toys & Entertainment .... ✓

$$ .... Prices
❸ .... Product availability
❸ .... Staff knowledge
❸ ....Customer service
❸ .... Decor

WWW.JCPENNEY.COM

SOUTH SIDE—7601 S CICERO AVE (AT FORD CITY SHOPPING CTR); 773.581.6600; M-F 10-9, SA 10-8, SU 11-6; PARKING IN FRONT OF BLDG

Jordan Marie ★★★★☆

"...very nice classic clothes—not too hip or overly trendy... upscale items for special occasions... the perfect place to buy shower gifts... be prepared for the big price tags... the cutest baby clothes ever... extremely cute items—they'll even put together custom baskets... nice sales staff... the online store is better... great clearance deals occasionally... the place to go for something fancy... the best baby gifts and you can even return on-line purchases at the retail stores which takes the worry out of shopping from home..."

Furniture, Bedding & Decor .... ✗
Gear & Equipment .... ✗
Nursing & Feeding .... ✗
Safety & Babycare .... ✗
Clothing, Shoes & Accessories ...... ✓
Books, Toys & Entertainment .... ✓

$$$$ .... Prices
❸ .... Product availability
❹ .... Staff knowledge
❹ ....Customer service
❹ .... Decor

WWW.JORDANMARIE.COM

RIVER NORTH/RIVER WEST—520 N MICHIGAN AVE (AT E GRAND AVE); 312.670.2229; M-SA 11-11; FREE PARKING

KB Toys ★★★☆☆

"...hectic and always buzzing... wall-to-wall plastic and blinking lights... more Fisher-Price, Elmo and Sponge Bob than the eye can handle... a toy super store with discounted prices... they always have some kind of special sale going on... if you're looking for the latest and greatest popular toy, then look no further—not the place for unique or unusual toys... perfect for bulk toy shopping—especially around the holidays..."

Furniture, Bedding & Decor .... ✗
Gear & Equipment .... ✗
Nursing & Feeding .... ✗
Safety & Babycare .... ✗
Clothing, Shoes & Accessories .... ✗
Books, Toys & Entertainment .... ✓

$$ .... Prices
❸ .... Product availability
❸ .... Staff knowledge
❸ ....Customer service
❸ .... Decor

WWW.KBTOYS.COM

FORD CITY—7601 S CICERO AVE (AT FORD CITY MALL); 773.767.6606; M-SA 10-9, SU 10-7; MALL PARKING

PORTAGE PARK—4620 W IRVING PARK RD (AT SIX CORNERS); 773.283.4852; M-SA 10-9, SU 10-7

Kid's Foot Locker

"...Nike, Reebok and Adidas for your little ones... hip, trendy and quite pricey... perfect for the sports addict dad who wants his kid sporting the latest NFL duds... shoes cost close to what the adult variety costs... generally good quality... they carry infant and toddler sizes..."

Furniture, Bedding & Decor	✗	$$$	Prices
Gear & Equipment	✗	❸	Product availability
Nursing & Feeding	✗	❸	Staff knowledge
Safety & Babycare	✗	❸	Customer service
Clothing, Shoes & Accessories	✓	❸	Decor
Books, Toys & Entertainment	✗		

WWW.KIDSFOOTLOCKER.COM

BELMONT CENTRAL—2700 N NARRAGANSETT AVE (AT W SCHUBERT AVE); 773.237.3837; M-SA 10-8, SU 11-6

FORD CITY—7601 S CICERO AVE (AT FORD CITY SHOPPING CTR); 773.581.7080; M-SA 10-9, SU 11-7

GARFIELD PARK—3900 W MADISON ST (AT S SPRINGFIELD AVE); 773.722.3560; M-F 10-7, SA 10-6, SU 11-5

LOOP—211 S STATE ST (AT W ADAMS ST); 312.957.9040; M-F 10-7, SA 10-6, SU 11-5

Kohl's

"...nice one-stop shopping for the whole family—everything from clothing to baby gear... great sales on clothing and a good selection of higher-end brands... stylish, inexpensive clothes for babies through 24 months... very easy shopping experience... dirt-cheap sales and clearance prices... nothing super fancy, but just right for those everyday romper outfits... Graco, Eddie Bauer and other well-known brands..."

Furniture, Bedding & Decor	✓	$$	Prices
Gear & Equipment	✓	❹	Product availability
Nursing & Feeding	✓	❸	Staff knowledge
Safety & Babycare	✓	❸	Customer service
Clothing, Shoes & Accessories	✓	❸	Decor
Books, Toys & Entertainment	✓		

WWW.KOHLS.COM

BUCKTOWN—2140 N ELSTON AVE (OFF ASHLAND AVE); 773.342.9032; M-SA 8-10, SU 10-8; FREE PARKING

Land of Nod

"...creative and fun decor and furnishings... lots of practical stuff that has a bit more flair than your typical furnishings store... nice, helpful staff... a truly terrific place to buy gifts... lots of cool, retro stuff that you don't find elsewhere... love their book and music selection... great ideas for decorating kids' bedrooms... fabulous customer service and knowledgeable staff... adorable furniture and bedding..."

Furniture, Bedding & Decor	✓	$$$$	Prices
Gear & Equipment	✗	❹	Product availability
Nursing & Feeding	✗	❹	Staff knowledge
Safety & Babycare	✗	❹	Customer service
Clothing, Shoes & Accessories	✗	❺	Decor
Books, Toys & Entertainment	✓		

WWW.LANDOFNOD.COM

LINCOLN PARK/DEPAUL/OLD TOWN—900 W NORTH AVE (AT N CLYBOURN AVE); 312.475.9903; M-F 10-9, SA 10-7, SU 11-6

Lego Store

"...a perfect place to take your children at any age... both of my sons love the hands on sections throughout the store... great staff—super friendly and if you are missing a piece to one of your Lego sets they have it—especially those small pieces we seem to vacuum up..."

Furniture, Bedding & Decor	✗	$$$	Prices
Gear & Equipment	✗	4	Product availability
Nursing & Feeding	✗	5	Staff knowledge
Safety & Babycare	✗	4	Customer service
Clothing, Shoes & Accessories	✗	5	Decor
Books, Toys & Entertainment	✗		

WWW.LEGO.COM

CHICAGO—520 N MICHIGAN AVE (AT NORTH BRIDGE MALL); 312.494.0760; M-SA 10-8, SU 11-6

Little Soles

"...cool selection of shoes and socks... the prices range from affordable to extravagant... the customer service is highly variable from amazing to nonexistent... excellent fitting for new shoes... we always stock up when they have big sales..."

Furniture, Bedding & Decor	✗	$$$	Prices
Gear & Equipment	✗	4	Product availability
Nursing & Feeding	✗	4	Staff knowledge
Safety & Babycare	✗	4	Customer service
Clothing, Shoes & Accessories	✓	4	Decor
Books, Toys & Entertainment	✗		

LINCOLN PARK/DEPAUL/OLD TOWN—2121 N CLYBOURN AVE (AT N WAYNE AVE); 773.525.7727; M-SA 10-6, SU 11-5

Little Threads

"...the coolest baby gear shop in the city—with the high prices to come with it... perfect shower gifts... moms can find T-shirts bearing sushi rolls, outfits from top designers and denim diaper bags... stroller central every day... a valuable addition to fertile Roscoe Village... especially cute dresses... very colorful displays... you don't feel smothered while shopping... fantastic selection of books, gifts, and clothes..."

Furniture, Bedding & Decor	✗	$$$$	Prices
Gear & Equipment	✓	4	Product availability
Nursing & Feeding	✗	4	Staff knowledge
Safety & Babycare	✗	4	Customer service
Clothing, Shoes & Accessories	✓	4	Decor
Books, Toys & Entertainment	✓		

NORTH CENTER/ST BEN'S—2033 W ROSCOE ST (AT N SEELEY AVE); 773.327.9310; SU-M 10-4, T-W 10-6, TH 10-7, F 10-6 SA 10-5; PARKING LOT

Madison & Friends

"...distinctive clothing and high-end gear... a terrific store with cutting edge fashion for kids... check out the cool clothes for Mom downstairs... very funky, modern clothing and accessories... pricey, but wonderful stuff... great place for baby gifts and layettes... not the place for those on a strict budget... if baby needs a leather bomber jacket, then this is the place for you... always crowded..."

Furniture, Bedding & Decor	✗	$$$$	Prices
Gear & Equipment	✓	4	Product availability
Nursing & Feeding	✗	4	Staff knowledge
Safety & Babycare	✗	4	Customer service
Clothing, Shoes & Accessories	✓	4	Decor
Books, Toys & Entertainment	✓		

WWW.MADISONANDFRIENDS.COM

EAST/WEST OLD TOWN GOLD COAST/STREETERVILLE—940 N RUSH ST (AT OAK ST); 312.642.6403; M-W 10-6, TH 10-7, F-SA 10-6:30, SU 12-5; STREET PARKING

My Child's Room

"...we bought everything here... some of the lowest prices on cribs, rockers and dressers... the store has everything you might need for a new baby, but you are not overwhelmed by the endless selection of a mega store... a range of styles, all with excellent quality... a little pricey but always have someone there to help you... it can get crowded so you're best going during the week... some of their regular prices seem high, but they have fantastic sales..."

Furniture, Bedding & Decor .... ✓
Gear & Equipment .... ✓
Nursing & Feeding .... ✓
Safety & Babycare .... ✗
Clothing, Shoes & Accessories .... ✓
Books, Toys & Entertainment .... ✓

$$$$ .... Prices
❸ .... Product availability
❸ .... Staff knowledge
❸ .... Customer service
❹ .... Decor

WWW.MYCHILDSROOM.NET

RIVER NORTH/RIVER WEST—640 N LA SALLE DR (AT W ONTARIO ST); 312.642.7126; M-F 10-9, SA 10-6, SU 12-6; STREET PARKING

Neiman Marcus

"...fairly traditional, high-end clothing... beautiful fancy dresses for little girls... I like their Ralph Lauren line for my son... Bugaboo frog strollers, Jack Spade bags and Cunill silver picture frames... Reed and Barton baby silver ware... only the best—you can never go wrong with Neiman's..."

Furniture, Bedding & Decor .... ✓
Gear & Equipment .... ✓
Nursing & Feeding .... ✗
Safety & Babycare .... ✗
Clothing, Shoes & Accessories .... ✓
Books, Toys & Entertainment .... ✓

$$$$$ .... Prices
❹ .... Product availability
❹ .... Staff knowledge
❹ .... Customer service
❹ .... Decor

WWW.NEIMANMARCUS.COM

RIVER NORTH/RIVER WEST—737 N MICHIGAN AVE (AT E CHICAGO AVE); 312.642.5900; M-SA 10-7 SU 12-5; PARKING LOT

Nordstrom

"...quality service and quality clothes... awesome kids shoe department—almost as good as the one for adults... free balloons in the children's shoe area as well as drawing tables... in addition to their own brand, they carry a very nice selection of other high-end baby clothing including Ralph Lauren, Robeez, etc... adorable baby clothes—they make great shower gifts... such a wonderful shopping experience—their lounge is perfect for breastfeeding and for changing diapers... well-rounded selection of baby basics as well as fancy clothes for special events..."

Furniture, Bedding & Decor .... ✓
Gear & Equipment .... ✓
Nursing & Feeding .... ✗
Safety & Babycare .... ✗
Clothing, Shoes & Accessories .... ✓
Books, Toys & Entertainment .... ✓

$$$$ .... Prices
❹ .... Product availability
❹ .... Staff knowledge
❹ .... Customer service
❹ .... Decor

WWW.NORDSTROM.COM

RIVER NORTH/RIVER WEST—55 E GRAND AVE (AT N WABASH AVE); 312.464.1515; M-SA 10-8, SU 11-6

Oilily

"...exclusive shop with fun, colorful clothing... prices are a bit steep, but if you value unique, well-designed clothes, this is the place... better selection for girls than boys but there are special items for either sex... your tot will definitely stand out from the crowd in these unique pieces... my kids love wearing their 'cool' clothes... whimsical items for mom, too..."

Furniture, Bedding & Decor	✗	$$$$	Prices
Gear & Equipment	✗	❹	Product availability
Nursing & Feeding	✗	❹	Staff knowledge
Safety & Babycare	✗	❹	Customer service
Clothing, Shoes & Accessories	✓	❹	Decor
Books, Toys & Entertainment	✗		

WWW.OILILYUSA.COM

RIVER NORTH/RIVER WEST—520 N MICHIGAN AVE (AT NORTH BRIDGE MALL); 312.527.5747; M-SA 10-8, SU 11-6

Old Navy

"...hip and 'in' clothes for infants and tots... plenty of steals on clearance items... T-shirts and pants for $10 or less... busy, busy, busy—long lines, especially on weekends... nothing fancy and you won't mind when your kids get down and dirty in these clothes... easy to wash, decent quality... you can shop for your baby, your toddler, your teen and yourself all at the same time... clothes are especially affordable when you hit their sales (post-holiday sales are amazing!)..."

Furniture, Bedding & Decor	✗	$$	Prices
Gear & Equipment	✗	❹	Product availability
Nursing & Feeding	✗	❸	Staff knowledge
Safety & Babycare	✗	❸	Customer service
Clothing, Shoes & Accessories	✓	❸	Decor
Books, Toys & Entertainment	✗		

WWW.OLDNAVY.COM

HUMBOLDT PARK—4905 W NORTH AVE (AT LAMON AVE); 773.862.1774; M-SA 9-9, SU 10-6

LOOP—35 N STATE ST (AT W CALHOUN PL); 312.551.0522; M-SA 9-9, SU 10-6

ROSCOE VILLAGE/WEST LAKEVIEW—1730 W FULLERTON AVE (AT N CLYBOURN AVE); 773.871.0601; M-SA 9-9, SU 10-6

SOUTH SIDE—7601 S CICERO AVE (AT FORD CITY SHOPPING CTR); 773.284.7710; M-SA 9-9, SU 10-6

WICKER PARK/UKRANIAN VILLAGE—1596 N KINGSBURY ST (AT W NORTH AVE); 312.397.0485; M-SA 10-9, SU 10-6

Once Upon A Child

"...new and used items... the place for bargain baby items in like-new condition... a great bargain spot with a wide variety of clothes for baby... some inexpensive furniture... good selection, staff and prices... cluttered and hard to get through the store with kids... good toys and gear... some items are definitely more than 'gently used'... a kid's play area... good end-of-season sales... expect to sort through items... cash for your old items..."

Furniture, Bedding & Decor	✓	$$	Prices
Gear & Equipment	✓	❸	Product availability
Nursing & Feeding	✗	❹	Staff knowledge
Safety & Babycare	✗	❹	Customer service
Clothing, Shoes & Accessories	✓	❸	Decor
Books, Toys & Entertainment	✓		

WWW.OUAC.COM

IRVING PARK/MAYFAIR—5316 N MILWAUKEE AVE (AT N CENTRAL AVE); 773.594.1705; M-F 10-8, SA 10-6, SU 11-5

Parkway Drugs

"...my favorite drug store for baby stuff... Gripe Water for baby and Murad for me... extremely reasonably prices... nice sales staff and pharmacists... they seem to have everything I need including breast pump rentals..."

Furniture, Bedding & Decor	×	$$$	Prices
Gear & Equipment	×	❹	Product availability
Nursing & Feeding	✓	❹	Staff knowledge
Safety & Babycare	×	❹	Customer service
Clothing, Shoes & Accessories	×	❹	Decor
Books, Toys & Entertainment	×		

LINCOLN PARK/DEPAUL/OLD TOWN—2346 N CLARK ST (AT W BELDEN AVE); 773.549.2720; M-F 8-7, SA 9-6, SU 10-4; STREET PARKING

RIVER NORTH/RIVER WEST—680 N LAKE SHORE DR (AT E ERIE ST); 312.943.2224; M-F 8-8, SA 8-6, SU 8-4

Payless Shoe Source

"...a good place for deals on children's shoes... staff is helpful with sizing... the selection and prices for kids' shoes can't be beat, but the quality isn't always spectacular... good leather shoes for cheap... great variety of all sizes and widths... I get my son's shoes here and don't feel like I'm wasting my money since he'll outgrow them in 3 months anyway..."

Furniture, Bedding & Decor	×	$$	Prices
Gear & Equipment	×	❸	Product availability
Nursing & Feeding	×	❸	Staff knowledge
Safety & Babycare	×	❸	Customer service
Clothing, Shoes & Accessories	✓	❸	Decor
Books, Toys & Entertainment	×		

WWW.PAYLESS.COM

LOOP—100 W RANDOLPH ST (AT CLARK ST); 312.726.3230

LOOP—13 N STATE ST (AT E MADISON ST); 312.201.1345; M-SA 8-8, SA 9-7, SU 11:30-5:30

LOOP—220 S STATE ST (AT W ADAMS ST); 312.427.4286; M-F 8-8:30, SA 12-7 SU 11-5:30

RIVER NORTH/RIVER WEST—444 N MICHIGAN AVE (AT E HUBBARD ST); 312.755.0482; M-F 9:30-8, SA 9-8, SU 11-6

WICKER PARK/UKRANIAN VILLAGE—1281 N MILWAUKEE AVE (AT N ASHLAND AVE); 773.384.2167; M-F 9:30-8, SA 9:30-7, SU 10-6

Petit Feet

"...a large shoe selection and limited clothes and socks... it is owned by a mom and daughter who are friendly and so helpful... this store had every style of Robeez shoes imaginable... I got the greatest pair of moccasins here for my daughter—they are soft and non-constricting and they don't fall off... shoes are reasonably priced..."

Furniture, Bedding & Decor	×	$$$$	Prices
Gear & Equipment	×	❹	Product availability
Nursing & Feeding	×	❸	Staff knowledge
Safety & Babycare	×	❹	Customer service
Clothing, Shoes & Accessories	✓	❹	Decor
Books, Toys & Entertainment	✓		

LAKEVIEW/WRIGLEYVILLE—3715 N SOUTHPORT AVE (AT W WAVELAND AVE); 773.472.3338; M-SA 10-5, SU 12-5; STREET PARKING

Piggy Toes

"...amazing Euro shoes... stylish indeed... soft leather bottoms made in Italy... high-end shoes for newborns to size 10 in women... store is a bit pricey, but well worth it if you can afford to spend the extra $30-$40 on a pair of children's shoes... generally you will find excellent help here..."

Furniture, Bedding & Decor	✗	$$$$	Prices
Gear & Equipment	✗	❹	Product availability
Nursing & Feeding	✗	❹	Staff knowledge
Safety & Babycare	✗	❹	Customer service
Clothing, Shoes & Accessories	✓	❹	Decor
Books, Toys & Entertainment	✗		

WWW.PTOES.COM

LINCOLN PARK/DEPAUL/OLD TOWN—2205 N HALSTED ST (AT W WEBSTER AVE); 773.281.5583; M-SA 10-7, SU 11-6

Pottery Barn Kids

"...stylish furniture, rugs, rockers and much more... they've found the right mix between quality and price... finally a company that stands behind what they sell—their customer service is great... gorgeous baby decor and furniture that will make your nursery to-die-for... the play area is so much fun—my daughter never wants to leave... a beautiful store with tons of ideas for setting up your nursery or kid's room... bright colors and cute patterns with basics to mix and match... if you see something in the catalog, but not in the store, just ask because they often have it in the back..."

Furniture, Bedding & Decor	✓	$$$$	Prices
Gear & Equipment	✗	❹	Product availability
Nursing & Feeding	✗	❹	Staff knowledge
Safety & Babycare	✗	❹	Customer service
Clothing, Shoes & Accessories	✗	❺	Decor
Books, Toys & Entertainment	✓		

WWW.POTTERYBARNKIDS.COM

LINCOLN PARK/DEPAUL/OLD TOWN—2111 N CLYBOURN AVE (AT N WAYNE AVE); 773.525.8349; M-SA 10-7, SU 11-6

Psychobaby

"...a hip store for hip kids... if you want something a little different than your run-of-the-mill baby clothes, then this is a store for you... most adorable baby clothes in town... cool place to shop if you have the money... price tags are worth it... one of a kind clothing and shoes... unique offerings... fun, funky and fashionable... friendly staff... a great store for baby gifts and special occasions..."

Furniture, Bedding & Decor	✗	$$$$	Prices
Gear & Equipment	✓	❹	Product availability
Nursing & Feeding	✗	❹	Staff knowledge
Safety & Babycare	✗	❹	Customer service
Clothing, Shoes & Accessories	✓	❹	Decor
Books, Toys & Entertainment	✓		

WWW.PSYCHOBABY.NET

BUCKTOWN—1630 N DAMEN AVE (AT W NORTH AVE); 773.772.2815; M-SA 10-6, SU 11-5

Rainbow Kids

"...fun clothing styles for infants and tots at low prices... the quality isn't the same as the more expensive brands, but the sleepers and play outfits always hold up well... great place for basics... cute trendy shoe selection for your little walker... we love the prices... up-to-date selection..."

Furniture, Bedding & Decor	✗	$$	Prices

Gear & Equipment ✓	❸ Product availability
Nursing & Feeding ×	❸ Staff knowledge
Safety & Babycare ×	❸ Customer service
Clothing, Shoes & Accessories ✓	❸ Decor
Books, Toys & Entertainment ✓	

WWW.RAINBOWSHOPS.COM

ARCHER HEIGHTS/BRIGHTON PARK/GAGE PARK—4717 S KEDZIE AVE (AT W 47TH ST); 773.869.0523; M-F 10-8, SA 10-6, SU 10-5; PARKING LOT

ASHBURN—3264 W 87TH ST (AT S KEDZIE AVE); 773.925.9551; M-FR 10-8,SA-SU10-6; PARKING LOT

CANARYVILLE/FULLER PARK—201 E 47TH ST (AT S INDIANA AVE); 773.373.2144; M-SA 10-7 SU 10-6; STREET PARKING

CHICAGO—1933 W 22ND ST (AT LEWIS AVE); 773.927.8255; M-SA 10-7 SU 10-6; STREET PARKING

CHICAGO—9125 S COMMERCIAL AVE (AT S SOUTH CHICAGO AVE); 773.374.0412; M-SA 10-7 SU 10-5; PARKING LOT

COLUMET HEIGHTS—9052 S COMMERCIAL AVE (AT S SOUTH CHICAGO AVE); 773.768.5966; M-SA10-7,SU 10-5; PARKING LOT

EDGEWATER—5231 N BROADWAY ST (AT W FOSTER AVE); 773.878.0284; DAILY 9-8

FORD CITY—7601 S CICERO AVE (AT S STATE RD); 773.284.8331; M-F 10-9, SA 10-7, SU 11-6

GARFIELD PARK—3900 W MADISON ST (AT N PULASKI RD); 773.533.2133; M-SA 10-7, SU 10-5:30; PARKING LOT

GARFIELD PARK—4049 W MADISON ST (AT N PULASKI RD); 773.722.4107; M-SA 10-7, SU 10-6; STREET PARKING

GRESHAM—105 W 87TH ST (AT HWY 94); 773.483.6867; DAILY 9-9

HAMILTON PARK—6312 HALSTEAD ST (AT W 63RD ST); 773.483.6255; DAILY 10-6; PARKING LOT

HUMBOLDT PARK—4001 W NORTH AVE (AT N PULASKI RD); 773.227.9939; DAILY 10-7; PARKING LOT

LITTLE VILLAGE—2539 W CERMAK RD (AT S WESTERN AVE); 773.376.8031; DAILY 9-8

MARQUETTE PARK—2414 W 63RD ST (AT S WESTERN AVE); 773.471.9707; DAILY 10-6

ROSELAND—11225 S MICHIGAN AVE (AT E 111TH ST); 773.568.4297; SU-W 10-6, TH-SA 10-7; PARKING LOT

SHERIDAN PARK/UPTOWN—4607 N BROADWAY ST (AT W LAWRENCE AVE); 773.271.0069; M-F 9-7, SA 9-6, SU 10-6

SOUTH SHORE—2545 E 79TH ST (AT S YATES BLVD); 773.221.2940; M-SA 10-6,SU 10-5; PARKING LOT

STONEY ISLAND—STONEY ISLAND PLAZA (AT STONEY ISLAND PLZ); 773.221.5230; M-FR 10-9, SA 10-7, SU 10-6; PARKING LOT

WICKER PARK/UKRANIAN VILLAGE—1333 N MILWAUKEE AVE (AT N ASHLAND AVE); 773.772.6265; M-SA 10-8, SU 10-6; STREET PARKING

WOODLAWN—6300 S COTTAGE GROVE AVE (AT E 63RD ST); 773.493.7494; DAILY 10-6

Red Balloon Company

“...you know this store is special as soon as you walk through the door... some of the best children's clothes in the city... unique designs, beautiful fabrics... lovely crib sheets... excellent customer service... unique clothes you won't find elsewhere... nice variety from books to booties... I really enjoy shopping here—even to just look at their wonderful displays...”

Furniture, Bedding & Decor ✓	$$$$ Prices
Gear & Equipment ×	❹ Product availability

Nursing & Feeding .... ✗
Safety & Babycare .... ✗
Clothing, Shoes & Accessories ...... ✓
Books, Toys & Entertainment .... ✓

❹ .... Staff knowledge
❺ ....Customer service
❺ .... Decor

WWW.THEREDBALLOON.COM

BUCKTOWN—2060 N DAMEN AVE (AT W DICKENS AVE); 773.489.9800; M-W 11-10:30, TH 11-1, F-SA 1-6, SU 12-5; STREET PARKING

Right Start, The ★★★★★

"...higher-end, well selected items... Britax, Maclaren, Combi, Mustela—all the cool brands under one roof... everything from bibs to bottles and even the Bugaboo stroller... prices seem a little high, but the selection is good and the staff knowledgeable and helpful... there are toys all over the store that kids can play with while you shop... I have a hard time getting my kids out of the store because they are having so much fun... a boutique-like shopping experience but they carry most of the key brands... their registry works well..."

Furniture, Bedding & Decor .... ✓
Gear & Equipment .... ✓
Nursing & Feeding .... ✓
Safety & Babycare .... ✓
Clothing, Shoes & Accessories ...... ✓
Books, Toys & Entertainment .... ✓

$$$ .... Prices
❹ .... Product availability
❹ .... Staff knowledge
❹ ....Customer service
❹ .... Decor

WWW.RIGHTSTART.COM

LINCOLN PARK—2121 N CLYBOURN AVE (AT N WAYNE AVE); 773.296.4420; M-SA 10-6, SU 11-5; PARKING LOT AT 2121 N CLYBOURN

Room & Board ★★★½☆

"...the store doesn't have a huge selection of baby furniture, but what's there is excellent quality... the staff is terrific... expect to receive fantastic customer service... terrific for the transition into a twin or bunk bed... a great furniture store with limited kids furniture, but good quality for the price..."

Furniture, Bedding & Decor .... ✓
Gear & Equipment .... ✗
Nursing & Feeding .... ✗
Safety & Babycare .... ✗
Clothing, Shoes & Accessories .... ✗
Books, Toys & Entertainment .... ✗

$$$$ .... Prices
❹ .... Product availability
❺ .... Staff knowledge
❹ ....Customer service
❺ .... Decor

WWW.ROOMANDBOARD.COM

CHICAGO—55 E OHIO ST (OFF WABASH AVE); 312.222.0970; M-F 10-7, SA 10-6, SU 11-6

Sears ★★★☆☆

"...a decent selection of clothes and basic baby equipment... check out the Kids Club program—it's a great way to save money... you go to Sears to save money, not to be pampered... the quality of their merchandise is better than Wal-Mart, but don't expect anything too special or different... not much in terms of gear, but tons of well-priced baby and toddler clothing..."

Furniture, Bedding & Decor .... ✓
Gear & Equipment .... ✓
Nursing & Feeding .... ✓
Safety & Babycare .... ✓
Clothing, Shoes & Accessories ...... ✓
Books, Toys & Entertainment .... ✓

$$ .... Prices
❸ .... Product availability
❸ .... Staff knowledge
❸ ....Customer service
❸ .... Decor

WWW.SEARS.COM

CHICAGO—1601 N HARLEM AVE (AT RT 43); 773.836.4100; M-F 9-9, SA 10-6, SU 11-5

ENGLEWOOD—6153 S WESTERN AVE (AT 61ST ST); 773.918.1400; M-F 10-9, SA 10-6, SU 11-5

FORD CITY—7601 S CICERO AVE (AT FORD CITY SHOPPING CTR); 773.284.4200; M-F 10-9, SA 8-8, SU 11-7

GRAND CROSSING—1334 E 79TH ST (AT CHICAGO SKWY); 773.933.1600; M-F 10-9, SA 10-9, SU 11-5

PORTAGE PARK—4730 W IRVING PARK RD (AT CICERO AVE); 773.202.2000; M-SA 9-9, SU 9-7:30

RIVER NORTH/RIVER WEST—2 N STATE ST (AT W MADISON ST); 312.373.6000; M-F 10-9, SA 10-9, SU 11-5

SHERIDAN PARK/UPTOWN—1900 W LAWRENCE AVE (AT DAMEN AVE); 773.769.8052; M-F 9-9, SA 8-9, SU 11-7

Second Child

"...great upscale thrift shop... slightly used, but in good condition... great clothing finds—I always find something nice to bring home... good brands for everything from strollers to clothes... twice a year sales are great—get on the mailing list... amazing deals and the staff is friendly..."

Furniture, Bedding & Decor	✓	$$	Prices
Gear & Equipment	✓	4	Product availability
Nursing & Feeding	✓	4	Staff knowledge
Safety & Babycare	✗	4	Customer service
Clothing, Shoes & Accessories	✓	3	Decor
Books, Toys & Entertainment	✓		

WWW.2NDCHILD.COM

LINCOLN PARK/DEPAUL/OLD TOWN—954 W ARMITAGE AVE (AT N SHEFFIELD AVE); 773.883.0880; M-SA 10-6, SU 12-5

Shop Elizabeth Marie

"...a quirky little store with cute, hand-picked items... bedding, furniture, gifts... they carry one or 2 styles of items ranging from blankets to gliders... store is only open by appointment which makes it hard to just stop in to browse... beautiful personalized gifts... the entire store is as big as a walk-in closet so leave the stroller at home..."

Furniture, Bedding & Decor	✓	$$$$	Prices
Gear & Equipment	✓	3	Product availability
Nursing & Feeding	✗	4	Staff knowledge
Safety & Babycare	✗	3	Customer service
Clothing, Shoes & Accessories	✗	3	Decor
Books, Toys & Entertainment	✓		

LAKEVIEW/WRIGGLEYVILLE—3612 N SOUTHPORT AVE (AT W ADDISON ST); 773.525.4100; M-F BY APPT ONLY, SA-SU 10:30-6:00

Strasburg Children

"...totally adorable special occasion outfits for babies and kids... classic baby, toddler, and kids clothes... dress-up clothes for kids... if you are looking for a flower girl or ring bearer outfit, look no further... handmade clothes that will last through multiple kids or generations... it's not cheap, but you can find great sales if you are patient..."

Furniture, Bedding & Decor	✗	$$$$	Prices
Gear & Equipment	✗	4	Product availability
Nursing & Feeding	✗	4	Staff knowledge
Safety & Babycare	✗	4	Customer service
Clothing, Shoes & Accessories	✓	4	Decor
Books, Toys & Entertainment	✗		

WWW.STRASBURGCHILDREN.COM

CHICAGO—650 PREMIUM OUTLETS BLVD (OFF RT 88); 630.978.9703; M-SA 10-9 SU 10-6

T-Shirt Deli, The

"...customized T-shirts for babies, parents, and friends... I received matching onesie and adult T-shirt for the arrival of my daughter—her outfit says 'rock me' and mine says 'rocker'... after they 'cook it up', your shirt will be rolled and wrapped in butcher paper, and served with a delicious sandwich and potato chips (really, it's true)... very fun shopping experience... you can choose from many different items that can be customized to your liking... friendly, fun, and you've got to check it out..."

Furniture, Bedding & Decor	✗	$$$	Prices
Gear & Equipment	✗	❹	Product availability
Nursing & Feeding	✗	❺	Staff knowledge
Safety & Babycare	✗	❹	Customer service
Clothing, Shoes & Accessories	✓	❹	Decor
Books, Toys & Entertainment	✗		

WWW.TSHIRTDELI.COM

BUCKTOWN—1739 N DAMEN AVE (AT W ST PAUL AVE); 773.276.6266; M-F 12-7, SA 11-6, SU 12-5; PARKING LOT

Talbots Kids

"...a nice alternative to the typical department store experience... expensive, but fantastic quality... great for holiday and special occasion outfits including christening outfits... well-priced, conservative children's clothing... cute selections for infants, toddlers and kids... sales are fantastic—up to half off at least a couple times a year... the best part is, you can also shop for yourself while shopping for baby..."

Furniture, Bedding & Decor	✗	$$$$	Prices
Gear & Equipment	✗	❹	Product availability
Nursing & Feeding	✗	❹	Staff knowledge
Safety & Babycare	✗	❹	Customer service
Clothing, Shoes & Accessories	✓	❹	Decor
Books, Toys & Entertainment	✗		

WWW.TALBOTS.COM

CHICAGO—700 N MICHIGAN AVE; 312.943.0255; M-F 10-7, SA 10-6, SU 12-5

Target

"...our favorite place to shop for kids' stuff—good selection and very affordable... guilt-free shopping—kids grow so fast so I don't want to pay high department-store prices... everything from diapers and sippy cups to car seats and strollers... easy return policy... generally helpful staff, but you don't go for the service—you go for the prices... decent registry that won't freak your friends out with outrageous prices... easy, convenient shopping for well-priced items... all the big-box brands available—Graco, Evenflo, Eddie Bauer, etc...."

Furniture, Bedding & Decor	✓	$$	Prices
Gear & Equipment	✓	❹	Product availability
Nursing & Feeding	✓	❸	Staff knowledge
Safety & Babycare	✓	❸	Customer service
Clothing, Shoes & Accessories	✓	❸	Decor
Books, Toys & Entertainment	✓		

WWW.TARGET.COM

ARCHER HEIGHTS/BRIGHTON PARK/GAGE PARK—4433 S PULASKI RD (AT W 44TH ST); 773.579.2120; M-SA 8-10, SU 8-9; PARKING IN FRONT OF BLDG

AVONDALE—2460 W GEORGE ST (AT N ELSTON AVE); 773.267.6141; M-SA 8-10, SU 8-9; PARKING IN FRONT OF BLDG

AVONDALE—2939 W ADDISON ST (AT N SACRAMENTO AVE); 773.604.7680; M-SA 8-10, SU 8-9; PARKING IN FRONT OF BLDG

ROSCOE VILLAGE/WEST LAKEVIEW—2656 N ELSTON AVE (AT W LOGAN BLVD); 773.252.1994; M-SA 8-10, SU 8-9; PARKING IN FRONT OF BLDG

SOUTH SIDE—7100 S CICERO AVE (AT W 72ND ST); 708.563.9050; M-SA 8-10, SU 8-9; PARKING IN FRONT OF BLDG

SOUTH SIDE—8560 S COTTAGE GROVE AVE (AT E 86TH ST); 773.371.8555; M-SA 8-10, SU 8-9; PARKING IN FRONT OF BLDG

Toys Et Cetera

"...this store is enormous and bountiful... toys, books, and gifts to please even the pickiest princess... the staff knows how to find you the right item... they have the standards—Whoozit, Early Years, Thomas, Brio, Lego, plus more unusual picks... don't miss the party favor area... fantastic store..."

Furniture, Bedding & Decor	✗	$$$	Prices
Gear & Equipment	✗	❺	Product availability
Nursing & Feeding	✗	❺	Staff knowledge
Safety & Babycare	✗	❺	Customer service
Clothing, Shoes & Accessories	✗	❹	Decor
Books, Toys & Entertainment	✓		

WWW.TOYSETCETERA.COM

HYDE PARK—5211 S HARPER AVE (AT E 52ND ST); 773.324.6039; M-SA 9:30-6, SU 11-5

LINCOLN PARK/DEPAUL/OLD TOWN—2037 N CLYBOURN (AT MAGNOLIA AVE); 773.348.1772; M-SA 9:30-7, SU 11-5

Toys R Us

"...not just toys, but also tons of gear and supplies including diapers and formula... a hectic shopping experience but the prices make it all worthwhile... I've experienced good and bad service at the same store on the same day... the stores are huge and can be overwhelming... most big brand-names available... leave the kids at home unless you want to end up with a cart full of toys..."

Furniture, Bedding & Decor	✓	$$$	Prices
Gear & Equipment	✓	❹	Product availability
Nursing & Feeding	✓	❸	Staff knowledge
Safety & Babycare	✓	❸	Customer service
Clothing, Shoes & Accessories	✓	❸	Decor
Books, Toys & Entertainment	✓		

WWW.TOYSRUS.COM

MONTECLAIRE—6420 W FULLERTON AVE (AT BRICKYARD SHOPPING CTR); 773.637.1166; M-SA 9:30-9:30, SU 10-7

ROSCOE VILLAGE/WEST LAKEVIEW—3330 N WESTERN AVE (AT W BELMONT AVE); 773.525.1690; M-SA 9:30-9:30, SU 10-7; PARKING IN FRONT OF BLDG

SOUTH SIDE—8900 LAFAYETTE ST (AT DAN RYAN EXPWY E); 773.846.2600; M-SA 9:30-9:30, SU 10-7

Unique So Chique

"...a tiny boutique with a small, but adorable kids selection... Jack Rabbit creations, Wiggle Wear, and Lillian Rose... toys, bags and some darling dresses... a fun place to pop into from time to time... we love the tea and chocolate room..."

Furniture, Bedding & Decor	✗	$$	Prices
Gear & Equipment	✗	❹	Product availability
Nursing & Feeding	✗	❹	Staff knowledge
Safety & Babycare	✗	❹	Customer service
Clothing, Shoes & Accessories	✓	❹	Decor
Books, Toys & Entertainment	✓		

WWW.UNIQUESOCHIQUE.COM

SHERIDAN PARK/UPTOWN—4600 N MAGNOLIA AVE (AT W WILSON AVE); 773.561.0324; T-TH 11:30-7:30, F 11:30-7:30, SA 10-6, SU 10-5; STREET PARKING

Value City

"...if you are looking for bargain merchandise for the whole family, you'll find it here... you can always find something and lots of inexpensive baby and toddler clothes... very low prices with many sizes... chaotic atmosphere and hard to find staff, once you do they are very helpful... lines can be long..."

Furniture, Bedding & Decor.......... ✓
Gear & Equipment........................ ✓
Nursing & Feeding .... ✓
Safety & Babycare....................... ✓
Clothing, Shoes & Accessories...... ✓
Books, Toys & Entertainment........ ✓

$$.. Prices
❸ .... Product availability
❸ .... Staff knowledge
❸ .... Customer service
❸ .... Decor

WWW.VALUECITY.COM

BACK OF THE YARDS—4500 S DAMEN AVE (AT W 47TH ST); 773.579.6850; M-SA 10-9:30, SU 11-7

Wesley Shoe Corral

Furniture, Bedding & Decor........... ✗
Nursing & Feeding .... ✗
Clothing, Shoes & Accessories...... ✓

✗ .... Gear & Equipment
✗ .... Safety & Babycare
✗ .... Books, Toys & Entertainment

OAKLAND/KENWOOD—1506 E 55TH ST (AT LAKE PARK AVE); 773.667.7463; M-F 9:30-7, SA 9:30-6, SU 12-5; PARKING AT 54TH & LAKE PARK AVE

Northwestern Suburbs

"lila picks"

★Babies R Us ★My Child's Room

★IKEA ★Pottery Barn Kids

April Cornell

"...beautiful, classic dresses and accessories for special occasions... I love the matching 'mommy and me' outfits... lots of fun knickknacks for sale... great selection of baby wear on their web site... rest assured your baby won't look like every other child in these adorable outfits... very frilly and girlie—beautiful..."

Furniture, Bedding & Decor .... ✗ | $$$ .... Prices
Gear & Equipment .... ✗ | ❸ .... Product availability
Nursing & Feeding .... ✓ | ❹ .... Staff knowledge
Safety & Babycare .... ✗ | ❹ .... Customer service
Clothing, Shoes & Accessories .... ✓ | ❹ .... Decor
Books, Toys & Entertainment .... ✗

WWW.APRILCORNELL.COM

DEER PARK—20530 N RAND RD (AT DEER PARK TOWN CTR); 847.540.5909; M-SA 10-9, SU 12-5

Babies N Beds

Furniture, Bedding & Decor .... ✓ | ✗ .... Gear & Equipment
Nursing & Feeding .... ✗ | ✗ .... Safety & Babycare
Clothing, Shoes & Accessories .... ✗ | ✗ .... Books, Toys & Entertainment

WWW.BABIESNBEDS.COM

STREAMWOOD—335 S BARTLETT RD (AT MONROE CT); 630.830.7701; M TH 11-8, W-SA 10-5, SU 12-5; PARKING LOT

Babies R Us

"...everything baby under one roof... they have a wide selection and carry most 'mainstream' items such as Graco, Fisher-Price, Avent and Britax... great customer service—given how big the stores are, I was pleasantly surprised at how attentive the staff was... easy return policy... super busy on weekends so try to visit on a weekday for the best service... keep an eye out for great coupons, deals and frequent sales... easy and comprehensive registry... shopping here is so easy—you've got to check it out..."

Furniture, Bedding & Decor .... ✓ | $$$ .... Prices
Gear & Equipment .... ✓ | ❹ .... Product availability
Nursing & Feeding .... ✓ | ❹ .... Staff knowledge
Safety & Babycare .... ✓ | ❹ .... Customer service
Clothing, Shoes & Accessories .... ✓ | ❹ .... Decor
Books, Toys & Entertainment .... ✓

WWW.BABIESRUS.COM

SCHAUMBURG—16 E GOLF RD (AT N ROSELLE RD); 847.781.8889; M-SA 9:30-9:30, SU 11-7; PARKING IN FRONT OF BLDG

VERNON HILLS—295 CENTER DR (AT HAWTHORN SHOPPING CTR); 847.573.1447; M-SA 9:30-8, SU 11-6; PARKING IN FRONT OF BLDG

Baby, Baby & More

"...this store carries many adorable items... difficult to maneuver a stroller and a double is out of the question... some of the cutest girl's clothes I've ever seen... pricey... best selection of socks... whimsical gift items..."

Furniture, Bedding & Decor	✓	$$$$	Prices
Gear & Equipment	✗	3	Product availability
Nursing & Feeding	✗	4	Staff knowledge
Safety & Babycare	✗	4	Customer service
Clothing, Shoes & Accessories	✓	3	Decor
Books, Toys & Entertainment	✓		

WWW.BABYBABYANDMORE.COM

LONG GROVE—407 ROBERT PARKER COFFIN RD (AT N OLD MCHENRY RD); 847.821.9296; M-SA 10-5, SU 12-5; STREET PARKING

Baby Depot At Burlington Coat Factory

"...a large, 'super store' layout with a ton of baby gear... wide aisles, packed shelves, barely existent customer service and awesome prices... everything from bottles, car seats and strollers to gliders, cribs and clothes... I always find something worth getting... a little disorganized and hard to locate items you're looking for... the staff is not always knowledgeable about their merchandise... return policy is store credit only..."

Furniture, Bedding & Decor	✓	$$	Prices
Gear & Equipment	✓	3	Product availability
Nursing & Feeding	✓	3	Staff knowledge
Safety & Babycare	✓	3	Customer service
Clothing, Shoes & Accessories	✓	3	Decor
Books, Toys & Entertainment	✓		

WWW.BABYDEPOT.COM

ARLINGTON HEIGHTS—30 W RAND RD (AT N EVERGREEN AVE); 847.577.7878; M-SA 10-9, SU 11-6; PARKING LOT

BabyGap/GapKids

"...colorful baby and toddler clothing in clean, well-lit stores... great return policy... it's the Gap, so you know what you're getting—colorful, cute and well-made clothing... best place for baby hats... prices are reasonable especially since there's always a sale of some sort going on... sales, sales, sales—frequent and fantastic... everything I'm looking for in infant clothing—snap crotches, snaps up the front, all natural fabrics and great styling... fun seasonal selections—a great place to shop for gifts as well as for your own kids... although it can get busy, staff generally seem accommodating and helpful..."

Furniture, Bedding & Decor	✗	$$$	Prices
Gear & Equipment	✗	4	Product availability
Nursing & Feeding	✗	4	Staff knowledge
Safety & Babycare	✗	4	Customer service
Clothing, Shoes & Accessories	✓	4	Decor
Books, Toys & Entertainment	✗		

WWW.GAP.COM

ARLINGTON HEIGHTS—585 E PALATINE RD (AT N PINETREE DR); 847.392.2991; M-SA 10-9, SU 11-6; PARKING IN FRONT OF BLDG

DEER PARK—20530 N RAND RD (AT W LONG GROVE RD); 847.540.1948; M-SA 10-9, SU 11-7

SCHAUMBURG—301 WOODFIELD MALL (AT GOLF RD); 847.330.1111; M-SA 10-9, SU 11-6; PARKING IN FRONT OF BLDG

VERNON HILLS—317 HAWTHORN CTR (AT HAWTHORN DR); 847.918.8706; M-SA 10-9, SU 11-6; PARKING IN FRONT OF BLDG

Bombay Kids

"...the kids section of this furniture store carries out-of-the-ordinary items... whimsical, pastel grandfather clocks... zebra bean bags... perfect for my eclectic taste... I now prefer my daughter's room to my own... clean bathroom with changing area and wipes... they have a little table with crayons and coloring books for the kids... easy and relaxed shopping destination..."

Furniture, Bedding & Decor	✓	$$$	Prices
Gear & Equipment	✗	❹	Product availability
Nursing & Feeding	✗	❹	Staff knowledge
Safety & Babycare	✗	❹	Customer service
Clothing, Shoes & Accessories	✗	❹	Decor
Books, Toys & Entertainment	✗		

WWW.BOMBAYKIDS.COM

SCHAUMBURG—1359 N MEACHAM RD (OFF GOLF RD); 847.995.0980; M-SA 10-9, SU 11-6

Costco

"...dependable place for bulk diapers, wipes and formula at discount prices... clothing selection is very hit-or-miss... avoid shopping there during nights and weekends if possible, because parking and checkout lines are brutal... they don't have a huge selection of brands, but the brands they do have are almost always in stock and at a great price... lowest prices around for diapers and formula... kid's clothing tends to be picked through, but it's worth looking for great deals on name-brand items like Carter's..."

Furniture, Bedding & Decor	✓	$$	Prices
Gear & Equipment	✓	❸	Product availability
Nursing & Feeding	✓	❸	Staff knowledge
Safety & Babycare	✓	❸	Customer service
Clothing, Shoes & Accessories	✓	❷	Decor
Books, Toys & Entertainment	✓		

WWW.COSTCO.COM

LAKE ZURICH—680 S RAND RD (AT ELA RD); 847.540.3053; M-F 11-8:30, SA 9:30-6, SU 10-6

SCHAUMBURG—1375 N MEACHAM RD (AT GOLF RD); 847.969.0790; M-F 11-8:30, SA 9:30-6, SU 10-6

FurnitureKidz

"...great furniture selection and a very helpful staff... it's a family run business and the owners and staff really take the time to help you make a good selection for your needs... rockers, step stools, artwork, and full bedroom gear... not cheap, but not over the top expensive either..."

Furniture, Bedding & Decor	✓	$$$$$	Prices
Gear & Equipment	✗	❹	Product availability
Nursing & Feeding	✗	❸	Staff knowledge
Safety & Babycare	✗	❹	Customer service
Clothing, Shoes & Accessories	✗	❸	Decor
Books, Toys & Entertainment	✗		

WWW.FURNITUREKIDZ.COM

ALGONQUIN—1552 E ALGONQUIN RD (AT RYAN PKWY); 847.854.4488; M-W F-SA 10-5, TH 10-8, SU 12-4

Gymboree

"...beautiful clothing and great quality... colorful and stylish baby and kids wear... lots of fun birthday gift ideas... easy exchange and return policy... items usually go on sale pretty quickly... save money with Gymbucks... many stores have a play area which makes shopping with my kids fun (let alone feasible)..."

Furniture, Bedding & Decor	✗	$$$	Prices
Gear & Equipment	✗	❹	Product availability
Nursing & Feeding	✗	❹	Staff knowledge
Safety & Babycare	✗	❹	Customer service
Clothing, Shoes & Accessories	✓	❹	Decor
Books, Toys & Entertainment	✓		

WWW.GYMBOREE.COM

DEER PARK—20530 N RAND RD (AT W LONG GROVE RD); 847.438.5564; M-SA 10-9, SU 12-5

SCHAUMBURG—348 WOODFIELD MALL (AT GOLF RD); 847.240.0818; M-SA 10-9, SU 11-6; MALL PARKING

VERNON HILLS—218 HAWTHORN CTR (AT HAWTHORN CTR); 847.549.0363; M-SA 10-9, SU 11-7; PARKING LOT AT CENTER

H & M

"...wonderful prices for trendy baby and toddler clothes... it's the 'Euro' Target... buy for yourself and for your kids... a fun shopping experience as long as your child doesn't mind the bright lights and loud music... decent return policy... incredible sale prices... store can get messy at peak hours... busy and hectic, but their inventory is fun and worth the visit..."

Furniture, Bedding & Decor	✗	$$	Prices
Gear & Equipment	✗	❸	Product availability
Nursing & Feeding	✗	❸	Staff knowledge
Safety & Babycare	✗	❸	Customer service
Clothing, Shoes & Accessories	✓	❸	Decor
Books, Toys & Entertainment	✓		

WWW.HM.COM

SCHAUMBURG—5 WOODFIELD SHOPPING CTR (AT GOLF RD); 847.619.9940; M-SA 10-9, SU 11-6; FREE PARKING

Hanna Andersson

"...top-notch, high-quality cotton clothes for babies and kids... pricey, but worth it for the durability and cuteness... girls clothes are beautifully designed... some stores have a train table for kids to play with while mom can shop... staff is always friendly... the long-john cotton pj's are the best... Hanna's cotton has no match—it looks new after being washed a billion times... neat kids' clothes—high-quality, bright colors and unique... clothes are soft, gorgeous and made to last... wonderful play dresses..."

Furniture, Bedding & Decor	✗	$$$$	Prices
Gear & Equipment	✗	❹	Product availability
Nursing & Feeding	✗	❹	Staff knowledge
Safety & Babycare	✗	❹	Customer service
Clothing, Shoes & Accessories	✓	❹	Decor
Books, Toys & Entertainment	✓		

WWW.HANNAANDERSSON.COM

SCHAUMBURG—WOODFIELD SHOPPING CENTER (AT WOODFIELD MALL); 847.413.9110; M-F 10-9, SA 10-9, SU 11-6

IKEA

"...the coolest-looking and best-priced bedding, bibs and eating utensils in town... fun, practical style and the prices are definitely right... one of the few stores around that lets kids climb and crawl on

furniture... the kids' area has a slide, tunnels, tents... is it an indoor playground or a store?.. unending decorating ideas for families on a budget (lamps, rugs, beds, bedding)... it's all about organization—cubbies, drawers, shelves, seats that double as a trunk and step stool... arts and crafts galore... free childcare while you shop... cheap eats if you get hungry... ”

Furniture, Bedding & Decor	✓	$$	Prices
Gear & Equipment	✗	❹	Product availability
Nursing & Feeding	✓	❹	Staff knowledge
Safety & Babycare	✓	❹	Customer service
Clothing, Shoes & Accessories	✗	❹	Decor
Books, Toys & Entertainment	✓		

WWW.IKEA.COM

SCHAUMBURG—1800 E MCCONNOR PKY (OFF GOLF RD); 847.969.9700; M-TH 10-9, F 10-10, SA 9-10, SU 10-8

Janie And Jack

“*...gorgeous clothing and some accessories (shoes, socks, etc.)... fun to look at, somewhat pricey, but absolutely adorable clothes for little ones... boutique-like clothes at non-boutique prices—especially on sale... high-quality infant and toddler clothes anyone would love—always good for a baby gift... I always check the clearance racks in the back of the store... their decor is darling—a really fun shopping experience...* ”

Furniture, Bedding & Decor	✗	$$$$	Prices
Gear & Equipment	✓	❹	Product availability
Nursing & Feeding	✗	❹	Staff knowledge
Safety & Babycare	✗	❹	Customer service
Clothing, Shoes & Accessories	✓	❹	Decor
Books, Toys & Entertainment	✗		

WWW.JANIEANDJACK.COM

SCHAUMBURG—WOODFIELD SHOPPING CTR (AT WOODFIELD SHOPPING CTR); 847.619.9921; M-SA 10-9, SU 11-6; MALL PARKING

JCPenney

“*...always a good place to find clothes and other baby basics... the registry process was seamless... staff is generally friendly but the lines always seem long and slow... they don't have the greatest selection of toddler clothes, but their baby section is great... we had some damaged furniture delivered but customer service was easy and accommodating... a pretty limited selection of gear, but what they have is priced right...* ”

Furniture, Bedding & Decor	✓	$$	Prices
Gear & Equipment	✓	❸	Product availability
Nursing & Feeding	✓	❸	Staff knowledge
Safety & Babycare	✓	❸	Customer service
Clothing, Shoes & Accessories	✓	❸	Decor
Books, Toys & Entertainment	✓		

WWW.JCPENNEY.COM

SCHAUMBURG—3 WOODFIELD MALL (AT GOLF RD); 847.240.5000; M-SA 10-10, SU 11-5; MALL PARKING

VERNON HILLS—480 E RING RD (AT HAWTHORN CTR); 847.367.0795; M-F 10-9, SA 10-7,SU 11-6

Jordan Marie

“*...very nice classic clothes—not too hip or overly trendy... upscale items for special occasions... the perfect place to buy shower gifts... be prepared for the big price tags... the cutest baby clothes ever... extremely cute items—they'll even put together custom baskets... nice sales staff... the online store is better... great clearance deals*

occasionally... the place to go for something fancy... the best baby gifts and you can even return on-line purchases at the retail stores which takes the worry out of shopping from home... ”

Furniture, Bedding & Decor	✗	$$$$	Prices
Gear & Equipment	✗	❸	Product availability
Nursing & Feeding	✗	❹	Staff knowledge
Safety & Babycare	✗	❹	Customer service
Clothing, Shoes & Accessories	✓	❹	Decor
Books, Toys & Entertainment	✓		

WWW.JORDANMARIE.COM

SCHAUMBURG—WOODFIELD MALL (AT GOLF & MEACHUMS RDS); 847.240.0035; M-SA 10-9, SU 11-6; PARKING AT RED ROBIN

KB Toys

“...hectic and always buzzing... wall-to-wall plastic and blinking lights... more Fisher-Price, Elmo and Sponge Bob than the eye can handle... a toy super store with discounted prices... they always have some kind of special sale going on... if you're looking for the latest and greatest popular toy, then look no further—not the place for unique or unusual toys... perfect for bulk toy shopping—especially around the holidays... ”

Furniture, Bedding & Decor	✗	$$	Prices
Gear & Equipment	✗	❸	Product availability
Nursing & Feeding	✗	❸	Staff knowledge
Safety & Babycare	✗	❸	Customer service
Clothing, Shoes & Accessories	✗	❸	Decor
Books, Toys & Entertainment	✓		

WWW.KBTOYS.COM

SCHAUMBURG—WOODFIELD MALL (AT GOLF RD); 847.619.1026; M-SA 10-9, SU 10-7; MALL PARKING

VERNON HILLS—HWY 60 & 21 (AT HAWTHORNE CTR); 847.680.7730; M-SA 10-9, SU 10-7

Kid's Foot Locker

“...Nike, Reebok and Adidas for your little ones... hip, trendy and quite pricey... perfect for the sports addict dad who wants his kid sporting the latest NFL duds... shoes cost close to what the adult variety costs... generally good quality... they carry infant and toddler sizes... ”

Furniture, Bedding & Decor	✗	$$$	Prices
Gear & Equipment	✗	❸	Product availability
Nursing & Feeding	✗	❸	Staff knowledge
Safety & Babycare	✗	❸	Customer service
Clothing, Shoes & Accessories	✓	❸	Decor
Books, Toys & Entertainment	✗		

WWW.KIDSFOOTLOCKER.COM

VERNON HILLS—224 HAWTHORN CTR (AT RING RD); 847.367.9630; M-SA 10-9, SU 11-6

Little Munchkins

“...lovely store with many one of a kind items... special order and custom bedding... clothes from Zutano, Le Top and more... a small, but well-chosen selection of decor items and furniture... keep them in mind for special occasion outfits—I bought a christening gown here that was just gorgeous... very cute and trendy boutique the kind of place to shop for someone who has it all and needs something unique... ”

Furniture, Bedding & Decor	✓	$$$$	Prices
Gear & Equipment	✓	❹	Product availability
Nursing & Feeding	✗	❹	Staff knowledge
Safety & Babycare	✗	❹	Customer service
Clothing, Shoes & Accessories	✓	❹	Decor

Books, Toys & Entertainment .... ✗

WWW.LITTLEMUNCHKINSINC.BIZ

BARRINGTON—141 S NORTHWEST HWY (AT LAKE COOK RD); 847.381.3960; M-SA 10-5

My Child's Room

"...we bought everything here... some of the lowest prices on cribs, rockers and dressers... the store has everything you might need for a new baby, but you are not overwhelmed by the endless selection of a mega store... a range of styles, all with excellent quality... a little pricey but always have someone there to help you... it can get crowded so you're best going during the week... some of their regular prices seem high, but they have fantastic sales..."

Furniture, Bedding & Decor	✓	$$$$	Prices
Gear & Equipment	✓	❸	Product availability
Nursing & Feeding	✓	❸	Staff knowledge
Safety & Babycare	✗	❸	Customer service
Clothing, Shoes & Accessories	✓	❹	Decor
Books, Toys & Entertainment	✓		

WWW.MYCHILDSROOM.NET

ARLINGTON HEIGHTS—1820 N ARLINGTON HEIGHTS RD (AT TOWN AND COUNTRY MALL); 847.253.4287; M-SA 10-8, SU 12-6; MALL PARKING

HOFFMAN ESTATES—2515 W GOLF RD (AT BARRINGTON RD); 847.885.2108; M-F 10-9, SA 10-6, SU 12-6; PARKING LOT

Old Navy

"...hip and 'in' clothes for infants and tots... plenty of steals on clearance items... T-shirts and pants for $10 or less... busy, busy, busy—long lines, especially on weekends... nothing fancy and you won't mind when your kids get down and dirty in these clothes... easy to wash, decent quality... you can shop for your baby, your toddler, your teen and yourself all at the same time... clothes are especially affordable when you hit their sales (post-holiday sales are amazing!)..."

Furniture, Bedding & Decor	✗	$$	Prices
Gear & Equipment	✗	❹	Product availability
Nursing & Feeding	✗	❸	Staff knowledge
Safety & Babycare	✗	❸	Customer service
Clothing, Shoes & Accessories	✓	❸	Decor
Books, Toys & Entertainment	✗		

WWW.OLDNAVY.COM

KILDEER—20505 N RAND RD (AT W LONG GROVE RD); 847.550.1485; M-SA 10-9, SU 11-7

SCHAUMBURG—1498 E GOLF RD (AT N PLAZA DR); 847.619.1715; M-SA 9-9, SU 10-6

Once Upon A Child

"...new and used items... the place for bargain baby items in like-new condition... a great bargain spot with a wide variety of clothes for baby... some inexpensive furniture... good selection, staff and prices... cluttered and hard to get through the store with kids... good toys and gear... some items are definitely more than 'gently used'... a kid's play area... good end-of-season sales... expect to sort through items... cash for your old items..."

Furniture, Bedding & Decor	✓	$$	Prices
Gear & Equipment	✓	❸	Product availability
Nursing & Feeding	✗	❹	Staff knowledge
Safety & Babycare	✗	❹	Customer service
Clothing, Shoes & Accessories	✓	❸	Decor
Books, Toys & Entertainment	✓		

WWW.OUAC.COM

SCHAUMBURG—1117 S ROSELLE RD (AT E WISE RD); 847.301.9250; M-F 10-8, SA 10-5, SU 11-4

Payless Shoe Source

"...a good place for deals on children's shoes... staff is helpful with sizing... the selection and prices for kids' shoes can't be beat, but the quality isn't always spectacular... good leather shoes for cheap... great variety of all sizes and widths... I get my son's shoes here and don't feel like I'm wasting my money since he'll outgrow them in 3 months anyway..."

Furniture, Bedding & Decor	✗	$$	Prices
Gear & Equipment	✗	❸	Product availability
Nursing & Feeding	✗	❸	Staff knowledge
Safety & Babycare	✗	❸	Customer service
Clothing, Shoes & Accessories	✓	❸	Decor
Books, Toys & Entertainment	✗		

WWW.PAYLESS.COM

ELK GROVE VILLAGE—MALLARD CROSSING SHOPPING CTR (AT BRANWOOD AVE); 847.985.5710

HOFFMAN ESTATES—GOLFROSE SHOPPING CTR (AT HASSEL RD); 847.882.0469; M-SA 9:30-9, SU 12-5

SCHAUMBURG—1476 E GOLF RD (AT N MEACHAM RD); 847.517.4401; M-SA 10-9, SU 10-6

SCHAUMBURG—WOODFIELD MALL (AT GOLF RD); 847.995.8910; M-SA 10-9, SU 11-6

Pottery Barn Kids

"...stylish furniture, rugs, rockers and much more... they've found the right mix between quality and price... finally a company that stands behind what they sell—their customer service is great... gorgeous baby decor and furniture that will make your nursery to-die-for... the play area is so much fun—my daughter never wants to leave... a beautiful store with tons of ideas for setting up your nursery or kid's room... bright colors and cute patterns with basics to mix and match... if you see something in the catalog, but not in the store, just ask because they often have it in the back..."

Furniture, Bedding & Decor	✓	$$$$	Prices
Gear & Equipment	✗	❹	Product availability
Nursing & Feeding	✗	❹	Staff knowledge
Safety & Babycare	✗	❹	Customer service
Clothing, Shoes & Accessories	✗	❺	Decor
Books, Toys & Entertainment	✓		

WWW.POTTERYBARNKIDS.COM

DEER PARK—20530 N RAND RD (AT W LONG GROVE RD); 847.438.4433; M-SA 10-9, SU 12-5

Rooms 4 Kids

"...a nice selection of beds, dressers and other furniture... children's rockers, step stools and tables... no cribs... the staff was very informative and courteous... decent prices for good quality furniture... store doesn't always have a ton of products... ordering times can be pretty long so plan ahead..."

Furniture, Bedding & Decor	✓	$$$	Prices
Gear & Equipment	✗	❹	Product availability
Nursing & Feeding	✗	❹	Staff knowledge
Safety & Babycare	✗	❹	Customer service
Clothing, Shoes & Accessories	✗	❹	Decor
Books, Toys & Entertainment	✗		

WWW.ROOMS4KIDS.COM

ARLINGTON HEIGHTS—1302 N RAND RD (AT OLIVIE); 847.259.5200; M W TH 10-9, T F 10-6, SA 10-5, SU 11-5; PARKING LOT

Sears

"...a decent selection of clothes and basic baby equipment... check out the Kids Club program—it's a great way to save money... you go to Sears to save money, not to be pampered... the quality of their merchandise is better than Wal-Mart, but don't expect anything too special or different... not much in terms of gear, but tons of well-priced baby and toddler clothing..."

Furniture, Bedding & Decor ✓
Gear & Equipment ✓
Nursing & Feeding ✓
Safety & Babycare ✓
Clothing, Shoes & Accessories ✓
Books, Toys & Entertainment ✓

$$ Prices
❸ Product availability
❸ Staff knowledge
❸ Customer service
❸ Decor

WWW.SEARS.COM

PALATINE—537 N HICKS RD (AT E BALDWIN); 847.221.0800; M-SA 8-10, SU 8-8

SCHAUMBURG—2 WOODFIELD MALL (AT GOLF RD); 847.330.2356; M-SA 10-9, SU 11-6

Target

"...our favorite place to shop for kids' stuff—good selection and very affordable... guilt-free shopping—kids grow so fast so I don't want to pay high department-store prices... everything from diapers and sippy cups to car seats and strollers... easy return policy... generally helpful staff, but you don't go for the service—you go for the prices... decent registry that won't freak your friends out with outrageous prices... easy, convenient shopping for well-priced items... all the big-box brands available—Graco, Evenflo, Eddie Bauer, etc...."

Furniture, Bedding & Decor ✓
Gear & Equipment ✓
Nursing & Feeding ✓
Safety & Babycare ✓
Clothing, Shoes & Accessories ✓
Books, Toys & Entertainment ✓

$$ Prices
❹ Product availability
❸ Staff knowledge
❸ Customer service
❸ Decor

WWW.TARGET.COM

ARLINGTON HEIGHTS—1700 E RAND RD (AT E THOMAS ST); 847.222.0925; M-SA 8-10, SU 8-9; PARKING IN FRONT OF BLDG

ELGIN—300 S RANDALL RD (AT SOUTH ST); 847.695.1992; M-SA 8-10, SU 8-9; PARKING IN FRONT OF BLDG

PALATINE—679 E DUNDEE RD (AT N HICKS RD); 847.202.5120; M-SA 8-10, SU 8-9; PARKING IN FRONT OF BLDG

SCHAUMBURG—1235 E HIGGINS RD (AT NATIONAL PKWY); 847.413.1080; M-SA 8-10, SU 8-9; PARKING IN FRONT OF BLDG

SCHAUMBURG—2621 W SCHAUMBURG RD (AT E SCHAUMBERG RD); 847.798.0192; M-SA 8-10, SU 8-9; PARKING IN FRONT OF BLDG

VERNON HILLS—313 E TOWNLINE RD (AT HAWTHORN CTR); 847.680.0723; M-SA 8-10, SU 8-9; PARKING IN FRONT OF BLDG

Tommy-Terri Shop

Furniture, Bedding & Decor ✗
Nursing & Feeding ✗
Clothing, Shoes & Accessories ✓

✗ Gear & Equipment
✗ Safety & Babycare
✓ Books, Toys & Entertainment

BARRINGTON—200 APPLEBEE ST (BTWN HARRISON & GARFIELD STS); 847.381.2005; M-SA 9:30-5:30, SU 12-4, TH 9:30-8

Toys R Us

"...not just toys, but also tons of gear and supplies including diapers and formula... a hectic shopping experience but the prices make it all worthwhile... I've experienced good and bad service at the same store on the same day... the stores are huge and can be overwhelming... most big brand-names available... leave the kids at home unless you want to end up with a cart full of toys..."

Furniture, Bedding & Decor .... ✓
Gear & Equipment .... ✓
Nursing & Feeding .... ✓
Safety & Babycare .... ✓
Clothing, Shoes & Accessories .... ✓
Books, Toys & Entertainment .... ✓

$$$ .... Prices
❹ .... Product availability
❸ .... Staff knowledge
❸ .... Customer service
❸ .... Decor

WWW.TOYSRUS.COM

ARLINGTON HEIGHTS—40 W RAND RD (AT N EVERGREEN AVE); 847.259.8697; M-SA 9:30-9:30, SU 10-7

SCHAUMBURG—1111 E GOLF RD (AT NATIONAL PKWY); 847.517.1300; M-SA 9:30-9:30, SU 10-7

VERNON HILLS—5555 TOWNLINE RD (AT RTE 21); 847.367.0029; M-SA 9:30-9:30, SU 10-7

Northern Suburbs

"lila picks"

- ★Babies R Us
- ★Chocolate Soup
- ★Galt Toys and Galt Baby
- ★Land of Nod
- ★Lazar's Juvenile Furniture
- ★My Child's Room
- ★Pottery Barn Kids
- ★The Right Start

Active Endeavors

"...adorable clothes for kids and moms too... all the hot kids brands for good prices... especially great for sporty boys and girls... terrific selection of shorts and summer play clothes... sizes can occasionally be tough to find..."

Furniture, Bedding & Decor	×	$$$	Prices
Gear & Equipment	×	❹	Product availability
Nursing & Feeding	×	❹	Staff knowledge
Safety & Babycare	×	❹	Customer service
Clothing, Shoes & Accessories	✓	❹	Decor
Books, Toys & Entertainment	✓		

WWW.ACTIVEENDEAVORS.COM

EVANSTON—1527 CHICAGO AVE (OFF DAVIS ST); 847.869.7070; M-TH 10-7, F, SA 10-6, SU 12-6

GLENCOE—694 VERNON AVE (AT PARK AVE); 847.835.3520; M-SA 10-6, SU 12-5; PARKING LOT

April Cornell

"...beautiful, classic dresses and accessories for special occasions... I love the matching 'mommy and me' outfits... lots of fun knickknacks for sale... great selection of baby wear on their web site... rest assured your baby won't look like every other child in these adorable outfits... very frilly and girlie—beautiful..."

Furniture, Bedding & Decor	×	$$$	Prices
Gear & Equipment	×	❸	Product availability
Nursing & Feeding	×	❹	Staff knowledge
Safety & Babycare	×	❹	Customer service
Clothing, Shoes & Accessories	✓	❹	Decor
Books, Toys & Entertainment	×		

NORTHBROOK—2228 NORTHBROOK CT (AT NORTHBROOK MALL); 847.564.8570; M-SA 10-9, SU 11-6

Babies R Us

"...everything baby under one roof... they have a wide selection and carry most 'mainstream' items such as Graco, Fisher-Price, Avent and Britax... great customer service—given how big the stores are, I was pleasantly surprised at how attentive the staff was... easy return

policy... super busy on weekends so try to visit on a weekday for the best service... keep an eye out for great coupons, deals and frequent sales... easy and comprehensive registry... shopping here is so easy—you've got to check it out... **”**

Furniture, Bedding & Decor	✓	$$$	Prices
Gear & Equipment	✓	❹	Product availability
Nursing & Feeding	✓	❹	Staff knowledge
Safety & Babycare	✓	❹	Customer service
Clothing, Shoes & Accessories	✓	❹	Decor
Books, Toys & Entertainment	✓		

WWW.BABIESRUS.COM

NILES—5660 TOUHY AVE (AT N CENTRAL AVE); 847.588.2081; M-SA 9:30-9:30, SU 11-7; PARKING IN FRONT OF BLDG

Baby Depot At Burlington Coat Factory ★★★½☆

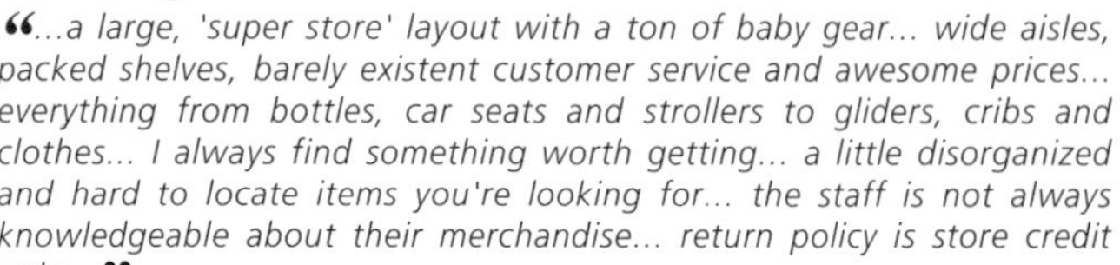

“*...a large, 'super store' layout with a ton of baby gear... wide aisles, packed shelves, barely existent customer service and awesome prices... everything from bottles, car seats and strollers to gliders, cribs and clothes... I always find something worth getting... a little disorganized and hard to locate items you're looking for... the staff is not always knowledgeable about their merchandise... return policy is store credit only...* **”**

Furniture, Bedding & Decor	✓	$$	Prices
Gear & Equipment	✓	❸	Product availability
Nursing & Feeding	✓	❸	Staff knowledge
Safety & Babycare	✓	❸	Customer service
Clothing, Shoes & Accessories	✓	❸	Decor
Books, Toys & Entertainment	✓		

WWW.BABYDEPOT.COM

GURNEE—6170 GRAND AVE (AT GURNEE MILLS MALL); 847.855.0565; M-F 10-9, SA 10-9:30, SU 11-7; MALL PARKING

MUNDELEIN—1555 S LAKE ST (AT HIGHWAY 45); 847.566.1295; M-SA 10-9, SU 11-6; PARKING LOT

BabyGap/GapKids

“*...colorful baby and toddler clothing in clean, well-lit stores... great return policy... it's the Gap, so you know what you're getting—colorful, cute and well-made clothing... best place for baby hats... prices are reasonable especially since there's always a sale of some sort going on... sales, sales, sales—frequent and fantastic... everything I'm looking for in infant clothing—snap crotches, snaps up the front, all natural fabrics and great styling... fun seasonal selections—a great place to shop for gifts as well as for your own kids... although it can get busy, staff generally seem accommodating and helpful...* **”**

Furniture, Bedding & Decor	✗	$$$	Prices
Gear & Equipment	✗	❹	Product availability
Nursing & Feeding	✗	❹	Staff knowledge
Safety & Babycare	✗	❹	Customer service
Clothing, Shoes & Accessories	✓	❹	Decor
Books, Toys & Entertainment	✗		

WWW.GAP.COM

GURNEE—6170 GRAND AVE (AT GURNEE MILLS MALL); 847.855.9311; M-F 10-9, SA 10-9:30, SU 11-7; MALL PARKING

HIGHLAND PARK—661 CENTRAL AVE (AT GREEN BAY RD); 847.266.0327; M-F 9:30-7, SA 9:30-6, SU 11-5; PARKING IN FRONT OF BLDG

LIBERTYVILLE—319 HAWTHORNE SHOPPING CTR (AT RING RD); 847.362.6363; M-SA 10-9, SU 11-6; PARKING IN FRONT OF BLDG

NORTHBROOK—1324 NORTHBROOK CT (AT NORTHBROOK SHOPPING CTR); 847.480.8848; M-SA 10-9, SU 11-6; PARKING IN FRONT OF BLDG

SKOKIE—175 OLD ORCHARD SHOPPING CTR (AT GOLF RD); 847.673.3529; M-F 10-9, SA 10-9, SU 11-6; PARKING LOT AT CENTER

Bellini

"...high-end furniture for a gorgeous nursery... if you're looking for the kind of furniture you see in magazines then this is the place to go... excellent quality... yes, it's pricey, but the quality is impeccable... free delivery and setup... their furniture is built to withstand the abuse my tots dish out... they sell very unique merchandise, ranging from cribs to bedding and even some clothes... our nursery design was inspired by their store decor... I wish they had more frequent sales..."

Furniture, Bedding & Decor	✓	$$$$	Prices
Gear & Equipment	×	❹	Product availability
Nursing & Feeding	×	❹	Staff knowledge
Safety & Babycare	×	❹	Customer service
Clothing, Shoes & Accessories	×	❹	Decor
Books, Toys & Entertainment	✓		

WWW.BELLINI.COM

HIGHLAND PARK—806 CENTRAL AVE (AT GREEN BAY RD); 847.433.5650; M-F 10-6, SA 10-5, SU 1-5

Carter's

"...always a great selection of inexpensive baby basics—everything from clothing to linens... I always find something at 'giveaway prices' during one of their frequent sales... busy and crowded—it can be a chaotic shopping experience... 30 to 50 percent less than what you would pay at other boutiques... I bought five pieces of baby clothing for less than $40... durable, adorable and affordable... most stores have a small play area for kids in center of store so you can get your shopping done..."

Furniture, Bedding & Decor	✓	$$	Prices
Gear & Equipment	×	❹	Product availability
Nursing & Feeding	×	❹	Staff knowledge
Safety & Babycare	×	❹	Customer service
Clothing, Shoes & Accessories	✓	❹	Decor
Books, Toys & Entertainment	✓		

WWW.CARTERS.COM

DEERFIELD—118 S WAUKEGAN RD (AT DEERBROOK MALL); 847.559.0434; M-SA 10-9, SU 10-7; MALL PARKING

Children's Place, The

"...great bargains on cute clothing... shoes, socks, swimsuits, sunglasses and everything in between... lots of '3 for $20' type deals on sleepers, pants and mix-and-match separates... so much more affordable than the other 'big chains'... don't expect the most unique stuff here, but it wears and washes well... cheap clothing for cheap prices... you can leave the store with bags full of clothes without putting a huge dent in your wallet..."

Furniture, Bedding & Decor	×	$$	Prices
Gear & Equipment	×	❹	Product availability
Nursing & Feeding	×	❹	Staff knowledge
Safety & Babycare	×	❹	Customer service
Clothing, Shoes & Accessories	✓	❹	Decor
Books, Toys & Entertainment	✓		

WWW.CHILDRENSPLACE.COM

DEERFIELD—720 WAUKEGAN RD (AT OSTERMAN AVE); 847.948.7582; M-F 9-7, SA 10-6, SU 11-5

Chocolate Soup ★★★★★

"...a great place to go and find out-of-the-ordinary items for your kids... the hippest clothes including my favorite brands like Baby Lulu and Le Top... very helpful staff... well worth the visit—their sales are awesome... tons of great merchandise at good prices... unique items—especially for girls... they have great sales, so be sure to sign up for mailing list... I'm never disappointed and always find something cute... a great variety of designer duds..."

Furniture, Bedding & Decor	✗	$$$	Prices
Gear & Equipment	✗	❹	Product availability
Nursing & Feeding	✗	❹	Staff knowledge
Safety & Babycare	✗	❹	Customer service
Clothing, Shoes & Accessories	✓	❸	Decor
Books, Toys & Entertainment	✗		

WINNETKA—602 GREEN BAY RD (AT PINE ST); 847.446.8951; M-W, F-SA 10-5:30, TH 10-8, SU 12-5 ; PARKING IN FRONT OF BLDG

Costco

"...dependable place for bulk diapers, wipes and formula at discount prices... clothing selection is very hit-or-miss... avoid shopping there during nights and weekends if possible, because parking and checkout lines are brutal... they don't have a huge selection of brands, but the brands they do have are almost always in stock and at a great price... lowest prices around for diapers and formula... kid's clothing tends to be picked through, but it's worth looking for great deals on name-brand items like Carter's..."

Furniture, Bedding & Decor	✓	$$	Prices
Gear & Equipment	✓	❸	Product availability
Nursing & Feeding	✓	❸	Staff knowledge
Safety & Babycare	✓	❸	Customer service
Clothing, Shoes & Accessories	✓	❷	Decor
Books, Toys & Entertainment	✓		

WWW.COSTCO.COM

GLENVIEW—2900 PATRIOT BLVD; 847.730.1003; M-F 10-8:30, SA 9:30-6, SU 10-6

NILES—7311 MELVINA AVE; 847.972.3003; M-F 10-8:30, SA 9:30-6, SU 10-6

Country Classics

Furniture, Bedding & Decor	✗	✗	Gear & Equipment
Nursing & Feeding	✗	✗	Safety & Babycare
Clothing, Shoes & Accessories	✓	✗	Books, Toys & Entertainment

GLENVIEW—1405 WAUKEGAN RD (AT E LAKE AVE); 847.998.4644; M-SA 9:30-6, SU 11-6, TH 9:30-8

Daydreams

"...trendy children boutique... my daughter has a better wardrobe than I do because of this store... adorable, but pricey... a definite treat if you feel like splurging..."

Furniture, Bedding & Decor	✗	$$$$	Prices
Gear & Equipment	✗	❹	Product availability
Nursing & Feeding	✗	❹	Staff knowledge
Safety & Babycare	✗	❹	Customer service
Clothing, Shoes & Accessories	✓	❹	Decor
Books, Toys & Entertainment	✗		

HIGHLAND PARK—482 CENTRAL AVE (AT SHERIDAN RD); 847.433.8055; M-F 10-5, SA 10-4

Euro Bimbi

Furniture, Bedding & Decor	✗	✗	Gear & Equipment
Nursing & Feeding	✗	✗	Safety & Babycare

Clothing, Shoes & Accessories....... ✓ ✗......... Books, Toys & Entertainment

HIGHLAND PARK—600 CENTRAL AVE (AT 1ST ST); 847.433.9020; M-F 10-6, SA 10-5; PARKING LOT

Galt Toys & Galt Baby

"...a wonderful neighborhood shopping destination for new parents... they carry strollers, baby products, and hard-to-find toys... we found things here that can't be found anyplace else... this store has just about everything you'll need for your baby (or they know how/where to get it)... very knowledgeable staff and excellent selection... a must-visit for new Chicago moms and dads..."

Furniture, Bedding & Decor .... ✗ $$$$ .... Prices
Gear & Equipment .... ✓ ❹...................... Product availability
Nursing & Feeding........................ ✓ ❹.......................... Staff knowledge
Safety & Babycare .... ✓ ❹........................ Customer service
Clothing, Shoes & Accessories....... ✓ ❹.. Decor
Books, Toys & Entertainment .... ✓

WWW.GALTTOYSGALTBABY.COM

NORTHBROOK—2012 NORTHBROOK CT (AT NORTHBROOK COURT SHOPPING CTR); 847.498.4660; M-SA 10-9, SU 11-6; PARKING LOT AT CENTER

Giggles & Giraffes

"...clothes and gear... new and trendy... one of the few places that carries the Mountain Buggy stroller... cool gear... well worth the prices for the professional selection and service..."

Furniture, Bedding & Decor .... ✗ $$$$ .... Prices
Gear & Equipment .... ✓ ❹...................... Product availability
Nursing & Feeding........................ ✗ ❹.......................... Staff knowledge
Safety & Babycare .... ✗ ❹........................ Customer service
Clothing, Shoes & Accessories....... ✓ ❺.. Decor
Books, Toys & Entertainment .... ✗

WILMETTE—1515 SHERIDAN RD (AT WESTERFIELD DR); 847.251.6665; M-SA 10-5; FREE PARKING

Gymboree

"...beautiful clothing and great quality... colorful and stylish baby and kids wear... lots of fun birthday gift ideas... easy exchange and return policy... items usually go on sale pretty quickly... save money with Gymbucks... many stores have a play area which makes shopping with my kids fun (let alone feasible)..."

Furniture, Bedding & Decor .... ✗ $$$ .... Prices
Gear & Equipment .... ✗ ❹...................... Product availability
Nursing & Feeding........................ ✗ ❹.......................... Staff knowledge
Safety & Babycare .... ✗ ❹........................ Customer service
Clothing, Shoes & Accessories....... ✓ ❹.. Decor
Books, Toys & Entertainment .... ✓

WWW.GYMBOREE.COM

NORTHBROOK—2056 NORTHBROOK CT (AT NORTHBROOK COURT SHOPPING CTR); 847.205.5113; M-SA 10-9, SU 11-6; PARKING LOT AT CENTER

SKOKIE—253 OLD ORCHARD CTR (AT GOLF RD); 847.982.0039; M-SA 10-9, SU 11-6; PARKING LOT AT CENTER

H & M

"...wonderful prices for trendy baby and toddler clothes... it's the 'Euro' Target... buy for yourself and for your kids... a fun shopping experience as long as your child doesn't mind the bright lights and loud music... decent return policy... incredible sale prices... store can get

messy at peak hours... busy and hectic, but their inventory is fun and worth the visit... ❞

Furniture, Bedding & Decor	✗	$$	Prices
Gear & Equipment	✗	❸	Product availability
Nursing & Feeding	✗	❸	Staff knowledge
Safety & Babycare	✗	❸	Customer service
Clothing, Shoes & Accessories	✓	❸	Decor
Books, Toys & Entertainment	✓		

WWW.HM.COM

GURNEE—6170 GRAND AVE (AT GURNEE MILLS MALL); 847.855.7847; M-F 10-9, SA 10-9:30, SU 11-7

Initial Choice ★★★★☆

❝*...from blankets to beach chairs, these guys will put names or initials on pretty much anything... I always love getting personalized gifts... all my baby gifts come from this store... quick and professional... tons of blankets, big and small...* ❞

Furniture, Bedding & Decor	✓	$$$	Prices
Gear & Equipment	✓	❺	Product availability
Nursing & Feeding	✗	❺	Staff knowledge
Safety & Babycare	✗	❺	Customer service
Clothing, Shoes & Accessories	✓	❹	Decor
Books, Toys & Entertainment	✓		

WWW.INITIALCHOICE.COM

LAKE FOREST—226 E WESTMINSTER RD (AT N MCKINLEY RD); 847.234.5884; M-F 9-5, SA 10-5

Jacadi ★★★★☆

❝*...beautiful French clothes, baby bumpers and quilts... elegant and perfect for special occasions... quite expensive, but the clothing is hip and the quality really good... many handmade clothing and bedding items... take advantage of their sales... more of a store to buy gifts than practical, everyday clothes... beautiful, special clothing—especially for newborns and toddlers... velvet pajamas, coordinated nursery items... stores are as pretty as the clothes... they have a huge (half-off everything) sale twice a year that makes it very affordable...* ❞

Furniture, Bedding & Decor	✓	$$$$	Prices
Gear & Equipment	✗	❹	Product availability
Nursing & Feeding	✗	❹	Staff knowledge
Safety & Babycare	✗	❹	Customer service
Clothing, Shoes & Accessories	✓	❹	Decor
Books, Toys & Entertainment	✓		

WWW.JACADIUSA.COM

NORTHBROOK—2056 NORTHBROOK CT (AT NORTHBROOK COURT SHOPPING CTR); 847.559.9205; M-SA 10-7, SU 11-6

Janie And Jack

❝*...gorgeous clothing and some accessories (shoes, socks, etc.)... fun to look at, somewhat pricey, but absolutely adorable clothes for little ones... boutique-like clothes at non-boutique prices—especially on sale... high-quality infant and toddler clothes anyone would love—always good for a baby gift... I always check the clearance racks in the back of the store... their decor is darling—a really fun shopping experience...* ❞

Furniture, Bedding & Decor	✗	$$$$	Prices
Gear & Equipment	✓	❹	Product availability
Nursing & Feeding	✗	❹	Staff knowledge
Safety & Babycare	✗	❹	Customer service
Clothing, Shoes & Accessories	✓	❹	Decor
Books, Toys & Entertainment	✗		

WWW.JANIEANDJACK.COM

NORTHBROOK—2228 NORTHBROOK CT (AT NORTHBROOK SHOPPING CTR); 847.480.5857; M-SA 10-9, SU 11-6; PARKING LOT AT CENTER

SKOKIE—253 OLD ORCHARD RD (AT GROSS POINT RD); 847.763.9223; M-SA 10-9, SU 11-6

JCPenney

"...always a good place to find clothes and other baby basics... the registry process was seamless... staff is generally friendly but the lines always seem long and slow... they don't have the greatest selection of toddler clothes, but their baby section is great... we had some damaged furniture delivered but customer service was easy and accommodating... a pretty limited selection of gear, but what they have is priced right..."

Furniture, Bedding & Decor	✓	$$	Prices
Gear & Equipment	✓	❸	Product availability
Nursing & Feeding	✓	❸	Staff knowledge
Safety & Babycare	✓	❸	Customer service
Clothing, Shoes & Accessories	✓	❸	Decor
Books, Toys & Entertainment	✓		

WWW.JCPENNEY.COM

NILES—220 GOLF MILL CTR (AT GREENWOOD AVE); 847.299.8888; M-SA 10-9, SU 10:30-7; PARKING LOT AT CENTER

Jump N Style

Furniture, Bedding & Decor	✗	✗	Gear & Equipment
Nursing & Feeding	✗	✗	Safety & Babycare
Clothing, Shoes & Accessories	✓	✗	Books, Toys & Entertainment

GLENVIEW—2737 PFINGSTEN RD (AT WILLOW RD); 847.291.6877; M-SA 10-6, TH 10-7

KB Toys

"...hectic and always buzzing... wall-to-wall plastic and blinking lights... more Fisher-Price, Elmo and Sponge Bob than the eye can handle... a toy super store with discounted prices... they always have some kind of special sale going on... if you're looking for the latest and greatest popular toy, then look no further—not the place for unique or unusual toys... perfect for bulk toy shopping—especially around the holidays..."

Furniture, Bedding & Decor	✗	$$	Prices
Gear & Equipment	✗	❸	Product availability
Nursing & Feeding	✗	❸	Staff knowledge
Safety & Babycare	✗	❸	Customer service
Clothing, Shoes & Accessories	✗	❸	Decor
Books, Toys & Entertainment	✓		

WWW.KBTOYS.COM

GURNEE—6170 W GRAND AVE (AT GURNEE MILLS); 847.855.0170; M-SA 10-9, SU 11-7

LINCOLNWOOD—3333 W TOUHY AVE (AT LINCOLNWOOD TOWN CTR); 847.674.8877; M-F 10-9, SA 10-8, SU 11-6

NILES—MILWAUKEE AVE & GOLF RD (AT GOLF MILL); 847.294.0290; M-F 10-9, SA-SU 10-6

Kid's Foot Locker

"...Nike, Reebok and Adidas for your little ones... hip, trendy and quite pricey... perfect for the sports addict dad who wants his kid sporting the latest NFL duds... shoes cost close to what the adult variety costs... generally good quality... they carry infant and toddler sizes..."

Furniture, Bedding & Decor	✗	$$$	Prices
Gear & Equipment	✗	❸	Product availability

Nursing & Feeding ✗ | ❸ Staff knowledge
Safety & Babycare ✗ | ❸ Customer service
Clothing, Shoes & Accessories ✓ | ❸ Decor
Books, Toys & Entertainment ✗

WWW.KIDSFOOTLOCKER.COM

NILES—239 GOLF MILL CTR (AT N GREENWOOD AVE); 847.768.1204; M-SA 10-9, SU 11-6

Kohl's ★★★★☆

"...nice one-stop shopping for the whole family—everything from clothing to baby gear... great sales on clothing and a good selection of higher-end brands... stylish, inexpensive clothes for babies through 24 months... very easy shopping experience... dirt-cheap sales and clearance prices... nothing super fancy, but just right for those everyday romper outfits... Graco, Eddie Bauer and other well-known brands..."

Furniture, Bedding & Decor ✓ | $$ Prices
Gear & Equipment ✓ | ❹ Product availability
Nursing & Feeding ✓ | ❸ Staff knowledge
Safety & Babycare ✓ | ❸ Customer service
Clothing, Shoes & Accessories ✓ | ❸ Decor
Books, Toys & Entertainment ✓

WWW.KOHLS.COM

GLENVIEW—2201 WILLOW RD (AT WILLOW HILL GOLF COURSE); 847.832.9400; M-SA 8-10, SU 10-8; FREE PARKING

LINCOLNWOOD—3333 TOUHY AVE (AT MCCORMICK BLVD); 847.673.9140; M-SA 8-10, SU 10-8; FREE PARKING

NILES—590 GOLF MILL CTR (AT GOLF RD); 847.296.7600; M-SA 8-10, SU 10-8; FREE PARKING

Land of Nod ★★★★★

"...creative and fun decor and furnishings... lots of practical stuff that has a bit more flair than your typical furnishings store... nice, helpful staff... a truly terrific place to buy gifts... lots of cool, retro stuff that you don't find elsewhere... love their book and music selection... great ideas for decorating kids' bedrooms... fabulous customer service and knowledgeable staff... adorable furniture and bedding..."

Furniture, Bedding & Decor ✓ | $$$$ Prices
Gear & Equipment ✗ | ❹ Product availability
Nursing & Feeding ✗ | ❹ Staff knowledge
Safety & Babycare ✗ | ❹ Customer service
Clothing, Shoes & Accessories ✗ | ❺ Decor
Books, Toys & Entertainment ✓

WWW.LANDOFNOD.COM

NORTHBROOK—2177 SHERMER RD (AT TECHNY RD); 847.656.4720; M-F 9-5, SA 9-5, SU 9-5

NORTHBROOK—NORTHBROOK COURT (AT NORTHBROOK COURT SHOPPING CTR); 847.291.9902; M-F 10-9, SA 10-7, SU 11-6; MALL PARKING

Lazar's Juvenile Furniture ★★★★★

"...incredible baby furniture and equipment store... their selection is fantastic—Bugaboo, BOB, Graco, Combi, Mountain Buggy... a great place to check out strollers—their staff is quite knowledgeable and is eager to help... if you have the money, buy all your baby stuff here... furniture will stay with your child forever... they deliver, set up and show you how to use everything... great customer service... weekends are crowded... although you need to order things far in advance, they will hold on to your stuff until the baby comes..."

Furniture, Bedding & Decor ✓ | $$$$ Prices
Gear & Equipment ✓ | ❹ Product availability
Nursing & Feeding ✓ | ❺ Staff knowledge

Safety & Babycare .... ✗ ❹........................ Customer service
Clothing, Shoes & Accessories...... ✗ ❹.. Decor
Books, Toys & Entertainment .... ✗

WWW.LAZARSFURNITURE.COM

LINCOLNWOOD—6557 N LINCOLN AVE (AT DEVON AVE); 847.679.6146; M-SA 10-5:30, SU 11-4; PARKING IN FRONT OF BLDG

Little Chick Shoe Shop ★★★★☆

"...the best place in Evanston to get quality children's shoes... excellent service... prices may be a little higher than some other stores, but the shoes are sure to fit and last for a while... they help you fit shoes properly... well worth the visit..."

Furniture, Bedding & Decor	✗	$$$$	Prices
Gear & Equipment	✗	❺	Product availability
Nursing & Feeding	✗	❺	Staff knowledge
Safety & Babycare	✗	❺	Customer service
Clothing, Shoes & Accessories	✓	❺	Decor
Books, Toys & Entertainment	✗		

EVANSTON—1627 SHERMAN AVE (AT DAVIS ST); 847.475.8333; M-W F 10-6, TH 10-7, SA 9-6, SU 11-5

Lollie ★★★★½

"...pricey beautiful baby clothes... just one sweater from this shop and your baby will look adorable and special all winter... Flora and Henri, Carmel Baby and Child and other name brands... also cool candy and of course lollipops..."

Furniture, Bedding & Decor	✗	$$$$	Prices
Gear & Equipment	✗	❹	Product availability
Nursing & Feeding	✗	❹	Staff knowledge
Safety & Babycare	✗	❹	Customer service
Clothing, Shoes & Accessories	✓	❹	Decor
Books, Toys & Entertainment	✗		

WWW.LOLLIESHOP.COM

EVANSTON—1312 CHICAGO AVE (AT DEMPSTER ST); 847.328.7303; T-F 10-6, SA 10-6, SU 12-5

Mud Pies ★★★☆☆

"...limited, but very cute selection for infants and newborns... they carry Robeez shoes... some adorable dress-up clothes—especially for girls... the store is jam packed with merchandise... maneuvering with a stroller can be tough..."

Furniture, Bedding & Decor	✗	$$$$	Prices
Gear & Equipment	✗	❹	Product availability
Nursing & Feeding	✗	❹	Staff knowledge
Safety & Babycare	✗	❹	Customer service
Clothing, Shoes & Accessories	✓	❸	Decor
Books, Toys & Entertainment	✗		

WWW.MUDPIESFORKIDS.COM

EVANSTON—2012 CENTRAL ST (AT GREEN BAY RD); 847.869.9191; M-F 10-6, SA 10-5, SU 11-4

My Child's Room ★★★★★

"...we bought everything here... some of the lowest prices on cribs, rockers and dressers... the store has everything you might need for a new baby, but you are not overwhelmed by the endless selection of a mega store... a range of styles, all with excellent quality... a little pricey but always have someone there to help you... it can get crowded so you're best going during the week... some of their regular prices seem high, but they have fantastic sales..."

Furniture, Bedding & Decor	✓	$$$$	Prices

Gear & Equipment ✓
Nursing & Feeding ✓
Safety & Babycare ✗
Clothing, Shoes & Accessories ✓
Books, Toys & Entertainment ✓

❸ Product availability
❸ Staff knowledge
❸ Customer service
❹ Decor

WWW.MYCHILDSROOM.NET

MUNDELEIN—8 OAK CREEK PLZ (AT HIGHWAY 60); 847.566.0763; M-F 10-9, SA 10-6, SU 12-6; PARKING LOT

NILES—5613 W TOUHY AVE (AT N CENTRAL AVE); 847.647.7005; M-SA 10-8, SU 12-6; PARKING LOT

Nordstrom ★★★★☆

"...quality service and quality clothes... awesome kids shoe department—almost as good as the one for adults... free balloons in the children's shoe area as well as drawing tables... in addition to their own brand, they carry a very nice selection of other high-end baby clothing including Ralph Lauren, Robeez, etc... adorable baby clothes—they make great shower gifts... such a wonderful shopping experience—their lounge is perfect for breastfeeding and for changing diapers... well-rounded selection of baby basics as well as fancy clothes for special events..."

Furniture, Bedding & Decor ✓
Gear & Equipment ✓
Nursing & Feeding ✗
Safety & Babycare ✗
Clothing, Shoes & Accessories ✓
Books, Toys & Entertainment ✓

$$$$ Prices
❹ Product availability
❹ Staff knowledge
❹ Customer service
❹ Decor

WWW.NORDSTROM.COM

SKOKIE—77 OLD ORCHARD SHOPPING CTR (AT GOLF RD); 847.677.2121; M-F 9-9, SA 9:30-9, SU 11-6

Oilily ★★★★½

"...exclusive shop with fun, colorful clothing... prices are a bit steep, but if you value unique, well-designed clothes, this is the place... better selection for girls than boys but there are special items for either sex... your tot will definitely stand out from the crowd in these unique pieces... my kids love wearing their 'cool' clothes... whimsical items for mom, too..."

Furniture, Bedding & Decor ✗
Gear & Equipment ✗
Nursing & Feeding ✗
Safety & Babycare ✗
Clothing, Shoes & Accessories ✓
Books, Toys & Entertainment ✗

$$$$ Prices
❹ Product availability
❹ Staff knowledge
❹ Customer service
❹ Decor

WWW.OILILYUSA.COM

NORTHBROOK—2090 NORTHBROOK CT (AT LAKE COOK RD); 847.562.0401; M-SA 10-9, SU 11-6

Old Navy ★★★★☆

"...hip and 'in' clothes for infants and tots... plenty of steals on clearance items... T-shirts and pants for $10 or less... busy, busy, busy—long lines, especially on weekends... nothing fancy and you won't mind when your kids get down and dirty in these clothes... easy to wash, decent quality... you can shop for your baby, your toddler, your teen and yourself all at the same time... clothes are especially affordable when you hit their sales (post-holiday sales are amazing!)..."

Furniture, Bedding & Decor ✗
Gear & Equipment ✗
Nursing & Feeding ✗

$$ Prices
❹ Product availability
❸ Staff knowledge

Safety & Babycare .... ✕	❸ .... Customer service
Clothing, Shoes & Accessories....... ✓	❸ .... Decor
Books, Toys & Entertainment .... ✕	

WWW.OLDNAVY.COM

GURNEE—6901 GRAND AVE (AT GURNEE MILLS MALL); 847.855.9890; M-SA 9-9, SU 11-6; MALL PARKING

LINCOLNWOOD—3333 W TOUHY AVE (AT N MCCORMICK BLVD); 847.677.1793; M-F 9-9, SA 9-8, SU 10-6

SKOKIE—9435 SKOKIE BLVD (AT GROSS POINT RD); 847.329.8505; M-SA 9-9, SU 10-6

OshKosh B'Gosh

"...cute, sturdy clothes for infants and toddlers... frequent sales make their high-quality merchandise a lot more affordable... doesn't every American kid have to get a pair of their overalls?.. great selection of cute clothes for boys... you can't go wrong here—their clothing is fun and worth the price... customer service is pretty hit-or-miss from store to store... we always walk out of here with something fun and colorful..."

Furniture, Bedding & Decor .... ✕	$$$ .... Prices
Gear & Equipment .... ✕	❹ .... Product availability
Nursing & Feeding .... ✕	❹ .... Staff knowledge
Safety & Babycare .... ✕	❹ .... Customer service
Clothing, Shoes & Accessories....... ✓	❹ .... Decor
Books, Toys & Entertainment .... ✕	

WWW.OSHKOSHBGOSH.COM

GURNEE —6170 W GRAND AVE (AT TRI STATE PKWY); 847.856.8172; M-F 10-9, SA 10-9:30, SU 11-7

Parkway Drugs

"...my favorite drug store for baby stuff... Gripe Water for baby and Murad for me... extremely reasonably prices... nice sales staff and pharmacists... they seem to have everything I need including breast pump rentals..."

Furniture, Bedding & Decor .... ✕	$$$ .... Prices
Gear & Equipment .... ✕	❹ .... Product availability
Nursing & Feeding .... ✓	❹ .... Staff knowledge
Safety & Babycare .... ✓	❹ .... Customer service
Clothing, Shoes & Accessories....... ✕	❹ .... Decor
Books, Toys & Entertainment .... ✕	

GLENCOE—353 PARK AVE (AT VERNON AVE); 847.835.0387; M-TH 8-8, F 8-7, SA 8-6, SU 9-5

WILMETTE—333 RIDGE RD (AT WILMETTE AVE); 847.256.1000; M-TH 7:30-8, F 7:30-7, SA 7:30-5, SU 9-5

Pottery Barn Kids

"...stylish furniture, rugs, rockers and much more... they've found the right mix between quality and price... finally a company that stands behind what they sell—their customer service is great... gorgeous baby decor and furniture that will make your nursery to-die-for... the play area is so much fun—my daughter never wants to leave... a beautiful store with tons of ideas for setting up your nursery or kid's room... bright colors and cute patterns with basics to mix and match... if you see something in the catalog, but not in the store, just ask because they often have it in the back..."

Furniture, Bedding & Decor .... ✓	$$$$ .... Prices
Gear & Equipment .... ✕	❹ .... Product availability
Nursing & Feeding .... ✕	❹ .... Staff knowledge
Safety & Babycare .... ✕	❹ .... Customer service
Clothing, Shoes & Accessories....... ✕	❺ .... Decor

Books, Toys & Entertainment .... ✓

WWW.POTTERYBARNKIDS.COM

SKOKIE—117 OLD ORCHARD CTR (AT GOLF RD); 847.673.8713; M-SA 10-9, SU 12-5

Right Start, The ★★★★★

"...higher-end, well selected items... Britax, Maclaren, Combi, Mustela—all the cool brands under one roof... everything from bibs to bottles and even the Bugaboo stroller... prices seem a little high, but the selection is good and the staff knowledgeable and helpful... there are toys all over the store that kids can play with while you shop... I have a hard time getting my kids out of the store because they are having so much fun... a boutique-like shopping experience but they carry most of the key brands... their registry works well..."

Furniture, Bedding & Decor	✓	$$$	Prices
Gear & Equipment	✓	❹	Product availability
Nursing & Feeding	✓	❹	Staff knowledge
Safety & Babycare	✓	❹	Customer service
Clothing, Shoes & Accessories	✓	❹	Decor
Books, Toys & Entertainment	✓		

WWW.RIGHTSTART.COM

HIGHLAND PARK—478 CENTRAL AVE (AT ST JOHNS AVE); 847.266.9270; DAILY 11-6

Room & Board

"...the store doesn't have a huge selection of baby furniture, but what's there is excellent quality... the staff is terrific... expect to receive fantastic customer service... terrific for the transition into a twin or bunk bed... a great furniture store with limited kids furniture, but good quality for the price..."

Furniture, Bedding & Decor	✓	$$$$	Prices
Gear & Equipment	✗	❹	Product availability
Nursing & Feeding	✗	❺	Staff knowledge
Safety & Babycare	✗	❹	Customer service
Clothing, Shoes & Accessories	✗	❺	Decor
Books, Toys & Entertainment	✗		

WWW.ROOMANDBOARD.COM

SKOKIE—10071 SKOKIE BLVD (AT OLD ORCHARD RD); 847.673.2655; M-F 10-9, SA 10-6, SU 12-5

Sears

"...a decent selection of clothes and basic baby equipment... check out the Kids Club program—it's a great way to save money... you go to Sears to save money, not to be pampered... the quality of their merchandise is better than Wal-Mart, but don't expect anything too special or different... not much in terms of gear, but tons of well-priced baby and toddler clothing..."

Furniture, Bedding & Decor	✓	$$	Prices
Gear & Equipment	✓	❸	Product availability
Nursing & Feeding	✓	❸	Staff knowledge
Safety & Babycare	✓	❸	Customer service
Clothing, Shoes & Accessories	✓	❸	Decor
Books, Toys & Entertainment	✓		

WWW.SEARS.COM

NILES—400 GOLF MILL CTR (AT GREENWOOD AVE); 847.803.7500; M-F 10-9, SA 8-9, SU 11-7

Strasburg Children

"...totally adorable special occasion outfits for babies and kids... classic baby, toddler, and kids clothes... dress-up clothes for kids... if

you are looking for a flower girl or ring bearer outfit, look no further... handmade clothes that will last through multiple kids or generations... it's not cheap, but you can find great sales if you are patient... ”

Furniture, Bedding & Decor	✗	$$$$	Prices
Gear & Equipment	✗	4	Product availability
Nursing & Feeding	✗	4	Staff knowledge
Safety & Babycare	✗	4	Customer service
Clothing, Shoes & Accessories	✓	4	Decor
Books, Toys & Entertainment	✗		

WWW.STRASBURGCHILDREN.COM

GLENVIEW—1911 TOWER DR (AT GLEN TOWN CTR); 847.724.6078; M-F 10-9, SA 10-6, SU 11-5

Stride Rite Shoes

“*...wonderful selection of baby and toddler shoes... sandals, sneakers, and even special-occasion shoes... decent quality shoes that last... they know a lot about kids' shoes and take the time to get it right—they always measure my son's feet before fittings... store sizes vary, but they always have something in stock that works... they've even special ordered shoes for my daughter... a fun 'first shoe' buying experience...* ”

Furniture, Bedding & Decor	✗	$$$	Prices
Gear & Equipment	✗	4	Product availability
Nursing & Feeding	✗	4	Staff knowledge
Safety & Babycare	✗	4	Customer service
Clothing, Shoes & Accessories	✓	4	Decor
Books, Toys & Entertainment	✗		

WWW.STRIDERITE.COM

NILES—247 GOLF MILL CTR (AT GREENWOOD AVE); 847.299.2575; M-SA 10-9, SU 11-6

NORTHBROOK—2076 NORTHBROOK CT (AT NORTHBROOK COURT SHOPPING CTR); 847.272.2299; M-SA 10-9, SU 11-6; PARKING LOT AT CENTER

Talbots Kids

“*...a nice alternative to the typical department store experience... expensive, but fantastic quality... great for holiday and special occasion outfits including christening outfits... well-priced, conservative children's clothing... cute selections for infants, toddlers and kids... sales are fantastic—up to half off at least a couple times a year... the best part is, you can also shop for yourself while shopping for baby...* ”

Furniture, Bedding & Decor	✗	$$$$	Prices
Gear & Equipment	✗	4	Product availability
Nursing & Feeding	✗	4	Staff knowledge
Safety & Babycare	✗	4	Customer service
Clothing, Shoes & Accessories	✓	4	Decor
Books, Toys & Entertainment	✗		

WWW.TALBOTS.COM

SKOKIE—90 OLD ORCHARD CTR (AT GOLF RD); 847.329.0670; M-SA 11-9, SU 11-6; PARKING LOT AT CENTER

Target

“*...our favorite place to shop for kids' stuff—good selection and very affordable... guilt-free shopping—kids grow so fast so I don't want to pay high department-store prices... everything from diapers and sippy cups to car seats and strollers... easy return policy... generally helpful staff, but you don't go for the service—you go for the prices... decent registry that won't freak your friends out with outrageous prices... easy, convenient shopping for well-priced items... all the big-box brands available—Graco, Evenflo, Eddie Bauer, etc....* ”

Furniture, Bedding & Decor .... ✓
Gear & Equipment .... ✓
Nursing & Feeding .... ✓
Safety & Babycare .... ✓
Clothing, Shoes & Accessories ...... ✓
Books, Toys & Entertainment .... ✓

$$ .... Prices
❹ .... Product availability
❸ .... Staff knowledge
❸ .... Customer service
❸ .... Decor

WWW.TARGET.COM

EVANSTON—2209 HOWARD ST (AT RIDGE AVE); 847.733.1144; M-SA 8-10, SU 8-9; PARKING IN FRONT OF BLDG

GLENVIEW—2241 WILLOW RD (AT OLD WILLOW RD); 847.657.0095; M-SA 8-10, SU 8-9

GURNEE—6601 GRAND AVE (AT N HUNT CLUB AVE); 847.244.4990; M-SA 8-10, SU 8-9; PARKING IN FRONT OF BLDG

NILES—6150 W TOUHY AVE (AT N MELVILLE AVE); 847.588.2800; M-SA 8-10, SU 8-9; PARKING IN FRONT OF BLDG

Toys Et Cetera ★★★★½

"...this store is enormous and bountiful... toys, books, and gifts to please even the pickiest princess... the staff knows how to find you the right item... they have the standards—Whoozit, Early Years, Thomas, Brio, Lego, plus more unusual picks... don't miss the party favor area... fantastic store..."

Furniture, Bedding & Decor .... ✗
Gear & Equipment .... ✗
Nursing & Feeding .... ✗
Safety & Babycare .... ✗
Clothing, Shoes & Accessories ...... ✗
Books, Toys & Entertainment .... ✓

$$$ .... Prices
❺ .... Product availability
❺ .... Staff knowledge
❺ .... Customer service
❹ .... Decor

WWW.TOYSETCETERA.COM

EVANSTON—711 MAIN ST (AT CHICAGO AVE); 847.475.7172; M-SA 9:30-6, SU 11-5; FREE PARKING

Toys R Us ★★★½☆

"...not just toys, but also tons of gear and supplies including diapers and formula... a hectic shopping experience but the prices make it all worthwhile... I've experienced good and bad service at the same store on the same day... the stores are huge and can be overwhelming... most big brand-names available... leave the kids at home unless you want to end up with a cart full of toys..."

Furniture, Bedding & Decor .... ✓
Gear & Equipment .... ✓
Nursing & Feeding .... ✓
Safety & Babycare .... ✓
Clothing, Shoes & Accessories ...... ✓
Books, Toys & Entertainment .... ✓

$$$ .... Prices
❹ .... Product availability
❸ .... Staff knowledge
❸ .... Customer service
❸ .... Decor

WWW.TOYSRUS.COM

HIGHLAND PARK—1610 DEERFIELD RD (AT CENTRAL AVE); 847.831.5500; M-SA 9:30-9:30, SU 10-7

NILES—9555 N MILWAUKEE AVE (AT GOLF MILL SHOPPING CTR); 847.967.9000; M-SA 9:30-9:30, SU 10-7

Von Maur ★★★½☆

"...nice small department store with a good selection of baby clothing... a very elegant store with a nice women's lounge area for nursing and diaper changing... their sales, while infrequent, are great... great train table for the kids... excellent customer service... not a lot of selection for boys... worthwhile kids' shoe department..."

Furniture, Bedding & Decor .... ✗
Gear & Equipment .... ✓
Nursing & Feeding .... ✗

$$$$ .... Prices
❹ .... Product availability
❹ .... Staff knowledge

Safety & Babycare .... ✗	❹ .... Customer service
Clothing, Shoes & Accessories .... ✓	❹ .... Decor
Books, Toys & Entertainment .... ✗	

WWW.VONMAUR.COM

GLENVIEW—1960 TOWER DR (AT CHESTNUT AVE); 847.724.4199; M-F 10-9, SA 10-7, SU 11-6

Vose-Sanders Bootery

"...expert shoe fitters—they even took a picture of my son getting his first pair of shoes... they really know what they are doing and aren't out to sell you the most expensive shoe... around for many years and hopefully for many more to come... they know their stuff..."

Furniture, Bedding & Decor .... ✗	$$$ .... Prices
Gear & Equipment .... ✗	❺ .... Product availability
Nursing & Feeding .... ✗	❺ .... Staff knowledge
Safety & Babycare .... ✗	❺ .... Customer service
Clothing, Shoes & Accessories .... ✓	❸ .... Decor
Books, Toys & Entertainment .... ✗	

EVANSTON—1924 CENTRAL ST (AT GREEN BAY RD); 847.864.8565; M-F 9-5:30, SA 9-5

WINNETKA—837 ELM ST (AT CHESTNUT ST); 847.446.1108; M-F 9-5:30, SA 9-5

Wild Child

"...fun, simple, everyday clothes... love the matching socks and hats... kid friendly store and nice salespeople... they also have wooden toys, soft toys, and slings... well made, durable clothes..."

Furniture, Bedding & Decor .... ✗	$$$$ .... Prices
Gear & Equipment .... ✓	❹ .... Product availability
Nursing & Feeding .... ✗	❹ .... Staff knowledge
Safety & Babycare .... ✗	❹ .... Customer service
Clothing, Shoes & Accessories .... ✓	❹ .... Decor
Books, Toys & Entertainment .... ✗	

WWW.WILDCHILDCLOTHES.COM

EVANSTON—612 DAVIS ST (AT CHICAGO AVE); 847.475.6225; M-SA 9:30-5:30, TH 9:30-7

Western Suburbs

"lila picks"

★Babies R Us ★My Child's Room

★Land of Nod ★The Right Start

A J Wright

"...it's like looking through racks of stuff that doesn't even sell at Ross or TJ Maxx... every now and then you will find something... really not all that interesting, a waste of time in my opinion... the prices are great, the clothes are name brand for a fraction of the cost..."

Furniture, Bedding & Decor	✗	$$	Prices
Gear & Equipment	✗	❸	Product availability
Nursing & Feeding	✗	❸	Staff knowledge
Safety & Babycare	✗	❸	Customer service
Clothing, Shoes & Accessories	✓	❷	Decor
Books, Toys & Entertainment	✗		

WWW.AJ-WRIGHT.COM

RIVER GROVE—8355 BELMONT AVE (AT N CUMBERLAND AVE); 708.456.0853; M-SA 9-9, SU 11-6; PARKING LOT

April Cornell

"...beautiful, classic dresses and accessories for special occasions... I love the matching 'mommy and me' outfits... lots of fun knickknacks for sale... great selection of baby wear on their web site... rest assured your baby won't look like every other child in these adorable outfits... very frilly and girlie—beautiful..."

Furniture, Bedding & Decor	✗	$$$	Prices
Gear & Equipment	✗	❸	Product availability
Nursing & Feeding	✗	❹	Staff knowledge
Safety & Babycare	✗	❹	Customer service
Clothing, Shoes & Accessories	✓	❹	Decor
Books, Toys & Entertainment	✗		

WWW.APRILCORNELL.COM

GENEVA—1510 COMMONS DR (AT GENEVA COMMONS); 630.845.0074; M-SA 10-9, SU 11-6

Babies R Us

"...everything baby under one roof... they have a wide selection and carry most 'mainstream' items such as Graco, Fisher-Price, Avent and Britax... great customer service—given how big the stores are, I was pleasantly surprised at how attentive the staff was... easy return policy... super busy on weekends so try to visit on a weekday for the best service... keep an eye out for great coupons, deals and frequent sales... easy and comprehensive registry... shopping here is so easy—you've got to check it out..."

Furniture, Bedding & Decor	✓	$$$	Prices
Gear & Equipment	✓	❹	Product availability

Nursing & Feeding ✓ | ❹ Staff knowledge
Safety & Babycare ✓ | ❹ Customer service
Clothing, Shoes & Accessories ✓ | ❹ Decor
Books, Toys & Entertainment ✓

WWW.BABIESRUS.COM

LOMBARD—481 E ROOSEVELT RD (AT S FAIRFIELD AVE); 630.495.9161; M-SA 9:30-9:30, SU 11-7; PARKING IN FRONT OF BLDG

NAPERVILLE—1955 GLACIER PARK AVE (AT MERIDIAN PKWY); 630.416.2225; M-SA 9:30-9:30, SU 11-7; PARKING IN FRONT OF BLDG

Baby Depot At Burlington Coat Factory

“...a large, 'super store' layout with a ton of baby gear... wide aisles, packed shelves, barely existent customer service and awesome prices... everything from bottles, car seats and strollers to gliders, cribs and clothes... I always find something worth getting... a little disorganized and hard to locate items you're looking for... the staff is not always knowledgeable about their merchandise... return policy is store credit only...”

Furniture, Bedding & Decor ✓ | $$ Prices
Gear & Equipment ✓ | ❸ Product availability
Nursing & Feeding ✓ | ❸ Staff knowledge
Safety & Babycare ✓ | ❸ Customer service
Clothing, Shoes & Accessories ✓ | ❸ Decor
Books, Toys & Entertainment ✓

WWW.BABYDEPOT.COM

BLOOMINGDALE—3 STRATFORD SQ MALL (AT ENTRANCE DR 1); 630.671.0364; M-SA 10-9, SU 11-6; MALL PARKING

COUNTRYSIDE—1 COUNTRYSIDE PLAZA (AT LA GRANGE RD); 708.354.2365; M-SA 10-9, SU 11-6; PARKING LOT

NAPERVILLE—510 S ROUTE 59 (AT AURORA RD); 630.428.1341; M-SA 10-9, SU 11-6

NORTH RIVERSIDE—2208 S HARLEM AVE (AT NORTH RIVERSIDE MALL); 708.447.4855; M-SA 10-9, SU 11-6; MALL PARKING

VILLA PARK—174 W ROOSEVELT RD (AT S MICHIGAN AVE); 630.832.4500; M-SA 9-9, SU 11-6; PARKING LOT

BabyGap/GapKids ★★★★☆

“...colorful baby and toddler clothing in clean, well-lit stores... great return policy... it's the Gap, so you know what you're getting—colorful, cute and well-made clothing... best place for baby hats... prices are reasonable especially since there's always a sale of some sort going on... sales, sales, sales—frequent and fantastic... everything I'm looking for in infant clothing—snap crotches, snaps up the front, all natural fabrics and great styling... fun seasonal selections—a great place to shop for gifts as well as for your own kids... although it can get busy, staff generally seem accommodating and helpful...”

Furniture, Bedding & Decor ✗ | $$$ Prices
Gear & Equipment ✗ | ❹ Product availability
Nursing & Feeding ✗ | ❹ Staff knowledge
Safety & Babycare ✗ | ❹ Customer service
Clothing, Shoes & Accessories ✓ | ❹ Decor
Books, Toys & Entertainment ✗

WWW.GAP.COM

AURORA—1262 FOX VALLEY CTR (AT NEW YORK ST); 630.851.9250; M-SA 10-9, SU 11-6; PARKING IN FRONT OF BLDG

BLOOMINGDALE—109 STRATFORD SQ MALL (AT SCHICK RD); 630.539.1467; M-SA 10-9, SU 11-6; PARKING IN FRONT OF BLDG

LOMBARD—237 YORKTOWN SHOPPING CTR (AT S HIGHLAND AVE); 630.620.6041; M-F 10-9, SA-SU 10-6; PARKING LOT AT CENTER

OAK BROOK—533 OAKBROOK CTR (AT SPRING RD); 630.571.3207; M-SA 10-9, SU 11-6; MALL PARKING

OAK PARK—435 N HARLEM AVE (AT LAKE ST); 708.358.1188; M-F 10-9, SA 10-8, SU 11-7; PARKING IN FRONT OF BLDG

Bellini

"...high-end furniture for a gorgeous nursery... if you're looking for the kind of furniture you see in magazines then this is the place to go... excellent quality... yes, it's pricey, but the quality is impeccable... free delivery and setup... their furniture is built to withstand the abuse my tots dish out... they sell very unique merchandise, ranging from cribs to bedding and even some clothes... our nursery design was inspired by their store decor... I wish they had more frequent sales..."

Furniture, Bedding & Decor	✓	$$$$	Prices
Gear & Equipment	✗	4	Product availability
Nursing & Feeding	✗	4	Staff knowledge
Safety & Babycare	✗	4	Customer service
Clothing, Shoes & Accessories	✗	4	Decor
Books, Toys & Entertainment	✓		

WWW.BELLINI.COM

OAKBROOK TERRACE—17 W 180 22ND STR (AT HIGHWAY 83); 630.941.7700; M-SA 10-6, SU 12-5

Bombay Kids

"...the kids section of this furniture store carries out-of-the-ordinary items... whimsical, pastel grandfather clocks... zebra bean bags... perfect for my eclectic taste... I now prefer my daughter's room to my own... clean bathroom with changing area and wipes... they have a little table with crayons and coloring books for the kids... easy and relaxed shopping destination..."

Furniture, Bedding & Decor	✓	$$$	Prices
Gear & Equipment	✗	4	Product availability
Nursing & Feeding	✗	4	Staff knowledge
Safety & Babycare	✗	4	Customer service
Clothing, Shoes & Accessories	✗	4	Decor
Books, Toys & Entertainment	✗		

WWW.BOMBAYKIDS.COM

LOMBARD—2830 S HIGHLAND AVE (OFF BUTTERFIELD RD); 630.620.5476; M-SA 10-9, SU 11-6

Carter's

"...always a great selection of inexpensive baby basics—everything from clothing to linens... I always find something at 'giveaway prices' during one of their frequent sales... busy and crowded—it can be a chaotic shopping experience... 30 to 50 percent less than what you would pay at other boutiques... I bought five pieces of baby clothing for less than $40... durable, adorable and affordable... most stores have a small play area for kids in center of store so you can get your shopping done..."

Furniture, Bedding & Decor	✓	$$	Prices
Gear & Equipment	✗	4	Product availability
Nursing & Feeding	✗	4	Staff knowledge
Safety & Babycare	✗	4	Customer service
Clothing, Shoes & Accessories	✓	4	Decor
Books, Toys & Entertainment	✓		

WWW.CARTERS.COM

AURORA—1650 PREMIUM OUTLETS BLVD (AT CHICAGO PREMIUM OUTLETS); 630.499.9407; M-SA 9-9, SU 9-7

BOLINGBROOK—127 S WEBER RD (AT BOLINGBROOK); 630.378.0801; M-SA 10-9, SU 10-7

GENEVA—1492 D-2 RANDALL RD (AT RANDALL SQUARE SHOPPING CTR); 630.845.2730; M-SA 10-9; FREE PARKING

Children's Place, The

"...great bargains on cute clothing... shoes, socks, swimsuits, sunglasses and everything in between... lots of '3 for $20' type deals on sleepers, pants and mix-and-match separates... so much more affordable than the other 'big chains'... don't expect the most unique stuff here, but it wears and washes well... cheap clothing for cheap prices... you can leave the store with bags full of clothes without putting a huge dent in your wallet..."

Furniture, Bedding & Decor	✗	$$	Prices
Gear & Equipment	✗	❹	Product availability
Nursing & Feeding	✗	❹	Staff knowledge
Safety & Babycare	✗	❹	Customer service
Clothing, Shoes & Accessories	✓	❹	Decor
Books, Toys & Entertainment	✓		

WWW.CHILDRENSPLACE.COM

BLOOMINGDALE—418 STRATFORD SQ MALL (AT STRATFORD SQUARE MALL); 630.980.4360; M-SA 10-9, SU 11-6; MALL PARKING

RIVER FOREST—7335 LAKE ST (AT GARDEN CT); 708.366.2390; M-TH 10-7, F-SA 10-8, SU 11-5

Costco

"...dependable place for bulk diapers, wipes and formula at discount prices... clothing selection is very hit-or-miss... avoid shopping there during nights and weekends if possible, because parking and checkout lines are brutal... they don't have a huge selection of brands, but the brands they do have are almost always in stock and at a great price... lowest prices around for diapers and formula... kid's clothing tends to be picked through, but it's worth looking for great deals on name-brand items like Carter's..."

Furniture, Bedding & Decor	✓	$$	Prices
Gear & Equipment	✓	❸	Product availability
Nursing & Feeding	✓	❸	Staff knowledge
Safety & Babycare	✓	❸	Customer service
Clothing, Shoes & Accessories	✓	❷	Decor
Books, Toys & Entertainment	✓		

WWW.COSTCO.COM

BLOOMINGDALE—505 W ARMY TRAIL RD; 630.351.3059; M-F 10-8:30, SA 9:30-6, SU 10-6

NAPERVILLE—1324 S RTE 59; 630.328.2900; M-F 11-8:30, SA 9:30-6, SU 10-6

OAK BROOK—1901 W 22ND ST; 630.928.0235; M-F 11-8:30, SA 9:30-6, SU 10-6

Cradles & All

"...a beautiful boutique carrying all that new babies might need... fun outfits, diaper bags, nursery furnishings and gifts... independently owned and providing fabulous service... a wonderful shopping experience... check out the 'Child In You' section for cute maternity wear..."

Furniture, Bedding & Decor	✓	$$$	Prices
Gear & Equipment	✓	❸	Product availability
Nursing & Feeding	✗	❸	Staff knowledge
Safety & Babycare	✗	❸	Customer service
Clothing, Shoes & Accessories	✓	❸	Decor
Books, Toys & Entertainment	✓		

WWW.CRADLESANDALL.COM

GENEVA—407 S 3RD ST (AT FULTON ST); 630.232.4030; M-SA 10-5, SU 12-4; STREET PARKING

Gymboree

"...beautiful clothing and great quality... colorful and stylish baby and kids wear... lots of fun birthday gift ideas... easy exchange and return policy... items usually go on sale pretty quickly... save money with Gymbucks... many stores have a play area which makes shopping with my kids fun (let alone feasible)..."

Furniture, Bedding & Decor	✗	$$$	Prices
Gear & Equipment	✗	❹	Product availability
Nursing & Feeding	✗	❹	Staff knowledge
Safety & Babycare	✗	❹	Customer service
Clothing, Shoes & Accessories	✓	❹	Decor
Books, Toys & Entertainment	✓		

WWW.GYMBOREE.COM

BLOOMINGDALE—406 STRATFORD SQ (AT BUTTERFIELD DR); 630.893.9844; M-SA 10-9, SU 11-6

LOMBARD—157F YORKTOWN CTR (AT HIGHLAND AVE); 630.629.5040; M-SA 10-9, SU 11-6

OAK BROOK—425 OAKBROOK CTR; 630.575.0338; M-SA 10-9, SU 11-6; MALL PARKING

SAINT CHARLES—3800 E MAIN ST (AT CHARLESTOWNE MALL); 630.587.2280; M-SA 10-9; FREE PARKING

H & M

"...wonderful prices for trendy baby and toddler clothes... it's the 'Euro' Target... buy for yourself and for your kids... a fun shopping experience as long as your child doesn't mind the bright lights and loud music... decent return policy... incredible sale prices... store can get messy at peak hours... busy and hectic, but their inventory is fun and worth the visit..."

Furniture, Bedding & Decor	✗	$$	Prices
Gear & Equipment	✗	❸	Product availability
Nursing & Feeding	✗	❸	Staff knowledge
Safety & Babycare	✗	❸	Customer service
Clothing, Shoes & Accessories	✓	❸	Decor
Books, Toys & Entertainment	✓		

WWW.HM.COM

AURORA—1276 FOX VALLEY CTR (AT NEW YORK ST); 630.499.5730; M-SA 10-9, SU 10-6; FREE PARKING

Hanna Andersson

"...top-notch, high-quality cotton clothes for babies and kids... pricey, but worth it for the durability and cuteness... girls clothes are beautifully designed... some stores have a train table for kids to play with while mom can shop... staff is always friendly... the long-john cotton pj's are the best... Hanna's cotton has no match—it looks new after being washed a billion times... neat kids' clothes—high-quality, bright colors and unique... clothes are soft, gorgeous and made to last... wonderful play dresses..."

Furniture, Bedding & Decor	✗	$$$$	Prices
Gear & Equipment	✗	❹	Product availability
Nursing & Feeding	✗	❹	Staff knowledge
Safety & Babycare	✗	❹	Customer service
Clothing, Shoes & Accessories	✓	❹	Decor
Books, Toys & Entertainment	✓		

WWW.HANNAANDERSSON.COM

OAK BROOK—20 OAKBROOK CTR (AT OAK BROOK CTR MALL); 630.684.0442; M-SA 10-9, SU 11-6

JCPenney

"...always a good place to find clothes and other baby basics... the registry process was seamless... staff is generally friendly but the lines always seem long and slow... they don't have the greatest selection of toddler clothes, but their baby section is great... we had some damaged furniture delivered but customer service was easy and accommodating... a pretty limited selection of gear, but what they have is priced right..."

Furniture, Bedding & Decor	✓	$$	Prices
Gear & Equipment	✓	❸	Product availability
Nursing & Feeding	✓	❸	Staff knowledge
Safety & Babycare	✓	❸	Customer service
Clothing, Shoes & Accessories	✓	❸	Decor
Books, Toys & Entertainment	✓		

WWW.JCPENNEY.COM

AURORA—4 FOX VALLEY CTR (AT NEW YORK ST); 630.851.6380; M-F 10-9, SA 10-7, SU 11-6

LOMBARD—175 YORKTOWN SHOPPING CTR (AT YORKTOWN CTR); 630.629.7750; M-F 10-9, SA 9:30-9, SU 11-6

NORTH RIVERSIDE—7507 W CERMAK RD (AT NORTH RIVERSIDE MALL); 708.442.6600; M-SA 10-9, SU 11-6; MALL PARKING

KB Toys

"...hectic and always buzzing... wall-to-wall plastic and blinking lights... more Fisher-Price, Elmo and Sponge Bob than the eye can handle... a toy super store with discounted prices... they always have some kind of special sale going on... if you're looking for the latest and greatest popular toy, then look no further—not the place for unique or unusual toys... perfect for bulk toy shopping—especially around the holidays..."

Furniture, Bedding & Decor	×	$$	Prices
Gear & Equipment	×	❸	Product availability
Nursing & Feeding	×	❸	Staff knowledge
Safety & Babycare	×	❸	Customer service
Clothing, Shoes & Accessories	×	❸	Decor
Books, Toys & Entertainment	✓		

WWW.KBTOYS.COM

AURORA—ROUTES 59 & 34 (AT FOX VALLEY CTR); 630.898.5155; M-SA 10-9, SU 10-7

BLOOMINGDALE—421 GARY AVE(N OF ARMY TRAIL) (AT STRATFORD SQUARE); 630.980.8473; M-SA 10-9, SU 10-7

LOMBARD—BUTTERFLD RD & HIGHLAND AV (AT YORKTOWN SHOPPING CTR); 630.629.3055; M-SA 10-9, SU 11-6

NORTH RIVERSIDE—7501 W CERMAK RD (AT NORTH RIVERSIDE PARK); 708.442.6998; M-SA 11-9, SU 11-7

Kid's Foot Locker

"...Nike, Reebok and Adidas for your little ones... hip, trendy and quite pricey... perfect for the sports addict dad who wants his kid sporting the latest NFL duds... shoes cost close to what the adult variety costs... generally good quality... they carry infant and toddler sizes..."

Furniture, Bedding & Decor	×	$$$	Prices
Gear & Equipment	×	❸	Product availability
Nursing & Feeding	×	❸	Staff knowledge
Safety & Babycare	×	❸	Customer service
Clothing, Shoes & Accessories	✓	❸	Decor
Books, Toys & Entertainment	×		

WWW.KIDSFOOTLOCKER.COM

LOMBARD—266 YORKTOWN SHOPPING CTR (AT HIGHLAND AVE); 630.268.8552; M-SA 10-9, SU 11-6

RIVERSIDE—7501 W CERMAK RD (AT NORTH RIVERSIDE MALL); 708.447.8417; M-SA 10-9, SU 11-6

Kohl's

"...nice one-stop shopping for the whole family—everything from clothing to baby gear... great sales on clothing and a good selection of higher-end brands... stylish, inexpensive clothes for babies through 24 months... very easy shopping experience... dirt-cheap sales and clearance prices... nothing super fancy, but just right for those everyday romper outfits... Graco, Eddie Bauer and other well-known brands..."

Furniture, Bedding & Decor	✓	$$	Prices
Gear & Equipment	✓	❹	Product availability
Nursing & Feeding	✓	❸	Staff knowledge
Safety & Babycare	✓	❸	Customer service
Clothing, Shoes & Accessories	✓	❸	Decor
Books, Toys & Entertainment	✓		

WWW.KOHLS.COM

ELMHURST—303 KINGERY HWY (AT ST CHARLES RD); 630.516.1200; M-SA 8-10, SU 10-8; FREE PARKING

NORTH RIVERSIDE—2200 HARLEM AVE (AT CERMAK RD); 708.447.8199; M-SA 8-10, SU 10-8; FREE PARKING

Lala Land

"...this is the store you go to when you want something different than what everyone else has and you don't mind paying for it... accessories, toys, full outfits, and all kids of gifts... upscale selection... off the beaten track..."

Furniture, Bedding & Decor	✗	$$$$	Prices
Gear & Equipment	✗	❹	Product availability
Nursing & Feeding	✗	❺	Staff knowledge
Safety & Babycare	✗	❺	Customer service
Clothing, Shoes & Accessories	✓	❺	Decor
Books, Toys & Entertainment	✓		

ELMHURST—112 S YORK ST (AT W ADELAIDE ST); 630.834.5252; M-SA 10-5:30, SU 11-2

Land of Nod

"...creative and fun decor and furnishings... lots of practical stuff that has a bit more flair than your typical furnishings store... nice, helpful staff... a truly terrific place to buy gifts... lots of cool, retro stuff that you don't find elsewhere... love their book and music selection... great ideas for decorating kids' bedrooms... fabulous customer service and knowledgeable staff... adorable furniture and bedding..."

Furniture, Bedding & Decor	✗	$$$$	Prices
Gear & Equipment	✗	❹	Product availability
Nursing & Feeding	✗	❹	Staff knowledge
Safety & Babycare	✗	❹	Customer service
Clothing, Shoes & Accessories	✗	❺	Decor
Books, Toys & Entertainment	✗		

WWW.LANDOFNOD.COM

OAK BROOK—35 OAKBROOK CTR (AT 22ND ST); 630.368.9990; M-F 10-9, SA 10-7, SU 11-6; FREE PARKING

Li'l Deb-N-Heir Children's Furniture

"...after you've tried shopping everywhere else, this is the place you're going to end up... very helpful and friendly staff... shop here if you

want quality furniture for your kids... top of the line products... Zooper strollers, Dutailier gliders and Ragazzi cribs... huge selection and variety of baby furniture... pricey, but top quality... ”

Furniture, Bedding & Decor .... ✓ | $$$$ .... Prices
Gear & Equipment .... ✓ | ❹ .... Product availability
Nursing & Feeding .... ✗ | ❹ .... Staff knowledge
Safety & Babycare .... ✗ | ❹ .... Customer service
Clothing, Shoes & Accessories .... ✗ | ❹ .... Decor
Books, Toys & Entertainment .... ✗

WWW.DEBNHEIR.COM

NAPERVILLE—540 E OGDEN AVE (AT NAPERVILKLE RD); 630.717.8100; M-W 10-6, TH-F 10-9, SA 10-5, SU 12-4; PARKING LOT

M & Em's

Furniture, Bedding & Decor .... ✗ | ✗ .... Gear & Equipment
Nursing & Feeding .... ✗ | ✗ .... Safety & Babycare
Clothing, Shoes & Accessories .... ✗ | ✗ .... Books, Toys & Entertainment

GLEN ELLYN—490 N MAIN ST (AT E WESLEY ST); 630.469.6040; M-W F-SA 9:30-5:30, TH 9:30-8, SU 12-4

My Child's Room

“*...we bought everything here... some of the lowest prices on cribs, rockers and dressers... the store has everything you might need for a new baby, but you are not overwhelmed by the endless selection of a mega store... a range of styles, all with excellent quality... a little pricey but always have someone there to help you... it can get crowded so you're best going during the week... some of their regular prices seem high, but they have fantastic sales...* ”

Furniture, Bedding & Decor .... ✓ | $$$$ .... Prices
Gear & Equipment .... ✓ | ❸ .... Product availability
Nursing & Feeding .... ✓ | ❸ .... Staff knowledge
Safety & Babycare .... ✗ | ❸ .... Customer service
Clothing, Shoes & Accessories .... ✓ | ❹ .... Decor
Books, Toys & Entertainment .... ✓

WWW.MYCHILDSROOM.NET

AURORA—443 S ROUTE 59 (AT AUDREY AVE); 630.978.5144; M-F 10-9, SA 10-6, SU 12-6

LOMBARD—1121 S MAIN ST (AT W EDWARD ST); 630.620.9198; M-F 10-9, SA 10-6, SU 12-6; PARKING LOT

Nordstrom

“*...quality service and quality clothes... awesome kids shoe department—almost as good as the one for adults... free balloons in the children's shoe area as well as drawing tables... in addition to their own brand, they carry a very nice selection of other high-end baby clothing including Ralph Lauren, Robeez, etc... adorable baby clothes—they make great shower gifts... such a wonderful shopping experience—their lounge is perfect for breastfeeding and for changing diapers... well-rounded selection of baby basics as well as fancy clothes for special events...* ”

Furniture, Bedding & Decor .... ✓ | $$$$ .... Prices
Gear & Equipment .... ✓ | ❹ .... Product availability
Nursing & Feeding .... ✗ | ❹ .... Staff knowledge
Safety & Babycare .... ✗ | ❹ .... Customer service
Clothing, Shoes & Accessories .... ✓ | ❹ .... Decor
Books, Toys & Entertainment .... ✓

WWW.NORDSTROM.COM

OAK BROOK—10 OAK BROOK CTR MALL (AT 22ND ST); 630.571.2121; M-F 10-9, SA 9:30-9, SU 11-6

Old Navy

“...hip and 'in' clothes for infants and tots... plenty of steals on clearance items... T-shirts and pants for $10 or less... busy, busy, busy—long lines, especially on weekends... nothing fancy and you won't mind when your kids get down and dirty in these clothes... easy to wash, decent quality... you can shop for your baby, your toddler, your teen and yourself all at the same time... clothes are especially affordable when you hit their sales (post-holiday sales are amazing!)... ”

Furniture, Bedding & Decor	✗	$$	Prices
Gear & Equipment	✗	❹	Product availability
Nursing & Feeding	✗	❸	Staff knowledge
Safety & Babycare	✗	❸	Customer service
Clothing, Shoes & Accessories	✓	❸	Decor
Books, Toys & Entertainment	✗		

WWW.OLDNAVY.COM

BLOOMINGDALE—346 W ARMY TRAIL RD (AT SPRINGFIELD DR); 630.671.0702; M-SA 9-9, SU 10-6; PARKING LOT

DOWNERS GROVE—1150-75TH ST (AT LEMONT AVE); 630.434.0028; M-SA 10-9, SU 10-6

GENEVA—1572 S RANDALL RD (AT BENT TREE DR); 630.262.8171; M-SA 9-9, SU 11-6

NAPERVILLE—220 S STATE RTE 59 (AT W JEFFERSON AVE); 630.717.5909; M-SA 9-9, SU 10-6

NORTH RIVERSIDE—7501 W CERMAK RD (AT NORTH RIVERSIDE MALL); 708.442.9375; M-SA 9-9, SU 11-6; MALL PARKING

OAK BROOK—2155 W 22ND ST (AT MIDWEST RD); 630.472.9201; M-SA 9-9, SU 10-6

OAK PARK—417 N HARLEM AVE (AT LAKE ST); 708.848.9103; HOURS: M-SA 9-9, SU 10-6

WHEATON—138 DANADA SQ W (AT S NAPERVILLE RD); 630.871.2312; M-SA 9-9, SU 10-6

Once Upon A Child

“...new and used items... the place for bargain baby items in like-new condition... a great bargain spot with a wide variety of clothes for baby... some inexpensive furniture... good selection, staff and prices... cluttered and hard to get through the store with kids... good toys and gear... some items are definitely more than 'gently used'... a kid's play area... good end-of-season sales... expect to sort through items... cash for your old items... ”

Furniture, Bedding & Decor	✓	$$	Prices
Gear & Equipment	✓	❸	Product availability
Nursing & Feeding	✗	❹	Staff knowledge
Safety & Babycare	✗	❹	Customer service
Clothing, Shoes & Accessories	✓	❸	Decor
Books, Toys & Entertainment	✓		

WWW.OUAC.COM

DOWNERS GROVE—1220C W 75TH ST (AT LEMONT RD); 630.663.9211; M-F 10-7, SA 10-5, SU 11-4

NAPERVILLE—572 S STATE RTE 59 (AT FOX VALLEY SHOPPING CTR); 630.416.9344; M-F 10-8, SA 10-6, SU 12-5; PARKING LOT AT CENTER

VILLA PARK—120 W ROOSEVELT RD (AT S ARDMORE AVE); 630.559.0285; M-F 10-8, SA 10-5, SU 11-4

Oshkosh B'gosh

“...cute, sturdy clothes for infants and toddlers... frequent sales make their high-quality merchandise a lot more affordable... doesn't every American kid have to get a pair of their overalls?.. great selection of

cute clothes for boys... you can't go wrong here—their clothing is fun and worth the price... customer service is pretty hit-or-miss from store to store... we always walk out of here with something fun and colorful... ”*

Furniture, Bedding & Decor .... ✗
Gear & Equipment .... ✗
Nursing & Feeding .... ✗
Safety & Babycare .... ✗
Clothing, Shoes & Accessories .... ✓
Books, Toys & Entertainment .... ✗

$$$ .... Prices
❹ .... Product availability
❹ .... Staff knowledge
❹ .... Customer service
❹ .... Decor

WWW.OSHKOSHBGOSH.COM

AURORA—1376 FOX VALLEY CTR (AT NEW YORK ST); 630.585.7750; M-SA 10-9, SU 11-6

AURORA—1650 PREMIUM OUTLET BLVD (AT BILTER RD); 630.236.0000; M-SA 10-9, SU 10-6

Payless Shoe Source

“...a good place for deals on children's shoes... staff is helpful with sizing... the selection and prices for kids' shoes can't be beat, but the quality isn't always spectacular... good leather shoes for cheap... great variety of all sizes and widths... I get my son's shoes here and don't feel like I'm wasting my money since he'll outgrow them in 3 months anyway... ”

Furniture, Bedding & Decor .... ✗
Gear & Equipment .... ✗
Nursing & Feeding .... ✗
Safety & Babycare .... ✗
Clothing, Shoes & Accessories .... ✓
Books, Toys & Entertainment .... ✗

$$ .... Prices
❸ .... Product availability
❸ .... Staff knowledge
❸ .... Customer service
❸ .... Decor

WWW.PAYLESS.COM

BLOOMINGDALE—BLOOMINGDALE CT (AT W SCHICK RD); 630.351.3273; M-SA 9:30-9, SU 11-6

Rainbow Kids

“...fun clothing styles for infants and tots at low prices... the quality isn't the same as the more expensive brands, but the sleepers and play outfits always hold up well... great place for basics... cute trendy shoe selection for your little walker... we love the prices... up-to-date selection... ”

Furniture, Bedding & Decor .... ✗
Gear & Equipment .... ✓
Nursing & Feeding .... ✗
Safety & Babycare .... ✗
Clothing, Shoes & Accessories .... ✓
Books, Toys & Entertainment .... ✓

$$ .... Prices
❸ .... Product availability
❸ .... Staff knowledge
❸ .... Customer service
❸ .... Decor

WWW.RAINBOWSHOPS.COM

NORTH RIVERSIDE—NORTH RIVERSIDE PLAZA (AT HARLEM AVE); 708.442.4910; DAILY 10-9

Right Start, The

“...higher-end, well selected items... Britax, Maclaren, Combi, Mustela—all the cool brands under one roof... everything from bibs to bottles and even the Bugaboo stroller... prices seem a little high, but the selection is good and the staff knowledgeable and helpful... there are toys all over the store that kids can play with while you shop... I have a hard time getting my kids out of the store because they are having so much fun... a boutique-like shopping experience but they carry most of the key brands... their registry works well... ”

Furniture, Bedding & Decor .... ✓
Gear & Equipment .... ✓

$$$ .... Prices
❹ .... Product availability

Nursing & Feeding	✓	❹	Staff knowledge
Safety & Babycare	✓	❹	Customer service
Clothing, Shoes & Accessories	✓	❹	Decor
Books, Toys & Entertainment	✓		

WWW.RIGHTSTART.COM

NAPERVILLE—30 W JEFFERSON AVE (AT S WASHINGTON ST); 630.548.2220; M-SA 10-6, SU 11-6

Rocking Horse ★★★★☆

"...geared to traditional styles of clothes and toys... best for the under 2 set... we love their selection of wooden toys... nice play area... they even have little tuxedos and flower girl dresses... frequent sales make their beautiful merchandise quite affordable..."

Furniture, Bedding & Decor	✗	$$$	Prices
Gear & Equipment	✗	❸	Product availability
Nursing & Feeding	✗	❹	Staff knowledge
Safety & Babycare	✗	❸	Customer service
Clothing, Shoes & Accessories	✓	❹	Decor
Books, Toys & Entertainment	✓		

WWW.ROCKINGHORSEBOUTIQUE.COM

OAK PARK—119 N MARION ST (AT LAKE ST); 708.383.2234; M-F 10-6, SA 11-5

Room & Board ★★★½☆

"...the store doesn't have a huge selection of baby furniture, but what's there is excellent quality... the staff is terrific... expect to receive fantastic customer service... terrific for the transition into a twin or bunk bed... a great furniture store with limited kids furniture, but good quality for the price..."

Furniture, Bedding & Decor	✓	$$$$	Prices
Gear & Equipment	✗	❹	Product availability
Nursing & Feeding	✗	❺	Staff knowledge
Safety & Babycare	✗	❹	Customer service
Clothing, Shoes & Accessories	✗	❺	Decor
Books, Toys & Entertainment	✗		

WWW.ROOMANDBOARD.COM

OAK BROOK—2525 W 22ND ST (OFF MIDWEST RD); 630.571.7801; M-F 10-9, SA 10-6, SU 12-6

Sears ★★★☆☆

"...a decent selection of clothes and basic baby equipment... check out the Kids Club program—it's a great way to save money... you go to Sears to save money, not to be pampered... the quality of their merchandise is better than Wal-Mart, but don't expect anything too special or different... not much in terms of gear, but tons of well-priced baby and toddler clothing..."

Furniture, Bedding & Decor	✓	$$	Prices
Gear & Equipment	✓	❸	Product availability
Nursing & Feeding	✓	❸	Staff knowledge
Safety & Babycare	✓	❸	Customer service
Clothing, Shoes & Accessories	✓	❸	Decor
Books, Toys & Entertainment	✓		

WWW.SEARS.COM

BLOOMINGDALE—5 STRATFORD SQ (AT S GARY AVE & W ARMY TRAIL RD); 630.924.8801; M-F 10-9

NORTH RIVERSIDE—7503 W CERMAK RD (AT NORTH RIVERSIDE MALL); 708.588.6600; M-F 10-9, SA 8-10, SU 10-6

OAK BROOK —2 OAKBROOK CLUB DR (AT OAK BROOK CTR MALL); 630.575.1800; M-F 10-9, SA 10-9, SU 11-7

SAINT CHARLES—3700 E MAIN ST (AT CHARLESTOWN MALL); 630.513.3200; M-F 10-9, SA 8-9, SU 10-6

Special Delivery

"...a terrific alternative to the mega stores... unusual and custom made nursery furniture and accessories... large selection of unique toys and clothing... furniture is special ordered so plan ahead... shipping is quite expensive and takes time for your order to arrive... very knowledgeable and helpful staff... if you have the money, then this is the place to spend it..."

Furniture, Bedding & Decor	✓	$$$$	Prices
Gear & Equipment	✓	❹	Product availability
Nursing & Feeding	✓	❹	Staff knowledge
Safety & Babycare	✗	❹	Customer service
Clothing, Shoes & Accessories	✓	❹	Decor
Books, Toys & Entertainment	✓		

WWW.SPECIAL-DELIVERYBABY.COM

GENEVA—220 S 3RD ST (AT FRANKLIN ST); 630.232.8980; M-SA 10-5, SU 12-4; STREET PARKING

Stride Rite Shoes

"...wonderful selection of baby and toddler shoes... sandals, sneakers, and even special-occasion shoes... decent quality shoes that last... they know a lot about kids' shoes and take the time to get it right—they always measure my son's feet before fittings... store sizes vary, but they always have something in stock that works... they've even special ordered shoes for my daughter... a fun 'first shoe' buying experience..."

Furniture, Bedding & Decor	✗	$$$	Prices
Gear & Equipment	✗	❹	Product availability
Nursing & Feeding	✗	❹	Staff knowledge
Safety & Babycare	✗	❹	Customer service
Clothing, Shoes & Accessories	✓	❹	Decor
Books, Toys & Entertainment	✗		

WWW.STRIDERITE.COM

NORTH RIVERSIDE—12-7501 W CERMAK RD; 708.442.7079; M-F 10-9, SA 10-9, SU 11-6

Talbots Kids

"...a nice alternative to the typical department store experience... expensive, but fantastic quality... great for holiday and special occasion outfits including christening outfits... well-priced, conservative children's clothing... cute selections for infants, toddlers and kids... sales are fantastic—up to half off at least a couple times a year... the best part is, you can also shop for yourself while shopping for baby..."

Furniture, Bedding & Decor	✗	$$$$	Prices
Gear & Equipment	✗	❹	Product availability
Nursing & Feeding	✗	❹	Staff knowledge
Safety & Babycare	✗	❹	Customer service
Clothing, Shoes & Accessories	✓	❹	Decor
Books, Toys & Entertainment	✗		

WWW.TALBOTS.COM

OAK BROOK—552 OAKBROOK CTR (AT 16TH ST); 630.572.1278; M-SA 10-9, SU 11-6; MALL PARKING

WHEATON—71 TOWN SQUARE; 630.690.5280; M-F 10-9, SA 10-6, SU 11-5

Target

"...our favorite place to shop for kids' stuff—good selection and very affordable... guilt-free shopping—kids grow so fast so I don't want to pay high department-store prices... everything from diapers and sippy

cups to car seats and strollers... easy return policy... generally helpful staff, but you don't go for the service—you go for the prices... decent registry that won't freak your friends out with outrageous prices... easy, convenient shopping for well-priced items... all the big-box brands available—Graco, Evenflo, Eddie Bauer, etc.... ”

Furniture, Bedding & Decor	✓	$$	Prices
Gear & Equipment	✓	❹	Product availability
Nursing & Feeding	✓	❸	Staff knowledge
Safety & Babycare	✓	❸	Customer service
Clothing, Shoes & Accessories	✓	❸	Decor
Books, Toys & Entertainment	✓		

WWW.TARGET.COM

GLENDALE HEIGHTS—175 W ARMY TRAIL RD (AT SCHMALE RD); 630.582.0043; M-SA 8-10, SU 8-9; PARKING IN FRONT OF BLDG

MELROSE PARK—850 W NORTH AVE (AT N 9TH AVE); 708.338.2784; M-SA 8-10, SU 8-9; PARKING IN FRONT OF BLDG

VILLA PARK—50 E NORTH AVE (AT N ARDMORE AVE); 630.833.7411; M-SA 8-10, SU 8-9; PARKING IN FRONT OF BLDG

Tiddlywinks & Scallywags

“*...fabulous washable wool booties... my daughter loves the ribbon tutus... you just can't go wrong with a gift from this store—whether it's for a baby or mom... geared toward girls, but you can find things for boys if you look hard enough... they also sell fabulous bolts of fabric if you feel inclined to make your own clothes...* ”

Furniture, Bedding & Decor	×	$$$$	Prices
Gear & Equipment	×	❺	Product availability
Nursing & Feeding	×	❺	Staff knowledge
Safety & Babycare	×	❺	Customer service
Clothing, Shoes & Accessories	✓	❺	Decor
Books, Toys & Entertainment	×		

WWW.BRITKID.COM

GLEN ELLYN—524 DUANE ST (AT N MAIN ST); 630.545.2715; M-SA 10-5

Toys R Us

“*...not just toys, but also tons of gear and supplies including diapers and formula... a hectic shopping experience but the prices make it all worthwhile... I've experienced good and bad service at the same store on the same day... the stores are huge and can be overwhelming... most big brand-names available... leave the kids at home unless you want to end up with a cart full of toys...* ”

Furniture, Bedding & Decor	✓	$$$	Prices
Gear & Equipment	✓	❹	Product availability
Nursing & Feeding	✓	❸	Staff knowledge
Safety & Babycare	✓	❸	Customer service
Clothing, Shoes & Accessories	✓	❸	Decor
Books, Toys & Entertainment	✓		

WWW.TOYSRUS.COM

AURORA—4070 FOX VALLEY CTR DR (AT FOX VALLEY SHOPPING CTR); 630.851.7600; M-SA 9:30-9:30, SU 10-7

BLOOMINGDALE—404 W ARMY TRAIL RD (AT STRATFOR SQUARE MALL); 630.529.3399; M-SA 9:30-9:30, SU 10-7; MALL PARKING

DOWNERS GROVE—1434 BUTTERFIELD RD (AT DOWNERS DR); 630.629.2200; M-SA 9:30-9:30, SU 10-6

DOWNERS GROVE—1500 75TH ST (AT DUNHAM RD); 630.964.7124; M-SA 9:30-9:30, SU 10-7

MELROSE PARK—9200 W N AVE (AT N 22ND AVE); 708.343.9000; M-SA 9:30-9:30, SU 10-7

NORTH RIVERSIDE—7451 W CERMAK RD (AT NORTH RIVERSIDE MALL); 708.442.5155; M-SA 9:30-9:30, SU 10-7; MALL PARKING

SAINT CHARLES—3880 E MAIN ST (AT CHARLESTOWNE MALL); 630.443.8697; M-SA 9:30-9:30, SU 10-7

Von Maur

"...nice small department store with a good selection of baby clothing... a very elegant store with a nice women's lounge area for nursing and diaper changing... their sales, while infrequent, are great... great train table for the kids... excellent customer service... not a lot of selection for boys... worthwhile kids' shoe department..."

Furniture, Bedding & Decor	✗	$$$$	Prices
Gear & Equipment	✓	❹	Product availability
Nursing & Feeding	✗	❹	Staff knowledge
Safety & Babycare	✗	❹	Customer service
Clothing, Shoes & Accessories	✓	❹	Decor
Books, Toys & Entertainment	✗		

WWW.VONMAUR.COM

LOMBARD—YORKTOWN CTR (AT 22ND ST); 630.953.8181; M-SA 10-9, SU 11-6

SAINT CHARLES—CHARLESTOWN MALL (AT MAIN ST); 630.377.9987; M-SA 10-9, SU 11-6

Southern Suburbs

"lila picks"

★Babies R Us ★My Own Little Room

Babies R Us

"...everything baby under one roof... they have a wide selection and carry most 'mainstream' items such as Graco, Fisher-Price, Avent and Britax... great customer service—given how big the stores are, I was pleasantly surprised at how attentive the staff was... easy return policy... super busy on weekends so try to visit on a weekday for the best service... keep an eye out for great coupons, deals and frequent sales... easy and comprehensive registry... shopping here is so easy—you've got to check it out..."

Furniture, Bedding & Decor	✓	$$$	Prices
Gear & Equipment	✓	4	Product availability
Nursing & Feeding	✓	4	Staff knowledge
Safety & Babycare	✓	4	Customer service
Clothing, Shoes & Accessories	✓	4	Decor
Books, Toys & Entertainment	✓		

WWW.BABIESRUS.COM

BURBANK—7750 S CICERO AVE (AT W 78TH ST); 708.424.8755; M-SA 9:30-9:30, SU 11-7 ; PARKING IN FRONT OF BLDG

LANSING—17675 S TORRENCE AVE (AT 177TH ST); 708.474.3222; M-SA 9:30-9:30, SU 11-7 ; PARKING IN FRONT OF BLDG

ORLAND PARK—15820 94TH AVE (AT ORLAND PARK PL); 708.873.9634; M-SA 9:30-9:30, SU 11-7 ; PARKING IN FRONT OF BLDG

Baby Depot At Burlington Coat Factory

"...a large, 'super store' layout with a ton of baby gear... wide aisles, packed shelves, barely existent customer service and awesome prices... everything from bottles, car seats and strollers to gliders, cribs and clothes... I always find something worth getting... a little disorganized and hard to locate items you're looking for... the staff is not always knowledgeable about their merchandise... return policy is store credit only..."

Furniture, Bedding & Decor	✓	$$	Prices
Gear & Equipment	✓	3	Product availability
Nursing & Feeding	✓	3	Staff knowledge
Safety & Babycare	✓	3	Customer service
Clothing, Shoes & Accessories	✓	3	Decor
Books, Toys & Entertainment	✓		

WWW.BABYDEPOT.COM

LANSING—16895 S TORRENCE AVE (AT E 170TH ST); 708.889.0213; M-SA 10-9, SU 11-6; PARKING LOT

MATTESON—4208 LINCOLN HWY (AT KILDARE AVE); 708.748.9393; M-SA 10-9:30, SU 11-7; PARKING LOT

TINLEY PARK—7061 159TH ST (AT BREMENTOWNE MALL); 708.614.1626; M-SA 10-9, SU 11-6; MALL PARKING

BabyGap/GapKids

"...colorful baby and toddler clothing in clean, well-lit stores... great return policy... it's the Gap, so you know what you're getting—colorful, cute and well-made clothing... best place for baby hats... prices are reasonable especially since there's always a sale of some sort going on... sales, sales, sales—frequent and fantastic... everything I'm looking for in infant clothing—snap crotches, snaps up the front, all natural fabrics and great styling... fun seasonal selections—a great place to shop for gifts as well as for your own kids... although it can get busy, staff generally seem accommodating and helpful..."

Furniture, Bedding & Decor .... ✗ | $$$ .... Prices
Gear & Equipment .... ✗ | ❹ .... Product availability
Nursing & Feeding .... ✗ | ❹ .... Staff knowledge
Safety & Babycare .... ✗ | ❹ .... Customer service
Clothing, Shoes & Accessories .... ✓ | ❹ .... Decor
Books, Toys & Entertainment .... ✗

WWW.GAP.COM

ORLAND PARK—460 ORLAND SQ DR (AT ORLAND SQUARE SHOPPING CTR); 708.349.0998; M-SA 10-9, SU 11-6; PARKING LOT AT CENTER

Bombay Kids

"...the kids section of this furniture store carries out-of-the-ordinary items... whimsical, pastel grandfather clocks... zebra bean bags... perfect for my eclectic taste... I now prefer my daughter's room to my own... clean bathroom with changing area and wipes... they have a little table with crayons and coloring books for the kids... easy and relaxed shopping destination..."

Furniture, Bedding & Decor .... ✓ | $$$ .... Prices
Gear & Equipment .... ✗ | ❹ .... Product availability
Nursing & Feeding .... ✗ | ❹ .... Staff knowledge
Safety & Babycare .... ✗ | ❹ .... Customer service
Clothing, Shoes & Accessories .... ✗ | ❹ .... Decor
Books, Toys & Entertainment .... ✗

WWW.BOMBAYKIDS.COM

ORLAND PARK—15159 S LAGRANGE RD (AT ORLAND PARK PL); 708.364.8349; M-SA 10-9, SU 11-6

Children's Orchard

"...a friendly resale boutique... the clothes and gear are super clean and sold at amazing prices... amazing prices on clothing that is hardly used and practically brand new... shoes, toys, furniture, hair pretties, crib sets, etc... fantastic deals on well-selected used items... prices are great and you can pretty much always find something useful... a great place to buy those everyday play outfits... a lot of name brands at steeply discounted prices..."

Furniture, Bedding & Decor .... ✓ | $$ .... Prices
Gear & Equipment .... ✓ | ❸ .... Product availability
Nursing & Feeding .... ✓ | ❹ .... Staff knowledge
Safety & Babycare .... ✓ | ❹ .... Customer service
Clothing, Shoes & Accessories .... ✓ | ❸ .... Decor
Books, Toys & Entertainment .... ✓

WWW.CHILDRENSORCHARD.COM

ORLAND PARK—15864 S LAGRANGE RD (AT W 159TH ST); 708.364.7300; M-F 10-7, SA 10-5, SU 12-5

Gymboree

"...beautiful clothing and great quality... colorful and stylish baby and kids wear... lots of fun birthday gift ideas... easy exchange and return policy... items usually go on sale pretty quickly... save money with Gymbucks... many stores have a play area which makes shopping with my kids fun (let alone feasible)..."

Furniture, Bedding & Decor	✗	$$$	Prices
Gear & Equipment	✗	❹	Product availability
Nursing & Feeding	✗	❹	Staff knowledge
Safety & Babycare	✗	❹	Customer service
Clothing, Shoes & Accessories	✓	❹	Decor
Books, Toys & Entertainment	✓		

WWW.GYMBOREE.COM

ORLAND PARK—620 ORLAND SQ (AT LAKEVIEW DR); 708.349.0300; M-SA 10-9, SU 11-6

H & M

"...wonderful prices for trendy baby and toddler clothes... it's the 'Euro' Target... buy for yourself and for your kids... a fun shopping experience as long as your child doesn't mind the bright lights and loud music... decent return policy... incredible sale prices... store can get messy at peak hours... busy and hectic, but their inventory is fun and worth the visit..."

Furniture, Bedding & Decor	✗	$$	Prices
Gear & Equipment	✗	❸	Product availability
Nursing & Feeding	✗	❸	Staff knowledge
Safety & Babycare	✗	❸	Customer service
Clothing, Shoes & Accessories	✓	❸	Decor
Books, Toys & Entertainment	✓		

WWW.HM.COM

ORLAND PARK—288 ORLAND SQUARE PARK (OFF 151ST ST); 708.364.7820; M-SA 10-9, SU 11-6

JCPenney

"...always a good place to find clothes and other baby basics... the registry process was seamless... staff is generally friendly but the lines always seem long and slow... they don't have the greatest selection of toddler clothes, but their baby section is great... we had some damaged furniture delivered but customer service was easy and accommodating... a pretty limited selection of gear, but what they have is priced right..."

Furniture, Bedding & Decor	✓	$$	Prices
Gear & Equipment	✓	❸	Product availability
Nursing & Feeding	✓	❸	Staff knowledge
Safety & Babycare	✓	❸	Customer service
Clothing, Shoes & Accessories	✓	❸	Decor
Books, Toys & Entertainment	✓		

WWW.JCPENNEY.COM

JOLIET—3340 MALL LOOP DR SPACE 2 (AT LOUIS JOLIET MALL); 815.439.1400; M-F 10-9, SA 10-7, SU 11-6; MALL PARKING

ORLAND PARK—3 ORLAND SQ DR (AT ORLAND SQUARE SHOPPING CTR); 708.349.7300; M-SA 10-9, SU 11-6

KB Toys

"...hectic and always buzzing... wall-to-wall plastic and blinking lights... more Fisher-Price, Elmo and Sponge Bob than the eye can handle... a toy super store with discounted prices... they always have some kind of special sale going on... if you're looking for the latest and greatest popular toy, then look no further—not the place for unique or

unusual toys... perfect for bulk toy shopping—especially around the holidays... ❞

Furniture, Bedding & Decor	×	$$	Prices
Gear & Equipment	×	❸	Product availability
Nursing & Feeding	×	❸	Staff knowledge
Safety & Babycare	×	❸	Customer service
Clothing, Shoes & Accessories	×	❸	Decor
Books, Toys & Entertainment	✓		

WWW.KBTOYS.COM

CHICAGO RIDGE—95TH ST (AT CHICAGO RIDGE MALL); 708.423.8848; DAILY 10-9; MALL PARKING

JOLIET—3340 MALL LOOP DR (AT LOUIS JOLIET MALL); 815.436.5099; M-SA 10-9, SU 11-6; MALL PARKING

ORLAND PARK—656 ORLAND SQUARE DR (AT ORLAND SQUARE); 708.349.7711; M-SA 10-9, SU 11-6

Kid's Foot Locker

❝*...Nike, Reebok and Adidas for your little ones... hip, trendy and quite pricey... perfect for the sports addict dad who wants his kid sporting the latest NFL duds... shoes cost close to what the adult variety costs... generally good quality... they carry infant and toddler sizes...* ❞

Furniture, Bedding & Decor	×	$$$	Prices
Gear & Equipment	×	❸	Product availability
Nursing & Feeding	×	❸	Staff knowledge
Safety & Babycare	×	❸	Customer service
Clothing, Shoes & Accessories	✓	❸	Decor
Books, Toys & Entertainment	×		

WWW.KIDSFOOTLOCKER.COM

MATTESON—129 LINCOLN MALL DR (AT LINCOLN HWY); 708.747.7860; M-SA 10-9, SU 11-6

Kohl's

❝*...nice one-stop shopping for the whole family—everything from clothing to baby gear... great sales on clothing and a good selection of higher-end brands... stylish, inexpensive clothes for babies through 24 months... very easy shopping experience... dirt-cheap sales and clearance prices... nothing super fancy, but just right for those everyday romper outfits... Graco, Eddie Bauer and other well-known brands...* ❞

Furniture, Bedding & Decor	✓	$$	Prices
Gear & Equipment	✓	❹	Product availability
Nursing & Feeding	✓	❸	Staff knowledge
Safety & Babycare	✓	❸	Customer service
Clothing, Shoes & Accessories	✓	❸	Decor
Books, Toys & Entertainment	✓		

WWW.KOHLS.COM

BURBANK—7608 S LA CROSSE AVE (AT CICERO AVE); 708.499.3900; M-SA 8-10, SU 10-8; FREE PARKING

COLUMET HEIGHTS—9700 S RIDGELAND AVE (AT CHICAGO RIDGE MALL); 708.425.7909; M-SA 8-10, SU 10-8; FREE PARKING

My Own Little Room

❝*...unique furniture, accessories and gifts for decorating your child's room... a great place to go to decorate a nursery if price is not an issue... the couple who owns the store are parents themselves, so they know what expecting parents are looking for... they will match any competitors price... unique boutique-type items not found at other places...* ❞

Furniture, Bedding & Decor	✓	$$$$	Prices
Gear & Equipment	×	❹	Product availability
Nursing & Feeding	×	❹	Staff knowledge

Safety & Babycare .... ✗
Clothing, Shoes & Accessories ...... ✓
Books, Toys & Entertainment .... ✓

❹ ....Customer service
❹ .... Decor

WWW.MYOWNLITTLEROOM.COM

ORLAND PARK—14490 S LA GRANGE RD (AT HWY 45); 708.364.7666; M T-W F 10-6, TH 10-8, SA 10-5

Old Navy ★★★★☆

"...hip and 'in' clothes for infants and tots... plenty of steals on clearance items... T-shirts and pants for $10 or less... busy, busy, busy—long lines, especially on weekends... nothing fancy and you won't mind when your kids get down and dirty in these clothes... easy to wash, decent quality... you can shop for your baby, your toddler, your teen and yourself all at the same time... clothes are especially affordable when you hit their sales (post-holiday sales are amazing!)..."

Furniture, Bedding & Decor .... ✗
Gear & Equipment .... ✗
Nursing & Feeding .... ✗
Safety & Babycare .... ✗
Clothing, Shoes & Accessories ...... ✓
Books, Toys & Entertainment .... ✗

$$... Prices
❹ .... Product availability
❸ .... Staff knowledge
❸ ....Customer service
❸ .... Decor

WWW.OLDNAVY.COM

CHICAGO RIDGE—238 COMMONS DR (AT RIDGELAND AVE); 708.857.9590; M-SA 10-9, SU 11-7

JOLIET—2711 PLAINFIELD RD (AT HENNEPIN DR); 815.439.9147; M-SA 9-9, SU 11-6

MATTESON—253 LINCOLN MALL DR (AT LINCOLN MALL); 708.503.4913; M-SA 9-9, SU 9-6; MALL PARKING

ORLAND PARK—120 ORLAND PARK PL (AT 94TH AVE); 708.364.0555; M-SA 9-9, SU 10-6

Rainbow Kids ★★½☆☆

"...fun clothing styles for infants and tots at low prices... the quality isn't the same as the more expensive brands, but the sleepers and play outfits always hold up well... great place for basics... cute trendy shoe selection for your little walker... we love the prices... up-to-date selection..."

Furniture, Bedding & Decor .... ✗
Gear & Equipment .... ✓
Nursing & Feeding .... ✗
Safety & Babycare .... ✗
Clothing, Shoes & Accessories ...... ✓
Books, Toys & Entertainment .... ✓

$$... Prices
❸ .... Product availability
❸ .... Staff knowledge
❸ ....Customer service
❸ .... Decor

WWW.RAINBOWSHOPS.COM

EVERGREEN PARK—9500 S WESTERN AVE (AT W 95TH ST); 708.636.3711; M-SA 10-9 SU 11-6 ; PARKING LOT

Target ★★★★☆

"...our favorite place to shop for kids' stuff—good selection and very affordable... guilt-free shopping—kids grow so fast so I don't want to pay high department-store prices... everything from diapers and sippy cups to car seats and strollers... easy return policy... generally helpful staff, but you don't go for the service—you go for the prices... decent registry that won't freak your friends out with outrageous prices... easy, convenient shopping for well-priced items... all the big-box brands available—Graco, Evenflo, Eddie Bauer, etc...."

Furniture, Bedding & Decor .... ✓
Gear & Equipment .... ✓
Nursing & Feeding .... ✓

$$... Prices
❹ .... Product availability
❸ .... Staff knowledge

Safety & Babycare .... ✓
Clothing, Shoes & Accessories....... ✓
Books, Toys & Entertainment .... ✓

❸ .... Customer service
❸ .... Decor

WWW.TARGET.COM

MATTESON—21600 CICERO AVE (AT N GATEWAY DR); 708.748.0990; M-SA 8-10, SU 8-9; PARKING IN FRONT OF BLDG

Toys R Us

"...not just toys, but also tons of gear and supplies including diapers and formula... a hectic shopping experience but the prices make it all worthwhile... I've experienced good and bad service at the same store on the same day... the stores are huge and can be overwhelming... most big brand-names available... leave the kids at home unless you want to end up with a cart full of toys..."

Furniture, Bedding & Decor .... ✓
Gear & Equipment .... ✓
Nursing & Feeding....................... ✓
Safety & Babycare .... ✓
Clothing, Shoes & Accessories....... ✓
Books, Toys & Entertainment .... ✓

$$$ .... Prices
❹ .... Product availability
❸ .... Staff knowledge
❸ .... Customer service
❸ .... Decor

WWW.TOYSRUS.COM

BURBANK—8148 S CICERO AVE (AT W 81TH ST); 708.636.4600; M-SA 10-9, SU 10-7

JOLIET—3128 VOYAGER LN (AT LOUIS JOLIET MALL); 815.439.1009; M-SA 9:30-9:30, SU 10-7; MALL PARKING

LANSING—16855 TORENCE AVE (AT E 170TH ST); 708.474.7707; M-SA 9:30-9:30, SU 10-7

MATTESON—5001 LINCOLN HWY (AT TOWN CTR RD); 708.748.1777; M-SA 9:30-9:30, SU 10-7

ORLAND PARK—45 ORLAND SQ DR (AT ORLAND SQUARE SHOPPING CTR); 708.460.9494; M-SA 9:30-9:30, SU 10-7

Online

"lila picks"

★babycenter.com ★babystyle.com

★babyuniverse.com ★joggingstroller.com

ababy.com

Furniture, Bedding & Decor	✓	✓	Gear & Equipment
Nursing & Feeding	✗	✓	Safety & Babycare
Clothing, Shoes & Accessories	✓	✗	Books, Toys & Entertainment

aikobaby.com ★★★☆☆

"...high end clothes that are so cute.. .everything from Catamini to Jack and Lily... you can find super expensive infant and baby clothes at discounted prices... amazing selection of diaper bags so you don't have to look like a frumpy mom (or dad)..."

Furniture, Bedding & Decor	✗	✓	Gear & Equipment
Nursing & Feeding	✗	✗	Safety & Babycare
Clothing, Shoes & Accessories	✓	✗	Books, Toys & Entertainment

albeebaby.com ★★★★☆

"...they offer a really comprehensive selection of baby gear... their prices are some of the best online... great discounts on Maclarens before the new models come out... good product availability—fast shipping and easy transactions... the site is pretty easy to use... the prices are surprisingly great..."

Furniture, Bedding & Decor	✓	✓	Gear & Equipment
Nursing & Feeding	✓	✓	Safety & Babycare
Clothing, Shoes & Accessories	✓	✓	Books, Toys & Entertainment

amazon.com ★★★★½

"...unless you've been living under a rock, you know that in addition to books, Amazon carries an amazing amount of baby stuff too... they have the best prices and offer free shipping on bigger purchases... you can even buy used items for dirt cheap... I always read the comments written by others—they're very useful in helping make my decisions... I love Amazon for just about everything, but their baby selection only carries the big box standards..."

Furniture, Bedding & Decor	✗	✓	Gear & Equipment
Nursing & Feeding	✓	✓	Safety & Babycare
Clothing, Shoes & Accessories	✓	✓	Books, Toys & Entertainment

arunningstroller.com ★★★★½

"...the prices are very competitive and the customer service is great... I talked to them on the phone for a while and they totally hooked me up with the right model... if you're looking for a new stroller, look no further... talk to Marilyn—she's the best... shipping costs are reasonable and their prices overall are good..."

Furniture, Bedding & Decor ✓ | ✓ Gear & Equipment
Nursing & Feeding ✗ | ✗ Safety & Babycare
Clothing, Shoes & Accessories ✗ | ✗ Books, Toys & Entertainment

babiesinthesun.com

★★★★☆

"...one-stop shopping for cloth diapers... run by a fantastic woman who had 3 cloth diapered babies herself and is a wealth of knowledge... if you live in South Florida, the owner will let you into her home to see the merchandise and ask questions... great selection and the customer service is the best..."

Furniture, Bedding & Decor ✗ | ✓ Gear & Equipment
Nursing & Feeding ✗ | ✓ Safety & Babycare
Clothing, Shoes & Accessories ✗ | ✗ Books, Toys & Entertainment

babiesrus.com

★★★★☆

"...terrific web site with all the baby gear you'll need... registering online made it easy for my family and friends... getting the registry activated was a bit tricky... super convenient and ideal for the moms-to-be who are on bedrest... web site prices are comparable to in-store prices... shipping is usually free... a very efficient way to buy and send baby gifts... our local Babies R Us said they will accept returns if they carry the same item... not all online items are available in your local store..."

Furniture, Bedding & Decor ✓ | ✓ Gear & Equipment
Nursing & Feeding ✓ | ✓ Safety & Babycare
Clothing, Shoes & Accessories ✓ | ✓ Books, Toys & Entertainment

babiestravellite.com

★★★★½

"...caters to traveling families... they deliver baby items to your hotel room anywhere in the country... all of the different baby supplies you will need when you travel with a baby or a toddler... they sell almost every major brand for each product and their prices are sometimes cheaper than you would find at your local store..."

Furniture, Bedding & Decor ✗ | ✗ Gear & Equipment
Nursing & Feeding ✓ | ✓ Safety & Babycare
Clothing, Shoes & Accessories ✗ | ✓ Books, Toys & Entertainment

babyage.com

★★★★☆

"...fast shipping and the best prices around... flat rate shipping is great after the baby has arrived and you don't have time to go to the store... very attentive customer service... clearance items are a great deal (regular items are very competitive too)... ordering and delivery were super smooth... I usually check this web site before I purchase any baby gear... sign up for their newsletter and they'll notify you when they are having a sale..."

Furniture, Bedding & Decor ✓ | ✓ Gear & Equipment
Nursing & Feeding ✓ | ✓ Safety & Babycare
Clothing, Shoes & Accessories ✓ | ✓ Books, Toys & Entertainment

babyant.com

★★★★☆

"...wide variety of brands and products available through their site... super easy to navigate... fun, whimsical ideas... nice people and helpful... easy to return items and you can call them with questions... often has the best prices and low shipping costs..."

Furniture, Bedding & Decor ✓ | ✓ Gear & Equipment
Nursing & Feeding ✓ | ✓ Safety & Babycare
Clothing, Shoes & Accessories ✓ | ✓ Books, Toys & Entertainment

babybazaar.com

"...high-end baby stuff available on an easy-to-use web site... lots of European styles... quick processing and shipping... mom's tips, educational toys, exclusive favorites Bugaboo and Stokke..."

Furniture, Bedding & Decor .... ✓ ✓ .... Gear & Equipment
Nursing & Feeding .... ✓ ✓ .... Safety & Babycare
Clothing, Shoes & Accessories ...... ✓ ✓ .... Books, Toys & Entertainment

babybestbuy.com

Furniture, Bedding & Decor .... ✓ ✓ .... Gear & Equipment
Nursing & Feeding .... ✓ ✓ .... Safety & Babycare
Clothing, Shoes & Accessories ...... ✓ ✓ .... Books, Toys & Entertainment

babycatalog.com ★★★★☆

"...great deals on many essentials... wide selection of rockers but fewer options in other categories... the web site could be more user-friendly... customer service and delivery was fast and efficient... check out their seasonal specials... the baby club is a great way to save additional money... sign up for their wonderful pregnancy/new baby email newsletter... check this web site before you buy anywhere else..."

Furniture, Bedding & Decor .... ✓ ✓ .... Gear & Equipment
Nursing & Feeding .... ✓ ✓ .... Safety & Babycare
Clothing, Shoes & Accessories ...... ✓ ✓ .... Books, Toys & Entertainment

babycenter.com ★★★★★

"...a terrific selection of all things baby, plus quick shipping... free shipping on big orders... makes shopping convenient for new parents... web site is very user friendly... they always email you about sale items and special offers... lots of useful information for parents... carries everything you may need... online registry is simple, easy and a great way to get what you need... includes helpful products ratings by parents... they've created a nice online community in addition to their online store..."

Furniture, Bedding & Decor .... ✓ ✓ .... Gear & Equipment
Nursing & Feeding .... ✓ ✓ .... Safety & Babycare
Clothing, Shoes & Accessories ...... ✓ ✓ .... Books, Toys & Entertainment

babydepot.com ★★★☆☆

"...carries everything you'll find in a big department store but at cheaper prices and with everything all in one place... be certain you know what you want because returns can be difficult... site could be more user-friendly... online selection can differ from instore selection... love the online registry..."

Furniture, Bedding & Decor .... ✓ ✓ .... Gear & Equipment
Nursing & Feeding .... ✓ ✓ .... Safety & Babycare
Clothing, Shoes & Accessories ...... ✓ ✓ .... Books, Toys & Entertainment

babygeared.com

Furniture, Bedding & Decor .... ✓ ✓ .... Gear & Equipment
Nursing & Feeding .... ✓ ✓ .... Safety & Babycare
Clothing, Shoes & Accessories ...... ✓ ✓ .... Books, Toys & Entertainment

babyphd.com

Furniture, Bedding & Decor .... ✓ ✗ .... Gear & Equipment
Nursing & Feeding .... ✗ ✗ .... Safety & Babycare
Clothing, Shoes & Accessories ...... ✓ ✓ .... Books, Toys & Entertainment

babystyle.com ★★★★★

"...their web site is just like their stores—terrific... an excellent source for everything a parent needs... fantastic maternity and baby clothes...

they always respond quickly by email... their site seems to have even more merchandise than their stores... I started shopping on their site after receiving a gift card—very easy and convenient... wonderful selection... ”

Furniture, Bedding & Decor ✓ ✓ Gear & Equipment
Nursing & Feeding ✓ ✓ Safety & Babycare
Clothing, Shoes & Accessories ✓ ✓ Books, Toys & Entertainment

babysupermall.com

Furniture, Bedding & Decor ✓ ✓ Gear & Equipment
Nursing & Feeding ✓ ✓ Safety & Babycare
Clothing, Shoes & Accessories ✓ ✓ Books, Toys & Entertainment

babyuniverse.com ★★★★★

“...nice large selection of specialty and basic items... easy-to-use web site with decent prices... carries Carter's clothes and many other popular brands... great bedding selection - they're one of the few places with the Kidsline bedding I wanted... adorable backpacks for toddlers and preschoolers... check out the site for strollers and car seats... this was my first online shopping experience and they made it so easy, convenient and fast, I was hooked... fine customer service... flat rate (if not free) shipping takes the 'ouch' factor out of those big ticket purchases... ”

Furniture, Bedding & Decor ✓ ✓ Gear & Equipment
Nursing & Feeding ✓ ✓ Safety & Babycare
Clothing, Shoes & Accessories ✓ ✓ Books, Toys & Entertainment

barebabies.com

Furniture, Bedding & Decor ✓ ✓ Gear & Equipment
Nursing & Feeding ✓ ✓ Safety & Babycare
Clothing, Shoes & Accessories ✓ ✓ Books, Toys & Entertainment

birthandbaby.com ★★★★☆

“...incredible site for buying a nursing bra... there is more information about different manufacturers than you can imagine... I've even received a phone call from the owner after placing an order to clarify something... free shipping, so it's easy to buy multiple sizes and send back the ones that don't fit... their selection of nursing bras is better than any other place I've found... if you are a hard to fit size, this is the place to go... ”

Furniture, Bedding & Decor ✗ ✓ Gear & Equipment
Nursing & Feeding ✓ ✓ Safety & Babycare
Clothing, Shoes & Accessories ✗ ✓ Books, Toys & Entertainment

blueberrybabies.com

Furniture, Bedding & Decor ✓ ✓ Gear & Equipment
Nursing & Feeding ✓ ✓ Safety & Babycare
Clothing, Shoes & Accessories ✓ ✓ Books, Toys & Entertainment

buybuybaby.com ★★★★½

“...this is the web site for the popular New York-based baby retailer... you name it, they've got it... all the items in their store can also be found on their web site... prices are fair - especially since things get shipped right to your door... we had some items that were damaged and their online customer service took care of it without any problems... ”

Furniture, Bedding & Decor ✓ ✓ Gear & Equipment
Nursing & Feeding ✓ ✓ Safety & Babycare
Clothing, Shoes & Accessories ✓ ✓ Books, Toys & Entertainment

childcarriers.com

Furniture, Bedding & Decor ✗ ✓ Gear & Equipment

Nursing & Feeding	✗	✗	Safety & Babycare
Clothing, Shoes & Accessories	✗	✗	Books, Toys & Entertainment

clothdiaper.com

Furniture, Bedding & Decor	✗	✓	Gear & Equipment
Nursing & Feeding	✓	✓	Safety & Babycare
Clothing, Shoes & Accessories	✗	✗	Books, Toys & Entertainment

cocoacrayon.com

Furniture, Bedding & Decor	✓	✓	Gear & Equipment
Nursing & Feeding	✓	✓	Safety & Babycare
Clothing, Shoes & Accessories	✓	✓	Books, Toys & Entertainment

cvs.com ★★★★☆

“...super convenient web site for any 'drug store' items... items are delivered in a reasonable amount of time... decent selection of baby products... prices are competitive and ordering online definitely beats making the trip out to the drugstore... order a bunch of stuff at a time so shipping is free... I used them for my baby announcements and everyone loved them... super easy to refill prescriptions... it was a real relief to order all my formula, baby wipes and diapers online...”

Furniture, Bedding & Decor	✗	✗	Gear & Equipment
Nursing & Feeding	✓	✓	Safety & Babycare
Clothing, Shoes & Accessories	✗	✗	Books, Toys & Entertainment

dreamtimebaby.com

Furniture, Bedding & Decor	✓	✓	Gear & Equipment
Nursing & Feeding	✓	✓	Safety & Babycare
Clothing, Shoes & Accessories	✓	✓	Books, Toys & Entertainment

drugstore.com ★★★★☆

Furniture, Bedding & Decor	✗	✗	Gear & Equipment
Nursing & Feeding	✓	✓	Safety & Babycare
Clothing, Shoes & Accessories	✗	✗	Books, Toys & Entertainment

ebay.com ★★★★☆

“...great way to save money on everything from maternity clothes to breast pumps... be careful with whom you do business... it's always worth checking out what's available... I picked up a brand new jogger for dirt cheap... great deals to be had if you have patience to browse and be willing to resell or exchange what you don't like... baby stuff is easily found and often reasonably priced... keep an eye on shipping costs when you're bidding...”

Furniture, Bedding & Decor	✓	✓	Gear & Equipment
Nursing & Feeding	✓	✓	Safety & Babycare
Clothing, Shoes & Accessories	✓	✓	Books, Toys & Entertainment

egiggle.com ★★★★☆

“...nice selection—not overwhelming... don't expect the big box store brands here—they carry higher-end, specialty items that you won't find elsewhere... smooth shopping experience... nice site—convenient and easy to use...”

Furniture, Bedding & Decor	✓	✓	Gear & Equipment
Nursing & Feeding	✓	✓	Safety & Babycare
Clothing, Shoes & Accessories	✓	✓	Books, Toys & Entertainment

gagagifts.com ★★★★☆

“...great online store that carries fun clothes and unique gifts and toys for kids and adults... unique and special gifts like designer diaper bags, Whoozit learning toys and handmade quilts... this site makes gift buying incredibly easy—I'm done in less than 5 minutes... prices are high but products are special...”

Furniture, Bedding & Decor .... ✓ ✓ .... Gear & Equipment
Nursing & Feeding .... ✓ ✓ .... Safety & Babycare
Clothing, Shoes & Accessories .... ✓ ✓ .... Books, Toys & Entertainment

gap.com ★★★★☆

"...I love the Gap's online store—all the cool things in their stores available via my computer... terrific selection of boys and girls clothes plus cute shoes... you can find awesome deals and return online purchases to Gap stores... their clothes are very durable... it's easy to purchase items online and delivery is prompt... a very practical and affordable way to shop... site makes it easy to quickly find what you need... sign up for the weekly newsletter and you'll find out about online sales..."

Furniture, Bedding & Decor .... ✓ ✓ .... Gear & Equipment
Nursing & Feeding .... ✗ ✗ .... Safety & Babycare
Clothing, Shoes & Accessories .... ✓ ✓ .... Books, Toys & Entertainment

geniusbabies.com ★★★½☆

"...the best selection available of developmental toys and gifts... the only place to order real puppets from the Baby Einstein video series... cool place for unique baby shower and birthday gifts... their site navigation could use an upgrade..."

Furniture, Bedding & Decor .... ✗ ✗ .... Gear & Equipment
Nursing & Feeding .... ✗ ✗ .... Safety & Babycare
Clothing, Shoes & Accessories .... ✗ ✓ .... Books, Toys & Entertainment

gymboree.com ★★★★☆

"...beautiful clothing and great quality... colorful and stylish baby and kids wear... lots of fun birthday gift ideas... easy exchange and return policy... items usually go on sale pretty quickly... save money with gymbucks... many stores have a play area which makes shopping with my kids fun (let alone feasible)..."

Furniture, Bedding & Decor .... ✗ ✗ .... Gear & Equipment
Nursing & Feeding .... ✗ ✗ .... Safety & Babycare
Clothing, Shoes & Accessories .... ✓ ✓ .... Books, Toys & Entertainment

hannaandersson.com

Furniture, Bedding & Decor .... ✓ ✗ .... Gear & Equipment
Nursing & Feeding .... ✓ ✗ .... Safety & Babycare
Clothing, Shoes & Accessories .... ✓ ✓ .... Books, Toys & Entertainment

jcpenney.com

Furniture, Bedding & Decor .... ✓ ✗ .... Gear & Equipment
Nursing & Feeding .... ✗ ✓ .... Safety & Babycare
Clothing, Shoes & Accessories .... ✓ ✗ .... Books, Toys & Entertainment

joggingstroller.com ★★★★★

"...an excellent resource when you're choosing a jogging stroller... the entire site is devoted to joggers... very helpful information that's worth checking whether you plan to buy from them or not... the best online guide for researching jogging strollers... includes helpful comparisons and parent reviews on the top strollers..."

Furniture, Bedding & Decor .... ✗ ✓ .... Gear & Equipment
Nursing & Feeding .... ✗ ✗ .... Safety & Babycare
Clothing, Shoes & Accessories .... ✗ ✗ .... Books, Toys & Entertainment

kidsurplus.com

Furniture, Bedding & Decor .... ✓ ✗ .... Gear & Equipment
Nursing & Feeding .... ✓ ✗ .... Safety & Babycare
Clothing, Shoes & Accessories .... ✓ ✓ .... Books, Toys & Entertainment

landofnod.com ★★★★☆

"...cool site with adorable and unique furnishings... hip kid style art work... fabulous furniture and bedding... the catalog is amusing and nicely laid out... lots of sweet selections for both boys and girls... good customer service... fun but small selection of music, books, toys and more... a great way to get ideas for putting rooms together..."

Furniture, Bedding & Decor .... ✓ | ✗ .... Gear & Equipment
Nursing & Feeding .... ✗ | ✗ .... Safety & Babycare
Clothing, Shoes & Accessories .... ✗ | ✓ .... Books, Toys & Entertainment

landsend.com ★★★★☆

"...carries the best quality in children's wear—their stuff lasts forever... durable and adorable clothing, shoes and bedding... they offer a huge variety of casual clothing and awesome pajamas... not as inexpensive as other sites, but you can't beat the quality... the very best diaper bags... site is easy to navigate and has great finds for the entire family... love the flannel sheets, maternity clothes and shoes for mom..."

Furniture, Bedding & Decor .... ✓ | ✗ .... Gear & Equipment
Nursing & Feeding .... ✗ | ✗ .... Safety & Babycare
Clothing, Shoes & Accessories ...... ✓ | ✗ .... Books, Toys & Entertainment

letsgostrolling.com

Furniture, Bedding & Decor .... ✓ | ✓ .... Gear & Equipment
Nursing & Feeding .... ✓ | ✗ .... Safety & Babycare
Clothing, Shoes & Accessories ...... ✓ | ✓ .... Books, Toys & Entertainment

llbean.com ★★★★☆

"...high quality clothing for babies, toddlers and kids at reasonable prices... the clothes are extremely durable and stand up to wear and tear very well... a great site for winter clothing and gear shopping... wonderful selection for older kids, too... fewer options for infants... an awesome way to shop for clothing basics... you can't beat the diaper bags..."

Furniture, Bedding & Decor .... ✗ | ✗ .... Gear & Equipment
Nursing & Feeding .... ✗ | ✗ .... Safety & Babycare
Clothing, Shoes & Accessories ...... ✓ | ✗ .... Books, Toys & Entertainment

modernseed.com

"...it was fun finding many unique items for my son's nursery... I wanted a contemporary theme and they had lots of wonderful items including crib linens, wall art and lighting... the place to find super cool baby and kid stuff and the best place for modern nursery decor... they also carry children and adult clothing and furniture and toys... not cheap but one of my favorite places..."

Furniture, Bedding & Decor .... ✓ | ✓ .... Gear & Equipment
Nursing & Feeding .... ✓ | ✓ .... Safety & Babycare
Clothing, Shoes & Accessories ...... ✓ | ✓ .... Books, Toys & Entertainment

naturalbaby-catalog.com

"...all natural products—clothes, toys, herbal medicines, bathing, etc... fine quality and a great alternative to the usual products... site is fairly easy to navigate and has a good selection... dealing with returns is pretty painless... love the catalogue and the products... excellent customer service... lots of organic clothing made with natural materials... high quality shoes in a range of prices..."

Furniture, Bedding & Decor .... ✓ | ✓ .... Gear & Equipment
Nursing & Feeding .... ✓ | ✓ .... Safety & Babycare
Clothing, Shoes & Accessories ...... ✓ | ✓ .... Books, Toys & Entertainment

netkidswear.com

Furniture, Bedding & Decor ....✓ ✓ .... Gear & Equipment
Nursing & Feeding ....✓ ✓ .... Safety & Babycare
Clothing, Shoes & Accessories.......✓ ✓ .... Books, Toys & Entertainment

nordstrom.com

★★★★☆

"...just like their stores, the site carries a great selection of high-quality items... you can't go wrong with Nordstrom—even online... quick shipping and easy site navigation... a little pricey, but great quality items... I've purchased a bunch of baby stuff from their website and have never had a problem... a great shoe selection for all ages..."

Furniture, Bedding & Decor ....✓ ✓ .... Gear & Equipment
Nursing & Feeding ....✗ ✓ .... Safety & Babycare
Clothing, Shoes & Accessories.......✓ ✓ .... Books, Toys & Entertainment

oldnavy.com

★★★★☆

"...shopping online with Old Navy makes it easy to find incredible bargains... site was easy to use and my products arrived quickly... site carries items that aren't necessarily available in their stores... an inexpensive way to get trendy baby clothes... you can return items directly to any store... check out the sale page of this web site for deep discounts on current season clothing... I signed up for the email savings and get free shipping several times a year..."

Furniture, Bedding & Decor ....✗ ✗ .... Gear & Equipment
Nursing & Feeding ....✗ ✗ .... Safety & Babycare
Clothing, Shoes & Accessories.......✓ ✗ .... Books, Toys & Entertainment

oliebollen.com

★★★★½

"...perfect for the busy mom looking for a fun baby shower gift... this online-only store has all the best brands—Catamini and Tea Collection to name a couple... great for gifts and home stuff, too... lots of style... very easy to use... 30 days full refund, 60 days store credit..."

Furniture, Bedding & Decor ....✓ ✗ .... Gear & Equipment
Nursing & Feeding ....✓ ✗ .... Safety & Babycare
Clothing, Shoes & Accessories.......✓ ✓ .... Books, Toys & Entertainment

onestepahead.com

★★★★½

"...one stop shopping site with everything parents are looking for... huge variety of items to choose from... I bought everything from a crib to a nursery bottle... high quality items, many of which are developmental in nature... great line of safety equipment... easy to order and fast delivery but you will pay for shipping... web site has helpful reviews... great site for hard to find items..."

Furniture, Bedding & Decor ....✓ ✓ .... Gear & Equipment
Nursing & Feeding ....✓ ✓ .... Safety & Babycare
Clothing, Shoes & Accessories.......✓ ✓ .... Books, Toys & Entertainment

peapods.com

Furniture, Bedding & Decor ....✓ ✓ .... Gear & Equipment
Nursing & Feeding ....✗ ✓ .... Safety & Babycare
Clothing, Shoes & Accessories.......✓ ✓ .... Books, Toys & Entertainment

pokkadots.com

Furniture, Bedding & Decor ....✓ ✓ .... Gear & Equipment
Nursing & Feeding ....✓ ✗ .... Safety & Babycare
Clothing, Shoes & Accessories.......✓ ✓ .... Books, Toys & Entertainment

poshtots.com

★★★★☆

"...incredible selection of whimsical and out-of-the-ordinary nursery decor... beautiful, unique designer room sets in multiple styles... they do boys and girls bedrooms... great for the baby that has everything—

including parents with an unlimited cash account... you can get great ideas about decor just from browsing the site, even if you don't buy... ”

Furniture, Bedding & Decor .... ✓ ✓ .... Gear & Equipment
Nursing & Feeding .... ✓ ✗ .... Safety & Babycare
Clothing, Shoes & Accessories ...... ✓ ✓ .... Books, Toys & Entertainment

potterybarnkids.com ★★★★½

“*...beautiful high end furniture and bedding... they have a way with matching everything perfectly and I am always a sucker for that look... adorable merchandise of great quality... you will get what you pay for: high quality furniture at high prices... web site is easy to navigate... items like hooded towels and plush blankets make this place special... if I could afford it I would buy everything in the store...* ”

Furniture, Bedding & Decor .... ✓ ✓ .... Gear & Equipment
Nursing & Feeding .... ✗ ✗ .... Safety & Babycare
Clothing, Shoes & Accessories .... ✗ ✓ .... Books, Toys & Entertainment

preemie.com

Furniture, Bedding & Decor .... ✗ ✓ .... Gear & Equipment
Nursing & Feeding .... ✓ ✓ .... Safety & Babycare
Clothing, Shoes & Accessories ...... ✓ ✓ .... Books, Toys & Entertainment

rei.com

Furniture, Bedding & Decor .... ✗ ✓ .... Gear & Equipment
Nursing & Feeding .... ✗ ✗ .... Safety & Babycare
Clothing, Shoes & Accessories ...... ✓ ✓ .... Books, Toys & Entertainment

royalnursery.com ★★★½☆

“*...this used to be a store in San Diego and now it is only online... if you need a silver rattle, luxury baby blanket or shower gift—this is the place... a beautiful site with elegant baby clothes, jewelry, and gifts...love the hand print kits—they are my current favorite gift... high end baby wear and gear... be sure to check out the sale items...* ”

Furniture, Bedding & Decor .... ✓ ✗ .... Gear & Equipment
Nursing & Feeding .... ✗ ✓ .... Safety & Babycare
Clothing, Shoes & Accessories ...... ✓ ✓ .... Books, Toys & Entertainment

showeryourbaby.com

Furniture, Bedding & Decor .... ✓ ✓ .... Gear & Equipment
Nursing & Feeding .... ✓ ✓ .... Safety & Babycare
Clothing, Shoes & Accessories ...... ✓ ✓ .... Books, Toys & Entertainment

snipsnsnails.com ★★★★½

“*...a great boys clothing store for infants to 14 years old... clothes for every occasion, from casual to special occasion... pajamas and swimsuits, too... pricey, but upscale and fun... items on the web site are not always in stock ...* ”

Furniture, Bedding & Decor .... ✓ ✗ .... Gear & Equipment
Nursing & Feeding .... ✗ ✗ .... Safety & Babycare
Clothing, Shoes & Accessories ...... ✓ ✗ .... Books, Toys & Entertainment

strollerdepot.com

Furniture, Bedding & Decor .... ✗ ✓ .... Gear & Equipment
Nursing & Feeding .... ✗ ✗ .... Safety & Babycare
Clothing, Shoes & Accessories .... ✗ ✓ .... Books, Toys & Entertainment

strollers4less.com ★★★½☆

“*...some of the best prices on strollers... I love this site... we purchased our stroller online for a lot less than it costs locally... online ordering went smoothly—from ordering through receiving... wide* *selection and some incredible deals... shipping is relatively fast... free shipping if you spend $100, which isn't hard to do...* ”

Furniture, Bedding & Decor .... ✗ ✓ .... Gear & Equipment
Nursing & Feeding .... ✗ ✗ .... Safety & Babycare
Clothing, Shoes & Accessories....... ✗ ✓ .... Books, Toys & Entertainment

target.com

★★★★☆

“*...our favorite place to shop for kids stuff—good selection and very affordable... guilt free shopping—kids grow so fast so I don't want to pay high department store prices... everything from diapers and sippy cups to car seats and strollers... easy return policy... decent registry that won't freak your friends out with outrageous prices... easy, convenient shopping for well-priced items... all the big box brands available—Graco, Evenflo, Eddie Bauer, etc....* ”

Furniture, Bedding & Decor .... ✓ ✓ .... Gear & Equipment
Nursing & Feeding .... ✓ ✓ .... Safety & Babycare
Clothing, Shoes & Accessories....... ✓ ✓ .... Books, Toys & Entertainment

teddylux.com

Furniture, Bedding & Decor .... ✗ ✗ .... Gear & Equipment
Nursing & Feeding .... ✗ ✗ .... Safety & Babycare
Clothing, Shoes & Accessories....... ✗ ✓ .... Books, Toys & Entertainment

thebabyhammock.com

★★★★☆

“*...a family owned business selling parent-tested products from morning sickness relief products to baby carriers, natural skincare, gift sets and more... fast friendly service... natural products and waldorf influenced toys...* ”

Furniture, Bedding & Decor .... ✓ ✓ .... Gear & Equipment
Nursing & Feeding .... ✓ ✓ .... Safety & Babycare
Clothing, Shoes & Accessories....... ✓ ✗ .... Books, Toys & Entertainment

thebabyoutlet.com

Furniture, Bedding & Decor .... ✗ ✓ .... Gear & Equipment
Nursing & Feeding .... ✓ ✓ .... Safety & Babycare
Clothing, Shoes & Accessories....... ✗ ✓ .... Books, Toys & Entertainment

tinyride.com

Furniture, Bedding & Decor .... ✗ ✓ .... Gear & Equipment
Nursing & Feeding .... ✓ ✗ .... Safety & Babycare
Clothing, Shoes & Accessories....... ✗ ✗ .... Books, Toys & Entertainment

toadsandtulips.com

Furniture, Bedding & Decor .... ✗ ✗ .... Gear & Equipment
Nursing & Feeding .... ✗ ✗ .... Safety & Babycare
Clothing, Shoes & Accessories....... ✗ ✗ .... Books, Toys & Entertainment

toysrus.com

★★★★☆

“*...makes shopping incredibly easy... well organized site with discount prices... makes registering for gifts super simple... even more products are online than in the actual stores... check out the outlet section and coupon codes for even more discounts... I did most of my Christmas shopping here, paid no shipping and had my gifts delivered in 3 days... web site includes helpful toy reviews... use this to send your wish lists to relatives...* ”

Furniture, Bedding & Decor .... ✓ ✓ .... Gear & Equipment
Nursing & Feeding .... ✓ ✓ .... Safety & Babycare
Clothing, Shoes & Accessories....... ✓ ✓ .... Books, Toys & Entertainment

tuttibella.com

★★★★☆

“*...well designed web site with beautiful, original clothing, toys, bedding and accessories... cute vintage stuff for babies and kids...*

stylish designer goods from here and abroad... your child will stand out among the Baby Gap-clothed masses... gorgeous fabrics... a great place to find that perfect gift for someone special and stylish... ❞

Furniture, Bedding & Decor .... ✓ ✓ .... Gear & Equipment
Nursing & Feeding .... ✗ ✗ .... Safety & Babycare
Clothing, Shoes & Accessories ...... ✓ ✗ .... Books, Toys & Entertainment

usillygoose.com

Furniture, Bedding & Decor .... ✓ ✗ .... Gear & Equipment
Nursing & Feeding .... ✗ ✗ .... Safety & Babycare
Clothing, Shoes & Accessories .... ✗ ✓ .... Books, Toys & Entertainment

walmart.com ★★★½☆

❝*...the site is packed with information, which can be a little difficult to navigate... anything and everything you need at a huge discount... good idea to browse the site and research prices before you visit a store... my order was delivered well before the estimated delivery date... I've found cheaper deals online than in the store...* ❞

Furniture, Bedding & Decor .... ✓ ✓ .... Gear & Equipment
Nursing & Feeding .... ✓ ✓ .... Safety & Babycare
Clothing, Shoes & Accessories ...... ✓ ✓ .... Books, Toys & Entertainment

maternity clothing

City of Chicago

"lila picks"

★A Pea In The Pod

★Belly Dance Maternity

★Gap Maternity

A Pea In The Pod

"...excellent if you are looking for stylish maternity clothes and don't mind paying for them... start here for special occasions and business wear... the decor is lovely and most of the clothes are beautiful... stylish fashion solutions, but expect to pay more than at department stores... keep your eyes open for the sale rack—the markdowns can be terrific... an upscale shop that carries everything from intimates to fancy dresses... stylish, fun and non-maternity-like..."

Casual wear ✓ | $$$$ Prices
Business wear ✓ | ❹ Product availability
Intimate apparel ✓ | ❹ Customer service
Nursing wear ✓ | ❹ Decor

WWW.APEAINTHEPOD.COM

EAST/WEST OLD TOWN GOLD COAST/STREETVILLE—46 E OAK ST (AT N RUSH ST); 312.944.3080; M-SA 10-6, SU 12-5

Baby Depot At Burlington Coat Factory

"...a surprisingly good selection of maternity clothes at great prices... staff can be hard to find so be prepared to dig... cute pants, skirts and sets... I wouldn't have thought that their selection would be as good as it is... not much other than casual items, but what they have is pretty good..."

Casual wear ✓ | $$ Prices
Business wear ✗ | ❸ Product availability
Intimate apparel ✗ | ❸ Customer service
Nursing wear ✗ | ❸ Decor

WWW.BABYDEPOT.COM

SOUTH SIDE—8320 S CICERO AVE (AT W 83RD ST); 708.636.8300; M-SA 10-9, SU 11-6; PARKING LOT

Belly Dance Maternity

"...thanks to Belly Dance Maternity I was able to be pregnant and somewhat stylish at the same time... fancy maternity gear from designers such as NOM, Cadeau, Earl Jean and more... great trendy items along with cool basics to make you feel cute... not cheap, but so worth the splurge... well laid out with lots of room—they even have a section for the kids while you shop..."

Casual wear ✓ | $$$$ Prices

Business wear .... ✓ ❹ .... Product availability
Intimate apparel .... ✓ ❹ .... Customer service
Nursing wear.............................. ✓ ❹ .... Decor

WWW.BELLYDANCEMATERNITY.COM

BUCKTOWN—1647 N DAMEN AVE (AT WABANSIA AVE); 773.862.1133; M-TH 11-7, F-SA 11-6, SU 12-5; PARKING LOT

Carson Pirie Scott ★★★½☆

"...although the maternity department isn't huge it has a nice variety—from T-shirt and shorts to evening gowns... unbelievable bargains... I found some classy maternity pieces here... there's always a sale going on so you can find plenty of nice items for less than $10..."

Casual wear .... ✓ $$$ .... Prices
Business wear .... ✓ ❸ .... Product availability
Intimate apparel .... ✗ ❸ .... Customer service
Nursing wear.............................. ✗ ❸ .... Decor

WWW.CARSONS.COM

LOOP—1 S STATE ST (AT E MADISON ST); 312.641.7000; M-F 9:45-8, SA 9-9, SU 11-6

Fleet Feet Sports ★★★☆☆

"...fine selection of workout clothes for active women..."

Casual wear .... ✓ $$$ .... Prices
Business wear .... ✗ ❸ .... Product availability
Intimate apparel .... ✗ ❺ .... Customer service
Nursing wear.............................. ✗ ❸ .... Decor

WWW.FLEETFEETCHICAGO.COM

LINCOLN PARK/DEPAUL/OLD TOWN—210 W NORTH AVE (AT N WELLS ST); 312.587.3338; M-F 10-8, SA 10-6, SU 12-5; FREE 1 HOUR CUSTOMER PARKING IN PIPERS'S ALLEY GARAGE (WITH VALIDATION)

Gap Maternity ★★★★★

"...the styles are very modern and attractive... the clothes are reasonably priced and wash well... comfy yet stylish basics... they have a great online resource and you can return online purchases at the store... average everyday prices, but catch a sale and you're golden... sizes run big so buy small... always a sale going on where you'll find hip items for a steal..."

Casual wear .... ✓ $$$ .... Prices
Business wear .... ✓ ❸ .... Product availability
Intimate apparel .... ✓ ❹ .... Customer service
Nursing wear.............................. ✓ ❸ .... Decor

WWW.GAP.COM

RIVER NORTH/RIVER WEST—555 N MICHIGAN AVE (AT E GRAND AVE); 312.494.8580; M-SA 9-9, SU 9-8

H & M ★★★½☆

"...hip, cute and cheap maternity clothes... wonderful stretch pants without the cutout for tummy... great style... lots of cool clothes, but need to visit often, as selection changes frequently... you can find some hip business type clothes on sale... not the place to go for personalized service..."

Casual wear .... ✓ $$ .... Prices
Business wear .... ✓ ❸ .... Product availability
Intimate apparel .... ✓ ❸ .... Customer service
Nursing wear.............................. ✗ ❸ .... Decor

WWW.HM.COM

EAST/WEST OLD TOWN GOLD COAST/STREETERVILLE—840 N MICHIGAN AVE (OFF CHICAGO AVE); 312.640.0060; M-SA 10-9, SU 10-7; FREE PARKING

LOOP—20 N STATE ST (OFF WASHINGTON ST); 312.263.4436; M-SA 10-9, SU 10-7; FREE PARKING

JCPenney

"...competitive prices and a surprisingly cute selection... they carry bigger sizes that are very hard to find at other stores... much cheaper than most maternity boutiques and they always seem to have some sort of sale going on... an especially large selection of maternity jeans for plus sizes... a more conservative collection than the smaller, hipper boutiques... good for casual basics, but not much for special occasions..."

Casual wear	✓	$$	Prices
Business wear	✓	❸	Product availability
Intimate apparel	✓	❸	Customer service
Nursing wear	✗	❸	Decor

WWW.JCPENNEY.COM

SOUTH SIDE—7601 S CICERO AVE (AT FORD CITY SHOPPING CTR); 773.581.6600; M-F 10-9, SA 10-8, SU 11-6; PARKING IN FRONT OF BLDG

Kohl's

"...a small maternity selection but I always manage to find several items I like... our favorite shopping destination—clean, wide open aisles... not a huge amount of maternity, but if you find something the price is always right... the selection is very inconsistent but sometimes you can find nice casuals... best for the bare-bone basics like T-shirts, shorts or casual pants..."

Casual wear	✓	$$	Prices
Business wear	✗	❸	Product availability
Intimate apparel	✗	❸	Customer service
Nursing wear	✗	❸	Decor

WWW.KOHLS.COM

BUCKTOWN—2140 N ELSTON AVE (OFF ASHLAND AVE); 773.342.9032; M-SA 8-10, SU 10-8; FREE PARKING

Krista K Boutique

"...friendly staff will help you put together a top quality maternity outfit... small shop, but well chosen stock... it's sometimes hard to find sizes... pricey... they call me whenever they get in new maternity styles... perfect place to find that something special... great selection of designer maternity jeans..."

Casual wear	✓	$$$$$	Prices
Business wear	✓	❸	Product availability
Intimate apparel	✗	❹	Customer service
Nursing wear	✗	❹	Decor

WWW.KRISTAK.COM

LAKEVIEW/WRIGLEYVILLE—3458 N SOUTHPORT AVE (AT N CORNELIA AVE); 773.248.1967; M-F 11-7, SA 10-6, SU 12-5

McShane's Exchange

"...shopped high and low to find cute, trendy maternity wear that wasn't going to break the bank... this second hand store is the only one I will shop at because of their good quality second hand clothes... many Pea in the Pod and Mimi, etc. brand clothes for rock bottom prices..."

Casual wear	✓	$$$	Prices
Business wear	✓	❸	Product availability
Intimate apparel	✓	❸	Customer service
Nursing wear	✓	❸	Decor

LINCOLN PARK/DEPAUL/OLD TOWN—815 W ARMITAGE AVE (AT N HALSTED ST); 773.525.0282; M-F 11-7, SA 10-6, SU 12-5

Mimi Maternity

"...it's definitely worth stopping here if you're still working and need some good-looking outfits... not cheap, but the quality is fantastic... not as expensive as A Pea In The Pod, but better quality than Motherhood Maternity... nice for basics that will last you through multiple pregnancies... perfect for work clothes, but pricey for the everyday stuff... good deals to be found on their sales racks... a good mix of high-end fancy clothes and items you can wear every day..."

Casual wear	✓	$$$	Prices
Business wear	✓	❹	Product availability
Intimate apparel	✓	❹	Customer service
Nursing wear	✓	❹	Decor

WWW.MIMIMATERNITY.COM

EAST/WEST OLD TOWN GOLD COAST/STREETERVILLE—835 N MICHIGAN AVE (AT E PEARSON AVE); 312.335.1818; M-SA 10-7, SU 12-6

LOOP—111 N STATE ST (AT N WASHINGTON ST); 312.629.9151; M-SA 9-8, SU 11-6

Motherhood Maternity

"...a wide variety of styles, from business to weekend wear, all at a good price... affordable and cute... everything from bras and swimsuits to work outfits... highly recommended for those who don't want to spend a fortune on maternity clothes... less fancy and pricey than their sister stores—A Pea in the Pod and Mimi Maternity... they have frequent sales, so you just need to keep dropping in—you're bound to find something good..."

Casual wear	✓	$$$	Prices
Business wear	✓	❹	Product availability
Intimate apparel	✓	❹	Customer service
Nursing wear	✓	❸	Decor

WWW.MOTHERHOOD.COM

LOOP—5 N STATE ST (AT W MADISON ST); 312.541.9210; M-F 10-7, SA 10-6, SU 12-5

ROSCOE VILLAGE/WEST LAKEVIEW—1730 W FULLERTON AVE (AT N CLYBOURNE AVE); 773.529.0564; M-F 10-9, SA 10-6, SU 12-5

SOUTH SIDE—7601 S CICERO AVE (AT FORD CITY SHOPPING CTR); 773.884.1805; M-SA 10-9, SU 11-6

Old Navy

"...the best for casual maternity clothing like stretchy T-shirts with Lycra and comfy jeans... prices are so reasonable it's ridiculous... not much for the workplace, but you can't beat the prices on casual clothes... not all Old Navy locations carry their maternity line... don't expect a huge or diverse selection... the staff is not always knowledgeable about maternity clothing and can't really help with questions about sizing... they have the best return policy—order online and return to the nearest store location... perfect for inexpensive maternity duds..."

Casual wear	✓	$$	Prices
Business wear	✗	❹	Product availability
Intimate apparel	✗	❸	Customer service
Nursing wear	✗	❸	Decor

WWW.OLDNAVY.COM

HUMBOLDT PARK—4905 W NORTH AVE (AT LAMON AVE); 773.862.1774; M-SA 9-9, SU 10-6

LOOP—35 N STATE ST (AT W CALHOUN PL); 312.551.0522; M-SA 9-9, SU 10-6

SOUTH SIDE—7601 S CICERO AVE (AT FORD CITY SHOPPING CTR); 773.284.7710; M-SA 9-9, SU 10-6

Sears

"...good place to get maternity clothes for a low price... the clearance rack always has good deals and their sales are quite frequent... not necessarily super high-quality, but if you just need them for nine months, who cares... good selection of nursing bras... I love the fact that they carry maternity wear in larger sizes—I got so tired of looking in those cutesy boutiques and then being disappointed because they didn't have my size... the only place I found maternity for plus-sized women..."

Casual wear	✓	$$	Prices
Business wear	✗	❸	Product availability
Intimate apparel	✓	❸	Customer service
Nursing wear	✓	❸	Decor

WWW.SEARS.COM

CHICAGO—1601 N HARLEM AVE (AT RT 43); 773.836.4100; M-F 9-9, SA 10-6, SU 11-5

ENGLEWOOD—6153 S WESTERN AVE (AT 61ST ST); 773.918.1400; M-F 10-9, SA 10-6, SU 11-5

FORD CITY—7601 S CICERO AVE (AT FORD CITY SHOPPING CTR); 773.284.4200; M-F 10-9, SA 8-8, SU 11-7

GRAND CROSSING—1334 E 79TH ST (AT CHICAGO SKWY); 773.933.1600; M-F 10-9, SA 10-9, SU 11-5

PORTAGE PARK—4730 W IRVING PARK RD (AT CICERO AVE); 773.202.2000; M-SA 9-9, SU 9-7:30

RIVER NORTH/RIVER WEST—2 N STATE ST (AT W MADISON ST); 312.373.6000; M-F 10-9, SA 10-9, SU 11-5

SHERIDAN PARK/UPTOWN—1900 W LAWRENCE AVE (AT DAMEN AVE); 773.769.8052; M-F 9-9, SA 8-9, SU 11-7

Swell Maternity

"...great selection of trendy maternity clothes that are hard to find elsewhere... pregnancy clothes you'll feel stylish in... you will be chic, but you are going to have to shell out some clams to do it... maternity section is in the back and they have a lot of merchandise, especially cute jeans and casual wear... unique and stylish..."

Casual wear	✓	$$$$	Prices
Business wear	✗	❸	Product availability
Intimate apparel	✓	❹	Customer service
Nursing wear	✗	❹	Decor

WWW.SWELLMATERNITY.COM

LINCOLN PARK/DEPAUL/OLD TOWN—1206 W WEBSTER AVE (AT N RACINE AVE); 773.935.7467; M-W 11-6, TH-F 11-7, SA 10-6, SU 10-5

Target

"...I was surprised at how fashionable their selection is—they carry Liz Lange and other really cute selections... the price is right—especially since you'll only be wearing these clothes for a few months... great for maternity basics—T-shirts, skirts, sweaters, even maternity bras... best of all, you can do some maternity shopping while you're shopping for other household basics... shirts for $10—you can't beat that... not the most exciting or romantic maternity shopping, but once you see the prices you'll get over it... as always, Target provides the perfectly priced solution..."

Casual wear	✓	$$	Prices
Business wear	✓	❸	Product availability
Intimate apparel	✓	❸	Customer service
Nursing wear	✓	❸	Decor

WWW.TARGET.COM

ARCHER HEIGHTS/BRIGHTON PARK/GAGE PARK—4433 S PULASKI RD (AT W 44TH ST); 773.579.2120; M-SA 8-10, SU 8-9; PARKING IN FRONT OF BLDG

AVONDALE—2460 W GEORGE ST (AT N ELSTON AVE); 773.267.6141; M-SA 8-10, SU 8-9; PARKING IN FRONT OF BLDG

AVONDALE—2939 W ADDISON ST (AT N SACRAMENTO AVE); 773.604.7680; M-SA 8-10, SU 8-9; PARKING IN FRONT OF BLDG

NEAR SOUTH SIDE—1154 S CLARK ST (AT W ROOSEVELT RD); 312.212.6300; M-SA 8-10, SU 8-9

ROSCOE VILLAGE/WEST LAKEVIEW—2656 N ELSTON AVE (AT W LOGAN BLVD); 773.252.1994; M-SA 8-10, SU 8-9; PARKING IN FRONT OF BLDG

SOUTH SIDE—7100 S CICERO AVE (AT W 72ND ST); 708.563.9050; M-SA 8-10, SU 8-9; PARKING IN FRONT OF BLDG

SOUTH SIDE—8560 S COTTAGE GROVE AVE (AT E 86TH ST); 773.371.8555; M-SA 8-10, SU 8-9; PARKING IN FRONT OF BLDG

Northwestern Suburbs

"lila picks"

★Gap Maternity

★Motherhood Maternity

Baby Depot At Burlington Coat Factory

"...a surprisingly good selection of maternity clothes at great prices... staff can be hard to find so be prepared to dig... cute pants, skirts and sets... I wouldn't have thought that their selection would be as good as it is... not much other than casual items, but what they have is pretty good..."

Casual wear	✓	$$	Prices
Business wear	✗	❸	Product availability
Intimate apparel	✗	❸	Customer service
Nursing wear	✗	❸	Decor

WWW.BABYDEPOT.COM

ARLINGTON HEIGHTS—30 W RAND RD (AT N EVERGREEN AVE); 847.577.7878; M-SA 10-9, SU 11-6; PARKING LOT

Gap Maternity

"...the styles are very modern and attractive... the clothes are reasonably priced and wash well... comfy yet stylish basics... they have a great online resource and you can return online purchases at the store... average everyday prices, but catch a sale and you're golden... sizes run big so buy small... always a sale going on where you'll find hip items for a steal..."

Casual wear	✓	$$$	Prices
Business wear	✓	❸	Product availability
Intimate apparel	✓	❹	Customer service
Nursing wear	✓	❸	Decor

WWW.GAP.COM

DEER PARK—20530 N RAND RD (AT W LONG GROVE RD); 847.540.1948; M-F 10-9, SA 9-9, SU 11-6

H & M

"...hip, cute and cheap maternity clothes... wonderful stretch pants without the cutout for tummy... great style... lots of cool clothes, but need to visit often, as selection changes frequently... you can find some hip business type clothes on sale... not the place to go for personalized service..."

Casual wear	✓	$$	Prices
Business wear	✓	❸	Product availability
Intimate apparel	✓	❸	Customer service
Nursing wear	✗	❸	Decor

WWW.HM.COM

SCHAUMBURG—5 WOODFIELD SHOPPING CTR (AT GOLF RD); 847.619.9940; M-SA 10-9, SU 11-6; FREE PARKING

JCPenney

"...competitive prices and a surprisingly cute selection... they carry bigger sizes that are very hard to find at other stores... much cheaper than most maternity boutiques and they always seem to have some sort of sale going on... an especially large selection of maternity jeans for plus sizes... a more conservative collection than the smaller, hipper boutiques... good for casual basics, but not much for special occasions..."

Casual wear	✓	$$	Prices
Business wear	✓	❸	Product availability
Intimate apparel	✓	❸	Customer service
Nursing wear	×	❸	Decor

WWW.JCPENNEY.COM

SCHAUMBURG—3 WOODFIELD MALL (AT GOLF RD); 847.240.5000; M-SA 10-10, SU 11-5; MALL PARKING

VERNON HILLS—480 E RING RD (AT HAWTHORN CTR); 847.367.0795; M-F 10-9, SA 10-7,SU 11-6

Mimi Maternity

"...it's definitely worth stopping here if you're still working and need some good-looking outfits... not cheap, but the quality is fantastic... not as expensive as A Pea In The Pod, but better quality than Motherhood Maternity... nice for basics that will last you through multiple pregnancies... perfect for work clothes, but pricey for the everyday stuff... good deals to be found on their sales racks... a good mix of high-end fancy clothes and items you can wear every day..."

Casual wear	✓	$$$	Prices
Business wear	✓	❹	Product availability
Intimate apparel	✓	❹	Customer service
Nursing wear	✓	❹	Decor

WWW.MIMIMATERNITY.COM

DEER PARK—20530 N RAND RD (AT W LONG GROVE RD); 847.540.7386; M-SA 10-9, SU 12-5

SCHAUMBURG—321 WOODFIELD MALL (AT GOLF RD); 847.413.9023; M-SA 10-9, SU 11-6; MALL PARKING

Motherhood Maternity

"...a wide variety of styles, from business to weekend wear, all at a good price... affordable and cute... everything from bras and swimsuits to work outfits... highly recommended for those who don't want to spend a fortune on maternity clothes... less fancy and pricey than their sister stores—A Pea in the Pod and Mimi Maternity... they have frequent sales, so you just need to keep dropping in—you're bound to find something good..."

Casual wear	✓	$$$	Prices
Business wear	✓	❹	Product availability
Intimate apparel	✓	❹	Customer service
Nursing wear	✓	❸	Decor

WWW.MOTHERHOOD.COM

ARLINGTON HEIGHTS—320 E RAND RD (AT N ARLINGTON HEIGHTS RD); 847.398.2114; M-F 10-8, SA 10-6, SU 12-5

SCHAUMBURG—317 WOODFIELD MALL (AT GOLF RD); 847.330.0084; M-SA 10-9, SU 11-6; MALL PARKING

SCHAUMBURG—GOLF RD AT 53 (AT WOODFIELD MALL); 847.330.0084; M-SA 10-9, SU 11-6

VERNON HILLS—329 HAWTHORNE CIR (AT HAWTHORN CTR); 847.680.4842; M-SA 10-9, SU 11-6

Old Navy

"...the best for casual maternity clothing like stretchy T-shirts with Lycra and comfy jeans... prices are so reasonable it's ridiculous... not much for the workplace, but you can't beat the prices on casual clothes... not all Old Navy locations carry their maternity line... don't expect a huge or diverse selection... the staff is not always knowledgeable about maternity clothing and can't really help with questions about sizing... they have the best return policy—order online and return to the nearest store location... perfect for inexpensive maternity duds..."

Casual wear	✓	$$	Prices
Business wear	✗	❹	Product availability
Intimate apparel	✗	❸	Customer service
Nursing wear	✗	❸	Decor

WWW.OLDNAVY.COM

KILDEER—20505 N RAND RD (AT W LONG GROVE RD); 847.550.1485; M-SA 10-9, SU 11-7

Sears

"...good place to get maternity clothes for a low price... the clearance rack always has good deals and their sales are quite frequent... not necessarily super high-quality, but if you just need them for nine months, who cares... good selection of nursing bras... I love the fact that they carry maternity wear in larger sizes—I got so tired of looking in those cutesy boutiques and then being disappointed because they didn't have my size... the only place I found maternity for plus-sized women..."

Casual wear	✓	$$	Prices
Business wear	✗	❸	Product availability
Intimate apparel	✓	❸	Customer service
Nursing wear	✓	❸	Decor

WWW.SEARS.COM

PALATINE—537 N HICKS RD (AT E BALDWIN); 847.221.0800; M-SA 8-10, SU 8-8

SCHAUMBURG—2 WOODFIELD MALL (AT GOLF RD); 847.330.2356; M-SA 10-9, SU 11-6

Target

"...I was surprised at how fashionable their selection is—they carry Liz Lange and other really cute selections... the price is right—especially since you'll only be wearing these clothes for a few months... great for maternity basics—T-shirts, skirts, sweaters, even maternity bras... best of all, you can do some maternity shopping while you're shopping for other household basics... shirts for $10—you can't beat that... not the most exciting or romantic maternity shopping, but once you see the prices you'll get over it... as always, Target provides the perfectly priced solution..."

Casual wear	✓	$$	Prices
Business wear	✓	❸	Product availability
Intimate apparel	✓	❸	Customer service
Nursing wear	✓	❸	Decor

WWW.TARGET.COM

ARLINGTON HEIGHTS—1700 E RAND RD (AT E THOMAS ST); 847.222.0925; M-SA 8-10, SU 8-9; PARKING IN FRONT OF BLDG

ELGIN—300 S RANDALL RD (AT SOUTH ST); 847.695.1992; M-SA 8-10, SU 8-9; PARKING IN FRONT OF BLDG

PALATINE—679 E DUNDEE RD (AT N HICKS RD); 847.202.5120; M-SA 8-10, SU 8-9; PARKING IN FRONT OF BLDG

SCHAUMBURG—1235 E HIGGINS RD (AT NATIONAL PKWY); 847.413.1080; M-SA 8-10, SU 8-9; PARKING IN FRONT OF BLDG

SCHAUMBURG—2621 W SCHAUMBURG RD (AT E SCHAUMBERG RD); 847.798.0192; M-SA 8-10, SU 8-9; PARKING IN FRONT OF BLDG

VERNON HILLS—313 E TOWNLINE RD (AT HAWTHORN CTR); 847.680.0723; M-SA 8-10, SU 8-9; PARKING IN FRONT OF BLDG

Northern Suburbs

"lila picks"

★A Pea In The Pod

★Belly Dance Maternity

A Pea In The Pod

"...excellent if you are looking for stylish maternity clothes and don't mind paying for them... start here for special occasions and business wear... the decor is lovely and most of the clothes are beautiful... stylish fashion solutions, but expect to pay more than at department stores... keep your eyes open for the sale rack—the markdowns can be terrific... an upscale shop that carries everything from intimates to fancy dresses... stylish, fun and non-maternity-like..."

Casual wear ✓ | $$$$ Prices
Business wear ✓ | ❹ Product availability
Intimate apparel ✓ | ❹ Customer service
Nursing wear ✓ | ❹ Decor

WWW.APEAINTHEPOD.COM

HIGHLAND PARK—600 CENTRAL AVE (AT 2ND ST); 847.266.7200; M-W 10-6, TH 10-7, F-SA 10-6, SU 12-5

Baby Depot At Burlington Coat Factory

"...a surprisingly good selection of maternity clothes at great prices... staff can be hard to find so be prepared to dig... cute pants, skirts and sets... I wouldn't have thought that their selection would be as good as it is... not much other than casual items, but what they have is pretty good..."

Casual wear ✓ | $$ Prices
Business wear ✗ | ❸ Product availability
Intimate apparel ✗ | ❸ Customer service
Nursing wear ✗ | ❸ Decor

WWW.BABYDEPOT.COM

GURNEE—6170 GRAND AVE (AT GURNEE MILLS MALL); 847.855.0565; M-F 10-9, SA 10-9:30, SU 11-7; MALL PARKING

MUNDELEIN—1555 S LAKE ST (AT HIGHWAY 45); 847.566.1295; M-SA 10-9, SU 11-6; PARKING LOT

Belly Dance Maternity

"...thanks to Belly Dance Maternity I was able to be pregnant and somewhat stylish at the same time... fancy maternity gear from designers such as NOM, Cadeau, Earl Jean and more... great trendy items along with cool basics to make you feel cute... not cheap, but so worth the splurge... well laid out with lots of room—they even have a section for the kids while you shop..."

Casual wear ✓ | $$$$ Prices

Business wear ✓	❹ Product availability
Intimate apparel ✓	❹ Customer service
Nursing wear ✓	❹ Decor

WWW.BELLYDANCEMATERNITY.COM

HIGHLAND PARK—1849 GREENBAY RD (AT RENAISSANCE PL); 847.926.0053; M-SA 10-6, SU 12-5; PARKING LOT

H & M

★★★½☆

"...hip, cute and cheap maternity clothes... wonderful stretch pants without the cutout for tummy... great style... lots of cool clothes, but need to visit often, as selection changes frequently... you can find some hip business type clothes on sale... not the place to go for personalized service..."

Casual wear ✓	$$ Prices
Business wear ✓	❸ Product availability
Intimate apparel ✓	❸ Customer service
Nursing wear ×	❸ Decor

WWW.HM.COM

GURNEE—6170 GRAND AVE (AT GURNEE MILLS MALL); 847.855.7847; M-F 10-9, SA 10-9:30, SU 11-7

JCPenney

★★★☆☆

"...competitive prices and a surprisingly cute selection... they carry bigger sizes that are very hard to find at other stores... much cheaper than most maternity boutiques and they always seem to have some sort of sale going on... an especially large selection of maternity jeans for plus sizes... a more conservative collection than the smaller, hipper boutiques... good for casual basics, but not much for special occasions..."

Casual wear ✓	$$ Prices
Business wear ✓	❸ Product availability
Intimate apparel ✓	❸ Customer service
Nursing wear ×	❸ Decor

WWW.JCPENNEY.COM

NILES—220 GOLF MILL CTR (AT GREENWOOD AVE); 847.299.8888; M-SA 10-9, SU 10:30-7; PARKING LOT AT CENTER

Kohl's

★★★☆☆

"...a small maternity selection but I always manage to find several items I like... our favorite shopping destination—clean, wide open aisles... not a huge amount of maternity, but if you find something the price is always right... the selection is very inconsistent but sometimes you can find nice casuals... best for the bare-bone basics like T-shirts, shorts or casual pants..."

Casual wear ✓	$$ Prices
Business wear ×	❸ Product availability
Intimate apparel ×	❸ Customer service
Nursing wear ×	❸ Decor

WWW.KOHLS.COM

GLENVIEW—2201 WILLOW RD (AT WILLOW HILL GOLF COURSE); 847.832.9400; M-SA 8-10, SU 10-8; FREE PARKING

LINCOLNWOOD—3333 TOUHY AVE (AT MCCORMICK BLVD); 847.673.9140; M-SA 8-10, SU 10-8; FREE PARKING

NILES—590 GOLF MILL CTR (AT GOLF RD); 847.296.7600; M-SA 8-10, SU 10-8; FREE PARKING

Mimi Maternity

"...it's definitely worth stopping here if you're still working and need some good-looking outfits... not cheap, but the quality is fantastic... not as expensive as A Pea In The Pod, but better quality than

Motherhood Maternity... nice for basics that will last you through multiple pregnancies... perfect for work clothes, but pricey for the everyday stuff... good deals to be found on their sales racks... a good mix of high-end fancy clothes and items you can wear every day... ”

Casual wear ✓	$$$ Prices
Business wear ✓	❹ Product availability
Intimate apparel ✓	❹ Customer service
Nursing wear ✓	❹ Decor

WWW.MIMIMATERNITY.COM

NORTHBROOK—1555 NORTHBROOK CT MALL (AT NORTHBROOK MALL); 847.559.8618; M-F 10-9, SA 9-10, SU 11-7; MALL PARKING

SKOKIE—1 OLD ORCHARD RD (AT GROSS POINT RD); 847.676.1218; M-F 10-9, SA 9-10, SU 11-7

SKOKIE—275 OLD ORCHARD CTR (AT GOLF RD); 847.679.7094; M-SA 10-9, SU 11-6

Motherhood Maternity

“...a wide variety of styles, from business to weekend wear, all at a good price... affordable and cute... everything from bras and swimsuits to work outfits... highly recommended for those who don't want to spend a fortune on maternity clothes... less fancy and pricey than their sister stores—A Pea in the Pod and Mimi Maternity... they have frequent sales, so you just need to keep dropping in—you're bound to find something good... ”

Casual wear ✓	$$$ Prices
Business wear ✓	❹ Product availability
Intimate apparel ✓	❹ Customer service
Nursing wear ✓	❸ Decor

WWW.MOTHERHOOD.COM

GURNEE—6170 GRAND AVE (AT GURNEE MILLS MALL); 847.855.9665; M-F 10-9, SA 10-9:30, SU 11-7; MALL PARKING

LINCOLNWOOD—3333 W TOUHY AVE (AT LINCOLNWOOD TOWN CTR); 847.677.2851; M-F 10-9, SA 10-8, SU 11-6

NILES—252 GOLF MILL CTR (AT GREENWOOD AVE); 847.298.5544; M-SA 10-9, SU 11-6

SKOKIE—34 OLD ORCHARD SHOPPING CTR (AT GOLF RD); 847.679.7094; M-SA 10-9, SU 11-6

Old Navy

“...the best for casual maternity clothing like stretchy T-shirts with Lycra and comfy jeans... prices are so reasonable it's ridiculous... not much for the workplace, but you can't beat the prices on casual clothes... not all Old Navy locations carry their maternity line... don't expect a huge or diverse selection... the staff is not always knowledgeable about maternity clothing and can't really help with questions about sizing... they have the best return policy—order online and return to the nearest store location... perfect for inexpensive maternity duds... ”

Casual wear ✓	$$ Prices
Business wear ✗	❹ Product availability
Intimate apparel ✗	❸ Customer service
Nursing wear ✗	❸ Decor

WWW.OLDNAVY.COM

LINCOLNWOOD—3333 W TOUHY AVE (AT N MCCORMICK BLVD); 847.677.1793; M-F 9-9, SA 9-8, SU 10-6

SKOKIE—9435 SKOKIE BLVD (AT GROSS POINT RD); 847.329.8505; M-SA 9-9, SU 10-6

Sears

"...good place to get maternity clothes for a low price... the clearance rack always has good deals and their sales are quite frequent... not necessarily super high-quality, but if you just need them for nine months, who cares... good selection of nursing bras... I love the fact that they carry maternity wear in larger sizes—I got so tired of looking in those cutesy boutiques and then being disappointed because they didn't have my size... the only place I found maternity for plus-sized women..."

Casual wear	✓	$$	Prices
Business wear	×	❸	Product availability
Intimate apparel	✓	❸	Customer service
Nursing wear	✓	❸	Decor

WWW.SEARS.COM

NILES—400 GOLF MILL CTR (AT GREENWOOD AVE); 847.803.7500; M-F 10-9, SA 8-9, SU 11-7

Target

"...I was surprised at how fashionable their selection is—they carry Liz Lange and other really cute selections... the price is right—especially since you'll only be wearing these clothes for a few months... great for maternity basics—T-shirts, skirts, sweaters, even maternity bras... best of all, you can do some maternity shopping while you're shopping for other household basics... shirts for $10—you can't beat that... not the most exciting or romantic maternity shopping, but once you see the prices you'll get over it... as always, Target provides the perfectly priced solution..."

Casual wear	✓	$$	Prices
Business wear	✓	❸	Product availability
Intimate apparel	✓	❸	Customer service
Nursing wear	✓	❸	Decor

WWW.TARGET.COM

EVANSTON—2209 HOWARD ST (AT RIDGE AVE); 847.733.1144; M-SA 8-10, SU 8-9; PARKING IN FRONT OF BLDG

GLENVIEW—2241 WILLOW RD (AT OLD WILLOW RD); 847.657.0095; M-SA 8-10, SU 8-9

GURNEE—6601 GRAND AVE (AT N HUNT CLUB AVE); 847.244.4990; M-SA 8-10, SU 8-9; PARKING IN FRONT OF BLDG

NILES—6150 W TOUHY AVE (AT N MELVILLE AVE); 847.588.2800; M-SA 8-10, SU 8-9; PARKING IN FRONT OF BLDG

Western Suburbs

"lila picks"

★A Pea In The Pod ★The Child In You

A Pea In The Pod

"...excellent if you are looking for stylish maternity clothes and don't mind paying for them... start here for special occasions and business wear... the decor is lovely and most of the clothes are beautiful... stylish fashion solutions, but expect to pay more than at department stores... keep your eyes open for the sale rack—the markdowns can be terrific... an upscale shop that carries everything from intimates to fancy dresses... stylish, fun and non-maternity-like..."

Casual wear	✓	$$$$	Prices
Business wear	✓	❹	Product availability
Intimate apparel	✓	❹	Customer service
Nursing wear	✓	❹	Decor

WWW.APEAINTHEPOD.COM

OAK BROOK—288 OAKBROOK CTR (AT OAK BROOK CTR MALL); 630.575.0211; M-SA 10-9, SU 11-6; MALL PARKING

Baby Depot At Burlington Coat Factory

"...a surprisingly good selection of maternity clothes at great prices... staff can be hard to find so be prepared to dig... cute pants, skirts and sets... I wouldn't have thought that their selection would be as good as it is... not much other than casual items, but what they have is pretty good..."

Casual wear	✓	$$	Prices
Business wear	✗	❸	Product availability
Intimate apparel	✗	❸	Customer service
Nursing wear	✗	❸	Decor

WWW.BABYDEPOT.COM

BLOOMINGDALE—3 STRATFORD SQ MALL (AT ENTRANCE DR 1); 630.671.0364; M-SA 10-9, SU 11-6; MALL PARKING

COUNTRYSIDE—1 COUNTRYSIDE PLAZA (AT LA GRANGE RD); 708.354.2365; M-SA 10-9, SU 11-6; PARKING LOT

NAPERVILLE—510 S ROUTE 59 (AT AURORA RD); 630.428.1341; M-SA 10-9, SU 11-6

NORTH RIVERSIDE—2208 S HARLEM AVE (AT NORTH RIVERSIDE MALL); 708.447.4855; M-SA 10-9, SU 11-6; MALL PARKING

VILLA PARK—174 W ROOSEVELT RD (AT S MICHIGAN AVE); 630.832.4500; M-SA 9-9, SU 11-6; PARKING LOT

Child In You, The

"...a cute shop with lots of unique stuff... higher end and pricier than other places, but I love their merchandise... a good selection of evening

and casual wear... very nice quality... plus sizes that can be hard to find elsewhere... nice staff... ”

Casual wear .... ✓ $$$ .... Prices
Business wear .... ✓ ❸ .... Product availability
Intimate apparel .... ✗ ❸ .... Customer service
Nursing wear.................................. ✓ ❸ .... Decor

WWW.THECHILDINYOU.COM

GENEVA—407 S 3RD ST (AT FULTON ST (INSIDE CRADLES & ALL)); 630.232.4030; M-SA 10-5, SU 12-4; STREET PARKING

H & M

“*...hip, cute and cheap maternity clothes... wonderful stretch pants without the cutout for tummy... great style... lots of cool clothes, but need to visit often, as selection changes frequently... you can find some hip business type clothes on sale... not the place to go for personalized service...* ”

Casual wear .... ✓ $$ .... Prices
Business wear .... ✓ ❸ .... Product availability
Intimate apparel .... ✓ ❸ .... Customer service
Nursing wear.................................. ✗ ❸ .... Decor

WWW.HM.COM

AURORA—1276 FOX VALLEY CTR (AT NEW YORK ST); 630.499.5730; M-SA 10-9, SU 10-6; FREE PARKING

JCPenney

“*...competitive prices and a surprisingly cute selection... they carry bigger sizes that are very hard to find at other stores... much cheaper than most maternity boutiques and they always seem to have some sort of sale going on... an especially large selection of maternity jeans for plus sizes... a more conservative collection than the smaller, hipper boutiques... good for casual basics, but not much for special occasions...* ”

Casual wear .... ✓ $$ .... Prices
Business wear .... ✓ ❸ .... Product availability
Intimate apparel .... ✓ ❸ .... Customer service
Nursing wear.................................. ✗ ❸ .... Decor

WWW.JCPENNEY.COM

AURORA—4 FOX VALLEY CTR (AT NEW YORK ST); 630.851.6380; M-F 10-9, SA 10-7, SU 11-6

LOMBARD—175 YORKTOWN SHOPPING CTR (AT YORKTOWN CTR); 630.629.7750; M-F 10-9, SA 9:30-9, SU 11-6

NORTH RIVERSIDE—7507 W CERMAK RD (AT NORTH RIVERSIDE MALL); 708.442.6600; M-SA 10-9, SU 11-6; MALL PARKING

Kohl's

“*...a small maternity selection but I always manage to find several items I like... our favorite shopping destination—clean, wide open aisles... not a huge amount of maternity, but if you find something the price is always right... the selection is very inconsistent but sometimes you can find nice casuals... best for the bare-bone basics like T-shirts, shorts or casual pants...* ”

Casual wear .... ✓ $$ .... Prices
Business wear .... ✗ ❸ .... Product availability
Intimate apparel .... ✗ ❸ .... Customer service
Nursing wear.................................. ✗ ❸ .... Decor

WWW.KOHLS.COM

ELMHURST—303 KINGERY HWY (AT ST CHARLES RD); 630.516.1200; M-SA 8-10, SU 10-8; FREE PARKING

NORTH RIVERSIDE—2200 HARLEM AVE (AT CERMAK RD); 708.447.8199; M-SA 8-10, SU 10-8; FREE PARKING

Marshall Fields

"...wide selection of maternity clothes and great big fitting rooms too... two racks of sale items, but while the rest of the women's floor seemed to be on sale, the majority of the maternity clothes were full price..."

Casual wear	✓	$$$$	Prices
Business wear	✓	❸	Product availability
Intimate apparel	✓	❸	Customer service
Nursing wear	✓	❹	Decor

WWW.FIELDS.COM

AURORA—1 FOX VALLEY CTR (AT NEW YORK ST); 630.978.5400; M-F 10-9, SA 9-10, SU 11-7

Mimi Maternity

"...it's definitely worth stopping here if you're still working and need some good-looking outfits... not cheap, but the quality is fantastic... not as expensive as A Pea In The Pod, but better quality than Motherhood Maternity... nice for basics that will last you through multiple pregnancies... perfect for work clothes, but pricey for the everyday stuff... good deals to be found on their sales racks... a good mix of high-end fancy clothes and items you can wear every day..."

Casual wear	✓	$$$	Prices
Business wear	✓	❹	Product availability
Intimate apparel	✓	❹	Customer service
Nursing wear	✓	❹	Decor

WWW.MIMIMATERNITY.COM

GENEVA—1440 COMMONS DR (AT WILLIAMSBURG AVE); 630.845.0407; M-SA 10-9, SU 11-6

WHEATON—101 TOWN SQ (AT S NAPERVILLE RD); 630.665.9009; M-F 10-9, SA 10-6, SU 11-5

Motherhood Maternity

"...a wide variety of styles, from business to weekend wear, all at a good price... affordable and cute... everything from bras and swimsuits to work outfits... highly recommended for those who don't want to spend a fortune on maternity clothes... less fancy and pricey than their sister stores—A Pea in the Pod and Mimi Maternity... they have frequent sales, so you just need to keep dropping in—you're bound to find something good..."

Casual wear	✓	$$$	Prices
Business wear	✓	❹	Product availability
Intimate apparel	✓	❹	Customer service
Nursing wear	✓	❸	Decor

WWW.MOTHERHOOD.COM

AURORA—2082 FOX VALLEY CTR (AT NEW YORK ST); 630.898.2820; M-SA 10-9, SU 11-6

BLOOMINGDALE—110 STRATFORD SQ MALL (AT ENTRANCE DR 1); 630.980.9015; M-SA 10-9, SU 11-6; MALL PARKING

LOMBARD—203 YORKTOWN SHOPPING CTR (AT MAJESTIC DR); 630.629.7144; M-F 10-9, SA 10-7, SU 11-6

NAPERVILLE—304 S STATE RTE 59 (AT AURORA AVE); 630.355.2004; M-F 10-9, SA 10-6, SU 11-6

NORTH RIVERSIDE—7501 CERMAK RD (AT NORTH RIVERSIDE MALL); 708.442.5330; M-SA 10-9, SU 10-5; MALL PARKING

OAK BROOK—521 OAKBROOK CTR (AT OAK BROOK CTR MALL); 630.572.8183; M-SA 10-9, SU 11-6; MALL PARKING

RIVER FOREST—7261 LAKE ST (AT BONNIE BREA PL); 708.488.0922; M-F 10-8, SA 10-6, SU 11-5; MALL PARKING

WOODRIDGE—1001 75TH ST (AT LEMONT RD); 630.985.5301; M-F 10-9, SA 10-6, SU 11-5

Old Navy

"...the best for casual maternity clothing like stretchy T-shirts with Lycra and comfy jeans... prices are so reasonable it's ridiculous... not much for the workplace, but you can't beat the prices on casual clothes... not all Old Navy locations carry their maternity line... don't expect a huge or diverse selection... the staff is not always knowledgeable about maternity clothing and can't really help with questions about sizing... they have the best return policy—order online and return to the nearest store location... perfect for inexpensive maternity duds..."

Casual wear	✓	$$	Prices
Business wear	×	❹	Product availability
Intimate apparel	×	❸	Customer service
Nursing wear	×	❸	Decor

WWW.OLDNAVY.COM

OAK BROOK—2155 W 22ND ST (AT MIDWEST RD); 630.472.9201; M-SA 9-9, SU 10-6

Sears

"...good place to get maternity clothes for a low price... the clearance rack always has good deals and their sales are quite frequent... not necessarily super high-quality, but if you just need them for nine months, who cares... good selection of nursing bras... I love the fact that they carry maternity wear in larger sizes—I got so tired of looking in those cutesy boutiques and then being disappointed because they didn't have my size... the only place I found maternity for plus-sized women..."

Casual wear	✓	$$	Prices
Business wear	×	❸	Product availability
Intimate apparel	✓	❸	Customer service
Nursing wear	✓	❸	Decor

WWW.SEARS.COM

BLOOMINGDALE—5 STRATFORD SQ (AT S GARY AVE & W ARMY TRAIL RD); 630.924.8801; M-F 10-9

NORTH RIVERSIDE—7503 W CERMAK RD (AT NORTH RIVERSIDE MALL); 708.588.6600; M-F 10-9, SA 8-10, SU 10-6

OAK BROOK —2 OAKBROOK CLUB DR (AT OAK BROOK CTR MALL); 630.575.1800; M-F 10-9, SA 10-9, SU 11-7

SAINT CHARLES—3700 E MAIN ST (AT CHARLESTOWN MALL); 630.513.3200; M-F 10-9, SA 8-9, SU 10-6

Target

"...I was surprised at how fashionable their selection is—they carry Liz Lange and other really cute selections... the price is right—especially since you'll only be wearing these clothes for a few months... great for maternity basics—T-shirts, skirts, sweaters, even maternity bras... best of all, you can do some maternity shopping while you're shopping for other household basics... shirts for $10—you can't beat that... not the most exciting or romantic maternity shopping, but once you see the prices you'll get over it... as always, Target provides the perfectly priced solution..."

Casual wear	✓	$$	Prices
Business wear	✓	❸	Product availability
Intimate apparel	✓	❸	Customer service
Nursing wear	✓	❸	Decor

WWW.TARGET.COM

GLENDALE HEIGHTS—175 W ARMY TRAIL RD (AT SCHMALE RD); 630.582.0043; M-SA 8-10, SU 8-9; PARKING IN FRONT OF BLDG

MELROSE PARK—850 W NORTH AVE (AT N 9TH AVE); 708.338.2784; M-SA 8-10, SU 8-9; PARKING IN FRONT OF BLDG

VILLA PARK—50 E NORTH AVE (AT N ARDMORE AVE); 630.833.7411; M-SA 8-10, SU 8-9; PARKING IN FRONT OF BLDG

Southern Suburbs

"lila picks"

★Gap Maternity

★Motherhood Maternity

★Old Navy

Baby Depot At Burlington Coat Factory

"...a surprisingly good selection of maternity clothes at great prices... staff can be hard to find so be prepared to dig... cute pants, skirts and sets... I wouldn't have thought that their selection would be as good as it is... not much other than casual items, but what they have is pretty good..."

Casual wear	✓	$$	Prices
Business wear	✗	3	Product availability
Intimate apparel	✗	3	Customer service
Nursing wear	✗	3	Decor

WWW.BABYDEPOT.COM

LANSING—16895 S TORRENCE AVE (AT E 170TH ST); 708.889.0213; M-SA 10-9, SU 11-6; PARKING LOT

TINLEY PARK—7061 159TH ST (AT BREMENTOWNE MALL); 708.614.1626; M-SA 10-9, SU 11-6; MALL PARKING

Gap Maternity

"...the styles are very modern and attractive... the clothes are reasonably priced and wash well... comfy yet stylish basics... they have a great online resource and you can return online purchases at the store... average everyday prices, but catch a sale and you're golden... sizes run big so buy small... always a sale going on where you'll find hip items for a steal..."

Casual wear	✓	$$$	Prices
Business wear	✓	3	Product availability
Intimate apparel	✓	4	Customer service
Nursing wear	✓	3	Decor

WWW.GAP.COM

ORLAND PARK—460 ORLAND SQ DR (AT ORLAND SQUARE SHOPPING CTR); 708.349.3135; M-F 10-9, SA 10-9, SU 11-5

H & M

"...hip, cute and cheap maternity clothes... wonderful stretch pants without the cutout for tummy... great style... lots of cool clothes, but need to visit often, as selection changes frequently... you can find some hip business type clothes on sale... not the place to go for personalized service..."

Casual wear	✓	$$	Prices
Business wear	✓	3	Product availability
Intimate apparel	✓	3	Customer service

Nursing wear .... ✗ ❸ .... Decor

WWW.HM.COM

ORLAND PARK—288 ORLAND SQUARE PARK (OFF 151ST ST); 708.364.7820; M-SA 10-9, SU 11-6

JCPenney ★★★☆☆

"...competitive prices and a surprisingly cute selection... they carry bigger sizes that are very hard to find at other stores... much cheaper than most maternity boutiques and they always seem to have some sort of sale going on... an especially large selection of maternity jeans for plus sizes... a more conservative collection than the smaller, hipper boutiques... good for casual basics, but not much for special occasions..."

Casual wear .... ✓ $$ .... Prices
Business wear .... ✓ ❸ .... Product availability
Intimate apparel .... ✓ ❸ .... Customer service
Nursing wear .... ✗ ❸ .... Decor

WWW.JCPENNEY.COM

JOLIET—3340 MALL LOOP DR SPACE 2 (AT LOUIS JOLIET MALL); 815.439.1400; M-F 10-9, SA 10-7, SU 11-6; MALL PARKING

ORLAND PARK—3 ORLAND SQ DR (AT ORLAND SQUARE SHOPPING CTR); 708.349.7300; M-SA 10-9, SU 11-6

Kohl's ★★★☆☆

"...a small maternity selection but I always manage to find several items I like... our favorite shopping destination—clean, wide open aisles... not a huge amount of maternity, but if you find something the price is always right... the selection is very inconsistent but sometimes you can find nice casuals... best for the bare-bone basics like T-shirts, shorts or casual pants..."

Casual wear .... ✓ $$ .... Prices
Business wear .... ✗ ❸ .... Product availability
Intimate apparel .... ✗ ❸ .... Customer service
Nursing wear .... ✗ ❸ .... Decor

WWW.KOHLS.COM

BURBANK—7608 S LA CROSSE AVE (AT CICERO AVE); 708.499.3900; M-SA 8-10, SU 10-8; FREE PARKING

COLUMET HEIGHTS—9700 S RIDGELAND AVE (AT CHICAGO RIDGE MALL); 708.425.7909; M-SA 8-10, SU 10-8; FREE PARKING

Martinelli's Maternity Wear ★★★☆☆

"...limited selection... knowledgeable and friendly staff... prices are on the high side..."

Casual wear .... ✗ $$$ .... Prices
Business wear .... ✗ ❸ .... Product availability
Intimate apparel .... ✓ ❸ .... Customer service
Nursing wear .... ✓ ❸ .... Decor

EVERGREEN PARK—3517 W 95TH ST (AT S ST LOUIS AVE); 708.425.6287; M TH 9:30-8, T-W F 9:30-6, SA 9:30-6; STREET PARKING

Mimi Maternity ★★★★☆

"...it's definitely worth stopping here if you're still working and need some good-looking outfits... not cheap, but the quality is fantastic... not as expensive as A Pea In The Pod, but better quality than Motherhood Maternity... nice for basics that will last you through multiple pregnancies... perfect for work clothes, but pricey for the everyday stuff... good deals to be found on their sales racks... a good mix of high-end fancy clothes and items you can wear every day..."

Casual wear .... ✓ $$$ .... Prices
Business wear .... ✓ ❹ .... Product availability

Intimate apparel .... ✓   ❹ .... Customer service
Nursing wear .... ✓   ❹ .... Decor

WWW.MIMIMATERNITY.COM

ORLAND PARK—118 ORLAND PARK PL (AT 94TH AVE); 708.364.1704; M-T F SA 10-6, W-TH 10-9, SU 11-5

Motherhood Maternity ★★★★★

"...a wide variety of styles, from business to weekend wear, all at a good price... affordable and cute... everything from bras and swimsuits to work outfits... highly recommended for those who don't want to spend a fortune on maternity clothes... less fancy and pricey than their sister stores—A Pea in the Pod and Mimi Maternity... they have frequent sales, so you just need to keep dropping in—you're bound to find something good..."

Casual wear .... ✓ $$$ .... Prices
Business wear .... ✓   ❹ .... Product availability
Intimate apparel .... ✓   ❹ .... Customer service
Nursing wear .... ✓   ❸ .... Decor

WWW.MOTHERHOOD.COM

CHICAGO RIDGE—444 CHICAGO RIDGE MALL DR (AT CHICAGO RIDGE MALL); 708.499.2656; M-F 10-6, SA 10-7, SU 10-9; MALL PARKING

JOLIET—1488 LOUIS JOLIET MALL (AT LOUIS JOLIET MALL); 815.254.3710; M-SA 10-9, SU 11-6; MALL PARKING

ORLAND PARK—152 ORLAND SQ DR (AT ORLAND SQUARE SHOPPING CTR); 708.403.5085; M-SA 10-9: SU 11-6

Old Navy ★★★★★

"...the best for casual maternity clothing like stretchy T-shirts with Lycra and comfy jeans... prices are so reasonable it's ridiculous... not much for the workplace, but you can't beat the prices on casual clothes... not all Old Navy locations carry their maternity line... don't expect a huge or diverse selection... the staff is not always knowledgeable about maternity clothing and can't really help with questions about sizing... they have the best return policy—order online and return to the nearest store location... perfect for inexpensive maternity duds..."

Casual wear .... ✓ $$ .... Prices
Business wear .... ✗   ❹ .... Product availability
Intimate apparel .... ✗   ❸ .... Customer service
Nursing wear .... ✗   ❸ .... Decor

WWW.OLDNAVY.COM

ORLAND PARK—120 ORLAND PARK PL (AT 94TH AVE); 708.364.0555; M-SA 9-9, SU 10-6

Target ★★★★☆

"...I was surprised at how fashionable their selection is—they carry Liz Lange and other really cute selections... the price is right—especially since you'll only be wearing these clothes for a few months... great for maternity basics—T-shirts, skirts, sweaters, even maternity bras... best of all, you can do some maternity shopping while you're shopping for other household basics... shirts for $10—you can't beat that... not the most exciting or romantic maternity shopping, but once you see the prices you'll get over it... as always, Target provides the perfectly priced solution..."

Casual wear .... ✓ $$ .... Prices
Business wear .... ✓   ❸ .... Product availability
Intimate apparel .... ✓   ❸ .... Customer service
Nursing wear .... ✓   ❸ .... Decor

WWW.TARGET.COM

MATTESON—21600 CICERO AVE (AT N GATEWAY DR); 708.748.0990; M-SA 8-10, SU 8-9; PARKING IN FRONT OF BLDG

Online

"lila picks"

★ breastisbest.com ★ gap.com

★ maternitymall.com ★ naissance maternity.com

babiesrus.com ★★★★☆

"...their online store is surprisingly plentiful for maternity wear in addition to all of the baby stuff... they carry everything from Mimi Maternity to Belly Basics... easy shopping and good return policy... the price is right and the selection is really good..."

Casual wear ✓ ✓ Nursing wear
Business wear ✓ ✓ Intimate apparel

babycenter.com ★★★★☆

"...it's babycenter.com—of course it's good... a small but well selected maternity section... I love being able to read other people's comments before purchasing... prices are reasonable and the convenience is priceless... great customer service and easy returns..."

Casual wear ✓ ✓ Nursing wear
Business wear ✗ ✗ Intimate apparel

babystyle.com ★★★★☆

"...beautiful selection of maternity clothes... very trendy, fashionable styles... take advantage of their free shipping offers to keep the cost down... items generally ship quickly... I found a formal maternity outfit for a benefit dinner, bought it on sale and received it on time... a nice variety of things and they ship in a timely manner..."

Casual wear ✓ ✓ Nursing wear
Business wear ✓ ✓ Intimate apparel

bellablumaternity.com

Casual wear ✓ ✓ Nursing wear
Business wear ✓ ✓ Intimate apparel

breakoutbras.com

Casual wear ✗ ✓ Nursing wear
Business wear ✗ ✓ Intimate apparel

breastisbest.com ★★★★★

"...by far the best resource for purchasing good quality nursing bras online... the site is easy to use and they have an extensive online fitting guide... returns are a breeze... since they are only online you may have to try a few before you get it exactly right..."

Casual wear ✓ ✓ Nursing wear
Business wear ✗ ✓ Intimate apparel

childishclothing.com

Casual wear ✓ ✗ Nursing wear
Business wear ✗ ✗ Intimate apparel

duematernity.com ★★★★☆

"...refreshing styles... fun and hip clothing... the site is easy to navigate and use... I've ordered a bunch of clothes from them and never had a problem... everything from casual wear to fun, funky items for special occasions... prices are reasonable..."

Casual wear ✓ ✓ Nursing wear
Business wear ✓ ✓ Intimate apparel

evalillian.com

Casual wear ✓ ✓ Nursing wear
Business wear ✓ ✓ Intimate apparel

expressiva.com ★★★★½

"...the best site for nursing clothes... prices are good and their selection is terrific... lots of selection on dressy, casual, sleep, workout and even bathing suits... if you're going to shop for maternity online then be sure not to miss this cool site... good customer service—quite prompt in answering questions about my order..."

Casual wear ✓ ✓ Nursing wear
Business wear ✗ ✓ Intimate apparel

gap.com ★★★★★

"...stylish maternity clothes delivered right to your doorstep... always something worth buying... the best place for functional, comfortable and affordable maternity clothes... classic styles, not too trendy... more available online than in a store... no fancy dresses but lots of casual outfits that are cheap, look good and I don't mind parting with them after my baby is born... easy to use site and deliveries are generally prompt... you can return them to any Gap store..."

Casual wear ✓ ✓ Nursing wear
Business wear ✓ ✓ Intimate apparel

japaneseweekend.com ★★★★☆

"...pregnancy clothes that scream 'I am proud of my pregnant body'... a must for comfy, stylish stuff... they make the best maternity pants which cradle your belly as it grows... a little expensive but I lived in their pants my entire pregnancy—I definitely got my money's worth... really nice clothing that just doesn't look and feel like your traditional pregnancy wear—I still wear a couple of the outfits (my baby is now 6 months old)..."

Casual wear ✓ ✓ Nursing wear
Business wear ✓ ✓ Intimate apparel

jcpenney.com ★★★☆☆

"...competitive prices and a surprisingly cute selection... they carry bigger sizes that are very hard to find at other stores... much cheaper than most maternity boutiques and they always seem to have some sort of sale going on... an especially large selection of maternity jeans for plus sizes... a more conservative collection than the smaller, hipper boutiques... good for casual basics, but not much for special occasions..."

Casual wear ✓ ✓ Nursing wear
Business wear ✓ ✓ Intimate apparel

lizlange.com ★★★★½

"...well-designed and cute... the real buys on this site are definitely in the sale section... cute, hip selection of jeans, skirts, blouses and

bathing suits... their evening and dressy clothes are the best with wonderful fabrics and designs... easy and convenient online shopping... practical but not frumpy styles—their web site made my maternity shopping so easy... ”

Casual wear ✓ ✗ Nursing wear
Business wear ✓ ✗ Intimate apparel

maternitymall.com ★★★★★

“*...I had great luck with maternitymall.com... a large selection of vendors in all price ranges... quick and easy without having to leave my house... found everything I needed... their merchandise tends to be true to size... site is a bit hard to navigate and cluttered with ads... sale and clearance prices are fantastic...* ”

Casual wear ✓ ✓ Nursing wear
Business wear ✓ ✓ Intimate apparel

mommygear.com

Casual wear ✓ ✓ Nursing wear
Business wear ✗ ✓ Intimate apparel

momsnightout.com

“*...for that fashionable-not-frumpy fancy occasion dress... beautiful store with gorgeous selection of dresses from cocktail to bridal... one on one attention... expensive but worth it...* ”

Casual wear ✗ ✗ Nursing wear
Business wear ✓ ✗ Intimate apparel

motherhood.com ★★★★☆

“*...a wide variety of styles, from business to weekend wear—all at a good price... affordable and cute... everything from bras and swimsuits to work outfits... highly recommended for those who don't want to spend a fortune on maternity clothes... less fancy and pricey than their sister stores—A Pea in the Pod and Mimi Maternity... they have frequent sales, so you just need to keep dropping in—you're bound to find something good...* ”

Casual wear ✓ ✓ Nursing wear
Business wear ✓ ✓ Intimate apparel

motherwear.com ★★★★½

“*...excellent selection of cute and practical nursing clothes at reasonable prices... sign up for their e-mail newsletter for great offers, including free shipping... top quality clothes... decent selection of hard to find plus sizes... golden return policy, you can return any item (even used!) you aren't 100% happy with... they sell the only nursing tops I could actually wear outside the house... cute styles that aren't frumpy... so easy... pricey but worth it for the quality... top notch customer service...* ”

Casual wear ✗ ✓ Nursing wear
Business wear ✗ ✓ Intimate apparel

naissancematernity.com ★★★★★

“*...the cutest maternity clothes around... hip and funky clothes for the artsy, well-dressed mom to be... their site is easy to navigate... if you can't make it down to the actual store in LA, just go online... clothes that make you look and feel sexy... it ain't cheap but you will look marvelous and the clothes will grow with you... web site is great and their phone order service was incredible...* ”

Casual wear ✓ ✗ Nursing wear
Business wear ✓ ✗ Intimate apparel

nordstrom.com ★★★☆☆

“...now that they don't carry maternity in stores anymore, this is the only way to get any maternity from Nordstrom... overpriced but nice... makes returns harder, since you have to ship everything instead of just going back to a store... they carry Cadeau, Liz Lange, Belly Basics, etc... nice stuff, not so nice prices...”

Casual wear ✓ ✓ Nursing wear
Business wear ✓ ✓ Intimate apparel

oldnavy.com ★★★★☆

“...since not all Old Navy stores carry maternity clothes, this is the easiest way to go... just like their regular clothes, the maternity selection is great for casual wear... cheap, cheap, cheap... the quality is good and the price is definitely right... frequent sales make great prices even better...”

Casual wear ✓ ✓ Nursing wear
Business wear ✗ ✗ Intimate apparel

onehotmama.com ★★★½☆

“...you'll find many things you must have... cool and very nice clothing... they carry everything from underwear and tights to formal dresses... you can find some real bargains online... super fast shipping... also, lots of choices for nursing and get-back-in-shape wear...”

Casual wear ✓ ✓ Nursing wear
Business wear ✓ ✓ Intimate apparel

showeryourbaby.com

Casual wear ✓ ✓ Nursing wear
Business wear ✗ ✓ Intimate apparel

target.com ★★★★☆

“...lots of Liz Lange at very fair prices... the selection is great and it's so easy to shop online—we bought most of our baby gear here and I managed to slip in a couple of orders for some maternity wear too... maternity shirts for $10—where else can you find deals like that...”

Casual wear ✓ ✓ Nursing wear
Business wear ✓ ✓ Intimate apparel

activities & outings

City of Chicago

"lila picks"

★Chicago Children's Museum

★Lincoln Park Zoo

★Old Town School Of Folk Music

★Shedd Aquarium

Adler Planetarium & Astronomy Museum

"...best for older kids—they have to be old enough to 'get' the wonders of space... the restaurant is a beautiful place to sit and feed your baby... lots of interesting exhibits... Far Out Fridays (4:30-10pm first Fridays of every month) are packed with activities for kids and adults... look through a telescope, sky shows, watch informative movies and listen to lectures by Adler astronomers... go to the library to get a free pass..."

Customer service........................❹ $ .... Prices
Age range.....................3 yrs and up

WWW.ADLERPLANETARIUM.ORG

SOUTH LOOP—1300 S LAKE SHORE DR (AT E 14TH ST); 312.322.0304; CHECK SCHEDULE ONLINE; PARKING GARAGE

Alliance Francaise

"...I cannot say enough positive things about my experiences there... I was nervous that my French would be rusty, but everyone I've met in the various classes that I've taken there has been supportive and friendly... they cultivate a very welcoming educational environment..."

Customer service........................❹ $$.. Prices
Age range................ 12 mths and up

WWW.AFCHICAGO.COM

CHICAGO—810 N DEARBORN ST (OFF CHICAGO AVE); 312.337.1070; CHECK SCHEDULE ONLINE

Art Institute Of Chicago

"...don't think of this as just a regular museum where you go and look at stuff... the Kraft Education Center is a great way to introduce children to the wonderful world of art... arts and crafts with paper, glue, paint, etc... all family programs are free with regular museum admission... best for school aged kids..."

Customer service........................❹ $$.. Prices
Age range.....................4 yrs and up

WWW.ARTIC.EDU/AIC/KIDS

LOOP—111 S MICHIGAN AVE (AT E MONROE ST); 312.443.3600; CHECK SCHEDULE ONLINE; STREET OR GARAGE PARKING

Baby PhD

WWW.BABYPHD.COM

OAKLAND/KENWOOD—5225 S HARPER AVE (AT 52ND ST); 773.684.8920; M-SA 10-6, SU 11-5; STREET PARKING

Barnes & Noble

"...wonderful weekly story times for all ages and frequent author visits for older kids... lovely selection of books and the story times are fun and very well done... they have evening story times—we put our kids in their pjs and come here as a treat before bedtime... they read a story, and then usually have a little craft or related coloring project... times vary by location so give them a call..."

Customer service .... ❹ $.. Prices

Age range .... 6 mths to 6 yrs

WWW.BARNESANDNOBLE.COM

GOLD COAST/STREETERVILLE—1130 N STATE ST (AT DIVISION ST); 312.280.8155; CALL FOR SCHEDULE

LAKEVIEW/WRIGLEYVILLE—659 W DIVERSEY (AT CLARK ST); 773.871.9004; CALL FOR SCHEDULE

LINCOLN PARK/DEPAUL/OLD TOWN—1441 W WEBSTER AVE (AT N CLYBOURN AVE); 773.871.3610; CALL FOR SCHEDULE; PARKING LOT

Belle Plaine Studio

CHICAGO—2014 W BELLE PLAINE (OFF IRVING PARK RD); 773.935.1890

Beverly Arts Center, The

"...lots of creative activities—dance, music, singing and just good old socializing with kids... mainly things for older kids since they require that they are potty trained... they have so many classes for adults and preschoolers... check out their 'Preschool of the Arts' program... class costs vary, but the preschool program is around $100 per month..."

Customer service .... ❹ $$...................................... Prices

Age range .... 3 yrs and up

WWW.BEVERLYARTCENTER.ORG

MORGAN PARK—2407 W 111TH ST (AT WESTERN AVE); 773.445.3838; CHECK SCHEDULE ONLINE

Borders Books

"...very popular weekly story time held in most branches (check the web site for locations and times)... call before you go since they are very popular and get extremely crowded... kids love the unique blend of songs, stories and dancing... Mr. Hatbox's appearances are a delight to everyone (unfortunately he doesn't make appearances at all locations)... large children's section is well categorized and well priced... they make it fun for young tots to browse through the board-book section by hanging toys around the shelves... the low-key cafe is a great place to have coffee with your baby and leaf through some magazines..."

Customer service .... ❹ $.. Prices

Age range .... 6 mths to 6 yrs

WWW.BORDERSSTORES.COM

BEVERLY—2210 W 95TH ST (AT S LEAVITT ST); 773.445.5471; CALL FOR SCHEDULE

EDGEWATER—6103 N LINCOLN AVE (AT N JERSEY AVE); 773.267.4822; CALL FOR SCHEDULE

GOLD COAST/STREETERVILLE—830 N MICHIGAN AVE (AT E PEARSON ST); 312.573.0564; CALL FOR SCHEDULE

LAKEVIEW/WRIGLEYVILLE—2817 N CLARK ST (AT W DIVERSEY PKY); 773.935.3909; CALL FOR SCHEDULE

LINCOLN PARK/DEPAUL/OLD TOWN—755 W NORTH AVE (AT N HALSTED ST); 312.266.8060; CALL FOR SCHEDULE

LOOP—150 N STATE ST (AT E RANDOLPH ST); 312.606.0750; CALL FOR SCHEDULE

OAKLAND/KENWOOD—1539 E 53RD ST (AT S LAKE PARK AVE); 773.752.8663; CALL FOR SCHEDULE

SHERIDAN PARK/UPTOWN—4718 N BROADWAY AVE (AT W LELAND AVE); 773.334.7338; CALL FOR SCHEDULE

Bubbles Academy

"...they have yoga for kids as well as arts & crafts... a terrific place, run by great people... nice atmosphere and the little ones love it, but it can be costly... the decor is really neat—truly enchanting... the baby music class is fun, warm and very interactive... yoga for children and mommy and me yoga classes, music and motion, language, creative movement, and mommy and me exercise classes are some off the fabulous classes offered for your little ones... $150 for 8 week program..."

Customer service........................❺ $$$.......................................Prices

Age range................3 mths to 12 yrs

WWW.BUBBLESACADEMY.COM

LINCOLN PARK/DEPAUL/OLD TOWN—1504 N FREMONT ST (AT W NORTH AVE); 312.944.7677; CALL FOR SCHEDULES; FREE PARKING

Build-A-Bear Workshop

"...design and make your own bear—it's a dream come true... the most cherished toy my daughter owns... they even come with birth certificates... the staff is fun and knows how to play along with the kids' excitement... the basic stuffed animal is only about $15, but the extras add up quickly... great for field trips, birthdays and special occasions... how darling—my nephew is 8 years old now, and still sleeps with his favorite bear..."

Customer service........................❹ $$$.......................................Prices

Age range.....................3 yrs and up

WWW.BUILDABEAR.COM

RIVER NORTH/RIVER WEST—700 E GRAND AVE (AT NAVY PIER); 312.832.0114; CALL FOR HOURS; FREE PARKING

Chicago Childrens Museum ★★★★★

"...a true Chicago gem with awesome exhibits and activities for tots... kids can play alone or with other kids in an educational and fun setting... excellent age-appropriate art activities—paper making, painting, glue projects—you name it... the children's exhibits all have a 'cruiser' area for non-walkers... there's a water exhibit and a game area with life-size chess, checkers and bowling for older kids... there's also a drop-in art activity room... definitely worth the trip and membership fee... $65 annual membership for family of four..."

Customer service........................❹ $$...Prices

Age range.............12 mths to 10 yrs

WWW.CHICHILDRENSMUSEUM.ORG

RIVER NORTH/RIVER WEST—700 E GRAND AVE (AT N STER DR); 312.527.1000; SU-W 10-5, TH 10-8, F 10-5, SA 10-8; PARKING AT NAVY PIER

Chicago Cultural Center

"...Chicago's Architectural Showplace for the Lively and Visual Arts and home of the city's official Visitor Center...this is a great family experience with both hands-on and educational exhibits...."

Customer service........................❹ $$$.......................................Prices

Age range............... 12 mths and up

WWW.CITYOFCHICAGO.ORG

LOOP—78 E WASHINGTON ST (AT N GARLAND CT); 312.744.6630; M-W 10-7, TH 10-9, F 10-6, SA 10-5, SU 11-5; FREE PARKING

Chicago Historical Society

"...the walking tour explores the city's beautiful and historic North Side—Lincoln Park, the Gold Coast, Old Town... your chance to discover Tarzan's home, find the Blues Brothers' secret speakeasy, and get a behind-the-scenes look at Chicago's legendary improvisational theater company... more appropriate for school-aged children..."

Customer service .... ❹ $$$ .... Prices
Age range .... 4 yrs and up

WWW.CHICAGOHS.ORG

CHICAGO—CLARK ST (AT NORTH AVE); 312.642.4600; M-W 12-8, TH-SA 9:30-4:30, SU 12-5; PARKING LOT $6 FLAT RATE

Chicago Water Tower

"...kids love the elevator... in a neighborhood where it's fun to walk around and explore... Chicago's most cherished landmark... here you can observe the Chicago WaterWorks at work... the gallery is a great place to learn about Chicago history..."

Customer service .... ❹ $$$ .... Prices
Age range .... 3 yrs and up

WWW.CITYOFCHICAGO.ORG

CHICAGO—806 N MICHIGAN AVE (AT E CHICAGO AVE); 312.742.0808; M-F 9:30-6, SA 10-6, SU 12-5; FREE PARKING

Children's Museum of Immigration (Swedish American Museum Center)

"...what a neat concept—a museum that teaches children about coming to America from a foreign country... the children's exhibits are so much fun—they can milk a cow, pretend to pack luggage... a very cute gift shop with lots of Swedish trinkets... my son loved the big boat (immigrant steamer)..."

Customer service .... ❺ $$ .... Prices
Age range .... 3 yrs to 12 yrs

WWW.SAMAC.ORG

EDGEWATER—5211 N CLARK ST (AT FOSTER); 773.728.8111; T-F 1-4, SA-SU 11-4; STREET PARKING

Chuck E Cheese's

"...lots of games, rides, playrooms and very greasy food... the kids can play and eat and parents can unwind a little... a good rainy day activity... the kids love the food, but it's a bit greasy for adults... always crowded and crazy—but that's half the fun... can you ever go wrong with pizza, games and singing?.. although they do have a salad bar for adults, remember, you're not going for the food—you're going because your kids will love it... just about the easiest birthday party around—just pay money and show up..."

Customer service .... ❸ $$ .... Prices
Age range .... 12 mths to 7 yrs

WWW.CHUCKECHEESE.COM

ARCHER HEIGHTS/BRIGHTON PARK/GAGE PARK—5080 S KEDZIE (AT W 51ST ST); 773.476.0500; SU-TH 9-10, F-SA 9-11; FREE PARKING

Corner Playroom

"...a room filled to the gills with different props for kids to play with... lots of play houses and other things to play in... take your kids and

activities & outings

have friends meet up there—you get to hang out while the kids play... they also have classes that help foster more structured play time... closed on weekends... they do birthday parties... $15 per visit... ”

Customer service........................ ❸ $$$..................................... Prices
Age range................ 6 mths to 5 yrs
WWW.MYCORNERPLAYROOM.COM
LINCOLN PARK/DEPAUL/OLD TOWN—2121 N CLYBOURN AVE (AT TREASURE ISLAND SHOPPING CTR); 773.388.2121; M-TH 8-5:30, F 8-3; FREE PARKING

DuSable Museum of African American History ★★★☆☆

“*...a museum that offers refreshingly different art and exhibits from the African American point of view... great story telling program every 3rd Wednesday... not geared specifically toward the preschool crowd, but worth visiting to take a look...* ”

Customer service........................ ❸ $$$..................................... Prices
Age range..................... 2 yrs and up
WWW.DUSABLEMUSEUM.ORG
WASHINGTON PARK—740 E 56TH PLACE (AT 57TH ST); 773.947.0600; CHECK SCHEDULE ONLINE

Ed & Annette's Monkeys & More ★★★★☆

“*...an animal show that comes to your house... a fun and educational birthday party... Ed, the owner, was great and knew how to make the kids feel comfortable with the animals, snakes and a real monkey—my daughter was ecstatic...* ”

Customer service........................ ❹ $$$..................................... Prices
Age range............... 12 mths and up
WWW.EDANDANNETTESMONKEYSANDMORE.COM
IRVING PARK/MAYFAIR—4301 W 47TH ST (AT S PULASKI RD); 773.376.0812; CALL FOR APPT

Eli's Cheescake Factory ★★★★½

“*...what a fun, different place to go... take a tour of the factory, make cheesecake and eat it... the grounds are very nice and make for a great picnic—inside and out...* ”

Customer service........................ ❺ $$.. Prices
Age range..................... 3 yrs and up
WWW.ELICHEESECAKE.COM
BIG OAKS—6701 W FOREST PRESERVE AVE (AT W MONTROSE AVE); 773.736.3417; M-F (BY APPT) 10-3

Emerald City Theater Company ★★★★☆

“*...this is what children's live theater should be all about... the staff is awesome and the productions the older kids put on are just precious... not much for really little kids, but my baby loves coming along to watch my preschooler... just about the coolest birthday party you can imagine—they create a neat fantasy for all...* ”

Customer service........................ ❹ $$.. Prices
Age range..................... 3 yrs and up
WWW.EMERALDCITYTHEATRE.COM
LAKEVIEW/WRIGLEYVILLE—2936 N SOUTHPORT AVE (AT N LINCOLN AVE); 773.529.2690; CALL FOR SCHEDULE; STREET PARKING

Fantasy Kingdom ★★★★½

“*...the best kid's party we've ever been to... play dress up, play house, play with other kids... no classes or scheduled time—you can just show* *up and start playing... a nice big, clean play area for little tots of all ages to romp around... $12 per person; additional siblings and kids under 1 are free...* ”

Customer service .... ❺ $$$ .... Prices
Age range ....6 mths to 6 yrs
WWW.FANTASYKINGDOM.ORG

WICKER PARK/UKRANIAN VILLAGE—1422 N KINGSBURY ST (AT NORTH AVE); 312.642.5437; M-F 9:30-5:30, SA-SU PRIVATE PARTIES ONLY; FREE PARKING

Field Museum, The ★★★★☆

“*...dinosaurs and big stuffed animals from long ago... kind of magical, they have story telling programs that are fun and keep little minds enthralled... plenty of family events—just ask... the animal area is definitely more appealing than the geology section... very educational—the stuff many questions are made of...* ”

Customer service .... ❹ $$ .... Prices
Age range .... 3 yrs and up
WWW.FIELDMUSEUM.ORG

CHICAGO—1400 S LAKE SHORE DR (OFF 18TH ST); 312.922.9410; DAILY 9-5

Garfield Park Conservatory ★★★☆☆

“*...this is a pretty special place for all ages... I used to come here just to get out and about when my daughter was a baby and now we come to visit the Children's Garden from time to time... the kids area is fairly small... the whole place is a working greenhouse so expect dirt and water all over the place... a wonderful outing for when you want to feel like you're in the jungle or a land far away—my son is totally mesmerized by this place... perfect for a cold, wintery afternoon...* ”

Customer service .... ❸ $$$ .... Prices
Age range ....3 mths and up
WWW.GARFIELD-CONSERVATORY.ORG

GARFIELD PARK—300 N CENTRAL PARK AVE (AT W FULTON BLVD); 312.746.5100; DAILY 9-5

Gymboree Play & Music ★★★★☆

“*...we've done several rounds of classes with our kids and they absolutely love it... colorful, padded environment with tons of things to climb and play on... a good indoor place to meet other families and for kids to learn how to play with each other... the equipment and play areas are generally neat and clean... an easy birthday party spot... a guaranteed nap after class... costs vary, so call before showing up...* ”

Customer service .... ❹ $$$ .... Prices
Age range .... birth to 5 yrs
WWW.GYMBOREE.COM

LAKEVIEW/WRIGLEYVILLE—3158 N LINCOLN AVE (AT N ASHLAND AVE); 773.296.4550; CHECK SCHEDULE ONLINE; STREET PARKING

LINCOLN PARK/DEPAUL/OLD TOWN—1030 W NORTH AVE (AT N KINGSBURY ST); 773.296.4550; CHECK SCHEDULE ONLINE; STREET PARKING

Hancock Observatory ★★★★★

“*...a fun outing to see the city from way up high... my son loves coming here because he likes to try to guess what all the buildings are... my 2 year old daughter was a little scared at first, but loved it once she got used to the sound of the wind... bring quarters for the telescopes...* ”

Customer service .... ❺ $$$$$.................................. Prices
Age range .... 3 yrs and up
WWW.HANCOCK-OBSERVATORY.COM

EAST/WEST OLD TOWN GOLD COAST/STREETERVILLE—875 N MICHIGAN AVE (AT E CHESTNUT ST); 888.875.8439; DAILY 9-11

Hands On Children's Art Museum

"...painting, drawing, dress up, clay—even computer classes for preschoolers... I love that I can take my preschooler and school-age kids here and have them both be entertained in such a constructive manner... very well organized—we always have fun... $50 membership provides discounts to classes and the store..."

Customer service........................❺ $$..Prices

Age range.............12 mths to 12 yrs

WWW.HANDSONART.ORG

SOUTH SIDE—1800 W 103RD ST (AT S WOOD ST); 773.233.9933; CHECK SCHEDULE ONLINE; PARKING BEHIND BLDG

Hyde Park Art Center

"...they hook you up with all the materials, and you get to go crazy with it... so much fun for all ages... I love that they provide preschooler classes in such an adult environment—it provides a nice atmosphere for kids to learn... their exhibits vary all the time so it's fun to come back often... class subjects rotate frequently too... get a membership—it will pay for itself quickly..."

Customer service........................❸ $$$......................................Prices

Age range....................2 yrs and up

WWW.HYDEPARKART.ORG

HYDE PARK—5307 S HYDE PARK BLVD (AT 53RD ST); 773.324.5520; CALL FOR SCHEDULE

Hyde Park School of Ballet

"...this is the real deal—they take their ballet to another level... we came to watch a class and frankly were intimidated by the intensity—it really is a dance class, not a movement program... tons of programs to choose from... the staff is very talented—my daughter loves taking ballet here..."

Customer service........................❸ $$$......................................Prices

Age range....................3 yrs and up

WWW.HYDEPARKSCHOOLOFBALLET.ORG

MARQUETTE PARK—5650 S WOODLAWN AVE (AT 56TH ST); 773.493.8498; CHECK SCHEDULE ONLINE

Jewish Community Center

"...programs vary from facility to facility, but most JCCs have outstanding early childhood programs... everything from mom and me music classes to arts and crafts for older kids... a wonderful place to meet other parents and make new friends... class fees are cheaper (if not free) for members, but still quite a good deal for nonmembers... a superb resource for new families looking for fun..."

Customer service........................❹ $$$......................................Prices

Age range.................3 mths and up

WWW.GOJCC.ORG

CHICAGO—1 S FRANKLIN ST (AT N UPPER WACKER DR); 313.357.4700; CALL FOR SCHEDULE

HYDE PARK—5200 S HYDE PARK BLVD (AT E HYDE PARK BLVD); 773.753.3080; CALL FOR SCHEDULE; STREET PARKING

LAKEVIEW/WRIGLEYVILLE—524 W MELROSE AVE (AT N LAKE SHORE DR); 773.871.6780; CALL FOR SCHEDULE; STREET PARKING

LOGAN SQUARE—3003 TOUHY AVE (AT N SACRAMENTO AVE); 773.761.9100; CALL FOR SCHEDULE; STREET PARKING

Lifeline Theatre

"...a great place to bring the kids... very interesting plays for kiddies... they also host a summer camp... Kidseries shows like Stuart Little, Brave Potatoes and more..."

Customer service .... ❺ $$$ .... Prices
Age range .... 5 yrs and up

WWW.LIFELINETHEATRE.COM

CHICAGO—6912 N GLENWOOD AVE (AT W FARWELL AVE); 773.761.4477; CHECK SCHEDULE ONLINE; STREET PARKING

Lillstreet Art Center

"...arts and crafts for all ages... their Kidstreet program is very well done... the staff is helpful, but not pushy with the kids and my boys always seem to have fun... prepare to get messy—paint and clay everywhere... many programs for older kids too, which lets me bring both my kids here... you can pay per class or for a full session (which is much cheaper)..."

Customer service .... ❸ $$$$$.................................... Prices
Age range .... 2 yrs and up

WWW.LILLSTREET.COM

CHICAGO—4401 N RAVENSWOOD (AT MONTROSE AVE); 773.769.4226; CHECK SCHEDULE ONLINE

Lincoln Park Conservatory

"...they have a great train display in the winter... a wonderful, free spot to visit on those cold, gray winter days... Chicago's largest park... worth a visit..."

Customer service .... ❹ $$ .... Prices
Age range .... 12 mths and up

WWW.CITYOFCHICAGO.ORG

LINCOLN PARK/DEPAUL/OLD TOWN—2400 N STOCKTON DR (AT W FULLERTON PKWY); 312.742.7736; DAILY 9-5

Lincoln Park Zoo

"...beautiful setting right on the lakefront, lots of brand new exhibits and it's all still free!.. usually not too crowded... very clean... don't miss the carousel... have a picnic outside the zoo for a relaxed lunch or snack... perfect for small children... main zoo has traditional zoo animals while the adjacent barnyard is great for domestic animals... don't miss the African exhibit—it's indoors, making it a great option for very hot or very cold days..."

Customer service .... ❹ $... Prices
Age range ....3 mths and up

WWW.LPZOO.COM

LINCOLN PARK/DEPAUL/OLD TOWN—2001 N CLARK ST (AT W ARMITAGE AVE); 312.742.2000; CHECK SCHEDULE ONLINE; PARKING LOT

Little Gym, The

"...a well thought-out program of gym and tumbling geared toward different age groups... a clean facility, excellent and knowledgeable staff... we love the small-sized gym equipment and their willingness to work with kids with special needs... activities are fun and personalized to match the kids' age... great place for birthday parties with a nice party room—they'll organize and do everything for you..."

Customer service .... ❹ $$$ .... Prices
Age range .... 4 mths to 12 yrs

WWW.THELITTLEGYM.COM

ROSCOE VILLAGE/WEST LAKEVIEW—3216 N LINCOLN AVE (AT W BELMONT AVE); 773.525.5750; CALL FOR SCHEDULE; STREET PARKING

Lookingglass Theatre

"...their Playtime program for infants consists of stories and playing... programs for older kids involve improvisational play... what a blast watching my boy play pretend—it's almost like he's starting to act... the social interaction in the classes is priceless... they'll even throw a birthday party for you..."

Customer service........................❸ $$$..Prices
Age range............... 12 mths and up
WWW.LOOKINGGLASSTHEATRE.ORG

LINCOLN PARK/DEPAUL/OLD TOWN—2936 N SOUTHPORT AVE (OFF LINCOLN AVE); 773.477.9257; CHECK SCHEDULE ONLINE

Menomonee Club

"...sports and socializing activities for older kids... the staff is awesome... this program has been around forever and is an incredible resource for local kids... where else are you going to find T-ball, puppet making, and tap dance under one roof... annual membership of $35 plus fees for additional classes..."

Customer service........................❸ $$$..Prices
Age range................. 4 yrs to 12 yrs
WWW.MENOMONEECLUB.ORG

CHICAGO—1535 N DAYTON ST (AT WEED ST); 312.664.4631; CHECK SCHEDULE ONLINE

LINCOLN PARK/DEPAUL/OLD TOWN—224 W WILLOW ST (AT N PARK AVE); 312.664.4515; CHECK SCHEDULE ONLINE

Mexican Fine Arts Center Museum

"...a great intro to Mexican art and culture... family days give your family the opportunity to do art together... older kids can participate in a bilingual summer camp... art classes all throughout the year... free admission..."

Customer service........................❹ $$..Prices
Age range....................4 yrs and up
WWW.MFACMCHICAGO.ORG

CHICAGO—1852 W 19TH ST (AT S WOOD ST); 312.738.1503; T-SU 10-5; STREET PARKING

Museum Of Science & Industry

"...a fantastic museum with tons of stuff to explore... kids of all ages love it... educational and free with your library's museum pass... my son loved the children's play area, where he got to climb around and play... water play, construction station and a very neat train exhibit... too much to see all in one day—you'll want to come back—guaranteed... adults $9; under 3 free..."

Customer service........................❹ $$..Prices
Age range............... 12 mths and up
WWW.MSICHICAGO.ORG

HYDE PARK—57TH ST AND LAKE SHORE DRIVE; 773.684.1414; CHECK SCHEDULE ONLINE; PARKING GARAGE

Music Together

"...the best mom and baby classes out there... music, singing, dancing—even instruments for tots to play with... liberal make-up policy, great venues, take home books, CDs and tapes which are different each semester... it's a national franchise so instructors vary and have their own style... different age groups get mixed up which makes it a good learning experience for all involved... the highlight of

our week—grandma always comes along... be prepared to have your tot sing the songs at home, in the car—everywhere... ”

Customer service .... ❹ $$$ .... Prices
Age range .... 2 mths to 5 yrs

WWW.MUSICTOGETHER.COM

CHICAGO—800.728.2692; CALL FOR SCHEDULE

CHICAGO—773.975.9874; CALL FOR SCHEDULE

CHICAGO—773.288.3815; CALL FOR SCHEDULE

Musical Magic

“*...they have created a wonderful program that stimulates babies by using puppets, colorful scarves, bubbles and, of course, music... my son has been attending classes since he was 5 months old... the music is very pleasant and doesn't get annoying or irritating... the teacher (Roseanne) is what makes this class so special... a wonderful introduction to music...* ”

Customer service .... ❺ $$$ .... Prices
Age range .... 3 mths to 4 yrs

WWW.MUSICALMAGIC.NET

ROSCOE VILLAGE/WEST LAKEVIEW—2255 W ROSCOE ST (AT N OAKLEY AVE); 773.529.5600; CHECK SCHEDULE ONLINE; STREET PARKING

My Gym Children's Fitness Center

★★★★☆

“*...a wonderful gym environment for parents with babies and older tots... classes range from tiny tots to school-aged children and the staff is great about making it fun for all ages... equipment and facilities are really neat—ropes, pulleys, swings, you name it... the kind of place your kids hate to leave... the staff's enthusiasm is contagious... great for memorable birthday parties... although it's a franchise, each gym seems to have its own individual feeling... awesome for meeting playmates and other parents...* ”

Customer service .... ❹ $$$ .... Prices
Age range .... 3 mths to 9 yrs

WWW.MY-GYM.COM

BUCKTOWN—1880 W FULLERTON AVE (AT N DAMEN AVE); 773.645.9600; CHECK SCHEDULE ONLINE; FREE PARKING

North Park Village Nature Center

“*...a great way to spend the day learning about trees, plants and nature... the walks aren't too long for little kids and it's a great way for them to get some exercise... on rainy or hot days kids stay inside and play in the room full of books, crayons and puppets... they even have classes for tots and parents... admission is free...* ”

Customer service .... ❹ $ .... Prices
Age range .... 6 mths and up

WWW.CHICAGOPARKDISTRICT.COM

NORTH RAVENSWOOD—5801 N PULASKI RD (AT W PETERSON AVE); 312.744.5472; DAILY 10-4; FREE PARKING

Old Town School Of Folk Music

“*...an outstanding music school with a tremendous selection of programs for kids... the wiggle worms class was awesome—totally worth the money and time... music, movement and language... fun kids instruments in the store... moms can meet other moms, while both baby and mom are stimulated and entertained... mix it up by doing*

Spanish or French classes once in a while... class was about half moms and half caregivers... all live music... ❞

Customer service........................❹ $$$..Prices
Age range..................6 mths and up

WWW.OLDTOWNSCHOOL.ORG

LINCOLN PARK/DEPAUL/OLD TOWN—909 W ARMITAGE AVE (AT N BISSELL ST); 773.728.6000; CHECK SCHEDULE ONLINE; STREET PARKING

RAVENSWOOD—4544 N LINCOLN AVE (AT W SUNNYSIDE AVE); 773.728.6000; CHECK SCHEDULE ONLINE; STREET PARKING

Oriental Institute Museum

Age range.....................3 yrs and up

WWW.OI.UCHICAGO.EDU

CHICAGO—1155 E 58TH ST (AT S WOODLAWN AVE); 773.702.9514; T 10-6, W 10-8:30, TH-SA 10-6, SU 12-6

Portage Park Center for the Arts

WWW.CHICAGOLEARNINGGUIDE.COM

PORTAGE PARK—3914 N MENARD AVE (AT W DAKIN ST); 773.205.0151; CALL FOR SCHEDULE; STREET PARKING

Portage Park Pool ★★★★☆

❝*...toddlers love this place—the small pool has an 'activity center' in knee-deep water... fun and always good for meeting new friends and families... a favorite summer outing for us... insanely crowded unless you go early in the day...* ❞

Customer service........................❹ $ ....Prices
Age range..................3 mths and up

WWW.CHICAGOPARKDISTRICT.COM

IRVING PARK/MAYFAIR—4100 N LONG AVE (AT W BELLE PLAINS AVE); 773.685.7235; M-F 7-8, SA 9-8, SU 9-6; FREE PARKING

Reel Moms (Loews Theatres) ★★★★☆

❝*...not really an activity for kids, but rather something you can easily do with your baby... first-run movies for people with babies... the sound is low, the lights turned up and no one cares if your baby cries... packed with moms changing diapers all over the place... so nice to be able to go see current movies... don't have to worry about baby noise... relaxed environment with moms, dads and babies wandering all over... the staff is very friendly and there is a real community feel... a great idea and very well done...* ❞

Customer service........................❹ $$..Prices
Age range................ 3 mths to 2 yrs

WWW.ENJOYTHESHOW.COM/REELMOMS

RIVER NORTH/RIVER WEST—600 N MICHIGAN AVE (AT E OHIO ST); 312.255.9347; CHECK SCHEDULE ONLINE; STREET PARKING

School of Ballet Chicago, The ★★★½☆

❝*...one of the more serious dance programs around... this is where the pros go, although they do have classes for little kids too... this can be costly, so be sure to get all the information in advance... $90 for a 5 week program...* ❞

Customer service........................❸ $$$..Prices
Age range.....................3 yrs and up

WWW.BALLETCHICAGO.ORG

LOOP—218 S WABASH AVE (AT ADAMS ST); 312.251.8838; CHECK SCHEDULE ONLINE

Sears Tower Skydeck

★★★★☆

"...the elevator ride is as fun as standing around at the top... what a view... good fun trying to point out the many sites of Chicago... my boy always like to point out where we live..."

Customer service .... ❹ $$ .... Prices

Age range .... 2 yrs and up

WWW.THE-SKYDECK.COM

LOOP—233 S WACKER DR (AT W ADAMS ST); 312.875.9696; DAILY 10-8, SUMMER 10-10; PARKING GARAGE

Shedd Aquarium

★★★★★

"...an absolutely fabulous aquarium... sharks, clown fish (think Nemo), sting rays and much, much more... a fun afternoon, but not cheap... a membership is key if you are going to be a frequent visitor... check for weekly free days during off season... good selection of food options... parking can be a challenge, but it is a pretty bike ride if you live close enough... $23 for adults; 2 and under free..."

Customer service .... ❹ $$$ .... Prices

Age range ....6 mths and up

WWW.SHEDDAQUARIUM.ORG

SOUTH LOOP—1200 S LAKE SHORE DR (AT E WM MCFETRIDGE DR); 312.939.2438; CHECK SCHEDULE ONLINE; FREE PARKING

Sherwood Conservatory Of Music

★★★☆☆

"...they offer Music Together classes in addition to percussion lessons... the variety of classes is really neat—a wonderful way of introducing children to music... the best part is that your kids can keep taking lessons here as they get older, which is especially nice because they'll get comfortable with the teachers... I wish classes were a little longer... $148 for a 10 week program..."

Customer service .... ❸ $$$ .... Prices

Age range ....1 mths and up

WWW.SHERWOODMUSIC.ORG

SOUTH LOOP—1312 S MICHIGAN AVE (AT E 13TH ST); 312.427.6267; CHECK SCHEDULE ONLINE; STREET PARKING

Sing 'n Dance

★★★☆☆

"...good energy and plenty to do... fun music and movement classes for tots... my daughter loved the class—everyone made us feel comfortable... fun props—hula hoops, instruments and group play... a very cool little community of moms having fun with their kids... check it out with their free introductory class..."

Customer service .... ❹ $$ .... Prices

Age range .... 2 mths to 3 yrs

WWW.SINGNDANCE.COM

LINCOLN PARK/DEPAUL/OLD TOWN—2632 N HALSTED (AT W WRIGHTWOOD AVE); 773.528.7464; CHECK SCHEDULE ONLINE; STREET PARKING

Suzuki-Orff School for Young Musicians

"...their Baby Steps program is wonderful... teachers are great and my baby was absolutely fascinated by the xylophone... parent participation is required for babies—older kids can be on their own... classes range from under an hour to an hour and a half... they even have a program for kids with special needs... a wonderful place..."

Customer service .... ❸ $$$ .... Prices

Age range ....6 mths and up

WWW.SUZUKIORFF.ORG

LINCOLN PARK/DEPAUL/OLD TOWN—1148 W CHICAGO AVE (AT MILWAUKEE AVE); 312.738.2646; CHECK SCHEDULE ONLINE

Ukrainian Village Children's Center

"...paper mache, painting, beading—a budding artists dream space... a totally creative fantasy world filled with props, furniture and all the tools to create... I still get compliments on the bead necklace my daughter made me... the head teacher is awesome with kids... Sarah is an accomplished artist and she has a wonderful way of engaging the kids... $10 classes are a bargain compared to many other programs around..."

Customer service........................❸ $$$....................................Prices

Age range................. 2 yrs to 12 yrs

HTTP://UVCC.HOME.MINDSPRING.COM

WICKER PARK/UKRANIAN VILLAGE—918 N DAMEN AVE (AT IOWA ST); 773.342.7415; CHECK SCHEDULE ONLINE

World Folk Music Company

"...the infant and toddler program is fun and interactive... a wonderful time to bond with my baby while watching her interact with teachers and other kids... fun, fun, fun—we're singing the melodies for the rest of the day... we end up playing many of the games at home too... only $70 for an 8 week session and class sizes are small..."

Customer service........................❺ $ ....Prices

Age range................ 6 mths to 3 yrs

WWW.WORLDFOLKMUSICCOMPANY.COM

SOUTH SIDE—1808 W 103RD ST (AT S WOOD ST); 773.779.7059; CHECK SCHEDULE ONLINE; STREET PARKING

Wrigley Field

"...a great family outing... a Chicago institution not to miss... all kids need to go see a Cubs game at some point in their life... every child should have the opportunity to experience this historic park, eat a hotdog and watch the Cubs... a little crowded, but that is part of the experience... wrap your baby in a scarf or baby carrier, and enjoy the game... older toddlers and preschoolers will feed off of the crowd's excitement and love all the snacks, colors and sounds..."

Customer service........................❸ $$$....................................Prices

Age range....................3 yrs and up

WWW.CUBS.COM

CHICAGO—1060 W ADDISON (AT N CLARK ST); 773.404.2827; CHECK SCHEDULE ONLINE

YMCA

"...most of the Ys in the area have classes and activities for kids... swimming, gym classes, dance—even play groups for the really little ones... ... some facilities are nicer than others, but in general their programs are worth checking out... prices are more than reasonable for what is offered... the best bang for your buck... they have it all—great programs that meet the needs of a diverse range of families... check out their camps during the summer and school breaks..."

Customer service........................❹ $$.......................................Prices

Age range................. 3 mths and up

WWW.YMCA.COM

CHICAGO—501 N CENTRAL AVE (AT W LAKE ST); 773.287.9120; M-F 6-9, SA-SU 7-7; PARKING LOT

CHINATOWN—1608 W 21ST PL (AT S ASHLAND AVE); 312.738.0282; M-F 8-6; STREET PARKING

COLUMET HEIGHTS—3039 E 91ST ST (AT S COMMERCIAL AVE); 773.721.9100; M-F 6-7:30, SA 7-3; PARKING LOT

EAST/WEST OLD TOWN GOLD COAST/STREETERVILLE—30 W CHICAGO AVE (AT N STATE ST); 312.944.6211; CHECK SCHEDULE ONLINE

HUMBOLDT PARK—1834 N LAWNDALE AVE (AT W ARMITAGE AVE); 773.235.2525; M-F 5:30-9, SA 8-3, SU 9-2; PARKING LOT

IRVING PARK/MAYFAIR—4251 W IRVING PARK (AT N KEELER AVE); 773.777.7500; CALL FOR SCHEDULES; FREE PARKING

LINCOLN PARK/DEPAUL/OLD TOWN—1515 N HALSTEAD (AT W CERMAK RD); 312.440.7272; CALL FOR SCHEDULE; STREET PARKING

NEAR SOUTH SIDE—3763 S WABASH AVE (AT E PERSHING RD); 773.285.0020; M-F 8-8:30, SA 9-2; STREET PARKING

ROSCOE VILLAGE/WEST LAKEVIEW—3333 N MARSHFIELD (AT N LINCOLN AVE); 773.248.3333; CALL FOR SCHEDULES; STREET PARKING

ROSELAND—4 E 111TH ST (AT S STATE ST); 773.785.9210; M-F 6-9, SA 9-5, SU 12-5

SAUGANASH—6235 S HOMAN AVE (AT W 63RD ST); 773.434.0300; M-F 9-9, SA 9-2; STREET PARKING

SOUTH LOOP—1001 W ROOSEVELT RD (AT UNIVERSITY OF ILLINOIS AT CHICAGO); 312.421.7800

WEST ROGERS PARK—2424 W TOUHY AVE (AT N WESTERN AVE); 773.262.8300; CALL FOR SCHEDULES; STREET PARKING

WOODLAWN—6330 S STONY ISLAND AVE (AT E 63RD ST); 773.947.0700; M-F 5:30-8:45, SA 6:30-4:15; PARKING LOT

Northwestern Suburbs

"lila picks"

- ★Gymboree Play & Music
- ★Reel Moms (Loews Theaters)
- ★Spring Valley Nature Center

Barnes & Noble

"...wonderful weekly story times for all ages and frequent author visits for older kids... lovely selection of books and the story times are fun and very well done... they have evening story times—we put our kids in their pjs and come here as a treat before bedtime... they read a story, and then usually have a little craft or related coloring project... times vary by location so give them a call..."

Customer service........................❹ $ .... Prices

Age range................ 6 mths to 6 yrs

WWW.BARNESANDNOBLE.COM

ARLINGTON HEIGHTS—13 W RAND RD (OFF N ARLINGTON HEIGHTS RD); 847.259.5304; CALL FOR SCHEDULE

CRYSTAL LAKE—5380 ROUTE 14 (AT MAIN ST); 815.444.0824; CALL FOR SCHEDULE

DEER PARK—20600 N RAND RD (AT LONG GROVE RD); 847.438.7444; CALL FOR SCHEDULE

SCHAUMBURG—590 E GOLF RD (AT PLUM GROVE RD); 847.310.0450; CALL FOR SCHEDULE

VERNON HILLS—720 HAWTHORNE CTR (OFF MILWAUKEE AVE); 847.247.1157; CALL FOR SCHEDULE

Borders Books

"...very popular weekly story time held in most branches (check the web site for locations and times)... call before you go since they are very popular and get extremely crowded... kids love the unique blend of songs, stories and dancing... Mr. Hatbox's appearances are a delight to everyone (unfortunately he doesn't make appearances at all locations)... large children's section is well categorized and well priced... they make it fun for young tots to browse through the board-book section by hanging toys around the shelves... the low-key cafe is a great place to have coffee with your baby and leaf through some magazines..."

Customer service........................❹ $ .... Prices

Age range................ 6 mths to 6 yrs

WWW.BORDERSSTORES.COM

ALGONQUIN—2216 S RANDALL RD (AT N COUNTRY LINE RD); 847.658.7548; CALL FOR SCHEDULE

CRYSTAL LAKE—6000 NORTHWEST HWY (AT S MAIN ST); 815.455.0302; CALL FOR SCHEDULE

SCHAUMBURG—1540 E GOLF RD (AT N MEACHAM RD); 847.330.0031; CALL FOR SCHEDULE

Build-A-Bear Workshop

"...design and make your own bear—it's a dream come true... the most cherished toy my daughter owns... they even come with birth certificates... the staff is fun and knows how to play along with the kids' excitement... the basic stuffed animal is only about $15, but the extras add up quickly... great for field trips, birthdays and special occasions... how darling—my nephew is 8 years old now, and still sleeps with his favorite bear..."

Customer service .... ❹ $$$ .... Prices

Age range .... 3 yrs and up

WWW.BUILDABEAR.COM

SCHAUMBURG—WOODFIELD SHOPPING CTR (AT E GOLF RD); 847.517.4155; M-SA 10-9, SU 11-6

VERNON HILLS—815 HAWTHORN CTR (AT E TOWNLINE RD); 847.680.8806; M-SA 10-9, SU 11-6

Chuck E Cheese's

"...lots of games, rides, playrooms and very greasy food... the kids can play and eat and parents can unwind a little... a good rainy day activity... the kids love the food, but it's a bit greasy for adults... always crowded and crazy—but that's half the fun... can you ever go wrong with pizza, games and singing?.. although they do have a salad bar for adults, remember, you're not going for the food—you're going because your kids will love it... just about the easiest birthday party around—just pay money and show up..."

Customer service .... ❸ $$ .... Prices

Age range .... 12 mths to 7 yrs

WWW.CHUCKECHEESE.COM

STREAMWOOD—990 S BARRINGTON RD (AT RAMBLEWOOD DR); 630.289.6700; SU-TH 9-10, F-SA 9-11; FREE PARKING

Forest Grove Athletic Club

"...a wonderful club with great daycare and swim programs... your kids can take lessons or jump in the pool with adults during weekend Family Swim... you need to be a member of the club in order to get into the pool..."

Customer service .... ❹ $$$$ .... Prices

Age range ....6 mths and up

WWW.FGAC.COM

PALATINE—1760 N HICKS RD (AT E DUNDEE RD); 847.991.4646; CHECK SCHEDULE ONLINE; FREE PARKING

Gymboree Play & Music

"...we've done several rounds of classes with our kids and they absolutely love it... colorful, padded environment with tons of things to climb and play on... a good indoor place to meet other families and for kids to learn how to play with each other... the equipment and play areas are generally neat and clean... an easy birthday party spot... a guaranteed nap after class... costs vary, so call before showing up..."

Customer service .... ❹ $$$ .... Prices

Age range .... birth to 5 yrs

WWW.GYMBOREE.COM

CRYSTAL LAKE—23 CRYSTAL LAKE PLZ (AT MARY LN); 815.477.7529; CHECK SCHEDULE ONLINE; GARAGE PARKING

Health World Children's Museum

"...exhibits that promote health and safety for children... wonderful for young and old—I learned a lot... tots can play with the shopping cart to buy fake food, milk a cow, go down the tree slide, check out a real ambulance... my daughter's favorite was the real bee hive... fake train ride with movie... a great rainy day outing... $7 per person; under 2 free..."

Customer service........................❹ $$..Prices
Age range....................2 yrs and up

WWW.HEALTHWORLDMUSEUM.ORG

BARRINGTON—1301 S GROVE AVE (AT E CORNELL AVE); 847.842.9100; T-SA 10-3; STREET PARKING

Jewish Community Center

"...programs vary from facility to facility, but most JCCs have outstanding early childhood programs... everything from mom and me music classes to arts and crafts for older kids... a wonderful place to meet other parents and make new friends... class fees are cheaper (if not free) for members, but still quite a good deal for nonmembers... a superb resource for new families looking for fun..."

Customer service........................❹ $$$......................................Prices
Age range.................3 mths and up

WWW.GOJCC.ORG

BUFFALO GROVE—370 HALF DAY RD (AT N BUFFALO GROVE RD); 847.955.0005; CALL FOR SCHEDULE

Little Gym, The

"...a well thought-out program of gym and tumbling geared toward different age groups... a clean facility, excellent and knowledgeable staff... we love the small-sized gym equipment and their willingness to work with kids with special needs... activities are fun and personalized to match the kids' age... great place for birthday parties with a nice party room—they'll organize and do everything for you..."

Customer service........................❹ $$$......................................Prices
Age range...............4 mths to 12 yrs

WWW.THELITTLEGYM.COM

SCHAUMBURG—540 E GOLF RD (AT BASEWOOD ST); 847.310.9160; CALL FOR SCHEDULE

Music Together

"...the best mom and baby classes out there... music, singing, dancing—even instruments for tots to play with... liberal make-up policy, great venues, take home books, CDs and tapes which are different each semester... it's a national franchise so instructors vary and have their own style... different age groups get mixed up which makes it a good learning experience for all involved... the highlight of our week—grandma always comes along... be prepared to have your tot sing the songs at home, in the car—everywhere..."

Customer service........................❹ $$$......................................Prices
Age range................ 2 mths to 5 yrs

WWW.MUSICTOGETHER.COM

BARRINGTON—847.322.4998; CALL FOR SCHEDULE

BUFFALO GROVE—847.322.4998; CALL FOR SCHEDULE

PALATINE—847.925.6659; CALL FOR SCHEDULE

My Gym Children's Fitness Center

"...a wonderful gym environment for parents with babies and older tots... classes range from tiny tots to school-aged children and the staff is great about making it fun for all ages... equipment and facilities are really neat—ropes, pulleys, swings, you name it... the kind of place your kids hate to leave... the staff's enthusiasm is contagious... great for memorable birthday parties... although it's a franchise, each gym seems to have its own individual feeling... awesome for meeting playmates and other parents..."

Customer service .... ❹ $$$ .... Prices
Age range .... 3 mths to 9 yrs

WWW.MY-GYM.COM

ARLINGTON HEIGHTS—780 E RAND RD (AT N DRYDEN AVE); 847.506.9600; CHECK SCHEDULE ONLINE

BUFFALO GROVE—166 MCHENRY RD (AT LAKE COOK RD); 847.229.1990; CHECK SCHEDULE ONLINE

SCHAUMBURG—247 W GOLF RD (AT ROSELLE RD); 847.882.6202; CHECK SCHEDULE ONLINE; FREE PARKING

Pirate's Cove

"...a theme park for tots of different ages—our whole family can go and have fun... a fun and affordable outing... caters to very young kids as well as older ones... nice atmosphere and cool activities... staffed by high school and college kids... unfortunately only open during the summer months..."

Customer service .... ❸ $$ .... Prices
Age range .... 2 yrs to 12 yrs

WWW.PARKS.ELKGROVE.ORG

ELK GROVE VILLAGE—999 LEICESTER RD (AT BIESTERFIELD RD); 847.439.2683; CHECK SCHEDULE ONLINE; FREE PARKING

Reel Moms (Loews Theatres)

"...not really an activity for kids, but rather something you can easily do with your baby... first-run movies for people with babies... the sound is low, the lights turned up and no one cares if your baby cries... packed with moms changing diapers all over the place... so nice to be able to go see current movies... don't have to worry about baby noise... relaxed environment with moms, dads and babies wandering all over... the staff is very friendly and there is a real community feel... a great idea and very well done..."

Customer service .... ❹ $$ .... Prices
Age range .... 3 mths to 2 yrs

WWW.ENJOYTHESHOW.COM/REELMOMS

SCHAUMBURG—601 N MARTINGALE RD (AT HIGGINS RD); 847.330.0720; CHECK SCHEDULE ONLINE; FREE PARKING

Seascape Family Aquatic Center

"...great summertime fun—well watched by the lifeguards... a huge outdoor pool packed with screaming kids... every hour they have a 15 minute adult swim time... my daughter loves the sand play area—you can actually make sand castles at the pool... they have seasonal hours so call ahead..."

Customer service .... ❸ $$$ .... Prices
Age range .... 2 yrs and up

WWW.HEPARKS.ORG/INDEX.PHP?LOC=SEA

HOFFMAN ESTATES—1300 MOON LAKE BLVD (AT VOLID DR); 847.310.3626; CALL FOR SCHEDULE; FREE PARKING

Spring Valley Nature Center & Heritage Farm

"...a great farm to visit... volunteers dress in period clothing on weekends and open the real 1840s buildings to visitors... see how the old kitchens were run and taste some food... visit the cabin for crafts... my kids love to check out the horses, cows, sheep, chickens and pigs... the best part is that it's free..."

Customer service........................❹ $ .... Prices
Age range.................6 mths and up

WWW.PARKFUN.COM

SCHAUMBURG—111 E SCHAUMBURG RD (AT MEACHAM RD); 847.985.2100; DAILY 9-5; PARKING LOT

Waterworks

"...an amazing indoor water play area... zero depth pool for toddlers... several water slides... clean and plenty of activities for a few hours... sometimes the water seems kind of cold... bring your own food—their cafe is expensive and only carries junk food..."

Customer service........................❸ $$$...................................... Prices
Age range....................2 yrs and up

WWW.PARKFUN.COM

SCHAUMBURG—505 N SPRINGINSGUTH RD (AT COTTINGTON DR); 847.490.2505; CALL FOR SCHEDULE; FREE PARKING

YMCA

"...most of the Ys in the area have classes and activities for kids... swimming, gym classes, dance—even play groups for the really little ones... ... some facilities are nicer than others, but in general their programs are worth checking out... prices are more than reasonable for what is offered... the best bang for your buck... they have it all—great programs that meet the needs of a diverse range of families... check out their camps during the summer and school breaks..."

Customer service........................❹ $$....................................... Prices
Age range.................3 mths and up

WWW.YMCA.COM

LAKE ZURICH—1025 OLD MCHENRY RD (AT RTE 53); 847.438.5300; M-F 5:15-10, SA 5:30-6, SU 8-5; PARKING LOT

PALATINE—1400 W NORTHWEST HWY (AT W COUNTRYSIDE DR); 847.359.2400; CALL FOR SCHEDULE

Northern Suburbs

"lila picks"

★ Chicago Botanic Garden

★ Exploritorium

★ Kohl's Children's Museum

Barnes & Noble

"...wonderful weekly story times for all ages and frequent author visits for older kids... lovely selection of books and the story times are fun and very well done... they have evening story times—we put our kids in their pjs and come here as a treat before bedtime... they read a story, and then usually have a little craft or related coloring project... times vary by location so give them a call..."

Customer service .... ❹ $.. Prices

Age range .... 6 mths to 6 yrs

WWW.BARNESANDNOBLE.COM

DEERFIELD—728 N WAUKEGAN RD (AT DEERFIELD RD); CALL FOR SCHEDULE

EVANSTON—1701 SHERMAN AVE (OFF CHICAGO AVE); 847.328.0883; CALL FOR SCHEDULE

SKOKIE—5405 TOUHY AVE (AT CARPENTER RD); 847.329.8460; CALL FOR SCHEDULE

SKOKIE—55 OLD ORCHARD CTR (OFF SKOKIE RD); 847.676.2230; CALL FOR SCHEDULE

Borders Books

"...very popular weekly story time held in most branches (check the web site for locations and times)... call before you go since they are very popular and get extremely crowded... kids love the unique blend of songs, stories and dancing... Mr. Hatbox's appearances are a delight to everyone (unfortunately he doesn't make appearances at all locations)... large children's section is well categorized and well priced... they make it fun for young tots to browse through the board-book section by hanging toys around the shelves... the low-key cafe is a great place to have coffee with your baby and leaf through some magazines..."

Customer service .... ❹ $.. Prices

Age range .... 6 mths to 6 yrs

WWW.BORDERSSTORES.COM

DEERFIELD—49 S WAUKEGAN RD (AT LAKE COOK RD); 847.559.1999; CALL FOR SCHEDULE

EVANSTON—1700 MAPLE AVE (AT CHURCH ST); 847.733.8852; CALL FOR SCHEDULE

GURNEE—6971 W GRAND AVE (AT N HUNT CLUB RD); 847.249.1845; CALL FOR SCHEDULE

HIGHLAND PARK—595 CENTRAL AVE (AT 1ST ST); 847.433.9130; CALL FOR SCHEDULE

WILMETTE—3232 LAKE AVE (AT SKOKIE RD); 847.256.3220; CALL FOR SCHEDULE

Chicago Botanic Garden

"...beautiful place to spend the afternoon with the kids... if you join for the entire year you can go as many times as you'd like... nice cafeteria style restaurant... wonderful train exhibit during the summer months... a very nice place to take your baby for a walk... a great place for city dwellers to let there kids run free... so clean and lovely..."

Customer service........................❹ $$..Prices

Age range....................3 yrs and up

WWW.CHICAGOBOTANIC.ORG

GLENCOE—1000 LAKE COOK RD (AT GREEN BAY RD); 847.835.5440; DAILY 8-SUNSET; FREE PARKING

Chuck E Cheese's

"...lots of games, rides, playrooms and very greasy food... the kids can play and eat and parents can unwind a little... a good rainy day activity... the kids love the food, but it's a bit greasy for adults... always crowded and crazy—but that's half the fun... can you ever go wrong with pizza, games and singing?.. although they do have a salad bar for adults, remember, you're not going for the food—you're going because your kids will love it... just about the easiest birthday party around—just pay money and show up..."

Customer service........................❸ $$..Prices

Age range...............12 mths to 7 yrs

WWW.CHUCKECHEESE.COM

SKOKIE—7142 CARPENTER RD (AT TOUHY AVE); 847.679.8192; SU-TH 9-10, F-SA 9-11; FREE PARKING

Deerfield Farmers Market

"...a great way to start the weekend... plenty of entertainment and food samples... it's fun to buy the produce from the farmers that grow it and to buy from local merchants..."

Customer service........................❸ $$..Prices

Age range................. 1 mths and up

WWW.DEERFIELD-IL.ORG

DEERFIELD—DEERFIELD RD (AT YORK AVE); 847.945.5000; JUN 18-OCT 15 SA 7-12:30; FREE PARKING

Exploritorium

"...a huge indoor play area with climbing, sliding, arts and crafts, dress up and even computers... it does cost a little money, but it's well worth it given how much fun the kids seem to have... my kids love coming here to get dressed up in all of the costumes they offer—wonderful for imaginative play... fun place to meet friends... great for birthday parties... adults $6 ($2 for residents); under 2 are free..."

Customer service........................❹ $$..Prices

Age range................. 2 yrs to 11 yrs

WWW.SKOKIEPARKDISTRICT.ORG

SKOKIE—4701 OAKTON ST (AT KILPATRICK AVE); 847.674.1500; M W F 9-6, SA 10-3

Gymboree Play & Music

"...we've done several rounds of classes with our kids and they absolutely love it... colorful, padded environment with tons of things to climb and play on... a good indoor place to meet other families and for kids to learn how to play with each other... the equipment and play

areas are generally neat and clean... an easy birthday party spot... a guaranteed nap after class... costs vary, so call before showing up... ”

Customer service .... ❹ $$$ .... Prices
Age range .... birth to 5 yrs

WWW.GYMBOREE.COM

MUNDELEIN—732 S BUTTERFIELD RD (AT ALLANSON RD); 847.996.0222; CHECK SCHEDULE ONLINE; GARAGE PARKING

NORTHBROOK—2042 NORTHBROOK CT (AT NORTHBROOK COURT SHOPPING CTR); 847.205.0080; CHECK SCHEDULE ONLINE; GARAGE PARKING

SKOKIE—70 OLD ORCHARD CTR (AT GOLF RD); 847.568.9880; CHECK SCHEDULE ONLINE; GARAGE PARKING

Heller Nature Center

Age range ....6 mths and up

WWW.HELLERNATURECENTER.ORG

HIGHLAND PARK—2821 RIDGE RD; 847.433.6901; CHECK SCHEDULE ONLINE

Jewish Community Center ★★★★☆

“*...programs vary from facility to facility, but most JCCs have outstanding early childhood programs... everything from mom and me music classes to arts and crafts for older kids... a wonderful place to meet other parents and make new friends... class fees are cheaper (if not free) for members, but still quite a good deal for nonmembers... a superb resource for new families looking for fun...* ”

Customer service .... ❹ $$$ .... Prices
Age range ....3 mths and up

WWW.GOJCC.ORG

NORTHBROOK—300 REVERE DR (AT LAKE COOK RD); 847.205.9480; CALL FOR SCHEDULE; STREET PARKING

SKOKIE—5050 W CHURCH ST (AT GROSSPOINT RD); 847.763.3520; CALL FOR SCHEDULE

Kohl's Children's Museum of Greater Chicago ★★★★★

“*...the new museum is twice as big as the old location... you can always count on Kohl's for a fun getaway... fun that is educational... nature exhibits, pretend supermarket and garage... a big ship to play on, a maze to play hide and seek in and a water exhibit to get soaked in... the best part is, the kids learn while playing... a very hands on environment... what an awesome, innovative place for kids to learn... $6.50 for adults; 1 and under free...* ”

Customer service .... ❹ $$ .... Prices
Age range ....6 mths to 8 yrs

WWW.KOHLCHILDRENSMUSEUM.ORG

GLENVIEW—2100 PATRIOT BLVD (AT LAKE AVE); 847.832.6600; PARKING LOT

Lamb's Farm ★★★★☆

“*...a wonderful home and training facility for adults with disabilities... I like that my kids can learn about disabilities, but also have fun at the same time... a must for the summer months... a wonderful outing for kids of all ages... our kids like riding the train, carousel and seeing the animals...* ”

Customer service .... ❹ $$ .... Prices
Age range ....6 mths and up

WWW.LAMBSFARM.ORG

LIBERTYVILLE—14245 W ROCKLAND RD (AT N BRADLEY RD); 847.362.4636; CHECK SCHEDULE ONLINE; FREE PARKING

Little Gym, The

"...a well thought-out program of gym and tumbling geared toward different age groups... a clean facility, excellent and knowledgeable staff... we love the small-sized gym equipment and their willingness to work with kids with special needs... activities are fun and personalized to match the kids' age... great place for birthday parties with a nice party room—they'll organize and do everything for you..."

Customer service........................❹ $$$..Prices

Age range................4 mths to 12 yrs

WWW.THELITTLEGYM.COM

GLENVIEW—1368 PATRIOT BLVD (AT E LAKE AVE); 847.724.4929; CALL FOR SCHEDULE; STREET PARKING

GURNEE—101 AMBROGIO DR (AT WASHINGTON); 847.244.4496; CALL FOR SCHEDULE; STREET PARKING

Music Together

"...the best mom and baby classes out there... music, singing, dancing—even instruments for tots to play with... liberal make-up policy, great venues, take home books, CDs and tapes which are different each semester... it's a national franchise so instructors vary and have their own style... different age groups get mixed up which makes it a good learning experience for all involved... the highlight of our week—grandma always comes along... be prepared to have your tot sing the songs at home, in the car—everywhere..."

Customer service........................❹ $$$..Prices

Age range................ 2 mths to 5 yrs

WWW.MUSICTOGETHER.COM

EVANSTON—847.869.9886; CALL FOR SCHEDULE

GLENVIEW—847.486.1368; CALL FOR SCHEDULE

WILMETTE—847.869.9886; CALL FOR SCHEDULE

My Gym Children's Fitness Center

"...a wonderful gym environment for parents with babies and older tots... classes range from tiny tots to school-aged children and the staff is great about making it fun for all ages... equipment and facilities are really neat—ropes, pulleys, swings, you name it... the kind of place your kids hate to leave... the staff's enthusiasm is contagious... great for memorable birthday parties... although it's a franchise, each gym seems to have its own individual feeling... awesome for meeting playmates and other parents..."

Customer service........................❹ $$$..Prices

Age range................ 3 mths to 9 yrs

WWW.MY-GYM.COM

SKOKIE—9446 SKOKIE BLVD (AT GROSS POINT RD); 847.675.9496; CHECK SCHEDULE ONLINE; FREE PARKING

Quig's Orchard

"...apple picking, pumpkins at Halloween and fun hay rides... a popular school field trip... the staff is great with the educational side of things... best known for their delicious variety of apples that you can pick yourself... a great hands-on way for kids to learn about fruits and vegetables... tasty cider donuts..."

Customer service........................❹ $$$..Prices

Age range....................2 yrs and up

WWW.QUIGS.COM

MUNDELEIN—300 S RT /83 (AT MIDLOTHIAN RD); 847.566.9130; CALL FOR HOURS; FREE PARKING

Reel Moms (Loews Theatres) ★★★★☆

"...not really an activity for kids, but rather something you can easily do with your baby... first-run movies for people with babies... the sound is low, the lights turned up and no one cares if your baby cries... packed with moms changing diapers all over the place... so nice to be able to go see current movies... don't have to worry about baby noise... relaxed environment with moms, dads and babies wandering all over... the staff is very friendly and there is a real community feel... a great idea and very well done..."

Customer service .... ❹ $$ .... Prices
Age range .... 3 mths to 2 yrs

WWW.ENJOYTHESHOW.COM/REELMOMS

SKOKIE—220 OLD ORCHARD CTR (AT GOLF RD); 847.674.0072; CHECK SCHEDULE ONLINE; FREE PARKING

Six Flags Hurricane Harbor

Age range .... 3 yrs and up

WWW.SIXFLAGS.COM

GURNEE—542 N ROUTE 21 (AT I-94); 847.249.4636; CHECK SCHEDULE ONLINE; FREE PARKING

YMCA

"...most of the Ys in the area have classes and activities for kids... swimming, gym classes, dance—even play groups for the really little ones... ... some facilities are nicer than others, but in general their programs are worth checking out... prices are more than reasonable for what is offered... the best bang for your buck... they have it all—great programs that meet the needs of a diverse range of families... check out their camps during the summer and school breaks..."

Customer service .... ❹ $$ .... Prices
Age range .... 3 mths and up

WWW.YMCACHGO.ORG

NILES—6300 W TOUHY AVE (AT N CALDWELL AVE); 847.647.8222; CALL FOR SCHEDULES; FREE PARKING

Western Suburbs

"lila picks"

★Brookfield Zoo

★DuPage Children's Museum

★Kiddieland

★My Gym Children's Fitness Center

Barnes & Noble

"...wonderful weekly story times for all ages and frequent author visits for older kids... lovely selection of books and the story times are fun and very well done... they have evening story times—we put our kids in their pjs and come here as a treat before bedtime... they read a story, and then usually have a little craft or related coloring project... times vary by location so give them a call..."

Customer service........................❹ $ ....Prices

Age range................ 6 mths to 6 yrs

WWW.BARNESANDNOBLE.COM

BLOOMINGDALE—200 S GARY AVE (AT STRATFORD SQ MALL); 630.671.9760; CALL FOR SCHEDULE

DOWNERS GROVE—1550 W 75TH (AT LEMONT RD); 630.663.0181; CALL FOR SCHEDULE

GENEVA—102 COMMONS DR (OFF RANDALL RD); 630.262.8568; CALL FOR SCHEDULE

NAPERVILLE—47 E CHICAGO AVE (AT WASHINGTON); 630.579.0200; CALL FOR SCHEDULE

OAKBROOK TERRACE—1 S 550 ROUTE 83 (ACROSS FROM OAKBROOK CTR); 630.571.0999; CALL FOR SCHEDULE

WHEATON—351 TOWN SQUARE WHEATON (AT NAPERVILLE RD); 630.653.2122; CALL FOR SCHEDULE

Bearfoot Fun & Fitness Center ★★★★☆

"...great indoor gym for children 9 months to 4 years old... classes are similar to Gymboree except they're less expensive... tots love to slide, play in the ball pit and crawl through the tunnels... they even have open gym hours twice a week ..."

Customer service........................❸ $$..Prices

Age range................ 9 mths to 4 yrs

ELMHURST—363 COMMONWEALTH LN (AT W BUTTERFIELD RD); 630.993.8937; CALL FOR SCHEDULES; FREE PARKING

Borders Books

"...very popular weekly story time held in most branches (check the web site for locations and times)... call before you go since they are very popular and get extremely crowded... kids love the unique blend of

songs, stories and dancing... Mr. Hatbox's appearances are a delight to everyone (unfortunately he doesn't make appearances at all locations)... large children's section is well categorized and well priced... they make it fun for young tots to browse through the board-book section by hanging toys around the shelves... the low-key cafe is a great place to have coffee with your baby and leaf through some magazines... ”

Customer service .... ❹ $ .... Prices
Age range .... 6 mths to 6 yrs

WWW.BORDERSSTORES.COM

BOLINGBROOK—161 N WEBER RD (AT VETERANS PKY); 630.771.9560; CALL FOR SCHEDULE

GENEVA—1660 S RANDALL RD (AT FARGO BLVD); 630.262.8747; CALL FOR SCHEDULE

NAPERVILLE—336 S ROUTE 59 (AT E NEW YORK ST); 630.637.9700; CALL FOR SCHEDULE

OAK BROOK—1500 16TH ST (AT KINGERY HWY); 630.574.0800; CALL FOR SCHEDULE

OAK PARK—1144 LAKE ST (AT N HARLEM AVE); 708.386.6927; CALL FOR SCHEDULE

SAINT CHARLES—3539 E MAIN ST (AT CHARLESTOWNE MALL); 630.443.8160; CALL FOR SCHEDULE

WHEATON—101 RICE LAKE SQUARE (AT BUTTERFIELD RD); 630.871.9595; CALL FOR SCHEDULE

Brookfield Zoo

“...can't say enough great things about the zoo... a clean, safe environment for the animals... we're members of the zoo and we go several times a year and the kids just love it... strollers are available for the little ones and there is tons of parking... don't miss the Hammil Family Play Zoo, where your child can imagine what it's like to be an animal, a zookeeper, a vet or a zoo planner... see and hold small household pet animals and don't forget to watch the animals being fed... ”

Customer service .... ❹ $$ .... Prices
Age range .... 3 mths and up

WWW.BROOKFIELDZOO.ORG

BROOKFIELD—8400 31ST ST (AT 1ST AVE); 708.485.2200; CHECK SCHEDULE ONLINE; PARKING LOT

Build-A-Bear Workshop

“...design and make your own bear—it's a dream come true... the most cherished toy my daughter owns... they even come with birth certificates... the staff is fun and knows how to play along with the kids' excitement... the basic stuffed animal is only about $15, but the extras add up quickly... great for field trips, birthdays and special occasions... how darling—my nephew is 8 years old now, and still sleeps with his favorite bear... ”

Customer service .... ❹ $$$ .... Prices
Age range .... 3 yrs and up

WWW.BUILDABEAR.COM

OAK BROOK—72 OAKBROOK CTR (AT KINGERY HWY); 630.928.0497; M-SA 10-9, SU 11-6

Chuck E Cheese's

“...lots of games, rides, playrooms and very greasy food... the kids can play and eat and parents can unwind a little... a good rainy day activity... the kids love the food, but it's a bit greasy for adults... always crowded and crazy—but that's half the fun... can you ever go wrong with pizza, games and singing?.. although they do have a salad bar for *adults, remember, you're not going for the food—you're going because your kids will love it... just about the easiest birthday party around—just pay money and show up...* ❞

Customer service........................ ❸ $$.. Prices
Age range...............12 mths to 7 yrs

WWW.CHUCKECHEESE.COM

NAPERVILLE—1154 E OGDEN AVE (AT IROQUOIS AVE); 630.369.2012; SU-TH 9-10, F-SA 9-11; FREE PARKING

VILLA PARK—200 W ROOSEVELT RD (AT S ARDMORE AVE); 630.833.6212; SU-TH 9-10, F-SA 9-11; FREE PARKING

Cosley Zoo ★★★★☆

❝*...a tiny zoo that's great for spending an hour or two... the little ones are just excited to be around animals... lots of farm animals like pigs and sheep to check out... best of all, it's free...* ❞

Customer service........................ ❸ $ .... Prices
Age range................. 6 mths and up

WWW.COSLEYZOO.ORG

WHEATON—1356 N GARY AVE (AT JEWELL RD); 630.665.5534; CHECK SCHEDULE ONLINE; PARKING AVAILABLE

DuPage Children's Museum ★★★★★

❝*...lots of creative activities for children and infants... great rainy day outing... our favorite activity is the water table—it twists and turns so kids can stand underneath while water pours down over them (don't worry, they don't actually get wet)... the bubble zone is great for older kids... the coolest kids museum we've been to... $7 per person; under 1 free...* ❞

Customer service........................ ❹ $$.. Prices
Age range...............6 mths to 10 yrs

WWW.DUPAGECHILDRENSMUSEUM.ORG

NAPERVILLE—301 N WASHINGTON ST (AT SPRING ST); 630.637.8000; M 9-1, T-W 9-5, TH 9-8, F-SA 9-5, SU 12-5; PARKING LOT

Early Notes Music Studio

Age range................ 3 mths to 6 yrs

NAPERVILLE—710 E OGDEN AVE (COLUMBIA AVE); 630.752.8443; CHECK SCHEDULE ONLINE; STREET PARKING

Gymboree Play & Music ★★★★½

❝*...we've done several rounds of classes with our kids and they absolutely love it... colorful, padded environment with tons of things to climb and play on... a good indoor place to meet other families and for kids to learn how to play with each other... the equipment and play areas are generally neat and clean... an easy birthday party spot... a guaranteed nap after class... costs vary, so call before showing up...* ❞

Customer service........................ ❹ $$$...................................... Prices
Age range....................birth to 5 yrs

WWW.GYMBOREE.COM

GENEVA—705 E STATE ST (AT SANDHOLM ST); 630.208.0774; CHECK SCHEDULE ONLINE; GARAGE PARKING

WESTMONT—504 E OGDEN AVE (AT OXFORD AVE); 630.654.1616; CHECK SCHEDULE ONLINE

WHEATON—1420 S GABLES BLVD (AT PLAMONTONDON RD); 630.260.9919; CHECK SCHEDULE ONLINE; GARAGE PARKING

Hal Tyrell Trailside Museum ★★★★☆

❝*...it's a wildlife rehabilitation center and you can visit the animals... the staff is nice and will answer any questions... free to get into and* *the animals are so cute... take a walk on the trail leading through the beautiful woods...* ”

Customer service .... ❹ $$$ .... Prices
Age range .... 2 yrs and up

WWW.FPDCC.COM

RIVER FOREST—738 THATCHER AVE (AT CHICAGO AVE); 708.366.6530; DAILY 10-4; STREET PARKING

Jeepers ★★★★☆

“*...they have a ton of video games and a few rides—flying bananas, bumper cars, Himalaya, monkey barrels and a train... plus, a tube for climbing and crawling... you can buy a wristband for unlimited use of the rides... awesome birthday parties... the snack bar serves up pizza, hot dogs and other 'standard' amusement park fare...* ”

Customer service .... ❸ $$ .... Prices
Age range .... 2 yrs to 12 yrs

WWW.JEEPERS.COM

GLENDALE HEIGHTS—91 N AVE (AT SWIFT RD); 630.510.7000; M-TH 11-9, F 11-10, SA 10-10, SU 11-8; FREE PARKING

Kiddieland ★★★★★

“*...traditional favorites like the carousel and Ferris wheel, as well as bigger rides for the more daring... a blast, but definitely an expensive outing... be sure to bring a change of clothes... rent a stroller for $5 if your tot gets tired of walking... a great amusement park that isn't too overwhelming for little ones...* ”

Customer service .... ❸ $$$$ .... Prices
Age range .... 3 yrs and up

WWW.KIDDIELAND.COM

MELROSE PARK—8400 W NORTH AVE (AT 1ST AVE); 708.343.8000; CALL FOR HOURS; STREET PARKING

Little Gym, The ★★★★☆

“*...a well thought-out program of gym and tumbling geared toward different age groups... a clean facility, excellent and knowledgeable staff... we love the small-sized gym equipment and their willingness to work with kids with special needs... activities are fun and personalized to match the kids' age... great place for birthday parties with a nice party room—they'll organize and do everything for you...* ”

Customer service .... ❹ $$$ .... Prices
Age range .... 4 mths to 12 yrs

WWW.THELITTLEGYM.COM

NAPERVILLE—2603 AURORA AVE (AT HIGHWAY 59); 630.637.0700; CALL FOR SCHEDULE

Morton Arboretum ★★★★☆

“*...beautiful trees—perfect for a quick outdoor adventure... the new maze garden is a fantastic—you really can get lost in this thing... beautiful any time of year... $5 for adults...* ”

Customer service .... ❹ $$ .... Prices
Age range .... 3 yrs and up

WWW.MORTONARB.ORG

LISLE—4100 ILLINOIS RTE 53 (AT HWY 56); 630.968.0074; CALL FOR HOURS; FREE PARKING

Music Together

“*...the best mom and baby classes out there... music, singing, dancing—even instruments for tots to play with... liberal make-up policy, great venues, take home books, CDs and tapes which are different each semester... it's a national franchise so instructors vary*

and have their own style... different age groups get mixed up which makes it a good learning experience for all involved... the highlight of our week—grandma always comes along... be prepared to have your tot sing the songs at home, in the car—everywhere... ❞

Customer service........................❹ $$$..Prices

Age range................ 2 mths to 5 yrs

WWW.MUSICTOGETHER.COM

BOLINGBROOK—630.527.0481; CALL FOR SCHEDULE

DOWNERS GROVE—630.927.3028; CALL FOR SCHEDULE

ELMHURST—630.325.4341; CALL FOR SCHEDULE

GLEN ELLYN—630.927.3028; CALL FOR SCHEDULE

NAPERVILLE—630.527.0481; CALL FOR SCHEDULE

OAK BROOK—630.325.4341; CALL FOR SCHEDULE

OAK PARK—708.406.1601; CALL FOR SCHEDULE

WHEATON—630.927.3028; CALL FOR SCHEDULE

WOODRIDGE—630.527.0481; CALL FOR SCHEDULE

My Gym Children's Fitness Center ★★★★★

❝*...a wonderful gym environment for parents with babies and older tots... classes range from tiny tots to school-aged children and the staff is great about making it fun for all ages... equipment and facilities are really neat—ropes, pulleys, swings, you name it... the kind of place your kids hate to leave... the staff's enthusiasm is contagious... great for memorable birthday parties... although it's a franchise, each gym seems to have its own individual feeling... awesome for meeting playmates and other parents...* ❞

Customer service........................❹ $$$..Prices

Age range................ 3 mths to 9 yrs

WWW.MY-GYM.COM

AURORA—4008 FOX VALLEY CTR DR (AT N COMMONS DR); 630.499.1299; CHECK SCHEDULE ONLINE

RIVER FOREST—7625 LAKE ST (AT LATHROP AVE); 708.209.1600; CHECK SCHEDULE ONLINE; FREE PARKING

Naper Settlement ★★★½☆

❝*...we've only been to Naper days, but loved it... excellent place to take school aged children... interesting, fun and a place where kids actually learn something... worth a day trip if you couple it with a visit to downtown Naperville...* ❞

Customer service........................❹ $$..Prices

Age range....................2 yrs and up

WWW.NAPERSETTLEMENT.ORG

NAPERVILLE—523 S WEBSTER ST (AT AURORA AVE); 630.420.6010; CHECK SCHEDULE ONLINE

Oak Park Conservatory ★★★☆☆

❝*...a really relaxing and peaceful place to bring your kids on a rainy day... a little slide indoors... on a sunny day kids can run around outside in the maze while you enjoy a picnic... a popular spot for play dates...* ❞

Customer service........................❸ $ ....Prices

Age range....................2 yrs and up

WWW.OPRF.COM/CONSERVATORY

OAK PARK—615 GARFIELD ST (AT CLARENCE AVE); 708.386.4700; M 2-4, T 10-4, W-SU 10-6; FREE PARKING

Oak Park Farmers Market

"...super fun for kids... parents come with kids in wagons... a live band provides hours of great entertainment... definitely a fun family outing... yummy food to take home (don't forget to try the fresh donuts)..."

Customer service .... ❸ $$$ .... Prices
Age range .... 1 wks and up
WWW.OAK-PARK.US
OAK PARK—460 LAKE ST (AT ELMWOOD AVE); 708.383.6400; JUN-OCT SA 7-1

Odyssey Fun World

"...highly recommended for parents who are looking to entertain children of different ages—especially during the Winter months when kids get stir crazy... there is a special area for infants and toddlers, and a big dragon balloon for the kids to jump in, climb in, and slide down... quite clean... video games and interactive games for older kids and a food area for pizza, pretzels, and the like... kind of like Chuck E Cheese..."

Customer service .... ❹ $$$ .... Prices
Age range .... 2 yrs and up
WWW.ODYSSEYFUNWORLD.COM
NAPERVILLE—3440 ODYSSEY CT (AT CELEBRATION DR); 630.416.2222; CHECK SCHEDULE ONLINE

Pelican Harbor Aquatic Park

"...a wonderful outdoor swim park... a zero-depth pool with water toys for babies... for older kids there are slides and a sand park... tons of staff on-hand to help... lots of water fountains and spray... good for all ages and you're guaranteed a solid nap from the little ones... $7 for adults; under 2 is free..."

Customer service .... ❹ $$$ .... Prices
Age range .... 3 mths and up
WWW.BOLINGBROOKPARKS.ORG
BOLINGBROOK—200 S LINDSEY LN (AT LILY CACHE LN); 630.739.1705; CHECK SCHEDULE ONLINE; FREE PARKING

Ridgeland Common Recreation Center

"...an indoor play area for only $2... not bad for a last-minute destination to get out of the house when it's too cold outdoors... the outdoor pool is huge..."

Customer service .... ❸ $$$ .... Prices
Age range .... 6 mths and up
WWW.OAKPARKPARKS.COM
OAK PARK—415 LAKE ST (AT N RIDGELAND AVE); 708.848.9661; CHECK SCHEDULE ONLINE; FREE PARKING

Wonder Works

"...it really isn't like a museum—it's more like a big open play area for children... plenty there to keep my 18-month-old entertained... a cozy, small museum with activities and programs for young children... fun for birthday parties... great for cold days when you want to do something indoors..."

Customer service .... ❹ $ .... Prices
Age range .... 18 mths to 10 yrs
WWW.WONDER-WORKS.ORG
OAK PARK—6445 W NORTH AVE (AT N NARRAGANSETT AVE); 708.383.4815; CALL FOR SCHEDULE

YMCA

"...most of the Ys in the area have classes and activities for kids... swimming, gym classes, dance—even play groups for the really little ones... ... some facilities are nicer than others, but in general their programs are worth checking out... prices are more than reasonable for what is offered... the best bang for your buck... they have it all—great programs that meet the needs of a diverse range of families... check out their camps during the summer and school breaks..."

Customer service........................❹ $$....................................Prices

Age range.................3 mths and up

WWW.YMCA.COM

DOWNERS GROVE—711 59TH ST (AT FAIRMOUNT AVE); 630.968.8400; M-F 5-10, SA 5-6, SU 9-5; PARKING LOT

ELMHURST—211 W 1ST ST (AT S YORK ST); 630.834.9200; CALL FOR SCHEDULES; STREET PARKING

Southern Suburbs

"lila picks"

★Children's Museum Of Oak Lawn

★My Gym Children's Fitness Center

Barnes & Noble

"...wonderful weekly story times for all ages and frequent author visits for older kids... lovely selection of books and the story times are fun and very well done... they have evening story times—we put our kids in their pjs and come here as a treat before bedtime... they read a story, and then usually have a little craft or related coloring project... times vary by location so give them a call..."

Customer service .... ❹ $.. Prices

Age range .... 6 mths to 6 yrs

WWW.BARNESANDNOBLE.COM

JOLIET—2621 PLAINFIELD RD (OFF HENNEPIN DR); 815.254.2253; CALL FOR SCHEDULE

ORLAND PARK—160 ORLAND PARK PLACE (AT 94TH AVE); 708.226.9092; CALL FOR SCHEDULE

Borders Books

"...very popular weekly story time held in most branches (check the web site for locations and times)... call before you go since they are very popular and get extremely crowded... kids love the unique blend of songs, stories and dancing... Mr. Hatbox's appearances are a delight to everyone (unfortunately he doesn't make appearances at all locations)... large children's section is well categorized and well priced... they make it fun for young tots to browse through the board-book section by hanging toys around the shelves... the low-key cafe is a great place to have coffee with your baby and leaf through some magazines..."

Customer service .... ❹ $.. Prices

Age range .... 6 mths to 6 yrs

WWW.BORDERSSTORES.COM

MATTESON—4824 W 211TH ST (AT CICERO AVE); 708.679.1835; CALL FOR SCHEDULE

ORLAND PARK—15260 S LA GRANGE RD (AT W 153RD ST); 708.460.7566; CALL FOR SCHEDULE

Bronzeville Children's Museum

Age range .... 3 yrs and up

WWW.BRONZEVILLECHILDRENSMUSEUM.COM

EVERGREEN PARK—EVERGREEN PLAZA (AT 95TH ST AND WESTERN AVE); 708.639.9504; T-SA 10-4

Build-A-Bear Workshop

"...design and make your own bear—it's a dream come true... the most cherished toy my daughter owns... they even come with birth certificates... the staff is fun and knows how to play along with the kids' excitement... the basic stuffed animal is only about $15, but the extras add up quickly... great for field trips, birthdays and special occasions... how darling—my nephew is 8 years old now, and still sleeps with his favorite bear..."

Customer service........................❹ $$$..Prices
Age range....................3 yrs and up

WWW.BUILDABEAR.COM

ORLAND PARK—448 ORLAND SQUARE DR (AT W 151ST ST); 708.226.1234; M-SA 10-9, SU 11-6; FREE PARKING

Children's Museum In Oak Lawn

"...lots of fun and interactive exhibits for kids to play with... we love coming here for a few hours—the membership is well worth it... puppet theater, water table... if your kids haven't had enough excitement you can play some more at the playground just outside... they'll be moving to a bigger location some time in 2006..."

Customer service........................❺ $ ....Prices
Age range................. 2 yrs to 10 yrs

WWW.CMOAKLAWN.ORG

OAK LAWN—9600 E SHORE DR (AT W 96TH ST); 708.423.6709; W-SA 10-3; PARKING LOT

Chuck E Cheese's

"...lots of games, rides, playrooms and very greasy food... the kids can play and eat and parents can unwind a little... a good rainy day activity... the kids love the food, but it's a bit greasy for adults... always crowded and crazy—but that's half the fun... can you ever go wrong with pizza, games and singing?.. although they do have a salad bar for adults, remember, you're not going for the food—you're going because your kids will love it... just about the easiest birthday party around—just pay money and show up..."

Customer service........................❸ $$..Prices
Age range...............12 mths to 7 yrs

WWW.CHUCKECHEESE.COM

JOLIET—1965 W JEFFERSON ST (AT S HAMMES AVE); 815.725.2044; SU-TH 9-10, F-SA 9-11

MATTESON—106 TOWN CENTER RD (AT HOLIDAY PLAZA DR); 708.747.5666; SU-TH 9-10, F-SA 9-11

TINLEY PARK—16090 S HARLEM AVE (AT RTE 6); 708.429.9230; SU-TH 9-10, F-SA 9-11; FREE PARKING

Jewish Community Center

"...programs vary from facility to facility, but most JCCs have outstanding early childhood programs... everything from mom and me music classes to arts and crafts for older kids... a wonderful place to meet other parents and make new friends... class fees are cheaper (if not free) for members, but still quite a good deal for nonmembers... a superb resource for new families looking for fun..."

Customer service........................❹ $$$..Prices
Age range.................3 mths and up

WWW.GOJCC.ORG

FLOSSMOOR—3400 W 196TH ST (AT HACKBERRY RD); 708.799.7650; CALL FOR SCHEDULE

My Gym Children's Fitness Center

"...a wonderful gym environment for parents with babies and older tots... classes range from tiny tots to school-aged children and the staff is great about making it fun for all ages... equipment and facilities are really neat—ropes, pulleys, swings, you name it... the kind of place your kids hate to leave... the staff's enthusiasm is contagious... great for memorable birthday parties... although it's a franchise, each gym seems to have its own individual feeling... awesome for meeting playmates and other parents..."

Customer service .... ❹ $$$ .... Prices
Age range .... 3 mths to 9 yrs
WWW.MY-GYM.COM

ORLAND PARK—9011 W 151ST ST (AT 94TH AVE); 708.349.0001; CHECK SCHEDULE ONLINE; FREE PARKING

Odyssey Fun World ★★★★☆

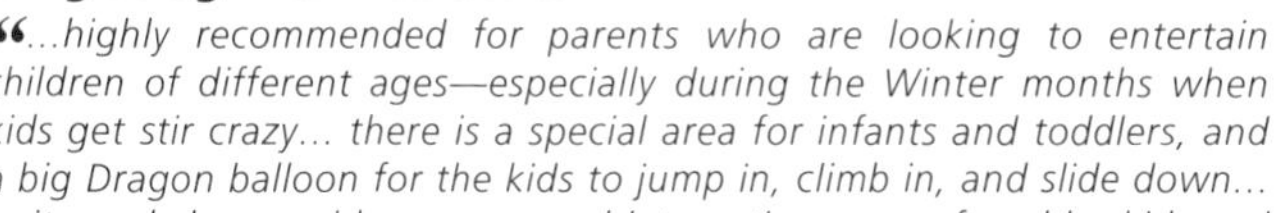

"...highly recommended for parents who are looking to entertain children of different ages—especially during the Winter months when kids get stir crazy... there is a special area for infants and toddlers, and a big Dragon balloon for the kids to jump in, climb in, and slide down... quite and clean... video games and interactive games for older kids and a food area for pizza, pretzels, and the like... kind of like Chuck E Cheese..."

Customer service .... ❹ $$$ .... Prices
Age range .... 2 yrs and up
WWW.ODYSSEYFUNWORLD.COM

TINLEY PARK—19111 S OAK PARK AVE (AT S HARLEM AVE); 708.429.3800; CALL FOR HOURS; FREE PARKING

YMCA

"...most of the Ys in the area have classes and activities for kids... swimming, gym classes, dance—even play groups for the really little ones... ... some facilities are nicer than others, but in general their programs are worth checking out... prices are more than reasonable for what is offered... the best bang for your buck... they have it all—great programs that meet the needs of a diverse range of families... check out their camps during the summer and school breaks..."

Customer service .... ❹ $$ .... Prices
Age range .... 3 mths and up
WWW.YMCA.COM

HARVEY—178 E 155TH ST (AT PARK AVE); 708.331.6500; M-F 9-8, SA 9-5; PARKING LOT

parks & playgrounds

City of Chicago

"lila picks"

★Fellger Park

★Indian Boundary Park

★Wicker Park

Archer Park

"...nice playground... the spary pool is great for those hot days during the summer... nice and always packed with kids..."

Equipment/play structures........... ❸ ❸ .... Maintenance

WWW.CHICAGOPARKDISTRICT.COM

KILBOURN PARK/KELVYN PARK/HERMOSA—4901 S KILBOURN AVE (AT W 49TH ST); 773.284.7029

Armour Square Park

"...the whole family enjoyed this park... very scenic... there's tennis, swimming, softball fields and a quarter mile trail... in 1906, the year after Armour Square opened to the public, President Theodore Roosevelt described the square as "the most notable civic achievement in any American city."..."

Equipment/play structures........... ❹ ❸ .... Maintenance

WWW.CHICAGOPARKDISTRICT.COM

BRIDGEPORT—3309 S SHIELDS AVE (AT W 33RD ST); 312.747.6012

Avalon Park

"...created in the 1920s with a long, interesting history... the church, community, and a local street pay homage to the English Isle of Avalon, believed to be the burial place of legendary King Arthur... includes play fields, a running track, tennis and horseshoe courts, and a combination shelter and comfort station..."

Equipment/play structures........... ❹ ❹ .... Maintenance

WWW.CHICAGOPARKDISTRICT.COM

SOUTH SIDE—1215 E 83RD ST (AT S AVALON AVE); 312.747.6015

Bessemer Park

"...offers several programs including boxing, swimming, and a Therapeutic Recreation Camp... come out and explore the Nature and Wildlife Gardens, these gardens have been planted with many native species that attract birds, butterflies, moths, and many other insects... kids love it and learn a lot about nature..."

Equipment/play structures........... ❺ ❹ .... Maintenance

WWW.CHICAGOPARKDISTRICT.COM

SOUTH SIDE—8930 S MUSKEGON AVE (AT E 90TH ST); 312.747.6023

Bixler Playlot

"...right in the heart of Hyde Park... great equipment for a variety of ages... water sprinkler all summer... a diverse scene—moms, dads and

nannies... of all the play areas in Hyde Park, this is probably the best known... there is a fence all around the playground... two different playgrounds—one for little ones and one for older kids... across the street from restaurants, a great coffee shop and a bank... ”

Equipment/play structures .... ❹ ❹ .... Maintenance

WWW.CHICAGOPARKDISTRICT.COM

SOUTH SIDE—5651 S KENWOOD AVE (AT 57TH)

Bogan Park ★★½☆☆

“*...this is a great park... lots of trees and interesting areas to go to... excellent softball and basketball programs...* ”

Equipment/play structures .... ❸ ❸ .... Maintenance

WWW.CHICAGOPARKDISTRICT.COM

FORD CITY—3939 W 79TH ST (AT S PULASKI RD); 312.747.6025

Brooks Park ★★★★☆

“*...a fun park for toddlers... good for playing, picnicking and people watching... Brooks Park houses baseball, softball, and soccer fields, a basketball court, a playground, tennis courts, and an indoor gym... programs, clubs, and classes are offered on a seasonal basis...* ”

Equipment/play structures .... ❹ ❹ .... Maintenance

WWW.CHICAGOPARKDISTRICT.COM

CHICAGO—7100 N HARLEM AVE (S OF TOUHY AVE); 773.631.4401

Caldwell Woods ★★★★☆

“*...we enjoy the great outdoors and the desirability of enjoying nature on foot which makes Caldwell Woods a great place for nature trails... I felt like a bird released from its cage and it seemed good to get one's feet on the earth and stride along... why not find out how good it feels to walk in the footsteps of history at Caldwell Woods...* ”

Equipment/play structures .... ❸ ❸ .... Maintenance

WWW.FOTP.ORG

PORTAGE PARK—6200 W DEVON AVE (AT N MERRIMAC AVE); DAILY 1-8; FREE PARKING

Calumet Park ★★★☆☆

“*...200 acres make up Calumet Park including the beach and some new play fields... the park's name pays tribute to the Calumet region, the name Calumet comes from the Norman-French word for peace pipes, "chamulet."... kids love the fishing, other activities include a model railroad club, basketball, and gymnastics...* ”

Equipment/play structures .... ❸ ❹ .... Maintenance

WWW.CHICAGOPARKDISTRICT.COM

SOUTH SIDE—9801 S AVE G (AT E 98TH ST); 312.747.6039

Chicago Beaches ★★★★☆

“*...the beaches are free, and it's always fun to have a picnic and build sand castles though... the beach is very close to a beautiful harbor, bird sanctuary, tall trees and an open park area for the little ones to run around... views from downtown beaches are extraordinary...* ”

Equipment/play structures .... ❸ ❸ .... Maintenance

WWW.CHICAGOPARKDISTRICT.COM

CHICAGO—312.747.2200; CHECK SCHEDULE ONLINE; FREE PARKING

Chicago River Walk ★★★☆☆

“*...beautiful during the day, but be careful after dark... ...* ”

Equipment/play structures .... ❸ ❸ .... Maintenance

WWW.CHICAGOPARKDISTRICT.COM

CHICAGO—E BRANCH OF THE CHICAGO RIVER; 312.742.7529; FREE PARKING

Chopin Park ★★★★★

"...this is a great park because all of the swings and sprinklers are fenced in... if you choose to walk around the park there is plenty of room even when there are baseball and football games going on... area by the sprinklers has benches and a cover for those hot summer days..."

Equipment/play structures........... ❹ ❹ .... Maintenance

WWW.CHICAGOPARKDISTRICT.COM

PORTAGE PARK—3420 N LONG AVE (AT W ROSCOE ST); 312.742.7606

Fellger Park ★★★★★

"...this is a wonderful park... there are so many fun things to play with, water for the kids, swings, slides and more, and a great area for picnics and sunbathing also... great park in great central location... very family-friendly—I've never been there when there weren't several kids around..."

Equipment/play structures........... ❹ ❹ .... Maintenance

WWW.CI.CHI.IL.US

ROSCOE VILLAGE/WEST LAKEVIEW—2000 W BELMONT AVE (AT N DAMEN AVE); 312.742.7785

Fellger Playlot ★★★★★

"...we love that they have a waterfall in this park... great for kids... be prepared for the ice cream truck and have water toys and bathing suits—there's some good water play here... there's also grass for picnicking on..."

Equipment/play structures........... ❺ ❹ .... Maintenance

WWW.CHICAGOPARKDISTRICT.COM

ROSCOE VILLAGE/WEST LAKEVIEW—2000 W BELMONT AVE (AT DAMEN AVE); 312.742.7785

Gill Park ★★★☆☆

"...a nice quiet little park... not much in the way of facilities, but it's a fun place to run around and play in..."

Equipment/play structures........... ❸ ❸ .... Maintenance

WWW.CHICAGOPARKDISTRICT.COM

LAKEVIEW/WRIGLEYVILLE—825 W SHERIDAN RD (AT N CLARENDON AVE); 312.742.7802

Goudy Square Playlot Park ★★★½☆

"...this park has something for all ages... it's big enough for the kids to really run around, yet small enough to make it easy to keep track of them... an extremely nice park... only problem is that it gets very crowded on the weekends..."

Equipment/play structures........... ❺ ❺ .... Maintenance

WWW.CHICAGOPARKDISTRICT.COM

EAST/WEST OLD TOWN GOLD COAST/STREETERVILLE—1255 N ASTOR ST (AT GOETHE ST); 312.742.7891

Grant Park ★★★★★

"...wonderful lakefront views make for relaxing walks with the stroller... if you have extra energy to burn off you can visit the aquarium... plenty of places to explore... lots of play structures spread through the park... always a good place for a picnic or birthday party..."

Equipment/play structures........... ❺ ❺ .... Maintenance

WWW.CHICAGOPARKDISTRICT.COM

LOOP—331 E RANDOLPH ST (AT S COLUMBUS DR); 312.742.7648

Gross Playground

"...the City of Chicago just redid the playground and landscaping... little playground with a spray pool and a sandbox... in the winter it's an ice rink... nice because you can easily watch your children..."

Equipment/play structures .... ❹ ❺ .... Maintenance

CHICAGO—2708 W LAWRENCE AVE (AT N CALIFORNIA AVE); 312.742.7528

Harold Washington Playlot Park

"...a good place to take the kids to play when you want some downtime by the lakefront... can get quite crowded when the local daycare and preschool groups show up... a big park with equipment for all ages... a little too close to Lakeshore Drive for my taste..."

Equipment/play structures .... ❹ ❹ .... Maintenance

WWW.CHICAGOPARKDISTRICT.COM

HYDE PARK—5200 S HYDE PARK BLVD (AT E HYDE PARK BLVD); 773.256.0903

Indian Boundary Park

"...a fantastic park... the biggest jungle gym in the city... a pond full of ducks and a big fountain for hot summer days... a huge sand box for kids to dig and build... great people watching... we love getting our play group together and going to this park... a cool field house in beautiful surroundings..."

Equipment/play structures .... ❺ ❹ .... Maintenance

WWW.CHICAGOPARKDISTRICT.COM

WEST ROGERS PARK—2500 W LUNT AVE (AT NORTH CAMPBELL AVE); DAILY 6-11, ZOO DAILY 8-4

Jefferson Playlot Park

"...beautiful park, well maintained, with equipment for young and older kids..."

Equipment/play structures .... ❺ ❺ .... Maintenance

WWW.CHICAGOPARKDISTRICT.COM

SOUTH LOOP—1640 S JEFFERSON ST (AT W 16TH ST); 773.685.3316

Juniper Park

"...great park although tiny... small, cute, friendly neighborhood park near the Southport Corridor... sandbox, baby swings and a water park for the warmer seasons!.."

Equipment/play structures .... ❹ ❹ .... Maintenance

WWW.CHICAGOPARKDISTRICT.COM

NORTH CENTER/ST BEN'S—3652 N GREENVIEW AVE (AT W ADDISON ST)

Lincoln Park

"...wonderful park with plenty of room to run around, picnic, etc... great place to take children for a bit of nature in the city..."

Equipment/play structures .... ❺ ❺ .... Maintenance

WWW.EGOV.CITYOFCHICAGO.ORG

LINCOLN PARK/DEPAUL/OLD TOWN—2045 N LINCOLN PARK W (AT N CLARK ST); 312.742.7529

Loyola Park

"...lots of activities here—swimming, great beach, playground... infant swings, wall painting and baseball field... a popular spot for summer events and picnics... the tot lot program at the park has been one of the best ways for us to meet new kids in the neighborhood..."

Equipment/play structures............❹ ❹ ....Maintenance

WWW.CHICAGOPARKDISTRICT.COM

SHERIDAN PARK/UPTOWN—1230 W GREENLEAF AVE (AT N SHERIDAN RD); 773.262.8605

Millennium Park ★★★★☆

"...the city has done a fantastic job of creating a beautiful Mecca right in the middle of the city—it has something for everyone! kids love the new fountain... the great lawn is magnificent with an acoustically perfect sound system... gardens and restaurants are very clean, though they do get crowded... free concerts, exhibitions, events and tours offer something for everyone!..."

Equipment/play structures............❺ ❺ ....Maintenance

WWW.CITYOFCHICAGO.ORG

LOOP—MICHIGAN AVE (AT MONROE AND RANDOLPH STS); 312.747.2200; DAILY 6-11; STREET PARKING

North Avenue Beach ★★★☆☆

"...the new beach house has upper decks and portholes for enjoying one of the best views in the city... bikers, runners, walkers and rollerbladers stream down the redesigned lakefront trail... can get rowdy there, thanks to the volleyball courts, outdoor gym, and bar..."

Equipment/play structures............❸ ❸ ....Maintenance

WWW.CHICAGOPARKDISTRICT.COM

LINCOLN PARK/DEPAUL/OLD TOWN—LAKE SHORE DR (AT NORTH AVE); 312.742.7529; MEMORIAL DAY-LABOR DAY DAILY 9-9:30PM; FREE PARKING

Oak Street Beach ★★★★★

"...seems to have an ideal atmosphere for families with small children... a calmer atmosphere than North Avenue beach, which is only 1/2 mile away..."

Equipment/play structures............❹ ❺ ....Maintenance

WWW.EGOV.CITYOFCHICAGO.ORG

EAST/WEST OLD TOWN GOLD COAST/STREETERVILLE—1000 N LAKE SHORE DR (AT N MICHIGAN AVE); 312.747.0832

Oz Park ★★★★☆

"...nice neighborhood park, with a good play area that is safely fenced in... great park for slightly older kids, the equipment is wood which makes me a little hesitant to go there as often as I would like... beautiful, larger park with lots of green space and a play area for toddlers and preschool age kids... plenty of shade for a picnic, too... my kids love it, but not ideal during school time as high school students are dismissing..."

Equipment/play structures............❹ ❹ ....Maintenance

WWW.CHICAGOPARKDISTRICT.COM

LINCOLN PARK/DEPAUL/OLD TOWN—2021 N BURLING ST (AT W DICKENS AVE); 312.742.7898

Peterson Park ★★★★½

"...a couple of playgrounds and lots of tennis and basketball courts... this park is probably best known for its fantastic gymnastics and dance programs at the field house... plenty of structures and space for kids to play... always busy and good for meeting new friends..."

Equipment/play structures............❺ ❺ ....Maintenance

WWW.CHICAGOPARKDISTRICT.COM

NORTH RAVENSWOOD—5801 N PULASKI (AT W THORNDALE AVE); 312.742.7584

Portage Park

"...been going here since i was a kid... beautiful park with lots to do... has everything, including a pool, large field, beautiful gardens, and a playground for infants and toddlers..."

Equipment/play structures .... ❺ ❺ .... Maintenance

WWW.CHICAGOPARKDISTRICT.COM

IRVING PARK/MAYFAIR—4100 N LONG AVE (AT W BELLE PLAINE AVE); 312.742.7634

Ridge Park

"...the park is very peaceful and in a wonderful setting... unfortunately it isn't always that well maintained and I wish the park service would clean it more often... the playground is nice and there are lots of trees to find shade... plenty of space for impromptu picnics..."

Equipment/play structures .... ❹ ❹ .... Maintenance

WWW.CHICAGOPARKDISTRICT.COM

SOUTH SIDE—9625 S LONGWOOD (AT W 96TH PL)

Sunshine Playlot

"...right off North Pond, you can feed the ducks and admire the juxtaposition of nature and downtown skyscrapers in the vista before running your little ones ragged at Sunshine Playlot... swings, sand box, monkey bars, tire swing and slides in this well worn, but loved playground..."

Equipment/play structures .... ❸ ❷ .... Maintenance

WWW.EGOV.CITYOFCHICAGO.ORG

LINCOLN PARK/DEPAUL/OLD TOWN—DEMING ST (AT LAKEVIEW ST)

Walsh Playground Park

"...a great park with the added bonus of an off-leash dog area—that way our whole family can go... the facilities are quite nice... lots of Wicker Park and Bucktown parents bring their kids here... pretty standard playground equipment that is well maintained..."

Equipment/play structures .... ❹ ❹ .... Maintenance

WWW.CHICAGOPARKDISTRICT.COM

BUCKTOWN—1722 N ASHLAND AVE (AT W WABANSIA AVE); 312.742.7529

Washington Square Park

WWW.CHICAGOPARKDISTRICT.COM

EAST/WEST OLD TOWN GOLD COAST/STREETERVILLE—901 N CLARK ST (AT W WALTON ST); 312.747.2200

Welles Park

"...pretty little park with a nice gazebo, which is used for outdoor concerts, and storytelling, and a great recreational program for preschoolers and toddlers... lots of activity and nice people ..."

Equipment/play structures .... ❹ ❹ .... Maintenance

WWW.CHICAGOPARKDISTRICT.COM

RAVENSWOOD—2333 W SUNNYSIDE AVE (BETWEEN MONTROSE AND WESTERN AVE)

Wicker Park

"...fun park with a brand new playground... it's our favorite place in the summer... fantastic playground, safe and fun equipment, lots of kids and parents, great location... beautiful grounds... dogs are usually kept to the dog run..."

Equipment/play structures .... ❹ ❹ .... Maintenance

WWW.CI.CHI.IL.US

WICKER PARK/UKRANIAN VILLAGE—1425 N DAMEN AVE (AT W SCHILLER ST); 312.742.7553

Northwestern Suburbs

Banta Park

"...Arlington Heights' central park with mature trees and bushes, play equipment for children of all ages, a paved area for basketball, and is the proposed site for a new splash park..."

Equipment/play structures .... ❸ ❸ .... Maintenance

WWW.AHPD.ORG

ARLINGTON HEIGHTS—S OF MINER ST (BTWN PHELPS & WATERMAN STS); DAILY 5-11

parks & playgrounds

Northern Suburbs

Heller Nature Center

WWW.HELLERNATURECENTER.ORG

HIGHLAND PARK—2821 RIDGE RD; 847.433.6901; CHECK SCHEDULE ONLINE

Village Green Park

"...3 large play areas with slides, ramps tunnels and swings... be prepared to empty lots of sand out of your kids' shoes... summer concerts in the Gazebo..."

Equipment/play structures............ ❸ ❸ ....Maintenance

WWW.NBPARKS.ORG

NORTHBROOK—SHERMER RD (AT WALTERS AVE)

Western Suburbs

"lila picks"

★Naperville Riverwalk

Camera Park ★★★★☆

"...a great park for families with younger and older children... it has separate little and big kid sections... a ton of open grassy areas—great to fly kites or just practice running... a nice path frames the entire park..."

Equipment/play structures .... ❹ ❺ .... Maintenance

WWW.GLENDALEHEIGHTS.ORG

GLENDALE HEIGHTS—101 E FULLERTON (AT PRESIDENT ST); 630.909.5302

Firetruck Park (Huntington Estates) ★★★☆☆

"...my son loves the fire truck/sandbox, but I wish there was more seating for parents and that the parking wasn't so far away..."

Equipment/play structures .... ❸ ❸ .... Maintenance

WWW.NAPERVILLE.IL.US

NAPERVILLE—828 ROCKBRIDGE DR (AT NAPER BLVD); 630.420.6111

Harvester Park ★★★★☆

"...lots of great activities for all ages... they have a special event every summer where everyone, including parents, will have hot dogs, chips and a drink... all the kids will participate in a park-wide scavenger hunt that will challenge their detective skills (parents are encouraged to help)..."

Equipment/play structures .... ❹ ❹ .... Maintenance

WWW.BRPARKS.ORG

BURR RIDGE—HARVESTER DR (AT S ELM ST)

Helmut Berens Park ★★★★★

"...my favorite place to take the children... been going there since I was a sprout myself... redeveloped in 2004: new youth and tot playground equipment, a spray park, batting cages, put golf, running/walking paths, baseball diamonds, and soccer fields..."

Equipment/play structures .... ❺ ❺ .... Maintenance

WWW.EPD.ORG

ELMHURST—493 N OAKLAWN AVE (AT W CROCKETT AVE); 630.993.8900

Hummer Park ★★★★☆

"...award winning park that has impeccable upkeep... lots to play on... also has huge shelter for parties/picnics..."

Equipment/play structures .... ❺ ❺ .... Maintenance

WWW.DOWNERS.US

DOWNERS GROVE—4833 FAIRVIEW (AT WILSON ST); 630.434.5500

Naperville Riverwalk ★★★★★

"...a beautifully landscaped riverwalk complete with covered bridges, fountains, seating areas, and grassy areas... a fabulous place to walk and watch performances in summertime evenings... don't forget to bring breadcrumbs to feed the ducks... know that there are rowdy teenagers who hang out here... what a great place to take a stroll with your family on a nice day..."

Equipment/play structures............❹ ❹..............................Maintenance

WWW.NAPERVILLE.IL.US

NAPERVILLE—300 E 5TH AVE (OFF WASHINGTON ST); 630.420.6111

Priory Park ★★★★½

"...a terrific, fun park with lots of newer well-maintained equipment that appeals to toddlers and grade-school aged children... well-lit and safe, with abundant parking, vending machines, restrooms available..."

Equipment/play structures............❹ ❹..............................Maintenance

WWW.OPRFCHAMBER.ORG

RIVER FOREST—7200 W DIVISION ST (AT N HARLEM AVE); 708.848.8151

Rehm Park ★★★★★

"...wonderful pool and lots of fun... a variety of people and beautifully maintained... great place to go if you want to meet people or just relax with your child..."

Equipment/play structures............❺ ❺..............................Maintenance

WWW.OAKPARKPARKS.COM

OAK PARK—900 GUNDERSON AVE (AT GARFIELD ST)

Ty Warner Park ★★★★★

"...offers a large variety of outdoor recreational opportunities... three multipurpose ball fields anchored by a concession building complete with handicapped accessible washrooms... courtyard laid out with benches, decorative lighting, stone masonry and brick work... a large garden gazebo on a great lawn is host to our annual summer series of "Concerts in the Park"..."

Equipment/play structures............❺ ❺..............................Maintenance

WWW.WPD4FUN.ORG/PARKS/TYWARNER.HTM

WESTMONT—PLAZA DR (AT N CASS AVE)

Wilder Park ★★★★★

"...beautiful setting, plenty of things for kids of all ages... love the tot playground for smaller toddlers... great walking paths, and plenty of parking... this is a great place to take the children... very clean next to a great downtown... you could even walk there from the train..."

Equipment/play structures............❺ ❺..............................Maintenance

WWW.EPD.ORG

ELMHURST—175 PROSPECT AVE (AT W ARTHUR ST); 630.993.8900

restaurants

City of Chicago

"lila picks"

- ★Ann Sather
- ★Ed Debevic's Short Orders Deluxe
- ★Kitsch'n
- ★Leona's
- ★Lou Malnati's Pizzeria
- ★Super Dawg
- ★Wishbone Restaurant

American Girl Place

"...fairy tale-like setting for a little girl's tea party... take your daughter for tea and have her bring her doll... lovely decor and fun atmosphere... high prices make this more of a special occasion place..."

Children's menu .... ✓ | $$$ .... Prices
Changing station .... ✗ | ❹ .... Customer service
Highchairs/boosters .... ✗ | ❸ .... Stroller access

WWW.AMERICANGIRLPLACE.COM

NEAR NORTH—111 E CHICAGO AVE (AT N RUSH ST); 312.943.9400; SU 9-7, M-TH 10-7, F 10-9, SA 9-9

Ann Sather

"...super Swedish food in a fun atmosphere... ABBA Brunch on the first Sunday of every month (Milwaukee Ave location)... great place for families... terrific food, great menu... you may have to wait, but it's often packed with babies and kids... Swedish pancakes are a must..."

Children's menu .... ✗ | $$ .... Prices
Changing station .... ✗ | ❹ .... Customer service
Highchairs/boosters .... ✓ | ❹ .... Stroller access

WWW.ANNSATHER.COM

EDGEWATER—5207 N CLARK ST (AT W FOSTER ST); 773.271.6677; M W TH-F 7-2:30 SA-SU 7-4

LAKEVIEW/WRIGLEYVILLE—3411 N BROADWAY ST (AT ROSCOE ST); 773.305.0024; M-F 7-3, SA-SU 7-4

LAKEVIEW/WRIGLEYVILLE—3416 N SOUTHPORT AVE (AT ROSCOE ST); 773.404.4475; DAILY 7-2

LAKEVIEW/WRIGLEYVILLE—929 W BELMONT AVE (OFF CLARK ST); 773.348.2378; M-T 7-3, W-SU 7-9

WICKER PARK/UKRANIAN VILLAGE—1448 N MILWAUKEE AVE (AT EVERGREEN AVE); 773.394.1812; DAILY 8-3

Benihana

"...stir-fry meals are always prepared in front of you—it keeps everyone entertained, parents and kids alike... chefs often perform especially for the little ones... tables sit about 10 people, so it

encourages talking with other diners... tend to be pretty loud so it's pretty family friendly... delicious for adults and fun for kids... ❞

Children's menu .... ✗ $$$ .... Prices
Changing station.......................... ✓ ❹........................ Customer service
Highchairs/boosters .... ✓ ❸............................Stroller access

WWW.BENIHANA.COM

EAST/WEST OLD TOWN GOLD COAST/STREETERVILLE—166 E SUPERIOR ST (AT N MICHIGAN AVE); 312.664.9643; M-TH 11:30-2, 5-10, F-SA 5-11, SU 1-9:30

Big Bowl ★★★★☆

❝*...surprisingly kid-friendly—they will bring you an order of white rice immediately, and have crayons, etc. for the kids... they immediately provide the children with something to nibble on and games to play... loud restaurant that hides noise well... the menu has mac and cheese for picky eaters and a couple of great appetizers... each kids' meal comes with a drink, a bowl of white rice, and a takeout Chinese container with crayons, chopsticks, and something to color on... overall a huge hit for both parents and kids...* ❞

Children's menu .... ✓ $$ .... Prices
Changing station.......................... ✓ ❹........................ Customer service
Highchairs/boosters .... ✓ ❹............................Stroller access

WWW.BIGBOWL.COM

GOLD COAST/STREETERVILLE—6 E CEDAR ST (AT N RUSH ST); 312.640.8888; SU-TH 11:30-10, F-SA 11:30-11; VALET PARKING

RIVER NORTH/RIVER WEST—60 EAST OHIO ST (BETWEEN RUSH ST AND WABASH AVE); 312.951.1888; SU-TH 11:30-10, F-SA 11-11

Cafe De Luca ★★★½☆

❝*...kid-friendly during the day... loud, but not too loud... they even gave us a free terry cloth bib... easy dining-spot with great service... lots to look at for baby ... service is fast and the food is very good... perfect lunch spot...* ❞

Children's menu .... ✓ $$ .... Prices
Changing station.......................... ✓ ❺........................ Customer service
Highchairs/boosters .... ✓ ❹............................Stroller access

BUCKTOWN—1721 N DAMEN AVE (AT N CLAREMONT AVE); 773.342.6000; M-TH 6-10, F-SA 7-12, SU 7-9; PARKING LOT

Cafe Selmarie ★★★★☆

❝*...this outdoor cafe is wonderful when the weather cooperates... excellent food... the staff is friendly and accommodating...* ❞

Children's menu .... ✓ $$$ .... Prices
Changing station.......................... ✓ ❸........................ Customer service
Highchairs/boosters .... ✓ ❸............................Stroller access

WW.CAFESELMARIE.COM

LINCOLN SQUARE—4729 N LINCOLN AVE (AT GIDDINGS PLAZA); 773.989.5595; M 11-3, T-TH 8-10, F 8-11, SA 8-11 SU 10-10; STREET PARKING

California Pizza Kitchen ★★★★½

❝*...you can't go wrong with their fabulous pizza... always clean... the food's great, the kids drinks all come with a lid... the staff is super friendly to kids... crayons and coloring books keep little minds busy... most locations have a place for strollers at the front... no funny looks or attitude when breastfeeding... open atmosphere with friendly service... tables are well spaced so you don't feel like your kid is annoying the diners nearby (it's usually full of kids anyway)...* ❞

Children's menu .... ✓ $$ .... Prices
Changing station.......................... ✓ ❹........................ Customer service

restaurants

Highchairs/boosters	✓	❹	Stroller access

WWW.CPK.COM

EAST/WEST OLD TOWN GOLD COAST/STREETERVILLE—835 N MICHIGAN AVE (AT E PEARSON AVE); 312.787.7300; M-SA 11-10, SU 12-9

RIVER NORTH/RIVER WEST—52 E OHIO ST (AT N WABASH AVE); 312.787.6075; M-TH 10:30-10, F-SA 10:30-11, SU 11:30-9:30

WICKER PARK/UKRANIAN VILLAGE—939 W N AVE (AT N SHEFFIELD AVE); 312.357.1281; M-TH 11-10 F-SA 11-11, SU 11:30-9

Caro Mio ★★★★½

"...a wonderful Italian restaurant featuring homemade specialties in a cozy neighborhood atmosphere... we've brought our daughter (now 6 months old) there a few times and always felt welcome... the staff is lovely and on the ball... it's a small space and a little tight for strollers, but they do have highchairs and I always see small children there... a great change of pace from other 'family' restaurants... it's a step up but not stuffy..."

Children's menu	×	$$	Prices
Changing station	×	❺	Customer service
Highchairs/boosters	✓	❹	Stroller access

WWW.CAROMIOCHICAGO.COM

RAVENSWOOD—1825 W WILSON AVE (AT N RAVENSWOOD AVE); 773.275.5000; M-TH 11-10, F 11-11, SA 4-11 SU 3-9

Cheesecake Factory, The ★★★★☆

"...although their cheesecake is good, we come here for the kid-friendly atmosphere and selection of good food... eclectic menu has something for everyone... they will bring your tot a plate of yogurt, cheese, bananas and bread free of charge... we love how flexible they are—they'll make whatever my kids want... lots of mommies here... always fun and always crazy... no real kids menu, but the pizza is great to share... waits can be really long..."

Children's menu	×	$$$	Prices
Changing station	✓	❹	Customer service
Highchairs/boosters	✓	❸	Stroller access

WWW.THECHEESECAKEFACTORY.COM

EAST/WEST OLD TOWN GOLD COAST/STREETERVILLE—875 N MICHIGAN AVE (AT E CHESTNUT ST); 312.337.1101; SU-TH 11-11:30, F-SA 11-12:30; PARKING AVAILABLE

RIVER NORTH/RIVER WEST—600 N MICHIGAN AVE (AT E OHIO ST); 312.254.0631; SU-TH 11-11:30, F-SA 11-12:30; PARKING AVAILABLE

Corner Bakery Cafe ★★★½☆

"...best kid's grilled cheese in town and excellent oatmeal raisin cookies... very nice, kid-friendly... a tastier and healthier alternative to fast food... selection ranges from sandwiches to pasta to salads and pizza... great for a quick bite... space is limited so strollers can be tricky ..."

Children's menu	✓	$$	Prices
Changing station	×	❹	Customer service
Highchairs/boosters	✓	❸	Stroller access

WWW.CORNERBAKERY.COM

CHICAGO—120 S LASALLE BLVD (AT MONROE ST); 312.269.9100; M-F 6:30-5

EAST/WEST OLD TOWN GOLD COAST/STREETERVILLE—1121 N STATE ST (OFF DIVISION ST); 312.787.1969; SU-TH 7-8, F-SA 7-9

LOOP—140 S DEARBORN ST (AT MARBLE PL); 312.920.9100; M-F 6:30-5:30

LOOP—1400 S LAKE SHORE DR (OFF ROOSEVELT RD); 312.588.1040; DAILY 9-5

LOOP—188 W WASHINGTON ST (AT WELLS ST); 312.263.4258; M-F 6:30-6

LOOP—200 N LASALLE BLVD (AT RANDOLPH ST); 312.726.7244; M-F 6:30-6

LOOP—224 S MICHIGAN AVE (AT ADAMS ST); 312.431.7600; M-F 6:30-8, SA 7:30-8, SU 7:30-5

LOOP—233 S WACKER DR (AT SEARS TOWER); 312.466.0200; M-F 6-5

LOOP—35 E MONROE ST (AT WABASH AVE); 312.372.0072; M-SA 6:30-8, SU 6:30-6

LOOP—360 N MICHIGAN AVE (OFF WACKER DR); 312.236.2400; M-F 6:30-6, SA 7-7, SU 7-5:30

LOOP—444 W JACKSON BLVD (AT CANAL ST); 312.575.1410; M-F 6-7, SA 8:30-2

LOOP—56 W RANDOLPH (AT DEARBORN ST); 312.346.9492; M-F 6:30-7:30, SA 8-7:30, SU 9-7:30

RIVER NORTH/RIVER WEST—516 N CLARK ST (AT LA SALLE BLVD); 312.644.8100; M-F 6:30-7, SA 7-6, SU 7-3

RIVER NORTH/RIVER WEST—676 N ST CLAIR ST (AT HURON ST); 312.266.2570; M-F 6:30-8, SA 7-7, SU 7-6

WEST LOOP—123 N WACKER DR (AT RANDOLPH ST); 312.372.3624; M-F 6-4

WEST LOOP—222 S RIVERSIDE PLAZA (AT ADAMS ST); 312.441.0821; M-F 6:30-8, SA 7:30-2:30, SU 7:30-1:30

WEST LOOP—500 W MADISON ST (AT WASHINGTON BLVD); 312.715.0800; M-F 7:30-7, SA 9-3

Deluxe Diner

Children's menu .... ✓ ✗ .... Changing station
Highchairs/boosters .... ✓

WWW.DELUXE-DINER.COM

EDGEWATER—6349 N CLARK ST (AT W HIGHLAND AVE); 773.743.8244; OPEN 24 HOURS

Ed Debevic's Short Orders Deluxe ★★★★★

"...classic 50's style diner... a popular place for kids and parents... the food is great and 'the help' is even better... servers make dining out with kids an enjoyable experience... plenty of entertainment, with the waitstaff dancing on the counters every half hour... great burgers and shakes..."

Children's menu .... ✓ $$ .... Prices
Changing station .... ✓ ❹ .... Customer service
Highchairs/boosters .... ✓ ❸ .... Stroller access

WWW.EDDEBEVICS.COM

RIVER NORTH/RIVER WEST—640 N WELLS ST (AT W ERIE ST); 312.664.1707; DAILY 11-10; STREET PARKING

El Cid 2

Children's menu .... ✗ ✗ .... Changing station
Highchairs/boosters .... ✓

LOGAN SQUARE—2645 N KEDZIE AVE (AT N MILWAUKEE AVE); 773.395.0505; SU-TH9-12, F-SA 9-2

ESPN Zone

"...loud and crazy with average food... kids like to play the arcade games and carry the beeper, which alerts diners when their table is ready... we avoid it during big sporting events... lots of room for strollers... staff is friendly and accommodating..."

Children's menu .... ✓ $$$ .... Prices
Changing station .... ✓ ❹ .... Customer service
Highchairs/boosters .... ✓ ❸ .... Stroller access

WWW.ESPNZONE.COM

RIVER NORTH—43 E OHIO ST (AT N WABASH AVE); 312.644.3776; SU-TH 11:30-12, F 11:30-1, SA 11-1

Feast

"...eclectic cuisine... they always seem to tolerate kids pretty well... plenty of space between tables to accommodate the highchairs... breakfast, lunch and dinner... enough sound so a baby's crying will not disturb the other patrons... not ideal for kids, but the brunch is always packed with kids and babies..."

Children's menu	✓	$$	Prices
Changing station	×	❹	Customer service
Highchairs/boosters	✓	❸	Stroller access

WWW.FEASTRESTAURANT.COM

WICKER PARK/UKRANIAN VILLAGE—1616 N DAMEN AVE (OFF MILWAUKEE AVE); 773.772.7100; M-TH 11:30-3 5:30-10, F 11:30-3 5:30-11, SA 9-3 5:30-11, SU 9-3 5-9; STREET PARKING

Flat Top Grill

"...you choose your food and they cook it... awesome Mongolian BBQ... especially fun for the little ones—lots to look at, good bread, and BBQ meat... you need at least two adults or a mobile kid because you have to leave your seat to make your meal... kids under 4 eat free..."

Children's menu	×	$$	Prices
Changing station	×	❹	Customer service
Highchairs/boosters	✓	❹	Stroller access

WWW.FLATTOPGRILL.COM

LAKEVIEW/WRIGLEYVILLE—3200 N SOUTHPORT AVE (AT ASHLAND AVE); 773.665.8100; SU-TH 11:30-10, F-SA 11:30-11

LINCOLN PARK/DEPAUL/OLD TOWN—319 W NORTH AVE (OFF LA SALLE BLVD); 312.787.7676; SU-TH 11:30-10, F-SA 11:30-11

WEST LOOP—1000 W WASHINGTON BLVD (AT N MORGAN ST); 312.829.4800; SU-TH 11-9:30, F-SA 11-10:30, SU 12-9:30

Gino's East Of Chicago

Children's menu	✓	✓	Changing station
Highchairs/boosters	✓		

WWW.GINOSEAST.COM

LAKEVIEW/WRIGLEYVILLE—2801 N LINCOLN AVE (AT N RACINE AVE); 773.327.3737; M-TH 11-10:30, F-SA 11-12, SU 12-10:30

RIVER NORTH/RIVER WEST—633 N WELLS ST (AT W ONTARIO ST); 312.943.1124; M-TH 11-9, F-SA 11-11, SU 12-9

Handlebar Bar & Grill

"...awesome... mostly veggie... kid-friendly... decor is great with most of the artwork revolving around bikes... small outdoor patio and great beer... good Sunday brunch..."

Children's menu	×	$	Prices
Changing station	×	❺	Customer service
Highchairs/boosters	✓	❺	Stroller access

WWW.HANDLEBARCHICAGO.COM

BUCKTOWN—2311 W N AVE (AT N OADLEY AVE); 773.384.9546; M-F 4-12AM, SA-SU 1-12AM; STREET PARKING

Hard Rock Cafe

"...fun and tasty if you can get in... the lines can be horrendous so be sure to check in with them first... a good spot if you have tots in tow—food tastes good and the staff is clearly used to messy eaters... hectic and loud... fun for adults as well as kids..."

Children's menu	✓	$$$	Prices

Changing station .... ✓ ❹ .... Customer service
Highchairs/boosters .... ✓ ❸ .... Stroller access

WWW.HARDROCK.COM

EAST/WEST OLD TOWN GOLD COAST/STREETERVILLE—63 W ONTARIO ST (AT DEARBORN ST); 312.943.2252; M-TH 11-12, F-SA 11-1, SU 11:30-12

Hilary's Urban Eatery

"...a wonderful dining experience... unless your child sits in a regular chair or you have a stroller with you, eat somewhere else—it can get crazy crowded... avoid the busy brunch time on weekends... wholesome yummy food, delightful decor, and the friendliest staffs... we love eating out on the patio..."

Children's menu .... ✓ $$ .... Prices
Changing station .... × ❺ .... Customer service
Highchairs/boosters .... ✓ ❸ .... Stroller access

WWW.HILARYSURBANEATERY.COM

WICKER PARK/UKRANIAN VILLAGE—1500 W DIVISION ST (AT N MILWAUKEE AVE); 773.235.4327; DAILY 8-10 EXCEPT W

Ina's

"...delicious breakfast food... nice staff—they make you feel like you're at your favorite Aunt's house... family friendly—you'll definitely see infants and toddlers at brunch on weekends..."

Children's menu .... ✓ $ .... Prices
Changing station .... ✓ ❺ .... Customer service
Highchairs/boosters .... ✓ ❸ .... Stroller access

WWW.BREAKFASTQUEEN.COM

WEST LOOP MARKET DISTRICT—1235 W RANDOLPH ST (AT ELIZABETH ST); 312.226.8227; M-TH 7-3 5-9, F 7-3 5-10, SA 8-3 5-10, SU 8-2 ; STREET PARKING

Indian Garden

"...fast and easy, it's a fun place to eat with kids... lunch buffet is a great way to have a nice and very tasty hot meal without having to worry about the wait... our 20-month-old loves to munch on the nan bread and slurp a mango lassi... lots of rice and vegetable options... fruit and yogurt is always available..."

Children's menu .... × $$$ .... Prices
Changing station .... × ❹ .... Customer service
Highchairs/boosters .... × ❸ .... Stroller access

RIVER NORTH/RIVER WEST—247 E ONTARIO ST (AT N MICHIGAN AVE); 312.280.4910; DAILY 11:30-2, 5-10

WEST ROGERS PARK—2546 W DEVON AVE (AT N MAPLEWOOD AVE); 773.338.2929; DAILY 11:30-3, 5-10,

John's Place

"...cozy and wonderful... great home-style cooking... good kiddies meals... a popular spot to bring babies on weekend mornings... friendly staff and gracious owner help kids feel welcome... look for the wine specials... a place where you can bring kids without a second thought..."

Children's menu .... ✓ $$$ .... Prices
Changing station .... ✓ ❹ .... Customer service
Highchairs/boosters .... ✓ ❸ .... Stroller access

LINCOLN PARK/DEPAUL/OLD TOWN—1200 W WEBSTER AVE (AT N RACINE AVE); 773.525.6670; T-TH 11-10, F 11-11, SA 8-11, SU 8-9; STREET PARKING

Johnny Rockets

"...burgers, fries and a shake served up in a 50's style diner... we love the singing waiters—they're always good for a giggle... my daughter is enthralled with the juke box and straw dispenser... sit at the counter and watch the cooks prepare the food... simple, satisfying and always a hit with the little ones..."

Children's menu ✓ | $$ Prices
Changing station ✗ | ❹ Customer service
Highchairs/boosters ✓ | ❸ Stroller access

WWW.JOHNNYROCKETS.COM

EAST/WEST OLD TOWN GOLD COAST/STREETERVILLE—901 N RUSH ST (AT DELAWARE PL); 312.337.3900; M-F 7-1, SA 7-2, SU 8-1; FREE PARKING

Julium Meinl Cafe

"...a popular meeting place for local moms and babies... strollers are allowed and there are plenty of highchairs for everyone .. staff seem to love babies, too..."

Children's menu ✗ | $$$ Prices
Changing station ✗ | ❺ Customer service
Highchairs/boosters ✓ | ❺ Stroller access

LAKEVIEW/WRIGLEYVILLE—3601 N SOUTHPORT AVE (AT W ADDISON ST); 773.868.1857; M-TH 6-10, F 6-11, SA 7-11, SU 7-10

Kitsch'n

"...delicious comfort food in a 70's retro scene... very 'groovy'... kids love playing with the toys on the tables... nice outdoor seating... great strolling in the neighborhood... a fun atmosphere, but not a lot of room for strollers... the back room is often filled with toddlers and parents—a good place to make new friends..."

Children's menu ✓ | $$ Prices
Changing station ✓ | ❹ Customer service
Highchairs/boosters ✓ | ❷ Stroller access

WWW.KITSCHN.COM

ROSCOE VILLAGE/WEST LAKEVIEW—2005 W ROSCOE ST (AT N DAMEN AVE); 773.248.7372; T-SA 9-10, SU-M 9-3; STREET PARKING

ROSCOE VILLAGE/WEST LAKEVIEW—600 W CHICAGO AVE (AT LARRABEE ST); 312.644.1500; M 8-9, T-F 8-10, SA 9-10, SU 9-9; STREET PARKING

Leona's ★★★★★

"...huge portions of tasty salads, pizza and other Italian goodies... thin crust and deep dish pizza... casual setting with awesome staff—the waitresses took turns walking our fussy daughter around while my husband and I finished our dinner... quick, friendly service except on weekends when it's busy... crayons, stickers, toddler cups with straws... good vegetarian (even vegan) items..."

Children's menu ✓ | $$ Prices
Changing station ✗ | ❹ Customer service
Highchairs/boosters ✓ | ❹ Stroller access

WWW.LEONAS.COM

AVONDALE—3877 N ELSTON AVE (AT DRAKE AVE); 773.267.7287; M-TH 11:30-10, F 11:30-11, SA 12-11, SU 12-10

EDGEWATER—6935 N SHERIDAN RD (AT W MORSE AVE); 773.764.5757; M-TH 11-11, F-SA 11-1, SU 11-10:30

HYDE PARK—1236 E 53RD ST (AT S WOODLAWN AVE); 773.363.2600; M-TH 11:30-10:30, F 11:30-12:30, SA 12-12:30, SU 12:30-10:30

LAKEVIEW/WRIGLEYVILLE—3215 N SHEFFIELD AVE (AT W BELMONT AVE); 773.327.8861; SU-TH 11-11:30, F-SA 11-1

MEDICAL VILLAGE—1419 W TAYLOR ST (AT S LOOMIS ST); 312.850.2222; DAILY 11-10; FREE PARKING

RIVER NORTH/RIVER WEST—646 N FRANKLIN ST (AT W ERIE ST); 312.867.0101; DAILY 11-10; FREE PARKING

SOUTH SIDE—11060 S WESTERN AVE (AT W 111TH ST); 773.881.7700; M-TH 11:30-10:30, F-SA 11:30-11:30, SU 12-10

WICKER PARK/UKRANIAN VILLAGE—1936 W AUGUSTA BLVD (AT N WINCHESTER AVE); 773.292.4300; M-TH 11-11, F-SA 11-1, SU 11-10:30

Leona's Daughters Restaurant

Children's menu ✓ ✓ Changing station
Highchairs/boosters ✓

WWW.LEONAS.COM

SHERIDAN PARK/UPTOWN—6935 N SHERIDAN RD (AT W MORSE AVE); 773.764.5757; M-TH 10:30-11, F-SA 11:30-12:30, SU 10:30-10:30

Lou Malnati's Pizzeria

"...all I can say is 'yum!'—simply the best pizza in the area... great food, not really stroller friendly, but sometimes it gets a little loud, so if your kids are restless, no one will even know... great food for kids and adults... prices are reasonable and the atmosphere is great..."

Children's menu ✗ $$$ Prices
Changing station ✗ ❹ Customer service
Highchairs/boosters ✓ ❸ Stroller access

WWW.LOUMALNATIS.COM

RIVER NORTH/RIVER WEST—439 N WELLS ST (AT W HUBBARD ST); 312.828.9800; M-TH 11-11, F-SA 11-12, SU 12-10

Lou Mitchell's Restaurant

Children's menu ✗ ✗ Changing station
Highchairs/boosters ✓

LOOP—565 W JACKSON BLVD (AT S CLINTON ST); 312.939.3111; M-SA 5:30-3, SU 7-3

Margies Candies

Children's menu ✗ ✗ Changing station
Highchairs/boosters ✗

WWW.MARGIESCANDIES.COM

CHICAGO—1960 N WESTERN AVE (AT W ARMITAGE AVE); 773.384.1035; M-TH 9-12 AM F-SA 9-1AM

McCormick & Schmicks

"...steak and seafood are the mainstay but the menu is broad... terrific happy-hour menu... a little more formal than your regular 'tot-friendly' restaurant, but the staff is great and goes out of their way to make sure you're comfortable... try to get one of the banquet rooms—it makes breastfeeding much easier... good food for adults and more than enough for the little ones too..."

Children's menu ✓ $$$ Prices
Changing station ✓ ❹ Customer service
Highchairs/boosters ✓ ❹ Stroller access

WWW.MCCORMICKANDSCHMICKS.COM

EAST/WEST OLD TOWN GOLD COAST/STREETERVILLE—41 E CHESTNUT ST (OFF CHICAGO AVE); 312.397.9500; M-SA 11:30-11:30, SU 11:30-10

Medici

"...good eatery close to University of Chicago campus... decent kid's menu, fun atmosphere, and several bigger tables that can accommodate multiple families... across the street from Bixler Playlot, they get a lot of family traffic... food can take a while to come, but they will give you crackers for the little ones..."

Children's menu ✓ $$ Prices

Changing station .... ✓ ❸ .... Customer service
Highchairs/boosters .... ✓ ❸ .... Stroller access

HYDE PARK—1327 E 57TH ST (AT S KIMBARK AVE); 773.667.7394; M-TH 11-11:30PM F11-12SA 9-12AM SU 9-11:30; STREET PARKING

Nordstrom Cafe ★★★★☆

"...a perfect shopping break or a destination of it's own... you generally need to wait in line to order food and the waiter will bring it to the table when ready... simple comfort food—sandwiches, mac and cheese, grilled cheese, etc... service is top notch and they don't mind substitutions..."

Children's menu .... ✓ $$ .... Prices
Changing station .... ✓ ❹ .... Customer service
Highchairs/boosters .... ✓ ❹ .... Stroller access

WWW.NORDSTROM.COM

RIVER NORTH/RIVER WEST—55 E GRAND AVE (AT STATE ST); 312.464.1515; M-SA 10-8, SU 11-6

Original Pancake House ★★★★½

"...consistently the best breakfast around... great flapjacks and appropriately-sized kids meals... food comes quickly... the most amazing apple pancakes ever... service is always friendly, but sometimes it can take a while to actually get the food... the highlight for my daughter is the free balloon when we leave... always a lot of families here with small children on the weekends, so you don't have to worry about being the only one..."

Children's menu .... ✓ $$ .... Prices
Changing station .... ✓ ❹ .... Customer service
Highchairs/boosters .... ✓ ❸ .... Stroller access

WWW.ORIGINALPANCAKEHOUSE.COM

CHICAGO—22 E BELLVUE (OFF DIVISION ST); 312.642.7917; M-F 7-3, SA-SU 7-5

LINCOLN PARK/DEPAUL/OLD TOWN—2020 N LINCOLN PARK W (AT N CLARK ST); 773.929.8130; M-F 7-3, SA-SU 7-5

SOUTH SIDE—10437 S WESTERN AVE (AT W 104TH ST); 773.445.6100; M-F 7-3, SA-SU 7-5

SOUTH SIDE—1517 E HYDE PARK BLVD (AT 51ST & LAKE PARK AVE); 773.288.2322; M-F 7-3, SA-SU 7-5

Panang Noodles & Rice

Children's menu .... ✓ ✓ .... Changing station
Highchairs/boosters .... ✓

EAST/WEST OLD TOWN GOLD COAST/STREETERVILLE—800 N CLARK ST (AT E CHICAGO AVE); 312.573.9999; SU-TH 11-10, F-SA 11-10:30

Penny's Noodle Shop

Children's menu .... ✗ ✗ .... Changing station
Highchairs/boosters .... ✓

BUCKTOWN—1542 N DAMEN AVE (AT NORTH AVE); 773.394.0100; DAILY 11-10, F-SA 11-10:30

LAKEVIEW/WRIGLEYVILLE—3400 N SHEFFIELD AVE (OFF BELMONT AVE); 773.281.8222; DAILY 11-10, F-SA 11-10:30

LINCOLN PARK/DEPAUL/OLD TOWN—950 W DIVERSEY PKWY (AT N SHEFFIELD AVE); 773.281.8448; DAILY 11-10, F-SA 11-10:30

PJ Clarke's ★★★½☆

"...small, but dark and loud so it is a good atmosphere for babies... hostess is so nice—we have been there only a few times and she remembered us and our baby..."

Children's menu .... ✗ | $$ .... Prices
Changing station.......................... ✗ | ❺ .... Customer service
Highchairs/boosters .... ✓ | ❶ ....Stroller access

WWW.PJCLARKESCHICAGO.COM

EAST/WEST OLD TOWN GOLD COAST/STREETERVILLE—1204 N STATE PKY (AT E DIVISION ST); 312.664.1650; M-SA 11-2AM, SU 10-2AM; GARAGE PARKING

RJ Grunt's ★★★★☆

"...right across from the zoo... the salad bar is the way to go so that you don't have to wait... cramped seating and hard to navigate with a stroller... they have stroller storage... parking impossible, but valet available..."

Children's menu .... ✓ | $$ .... Prices
Changing station.......................... ✓ | ❹ .... Customer service
Highchairs/boosters .... ✓ | ❸ ....Stroller access

LINCOLN PARK/DEPAUL/OLD TOWN—2056 N LINCOLN PARK WEST (AT W DICKENS AVE); 773.929.5363; M-TH 11:30-9:30, F-SA 11:30-10:30, SU 11:30-9

restaurants

Scoozi ★★★★☆

"...on Sunday's they have make your own pizza night..."

Children's menu .... ✗ | $$ .... Prices
Changing station.......................... ✗ | ❸ .... Customer service
Highchairs/boosters .... ✓ | ❸ ....Stroller access

WWW.LEYE.COM

EAST/WEST OLD TOWN GOLD COAST/STREETERVILLE—410 W HURON ST (AT N SEDGWICK ST); 312.943.5900; M-TH 5:30-9, F 5:30-10, SA 5-10, SU 5-9; VALET

Stella's Diner ★★★★★

"...owned by a very nice Greek family that will get to know and love your kids... no kid menu, but good pricing—I highly recommend for breakfast..."

Children's menu .... ✗ | $$$ .... Prices
Changing station.......................... ✗ | ❺ .... Customer service
Highchairs/boosters .... ✓ | ❺ ....Stroller access

LAKEVIEW/WRIGLEYVILLE—3042 N BROADWAY ST (AT W WELLINGTON AVE); 773.472.9040; DAILY 6-10

SuperDawg ★★★★★

"...first rate for a lunch in the car, the waitresses bring your food to the car, with trays that fit in the door... can sit outside on the picnic tables, just off Milwaukee Ave so it can be a bit noisy... hot-dogs are delicious and so are the fries... shakes are awesome, too..."

Children's menu .... ✗ | $$ .... Prices
Changing station.......................... ✗ | ❹ .... Customer service
Highchairs/boosters .... ✗ | ❸ ....Stroller access

WWW.SUPERDAWG.COM

EDGEBROOK—6363 N MILWAUKEE AVE (AT N NAGEL AVE); 773.763.0660; SU-TH 11-1AM, F-SA 11-2AM

Sweet Occasions

Children's menu .... ✗ | ✗ .... Changing station
Highchairs/boosters .... ✗

WWW.SWEETOCCASIONSANDMORE.COM

CHICAGO—4639 N DAMEN AVE (AT W LAWRENCE AVE); 773.293.3080; M-F 6:30AM-11PM, SA 8 AM-11PM, SU 8AM-10PM

TGI Friday's ★★★★☆

"...good old American bar food with a reasonable selection for the healthier set as well... I love that the kids meal includes salad... my daughter requests the potato skins on a regular basis (which is good because they are also my favorite)... moderately priced... cheerful servers are used to the mess my kids leave behind... relaxed scene... I'd steer clear on a Friday night unless you don't mind waiting and watching the singles scene..."

Children's menu........................ ✓ $$.. Prices
Changing station........................ ✓ ❹ ....Customer service
Highchairs/boosters.................... ✓ ❸ .... Stroller access

WWW.TGIFRIDAYS.COM

RIVER NORTH/RIVER WEST—153 E ERIE ST (AT N MICHIGAN AVE); 312.664.9820; M-TH 11-10:30, F-SA 11-12:30, SU 11-10

Toast Two

"...yum!.. daughter's first table food out experience... kid's menu is great... even the kid's French toast is enough for two... came with a bowl of fruit on the side... lots of moms are here with their kids on weekdays... conveniently located across the street from the Bucktown library..."

Children's menu........................ ✓ $$.. Prices
Changing station........................ × ❹ ....Customer service
Highchairs/boosters.................... ✓ ❸ .... Stroller access

BUCKTOWN—2046 N DAMEN AVE (AT W ARMITAGE AVE); 773.772.5600; M-F 8-3, SA-SU 8-4

Uncommon Ground

"...first-class find, even better when the weather is nice since they have lots of outdoor seating... food is renowned and so is the service, and they just expanded so there is even more room... weekend brunches and weekday dinners are best for kids..."

Children's menu........................ ✓ $$.. Prices
Changing station........................ × ❹ ....Customer service
Highchairs/boosters.................... ✓ ❹ .... Stroller access

WWW.UNCOMMONGROUND.COM

LAKEVIEW/WRIGLEYVILLE—1214 W GRACE ST (AT N CLARK ST); 773.929.3680; SU-TH 9-11, F-SA 9-12AM

Wishbone Restaurant

"...excellent southern-style comfort food... tends to draw a crowd (with long waits) during peak hours... expect to find a lot of babies during the early dinner hour... kids gets crayons, coloring place mats and corn muffins to make the sometimes lengthy wait more enjoyable... excellent breakfast food..."

Children's menu........................ ✓ $$.. Prices
Changing station........................ ✓ ❹ ....Customer service
Highchairs/boosters.................... ✓ ❹ .... Stroller access

WWW.WISHBONECHICAGO.COM

ROSCOE VILLAGE/WEST LAKEVIEW—3300 N LINCOLN AVE (AT W SCHOOL ST); 773.549.2663; M 7-3, T-F 7-3 & 5-10, SA 8-2:30 & 5-10, SU 8-2:30 & 5-9

WEST LOOP—1001 W WASHINGTON BLVD (AT N MORGAN ST); 312.850.2663; M-F 7-3, T-SA 5-10, SA-SU 8-3; STREET & VALET PARKING

Yoshi's Cafe

"...seasonal favorites... blend of flavors... the owners have children and bend over backwards to accommodate kids... they even offered PB and J for my son... they also brought the children free fruit... they never complained about dropped food or silverware and picked everything up with a smile... great place for a nice meal with the whole family..."

Children's menu ✓
Changing station ✓
Highchairs/boosters ✓

$$$$ ... Prices
❺ ... Customer service
❹ ... Stroller access

LAKEVIEW/WRIGLEYVILLE—3257 N HALSTED ST (AT W ALDINE AVE); 773.248.6160; T-TH 5-10:30, F-SA 5-11, SU 5-9:30; STREET PARKING

Northwestern Suburbs

"lila picks"

★Chevy's Fresh Mex

★California Pizza Kitchen

★Lou Malnati's Pizzeria

Big Bowl

"...surprisingly kid-friendly—they will bring you an order of white rice immediately, and have crayons, etc. for the kids... they immediately provide the children with something to nibble on and games to play... loud restaurant that hides noise well... the menu has mac and cheese for picky eaters and a couple of great appetizers... each kids' meal comes with a drink, a bowl of white rice, and a takeout Chinese container with crayons, chopsticks, and something to color on... overall a huge hit for both parents and kids..."

Children's menu .... ✓ $$ .... Prices
Changing station .... ✓ ❹ .... Customer service
Highchairs/boosters .... ✓ ❹ .... Stroller access

WWW.BIGBOWL.COM

SCHAUMBURG—1950 E HIGGINS RD (AT N MARTINGDALE RD); 847.517.8881; M-SA 11-10; FREE PARKING

California Pizza Kitchen

"...you can't go wrong with their fabulous pizza... always clean... the food's great, the kids drinks all come with a lid... the staff is super friendly to kids... crayons and coloring books keep little minds busy... most locations have a place for strollers at the front... no funny looks or attitude when breastfeeding... open atmosphere with friendly service... tables are well spaced so you don't feel like your kid is annoying the diners nearby (it's usually full of kids anyway)..."

Children's menu .... ✓ $$ .... Prices
Changing station .... ✓ ❹ .... Customer service
Highchairs/boosters .... ✓ ❹ .... Stroller access

WWW.CPK.COM

ARLINGTON HEIGHTS—3 S EVERGREEN AVE (AT E CAMPBELL ST); 847.590.0801; M-TH 11-10, F-SA 11-11, SU 11-9

DEER PARK—20502 N RAND RD (AT W LONG GROVE RD); 847.550.0273; M-TH 11-10, F-SA 11-11, SU 11-9

SCHAUMBURG—1550 E GOLF RD (AT WOODFIELD MALL); 847.413.9200; M-TH 11-10, F-SA 11-11, SU 11-9; MALL PARKING

Chevys Fresh Mex

"...a nice combo of good food for adults and a nice kid's menu... always a sure bet with tots in tow... tasty Mexican food with a simple kids menu (especially the quesedillas)... the tortilla making machine is

sure to grab your toddler's attention until the food arrives... an occasional balloon making man... party-like atmosphere with colorful decorations... huge Margaritas for mom and dad... service generally excellent and fast, but you may have to wait for a table at peak hours... long tables can accommodate the multifamily get-together... ”

Children's menu ✓ — $$ Prices
Changing station ✓ — ❹ Customer service
Highchairs/boosters ✓ — ❹ Stroller access

WWW.CHEVYS.COM

SCHAUMBURG—1180 N PLZ DR (AT WOODFIELD MALL); 847.413.9100; SU-TH 11-10, F-SA 11-11; MALL PARKING

Corner Bakery Cafe

“*...best kid's grilled cheese in town and excellent oatmeal raisin cookies... very nice, kid-friendly... a tastier and healthier alternative to fast food... selection ranges from sandwiches to pasta to salads and pizza... great for a quick bite... space is limited so strollers can be tricky ...* ”

Children's menu ✓ — $$ Prices
Changing station × — ❹ Customer service
Highchairs/boosters ✓ — ❸ Stroller access

WWW.CORNERBAKERY.COM

ARLINGTON HEIGHTS—470 E RAND RD (OFF PALATINE RD); 847.394.4661; M-SA 7:30-8, SU 7:30-7

CRYSTAL LAKE—815 COG CIR (AT PINGREE RD); 815.788.8620; SU-TH 7-8, F-SA 7-9

SCHAUMBURG—1901 E WOODFIELD RD (AT FRONTAGE RD); 847.240.1111; M-SA 7:30-9, SU 7:30-8

Fuddruckers

“*...a super burger chain with fresh and tasty food... colorful and noisy with lots of distraction until the food arrives... loads of fresh toppings so that you can make your perfectly cooked burger even better... great kids deals that come with a free treat... noise not a problem in this super casual atmosphere... some locations have video games in the back which will buy you an extra half hour if you need it... low-key and very family friendly...* ”

Children's menu ✓ — $$ Prices
Changing station ✓ — ❹ Customer service
Highchairs/boosters ✓ — ❹ Stroller access

WWW.FUDDRUCKERS.COM

PALATINE—1151 E DUNDEE RD (AT N RAND RD); 847.359.4422; DAILY 11-9; FREE PARKING

SCHAUMBURG—436 E GOLF RD (AT BASSWOOD RD); 847.519.9390; M-TH 11-9, F-SA 11-10

Hunan Beijing

“*...excellent family owned Chinese restaurant ... nothing too fancy here ... buffet on Sunday... cooks will make chicken noodle soup for the kids, just ask... also, soft serve ice cream machine for dessert helps me get my kids to eat their veggies first...* ”

Children's menu × — $$ Prices
Changing station × — ❺ Customer service
Highchairs/boosters ✓ — ❺ Stroller access

WWW.BAMBOO-GARDENS.COM

HOFFMAN ESTATES—1004 W GOLF RD (AT GAMMON RD); 847.885.3777

IKEA

“*...Swedish meatballs and funny berry drinks—all very yummy and cheap... a clean, comfortable place to eat... the restaurant sells baby*

restaurants

food and has bottle/jar warmers... worth visiting even if you aren't shopping—the food is cheap, but good... totally kid-friendly... lines can sometimes be long—especially during peak shopping hours... ”

Children's menu .... ✓ $$ .... Prices
Changing station .... ✓ ❹ .... Customer service
Highchairs/boosters .... ✓ ❹ .... Stroller access

WWW.IKEA.COM

SCHAUMBURG—1800 E MCCONNOR PKY (OFF GOLF RD); 847.969.9700; M-TH 10-9, F 10-10, SA 9-10, SU 10-8

Lou Malnati's Pizzeria

“*...all I can say is 'yum!'—simply the best pizza in the area... great food, not really stroller friendly, but sometimes it gets a little loud, so if your kids are restless, no one will even know... great food for kids and adults... prices are reasonable and the atmosphere is great...* ”

Children's menu .... ✕ $$$ .... Prices
Changing station .... ✕ ❹ .... Customer service
Highchairs/boosters .... ✕ ❸ .... Stroller access

WWW.LOUMALNATIS.COM

SCHAUMBURG—1 S ROSELLE RD (AT E SCHAUMBURG RD); 847.985.1525; DAILY 11-11, SA 11-11

Olive Garden

“*...finally a place that is both kid and adult friendly... tasty Italian chain with lot's of convenient locations... the staff consistently attends to the details of dining with babies and toddlers—minimizing wait time, highchairs offered spontaneously, bread sticks brought immediately... food is served as quickly as possible... happy to create special orders... our waitress even acted as our family photographer...* ”

Children's menu .... ✓ $$ .... Prices
Changing station .... ✓ ❹ .... Customer service
Highchairs/boosters .... ✓ ❹ .... Stroller access

WWW.OLIVEGARDEN.COM

ARLINGTON HEIGHTS—630 E RAND RD (AT TOWN & COUNTRY MALL); 847.818.8821; SU-TH 11-10, F-SA 11-11

SCHAUMBURG—1925 E GOLF RD (AT WOODFIELD MALL); 847.619.9095; SU-TH 11-10, F-SA 11-11; MALL PARKING

VERNON HILLS—701 N MILWAUKEE AVE (AT HAWTHORN CTR); 847.816.0293; SU-TH 11-10, F-SA 11-11

Original Pancake House

“*...consistently the best breakfast around... great flapjacks and appropriately-sized kids meals... food comes quickly... the most amazing apple pancakes ever... service is always friendly, but sometimes it can take a while to actually get the food... the highlight for my daughter is the free balloon when we leave... always a lot of families here with small children on the weekends, so you don't have to worry about being the only one...* ”

Children's menu .... ✓ $$ .... Prices
Changing station .... ✓ ❹ .... Customer service
Highchairs/boosters .... ✓ ❸ .... Stroller access

WWW.ORIGINALPANCAKEHOUSE.COM

ARLINGTON HEIGHTS—825 DUNDEE RD (AT ARLINGTON HEIGHTS RD); 847.392.6600; DAILY 6:30-10

LAKE ZURICH—767 S RAND RD (OF ELA RD); 847.550.0006; DAILY 6:30-10

Red Robin

“*...very kid-oriented—loud, balloons, bright lights, colorful decor and a cheerful staff make Red Robin a favorite among parents and children... the food is mainly burgers (beef or chicken)... loud music*

covers even the most boisterous of screaming... lots of kids—all the time... sometimes the wait can be long, but the arcade games and balloons help pass the time... ”

Children's menu ✓ $$ Prices
Changing station ✓ ❹ Customer service
Highchairs/boosters ✓ ❹ Stroller access

WWW.REDROBIN.COM

ALGONQUIN—441 S RANDALL RD (AT HUNINGTON DR); 847.458.6655; SU-TH 11-10, F-SA 11-11

SCHAUMBURG—120 WOODFIELD MALL (AT GOLF RD); 847.517.4476; M-TH 11-9, F-SA 11-10, SU 22-7; MALL PARKING

Romano's Macaroni Grill

“*...family oriented and tasty... noisy so nobody cares if your kids make noise... the staff goes out of their way to make families feel welcome... they even provide slings by the table for infant carriers... the noise level is pretty constant so it's not too loud, but loud enough so that crying babies don't disturb the other patrons... good kids' menu with somewhat healthy items... crayons for kids to color on the paper tablecloths...* ”

Children's menu ✓ $$$ Prices
Changing station ✓ ❹ Customer service
Highchairs/boosters ✓ ❹ Stroller access

WWW.MACARONIGRILL.COM

HOFFMAN ESTATES—2575 W HIGGINS RD (AT BARRIINGTON RD); 847.882.6676; SU-TH 11-10, F-SA 11-11

Smokey Bones BBQ

“*...reasonably healthy food for kids—not fried chicken fingers and fries... lots of TVs to entertain kids so adults can have a little time to talk... volume control at each table, stations often set to Nickelodeon... unique holders for car seats that cradle the seats...* ”

Children's menu ✓ $$$ Prices
Changing station ✓ ❹ Customer service
Highchairs/boosters ✓ ❹ Stroller access

WWW.SMOKEYBONES.COM

SCHAUMBURG—680 N MALL DR (OFF HIGGINS RD); 847.605.0889; SU-TH 11-10, F-SA 11-11

Souplantation/Sweet Tomatoes

“*...you can't beat the price and selection of healthy foods... all you can eat—serve yourself soup and salad bar... lots of healthy choices plus pizza and pasta... great for picky eaters... free for 2 and under and only $3 for kids under 5... booths for comfy seating and discreet breastfeeding... helps to have another adult along since it is self serve... they always bring fresh cookies to the table and offer to refill drinks...* ”

Children's menu ✓ $$ Prices
Changing station ✓ ❹ Customer service
Highchairs/boosters ✓ ❹ Stroller access

WWW.SOUPLANTATION.COM

SCHAUMBURG—1951 E MCCONNOR PKY (AT E GOLF RD); 847.619.1271; SU-TH 11-9, F-SA 11-10

TGI Friday's

“*...good old American bar food with a reasonable selection for the healthier set as well... I love that the kids meal includes salad... my daughter requests the potato skins on a regular basis (which is good because they are also my favorite)... moderately priced... cheerful*

servers are used to the mess my kids leave behind... relaxed scene... I'd steer clear on a Friday night unless you don't mind waiting and watching the singles scene... **”**

Children's menu	✓	$$	Prices
Changing station	✓	❹	Customer service
Highchairs/boosters	✓	❸	Stroller access

WWW.TGIFRIDAYS.COM

CRYSTAL LAKE—835 COG CIR (OFF RT 14); 815.788.9440; SU-TH 11-10, F-SA 11-11

HOFFMAN ESTATES—1795 BARRINGTON RD (AT HIGGINS RD); 847.843.9930; M-TH 11-1, F 11-2, SA 11:30-2, SU 11:30-1

LAKE ZURICH—676 S RAND RD (AT RT 12); 847.726.8237; SU-TH 11-1, F-SA 11-1:30

SCHAUMBURG—1695 E GOLF RD (AT WOODFIELD MALL); 847.969.0126; SU-TH 11-12, SA-SU 11-1

VERNON HILLS—151 E TOWNLINE RD (AT HAWTHORNE CTR); 847.680.9980; SU-TH 11-12, F-SA 11-1; PARKING LOT

Village Tavern & Grill ★★★★☆

“*...the best chicken fingers around... very kid-friendly... infant car seat stands and Koala changing stations in the bathroom... terrific neighborhood place that is just fine for a family dinner... wide selections and variety... you will likely see your friends there, too...* **”**

Children's menu	✓	$$	Prices
Changing station	✓	❹	Customer service
Highchairs/boosters	✓	❸	Stroller access

WWW.VILLAGETAVERNANDGRILL.COM

SCHAUMBURG—901 W WISE RD (AT WRIGHT BLVD); 847.891.8866; SU-TH 11-11, F-SA 11-12

Northern Suburbs

"lila picks"

★Michael's Chicago Style Red Hots

★Walker Brothers Original Pancake House

restaurants

Applebee's Neighborhood Grill

"...geared to family dining—they expect you to be loud and leave a mess... Macaroni & Cheese, Hot Dogs, and tasty grilled cheese... activity book and special kids cup are a bonus... service can be slow, but they will cover you with things to snack on... stay clear on Friday and Saturday nights... comfort food in a casual atmosphere... even though it's part of a very large chain you get the feeling it's a neighborhood-type place..."

Children's menu .... ✓ $$ .... Prices
Changing station.......................... ✓ ❹.......................... Customer service
Highchairs/boosters .... ✓ ❸.............................Stroller access

WWW.APPLEBEES.COM

GURNEE—6447 GRAND AVE (AT GURNEE MILLS MALL); 847.855.2748; M-TH 11-11, F-SA 11-12, SU 11-10

Baja Fresh

"...Mexican food using all fresh ingredients... many restaurants have a nice outdoor courtyard—which is good if you are self-conscious about a loud baby... casual atmosphere... my son loves the fresh salsa... I was able to keep the stroller next to me throughout my meal... I was able to get milk and juice for my kid's meal..."

Children's menu .... ✓ $$ .... Prices
Changing station.......................... × ❹.......................... Customer service
Highchairs/boosters .... ✓ ❸.............................Stroller access

WWW.BAJAFRESH.COM

DEERFIELD—100 S WAUKEGAN RD (AT LAKE COOK RD); 847.480.8746; M-SA 11-9, F-SA 11-10

Bravo Cucina Italiana

"...good food, decent prices and family friendly... we like it because it isn't a 'kids' restaurant—it definitely caters primarily to adults, but they are great with kids... my son is always welcomed there with balloons and lots of attention... great kids menu and friendly staff..."

Children's menu .... ✓ $$$ .... Prices
Changing station.......................... ✓ ❹.......................... Customer service
Highchairs/boosters .... ✓ ❹.............................Stroller access

WWW.BRAVOITALIAN.COM

GLENVIEW—2600 NAVY BLVD; 847.724.8400; SU-TH 11-10, F-SA 11-11

California Pizza Kitchen

"...you can't go wrong with their fabulous pizza... always clean... the food's great, the kids drinks all come with a lid... the staff is super friendly to kids... crayons and coloring books keep little minds busy... most locations have a place for strollers at the front... no funny looks or attitude when breastfeeding... open atmosphere with friendly service... tables are well spaced so you don't feel like your kid is annoying the diners nearby (it's usually full of kids anyway)..."

Children's menu .... ✓ $$ .... Prices
Changing station .... ✓ ❹ .... Customer service
Highchairs/boosters .... ✓ ❹ .... Stroller access

WWW.CPK.COM

SKOKIE—374 OLD ORCHARD SHOPPING CTR (AT GOLF RD); 847.673.1144; M-TH 11-10, F-SA 11-11, SU 11:30-9; PARKING LOT AT CENTER

Champps Restaurant

"...a spot that's tailored to families... the staff is extremely accommodating... some nights they have a man who visits each table and makes balloon animals for the kids... eat free on Tuesday night... lots of pasta and a wide variety of everything else..."

Children's menu .... ✓ $$$ .... Prices
Changing station .... ✓ ❹ .... Customer service
Highchairs/boosters .... ✓ ❹ .... Stroller access

WWW.CHAMPPS.COM

SKOKIE—134 OLD ORCHARD SHOPPING CTR (AT GOLF RD); 847.673.4778; M-W 11-11, TH-SA 11-12, SU 11-10:30; PARKING LOT AT CENTER

Cheeburger Cheeburger

"...old time feel... classic 50's and 60's rock and roll on the radio... big, big burgers... salads too... you can choose what ever topping you want for your burgers and salads... great shakes... don't miss the clown on Friday nights—free face painting and my kids love it... good food and a very relaxed environment..."

Children's menu .... ✓ $$ .... Prices
Changing station .... ✓ ❹ .... Customer service
Highchairs/boosters .... ✓ ❸ .... Stroller access

WWW.CHEEBURGER.COM

GLENVIEW—1839 TOWER DR (AT CHESTNUT AVE); 847.729.3340; M-TH 11-9, F-SA 11-10, SU 12-9; FREE PARKING

Corner Bakery Cafe

"...best kid's grilled cheese in town and excellent oatmeal raisin cookies... very nice, kid-friendly... a tastier and healthier alternative to fast food... selection ranges from sandwiches to pasta to salads and pizza... great for a quick bite... space is limited so strollers can be tricky..."

Children's menu .... ✓ $$ .... Prices
Changing station .... ✗ ❹ .... Customer service
Highchairs/boosters .... ✓ ❸ .... Stroller access

WWW.CORNERBAKERY.COM

GLENVIEW—1378 PATRIOT BLVD (AT LAKE AVE); 847.998.4745; M-SA 8-8:30, SU 8-7

HIGHLAND PARK—638 CENTRAL AVE (AT 2ND ST); 847.433.4638; M-TH 7:30-8, SU 7:30-6

NORTHBROOK—1515 LAKE COOK RD (AT NORTHBROOK SHOPPING CTR); 847.753.9665; M-SA 8:30-10, SU 8:30-7

SKOKIE—175 OLD ORCHARD CTR (AT GOLF RD); 847.933.1555; M-TH 8-9, F-SA 8-10, SU 8-8

SKOKIE—5369 TOUHY AVE (AT CENTRAL AVE); 847.763.0735; M-SA 7:30-9:30, SU 8-8

Country Kitchen

"...our daughter (12 months old) was really entertained by everyone in the restaurant ... we had time to eat our meal as a result ... staff is friendly and really cater to families ... you can park your stroller right at the table and they don't care... totally kid-friendly place with a great variety on the menu... awesome omelets..."

Children's menu .... ✗ $$ .... Prices
Changing station.......................... ✗ ❺ .... Customer service
Highchairs/boosters .... ✗ ❹ .... Stroller access

HIGHLAND PARK—446 CENTRAL AVE (AT SHERIDAN RD); 847.432.7500

Flat Top Grill

"...you choose your food and they cook it... awesome Mongolian BBQ... especially fun for the little ones—lots to look at, good bread, and BBQ meat... you need at least two adults or a mobile kid because you have to leave your seat to make your meal... kids under 4 eat free..."

Children's menu .... ✗ $$ .... Prices
Changing station.......................... ✗ ❹ .... Customer service
Highchairs/boosters .... ✓ ❹ .... Stroller access

WWW.FLATTOPGRILL.COM

EVANSTON—707 CHURCH ST (AT CHICAGO AVE); 847.570.0100; M-TH 11-10, F-SA 11-11, SU 11-9:30

Fuddruckers

"...a super burger chain with fresh and tasty food... colorful and noisy with lots of distraction until the food arrives... loads of fresh toppings so that you can make your perfectly cooked burger even better... great kids deals that come with a free treat... noise not a problem in this super casual atmosphere... some locations have video games in the back which will buy you an extra half hour if you need it... low-key and very family friendly..."

Children's menu .... ✓ $$ .... Prices
Changing station.......................... ✓ ❹ .... Customer service
Highchairs/boosters .... ✓ ❹ .... Stroller access

WWW.FUDDRUCKERS.COM

HIGHLAND PARK—1538 CLAVEY RD (AT SKOKIE HWY); 847.831.2501; SU-TH 11-9, F-SA 11-10

Jack's Family Restaurant

"...this place is great for babies—-they always are very attentive and accommodating... heating up food or milk... bringing crackers or bread... neat and clean... the employees are wonderful and keep us coming back for a dinner out..."

Children's menu .... ✓ $$ .... Prices
Changing station.......................... ✓ ❹ .... Customer service
Highchairs/boosters .... ✓ ❸ .... Stroller access

SKOKIE—5201 TOUHY AVE (AT LARAMINE AVE); 847.674.5532; DAILY 6-1AM

Johnny Rockets

"...burgers, fries and a shake served up in a 50's style diner... we love the singing waiters—they're always good for a giggle... my daughter is enthralled with the juke box and straw dispenser... sit at the counter and watch the cooks prepare the food... simple, satisfying and always a hit with the little ones..."

Children's menu .... ✓ $$ .... Prices
Changing station.......................... ✗ ❹ .... Customer service

restaurants

Highchairs/boosters .... ✓ ❸ .... Stroller access

WWW.JOHNNYROCKETS.COM

NORTHBROOK—2338 NORTHBROOK COURT (AT NORTHBROOK MALL); 847.562.8720; M-TH 9-10, F-SA 9-11, SU 9-9; MALL PARKING

SKOKIE—45 OLD ORCHARD CTR (AT GOLF RD); 847.677.6039; M-TH 10:30-9, F-SA 10:30-10, SU 10:30-8; FREE PARKING

Little Louie's Red Hots ★★★★☆

"...a Northbrook tradition... it's best to go on a warm spring day and take your food to the Village Green across the street to eat and play in the park... there is a new party room that has been added to the restaurant as well... oh, and they make cherry coke the old fashioned way..."

Children's menu .... × $ .... Prices
Changing station .... × ❹ ....Customer service
Highchairs/boosters .... × ❹ .... Stroller access

NORTHBROOK—1342 SHERMER RD (AT MEADOW RD); 847.498.1033; M-SA 11-8, SU 11-7

Michael's Chicago Style Red Hots ★★★★★

"...hot dogs, burgers, pizza, potatoes, wraps... you are bound to have plenty of choices here... amazing salad bar with all fresh ingredients... they chop the salads on request and have over 20 salad dressings to choose from... huge open space for your kids to run around..."

Children's menu .... ✓ $ .... Prices
Changing station .... ✓ ❹ ....Customer service
Highchairs/boosters .... ✓ ❹ .... Stroller access

WWW.MICHAELSHOTDOGS.COM

HIGHLAND PARK—1879 2ND ST (AT CENTRAL AVE); 847.432.3338; M-SA 10:30-8, SU 11-8

Olive Garden ★★★★☆

"...finally a place that is both kid and adult friendly... tasty Italian chain with lot's of convenient locations... the staff consistently attends to the details of dining with babies and toddlers—minimizing wait time, highchairs offered spontaneously, bread sticks brought immediately... food is served as quickly as possible... happy to create special orders... our waitress even acted as our family photographer..."

Children's menu .... ✓ $$ .... Prices
Changing station .... ✓ ❹ ....Customer service
Highchairs/boosters .... ✓ ❹ .... Stroller access

WWW.OLIVEGARDEN.COM

LINCOLNWOOD—3303 W TOUHY AVE (AT N MCCORMICK BLVD); 847.679.4498; SU-TH 11-10, F-SA 11-11

Once Upon A Bagel ★★★★☆

"...every possible bagel you could imagine with all the cream cheeses in low fat flavors... incredible chicken soup... they've got all the deli standards—ruebens, pastrami, salads... you can even get a huge 10 pound bagel for parties... bright decor that is pretty kid proof..."

Children's menu .... × $$ .... Prices
Changing station .... × ❹ ....Customer service
Highchairs/boosters .... ✓ ❸ .... Stroller access

WWW.ONCEUPONABAGEL.COM

HIGHLAND PARK—1888 1ST ST (AT 1ST ST); 847.433.1411; M-F 6-5, SA 6-5:30, SU 6-2

Original Pancake House

"...consistently the best breakfast around... great flapjacks and appropriately-sized kids meals... food comes quickly... the most amazing apple pancakes ever... service is always friendly, but sometimes it can take a while to actually get the food... the highlight for my daughter is the free balloon when we leave... always a lot of families here with small children on the weekends, so you don't have to worry about being the only one..."

Children's menu ✓ — $$ Prices
Changing station ✓ — ❹ Customer service
Highchairs/boosters ✓ — ❸ Stroller access

WWW.ORIGINALPANCAKEHOUSE.COM

GLENVIEW—1615 WAUKEGAN RD (OFF CHESTNUT AVE); 847.724.0220; DAILY 6:30-9:30

LINCOLNSHIRE—200 MARRIOTT DR (OFF HALF DAY RD); 847.634.2220; DAILY 6:30-9:30

Red Robin

"...very kid-oriented—loud, balloons, bright lights, colorful decor and a cheerful staff make Red Robin a favorite among parents and children... the food is mainly burgers (beef or chicken)... loud music covers even the most boisterous of screaming... lots of kids—all the time... sometimes the wait can be long, but the arcade games and balloons help pass the time..."

Children's menu ✓ — $$ Prices
Changing station ✓ — ❹ Customer service
Highchairs/boosters ✓ — ❹ Stroller access

WWW.REDROBIN.COM

LINCOLNSHIRE—295 PKY DR (AT W APTAKISIC RD); 847.520.4747; SU-TH 11-10, F-SA 11-11

Romano's Macaroni Grill

"...family oriented and tasty... noisy so nobody cares if your kids make noise... the staff goes out of their way to make families feel welcome... they even provide slings by the table for infant carriers... the noise level is pretty constant so it's not too loud, but loud enough so that crying babies don't disturb the other patrons... good kids' menu with somewhat healthy items... crayons for kids to color on the paper tablecloths..."

Children's menu ✓ — $$$ Prices
Changing station ✓ — ❹ Customer service
Highchairs/boosters ✓ — ❹ Stroller access

WWW.MACARONIGRILL.COM

SKOKIE—7016 CARPENTER RD (AT TOUHY AVE); 847.679.8478; SU-TH 11-10, F-SA 11-11

Souplantation/Sweet Tomatoes

"...you can't beat the price and selection of healthy foods... all you can eat—serve yourself soup and salad bar... lots of healthy choices plus pizza and pasta... great for picky eaters... free for 2 and under and only $3 for kids under 5... booths for comfy seating and discreet breastfeeding... helps to have another adult along since it is self serve... they always bring fresh cookies to the table and offer to refill drinks..."

Children's menu ✓ — $$ Prices
Changing station ✓ — ❹ Customer service
Highchairs/boosters ✓ — ❹ Stroller access

WWW.SOUPLANTATION.COM

GLENVIEW—2351 WILLOW RD (AT OLD WILLOW RD); 847.657.8141; SU-TH 11-9, F-SA 11-10

TGI Friday's

"...good old American bar food with a reasonable selection for the healthier set as well... I love that the kids meal includes salad... my daughter requests the potato skins on a regular basis (which is good because they are also my favorite)... moderately priced... cheerful servers are used to the mess my kids leave behind... relaxed scene... I'd steer clear on a Friday night unless you don't mind waiting and watching the singles scene..."

Children's menu.......................... ✓ $$.. Prices
Changing station .... ✓ ❹ .... Customer service
Highchairs/boosters..................... ✓ ❸ .... Stroller access

WWW.TGIFRIDAYS.COM

GLENVIEW—4513 W LAKE AVE (OFF RT 294); 847.298.9966; M-TH 11-12, F 11-12:30, SA 11:30-12:30, SU 11:30-11

GURNEE—6577 GRAND AVE (AT N HUNT CLUB RD); 847.855.0007; DAILY 11-2

Walker Brothers Original Pancake House

"...consistently the best breakfast around... great flapjacks and appropriately-sized kids meals... food comes quickly... the most amazing apple pancakes ever... service is always friendly, but sometimes it can take a while to actually get the food... the highlight for my daughter is the free balloon when we leave... always a lot of families here with small children on the weekends, so you don't have to worry about being the only one..."

Children's menu.......................... ✓ $$.. Prices
Changing station .... ✓ ❺ .... Customer service
Highchairs/boosters..................... ✓ ❸ .... Stroller access

HIGHLAND PARK—620 CENTRAL AVE (AT 1ST ST); 847.432.0660; M-TH 7-10, F-SU 7-11

WILMETTE—153 GREEN BAY RD (AT ISABELLA AVE); 847.251.6000; DAILY 6:30-10

Western Suburbs

"lila picks"

★Chevys Fresh Mex

★Ed Debevic's Short Orders Deluxe

★Leona's

restaurants

Alfie's Inn

"...family atmosphere with crayons on the table... kid menu... adults find salads to ribs and steaks ... known for their loin burgers ... one of our favorites through three generations..."

Children's menu	✓	$$	Prices
Changing station	×	❹	Customer service
Highchairs/boosters	✓	❸	Stroller access

WWW.ALFIESINN.COM

GLEN ELLYN—425 ROOSEVELT RD (AT N MAIN ST); 630.858.2506; DAILY 11-11

Beef O'Brady's

"...good place for a quick bite and a beer... the best wings around... dim lighting and layout can make it tricky to navigate a stroller... the O'Bradys burger is great... family-friendly atmosphere—kids can play and have a good time without disturbing other patrons..."

Children's menu	✓	$$	Prices
Changing station	✓	❹	Customer service
Highchairs/boosters	✓	❹	Stroller access

WWW.BEEFOBRADYS.COM

GLEN ELLYN—940 ROOSEVELT RD (AT BRYANT AVE); 630.545.2333; DAILY 11-11

Buffalo Wild Wings

"...watch sports with Dad and have lunch/dinner with the family... kids meals include standards like chicken tenders, mac and cheese, and corn dogs... babies and grownups welcome—the staff loves to joke around with my son..."

Children's menu	✓	$$	Prices
Changing station	✓	❹	Customer service
Highchairs/boosters	✓	❹	Stroller access

WWW.BUFFALOWILDWINGS.COM

ELMHURST—149 N YORK ST (AT N PALMER DR); 630.832.2999; SU-TH 11-1, F-SA 11-2

Buzz Cafe

Children's menu	✓	×	Changing station
Highchairs/boosters	✓		

WWW.THEBUZZCAFE.COM

OAK PARK—905 S LOMBARD AVE (AT HARRISON ST); 708.524.2899; M-F 6AM-9PM, SA 7AM-9PM, SU 8AM-2PM

Cafe Winberie

"...after spending time at the library, it's an easy walk for a good lunch or dinner... my toddler loves their kids menu... they bring crayons and paper to the table and are tolerant of kids behavior... for parents, the food is much better than in many kid-friendly places (goes far beyond burgers and fries)... Sunday brunch is a good family friendly option..."

Children's menu .... ✓ $$$ .... Prices
Changing station .... ✓ ❹ .... Customer service
Highchairs/boosters .... ✓ ❸ .... Stroller access

WWW.SELECTRESTAURANTS.COM

OAK PARK—151 N OAK PARK AVE (AT LAKE ST); 708.386.2600; M-TH 11-10, F-SA 11-11, SU 10-9

California Pizza Kitchen

"...you can't go wrong with their fabulous pizza... always clean... the food's great, the kids drinks all come with a lid... the staff is super friendly to kids... crayons and coloring books keep little minds busy... most locations have a place for strollers at the front... no funny looks or attitude when breastfeeding... open atmosphere with friendly service... tables are well spaced so you don't feel like your kid is annoying the diners nearby (it's usually full of kids anyway)..."

Children's menu .... ✓ $$ .... Prices
Changing station .... ✓ ❹ .... Customer service
Highchairs/boosters .... ✓ ❹ .... Stroller access

WWW.CPK.COM

GENEVA—1202 COMMONS DR (AT BRICHER RD); 630.845.1731; M-TH 11-10, F-SA 11-11, SU 11-9

Cheesecake Factory, The

"...although their cheesecake is good, we come here for the kid-friendly atmosphere and selection of good food... eclectic menu has something for everyone... they will bring your tot a plate of yogurt, cheese, bananas and bread free of charge... we love how flexible they are—they'll make whatever my kids want... lots of mommies here... always fun and always crazy... no real kids menu, but the pizza is great to share... waits can be really long..."

Children's menu .... ✗ $$$ .... Prices
Changing station .... ✓ ❹ .... Customer service
Highchairs/boosters .... ✓ ❸ .... Stroller access

WWW.THECHEESECAKEFACTORY.COM

OAK BROOK—2020 SPRING RD (AT OAK BROOK CTR MALL); 630.573.1800; M-TH 11-11:30, F-SA 11-12:30, SU 10-11:30

Chevys Fresh Mex

"...a nice combo of good food for adults and a nice kid's menu... always a sure bet with tots in tow... tasty Mexican food with a simple kids menu (especially the quesedillas)... the tortilla making machine is sure to grab your toddler's attention until the food arrives... an occasional balloon making man... party-like atmosphere with colorful decorations... huge Margaritas for mom and dad... service generally excellent and fast, but you may have to wait for a table at peak hours... long tables can accommodate the multifamily get-together..."

Children's menu .... ✓ $$ .... Prices
Changing station .... ✓ ❹ .... Customer service
Highchairs/boosters .... ✓ ❹ .... Stroller access

WWW.CHEVYS.COM

NAPERVILLE—1633 N NAPER BLVD (AT N NAPSVILLE RD); 630.505.7037; M-TH 11-10, F 11-11, SA 10-11, SU 10-10

Chili's Grill & Bar

"...family-friendly, mild Mexican fare... delicious ribs, soups, salads... kids' menu and crayons as you sit down... on the noisy side, so you don't mind if your kids talk in their usual loud voices... service is excellent... fun night out with the family... a wide variety of menu selections for kids and their parents—all at a reasonable price... best chicken fingers on any kids' menu..."

Children's menu ✓ | $$ Prices
Changing station ✓ | ❹ Customer service
Highchairs/boosters ✓ | ❹ Stroller access

WWW.CHILIS.COM

BLOOMINGDALE—310 W ARMY TRAIL RD (AT SCHMALE RD); 630.894.9966; SU-TH 11-11, F-SA 11-12AM

Corner Bakery Cafe

"...best kid's grilled cheese in town and excellent oatmeal raisin cookies... very nice, kid-friendly... a tastier and healthier alternative to fast food... selection ranges from sandwiches to pasta to salads and pizza... great for a quick bite... space is limited so strollers can be tricky ..."

Children's menu ✓ | $$ Prices
Changing station ✗ | ❹ Customer service
Highchairs/boosters ✓ | ❸ Stroller access

WWW.CORNERBAKERY.COM

GENEVA—1614 COMMONS DR (AT WILLIAMSBURG AVE); 630.845.1738; M-SA 8-8, SU 8-7

HINSDALE—40 E HINSDALE AVE (AT GARFIELD AVE); 630.850.7587; M-F 7-8, SA 8-8, SU 11-5

LA GRANGE—39 N LAGRANGE RD (AT 47TH ST); 708.579.5410; M-F 7:30-8, SA-SU 8-8

NAPERVILLE—47 E CHICAGO AVE (AT WASHINGTON ST); 630.420.1900; M-SA 8-8, SU 8-5

OAK BROOK—240 OAK BROOK CTR (AT 22ND ST); 630.368.0505; M-SA 7:30-9, SU 7:30-8

Denny's

"...inexpensive, coloring books, crayons and a good kids menu... you can customize your order to accommodate your tots needs... the layout is roomy so strollers can be parked right next to your table... booths provide plenty of cover if you need to breastfeed... nothing fancy, but very convenient if you need to quickly find a place to rest up with your babes..."

Children's menu ✓ | $$ Prices
Changing station ✓ | ❹ Customer service
Highchairs/boosters ✓ | ❹ Stroller access

WWW.DENNYS.COM

MELROSE PARK—8349 N AVE (AT THATCHER AVE); 708.450.0026; SU-TH 6-12, F-SA 6-1

OAK PARK—711 N HARLEM AVE (AT ERIE ST); 708.386.6964; M-W 6-12, TH-SU 6-1

OAKBROOK TERRACE—17W 660 22ND ST (AT OAKBROOK CTR MALL); 630.932.1888; OPEN 24 HOURS; MALL PARKING

Ed Debevic's Short Orders Deluxe

"...classic 50's style diner... a popular place for kids and parents... the food is great and 'the help' is even better... servers make dining out with kids an enjoyable experience... plenty of entertainment, with the waitstaff dancing on the counters every half hour... great burgers and shakes..."

Children's menu .... ✓ | $$ .... Prices
Changing station .... ✓ | ❹ .... Customer service
Highchairs/boosters .... ✓ | ❸ .... Stroller access

WWW.EDDEBEVICS.COM

LOMBARD—157 YORKTOWN SHOPPING CTR (AT HIGHLAND AVE); 630.495.60148; CALL FOR HOURS; STREET PARKING

Flat Top Grill

"...you choose your food and they cook it... awesome Mongolian BBQ... especially fun for the little ones—lots to look at, good bread, and BBQ meat... you need at least two adults or a mobile kid because you have to leave your seat to make your meal... kids under 4 eat free..."

Children's menu .... ✗ | $$ .... Prices
Changing station .... ✗ | ❹ .... Customer service
Highchairs/boosters .... ✓ | ❹ .... Stroller access

WWW.FLATTOPGRILL.COM

OAK PARK—726 LAKE ST (AT OAK PARK AVE); 708.358.8200; SU-TH 11-9:30, F-SA 11-10:30

Francesca's Amici

"...wonderful dining experience that you can experience with babies and children... good place for date night without the kids or family dinner ... accommodating to the youngsters (provided ketchup to my 1-year-old) ... didn't mind my toddler throwing food on the floor even though its a nice place..."

Children's menu .... ✗ | $$$ .... Prices
Changing station .... ✗ | ❺ .... Customer service
Highchairs/boosters .... ✓ | ❷ .... Stroller access

WWW.MIAFRANCESCA.COM

ELMHURST—174 N YORK ST (AT N PALMER DR); 630.279.7970; M-F 11:30-2 SU-W 5-9 TH 5-9:30, F-SA 5-10

Fuddruckers

"...a super burger chain with fresh and tasty food... colorful and noisy with lots of distraction until the food arrives... loads of fresh toppings so that you can make your perfectly cooked burger even better... great kids deals that come with a free treat... noise not a problem in this super casual atmosphere... some locations have video games in the back which will buy you an extra half hour if you need it... low-key and very family friendly..."

Children's menu .... ✓ | $$ .... Prices
Changing station .... ✓ | ❹ .... Customer service
Highchairs/boosters .... ✓ | ❹ .... Stroller access

WWW.FUDDRUCKERS.COM

ADDISON—1000 N ROHLWING RD (AT LAKE ST); 630.268.8080; SU-TH 11-9, F-SA 11-10; FREE PARKING

AURORA—4250 FOX VALLEY CTR DR (AT NEW YORK ST); 630.851.9450; SU-TH 11-9, F-SA 11-10; FREE PARKING

DOWNERS GROVE—1500 BRANDING LN (AT FINLEY RD); 630.963.0404; SU-TH 11-9, F-SA 11-10; FREE PARKING

DOWNERS GROVE—7231 LEMONT RD (AT MAIN ST); 630.960.1122; SU-TH 11-9, F-SA 11-10

Leona's

"...huge portions of tasty salads, pizza and other Italian goodies... thin crust and deep dish pizza... casual setting with awesome staff—the waitresses took turns walking our fussy daughter around while my husband and I finished our dinner... quick, friendly service except on weekends when it's busy... crayons, stickers, toddler cups with straws... good vegetarian (even vegan) items..."

Children's menu ✓ | $$ Prices
Changing station ✗ | ❹ Customer service
Highchairs/boosters ✓ | ❹ Stroller access

WWW.LEONAS.COM

HILLSIDE—4431 W ROOSEVELT RD (AT ORCHARD AVE); 708.449.0101; T-TH 11-10, F11-11, SA 12-11, SU 12-9

OAK PARK—848 W MADISON ST (AT CARPENTER AVE); 708.445.0101; M-TH 3-10, F 11:30-11, SA 12-11, SU 1-10

Max & Erma's

"...extremely child-friendly... lots of highchairs, themed activities for children... a little noisy, but fun..."

Children's menu ✓ | $$ Prices
Changing station ✓ | ❹ Customer service
Highchairs/boosters ✓ | ❹ Stroller access

WWW.MAXANDERMAS.COM

BURR RIDGE—201 BRIDEWELL DR (AT BURR RIDGE PKY); 630.794.0800; M-TH 11-11, F-SA 11-12, SU 10-10; FREE PARKING

Moondance Diner

"...swell food... full of kids and babies on weekend mornings and the staff is cooperative in seating you where it is convenient with kids..."

Children's menu ✓ | $$$ Prices
Changing station ✓ | ❸ Customer service
Highchairs/boosters ✓ | ❸ Stroller access

BURR RIDGE—78 BURR RIDGE PKY (AT S COUNTY LINE RD); 630.455.5504; DAILY 7-2:30AM

Olive Garden

"...finally a place that is both kid and adult friendly... tasty Italian chain with lot's of convenient locations... the staff consistently attends to the details of dining with babies and toddlers—minimizing wait time, highchairs offered spontaneously, bread sticks brought immediately... food is served as quickly as possible... happy to create special orders... our waitress even acted as our family photographer..."

Children's menu ✓ | $$ Prices
Changing station ✓ | ❹ Customer service
Highchairs/boosters ✓ | ❹ Stroller access

WWW.OLIVEGARDEN.COM

BLOOMINGDALE—332 W ARMY TRAIL RD (AT SPRINGFIELD DR); 630.307.7080; SU-TH 11-10, F-SA 11-11

BOLINGBROOK—215 S WEBER RD (AT VETERANS PKY); 630.759.5191; SU-TH 11-10, F-SA 11-11

DOWNERS GROVE—1211 BUTTERFIELD RD (AT S HIGHLAND AVE); 630.852.4224; SU-TH 11-10, F-SA 11-11

NAPERVILLE—620 S STATE RTE 59 (AT FOX VALLEY SHOPPING CTR); 630.355.2818; M-TH 11-10, F-SU 11-11

NORTH RIVERSIDE—7513 W CERMAK RD (AT NORTH RIVERSIDE MALL); 708.447.0666; SU-TH 11-10, F-SA 11-11; MALL PARKING

SAINT CHARLES—3785 E MAIN ST (AT CHARLESTOWNE MALL); 630.443.1122; SU-TH 11-10, F-SA 11-11

Original Pancake House ★★★★½

"...consistently the best breakfast around... great flapjacks and appropriately-sized kids meals... food comes quickly... the most amazing apple pancakes ever... service is always friendly, but sometimes it can take a while to actually get the food... the highlight for my daughter is the free balloon when we leave... always a lot of families here with small children on the weekends, so you don't have to worry about being the only one..."

Children's menu .... ✓ $$ .... Prices
Changing station .... ✓ ❹ .... Customer service
Highchairs/boosters .... ✓ ❸ .... Stroller access

WWW.ORIGINALPANCAKEHOUSE.COM

LA GRANGE PARK—531 LA GRANGE RD (OFF WOODLAWN AVE); 708.354.2112

OAK PARK—954 LAKE ST (OFF OAK PARK AVE); 708.524.0955; DAILY 6:30-9:30

Penny's Noodle Shop

Children's menu .... ✗ ✗ .... Changing station
Highchairs/boosters .... ✓

OAK PARK—1130 CHICAGO AVE (AT HARLEM AVE); 708.660.1300; DAILY 11-10, F-SA 11-10:30

Red Apple Pancake House

Children's menu .... ✓ ✓ .... Changing station
Highchairs/boosters .... ✓

CAROL STREAM—414 S SCHMALE RD (AT THORNHILL DR); 630.871.2911; DAILY 6-3

Red Robin ★★★½☆

"...very kid-oriented—loud, balloons, bright lights, colorful decor and a cheerful staff make Red Robin a favorite among parents and children... the food is mainly burgers (beef or chicken)... loud music covers even the most boisterous of screaming... lots of kids—all the time... sometimes the wait can be long, but the arcade games and balloons help pass the time..."

Children's menu .... ✓ $$ .... Prices
Changing station .... ✓ ❹ .... Customer service
Highchairs/boosters .... ✓ ❹ .... Stroller access

WWW.REDROBIN.COM

WARRENVILLE—28260 DIEHL RD (AT WINFIELD RD); 630.836.8870; SU-TH 11-10, F-SA 11-11

WHEATON—51 TOWN SQ (AT S NAPERVILLE RD); 630.784.9055; M-TH 11-10, F-SA 11-11, SU 11-9; PARKING LOT

Romano's Macaroni Grill ★★★★☆

"...family oriented and tasty... noisy so nobody cares if your kids make noise... the staff goes out of their way to make families feel welcome... they even provide slings by the table for infant carriers... the noise level is pretty constant so it's not too loud, but loud enough so that crying babies don't disturb the other patrons... good kids' menu with somewhat healthy items... crayons for kids to color on the paper tablecloths..."

Children's menu .... ✓ $$$ .... Prices
Changing station .... ✓ ❹ .... Customer service
Highchairs/boosters .... ✓ ❹ .... Stroller access

WWW.MACARONIGRILL.COM

WHEATON—21 BLANCHARD CIR (AT S NAPERVILLE RD); 630.668.9366; SU-TH 11-10, F-SA 11-11

Ruby Tuesday

“...nice variety of healthy choices on the kids' menu—turkey, spaghetti, chicken tenders... you can definitely find something healthy here... prices are on the high side, but at least everyone can find something they like... service is fast and efficient... my daughter makes a mess and they never let me clean it up... your typical chain, but it works—you'll be happy to see ample aisle space, storage for your stroller, and attentive staff...”

Children's menu .... ✓ $$ .... Prices
Changing station.......................... ✓ ❹ .... Customer service
Highchairs/boosters .... ✓ ❸ .... Stroller access

WWW.RUBYTUESDAY.COM

DOWNERS GROVE—1570 BUTTERFIELD RD (AT FINLEY RD); 630.627.4228; SU-TH 11-11, F-SA 11-12AM

Smokey Bones BBQ

“...reasonably healthy food for kids—not fried chicken fingers and fries... lots of TVs to entertain kids so adults can have a little time to talk... volume control at each table, stations often set to Nickelodeon... unique holders for car seats that cradle the seats...”

Children's menu .... ✓ $$$ .... Prices
Changing station.......................... ✓ ❹ .... Customer service
Highchairs/boosters .... ✓ ❹ .... Stroller access

WWW.SMOKEYBONES.COM

AURORA—4435 FOX VALLEY CTR DR (OFF RT 59); 630.236.9630; SU-TH 11-10, F-SA 11-11

Souplantation/Sweet Tomatoes

“...you can't beat the price and selection of healthy foods... all you can eat—serve yourself soup and salad bar... lots of healthy choices plus pizza and pasta... great for picky eaters... free for 2 and under and only $3 for kids under 5... booths for comfy seating and discreet breastfeeding... helps to have another adult along since it is self serve... they always bring fresh cookies to the table and offer to refill drinks...”

Children's menu .... ✓ $$ .... Prices
Changing station.......................... ✓ ❹ .... Customer service
Highchairs/boosters .... ✓ ❹ .... Stroller access

WWW.SOUPLANTATION.COM

SAINT CHARLES—2801 E MAIN ST (AT N KIRK RD); 630.377.3309; SU-TH 11-9, F-SA 11-10

TGI Friday's

“...good old American bar food with a reasonable selection for the healthier set as well... I love that the kids meal includes salad... my daughter requests the potato skins on a regular basis (which is good because they are also my favorite)... moderately priced... cheerful servers are used to the mess my kids leave behind... relaxed scene... I'd steer clear on a Friday night unless you don't mind waiting and watching the singles scene...”

Children's menu .... ✓ $$ .... Prices
Changing station.......................... ✓ ❹ .... Customer service
Highchairs/boosters .... ✓ ❸ .... Stroller access

WWW.TGIFRIDAYS.COM

AURORA—888 N ROUTE 59 (AT AMTRAK RAIL); 630.851.6565; SU-TH 11-12, F-SA 11-1

BLOOMINGDALE—302 W ARMY TRAIL RD (AT SCHMALE RD); 630.307.8126; DAILY 11:30-1:30

BOLINGBROOK—157 S WEBER RD (AT LILY COACH LN); 630.771.9860; DAILY 11:30-1:30

LOMBARD—601 E BUTTERFIELD RD (AT MAXANT DR); 630.964.3743; SU-TH 11-1, F-SA 11-2

NAPERVILLE—1516 N NAPER BLVD (AT RT 34); 630.505.9076; M-TH 11-12, F-SA 11-1, SU 11-11

OAK PARK—401 N HARLEM AVE (AT CENTRAL AVE); 708.445.8249; SU-TH 11-12, F-SA 11-1; PARKING LOT

SAINT CHARLES—3875 E MAIN ST (AT SMITH RD); 630.443.6528; SU-TH 11-11:30, F-SA 11-12:30; PARKING LOT

Village Tavern & Grill

"...the best chicken fingers around... very kid-friendly... infant car seat stands and Koala changing stations in the bathroom... terrific neighborhood place that is just fine for a family dinner... wide selections and variety... you will likely see your friends there, too..."

Children's menu .... ✓ $$ .... Prices
Changing station .... ✓ ❹ .... Customer service
Highchairs/boosters .... ✓ ❸ .... Stroller access

WWW.VILLAGETAVERNANDGRILL.COM

CAROL STREAM—291 S SCHMALE RD (AT ST CHARLES RD); 630.668.1101; DAILY 11-1AM

Southern Suburbs

"lila picks"

★Fuddrucker's ★Leona's

restaurants

Applebee's Neighborhood Grill ★★★½☆

"...geared to family dining—they expect you to be loud and leave a mess... Macaroni & Cheese, Hot Dogs, and tasty grilled cheese... activity book and special kids cup are a bonus... service can be slow, but they will cover you with things to snack on... stay clear on Friday and Saturday nights... comfort food in a casual atmosphere... even though it's part of a very large chain you get the feeling it's a neighborhood-type place..."

Children's menu ✓ $$ Prices
Changing station ✓ ❹ Customer service
Highchairs/boosters ✓ ❸ Stroller access

WWW.APPLEBEES.COM

JOLIET—2795 PLAINFIELD RD (AT HENNEPIN DR); 815.254.9070; M-TH 11-11, F-SA 11-12, SU 11-10

Chili's Grill & Bar ★★★½☆

"...family-friendly, mild Mexican fare... delicious ribs, soups, salads... kids' menu and crayons as you sit down... on the noisy side, so you don't mind if your kids talk in their usual loud voices... service is excellent... fun night out with the family... a wide variety of menu selections for kids and their parents—all at a reasonable price... best chicken fingers on any kids' menu..."

Children's menu ✓ $$ Prices
Changing station ✓ ❹ Customer service
Highchairs/boosters ✓ ❹ Stroller access

WWW.CHILIS.COM

ORLAND PARK—15735 S HARLEM AVE (AT W 157TH ST); 708.342.1626; M-TH 11-11, F-SA 11-12, SU 11-10:30

Corner Bakery Cafe ★★★½☆

"...best kid's grilled cheese in town and excellent oatmeal raisin cookies... very nice, kid-friendly... a tastier and healthier alternative to fast food... selection ranges from sandwiches to pasta to salads and pizza... great for a quick bite... space is limited so strollers can be tricky ..."

Children's menu ✓ $$ Prices
Changing station ✗ ❹ Customer service
Highchairs/boosters ✓ ❸ Stroller access

WWW.CORNERBAKERY.COM

ORLAND PARK—14650 S LAGRANGE RD (AT 147TH ST); 708.460.8202; M-TH 7:30-8, F-SA 7:30-9, SU 8-7

Denny's

"...inexpensive, coloring books, crayons and a good kids menu... you can customize your order to accommodate your tots needs... the layout is roomy so strollers can be parked right next to your table... booths provide plenty of cover if you need to breastfeed... nothing fancy, but very convenient if you need to quickly find a place to rest up with your babes..."

Children's menu .... ✓ $$ .... Prices
Changing station .... ✓ ❹ .... Customer service
Highchairs/boosters .... ✓ ❹ .... Stroller access

WWW.DENNYS.COM

OAK LAWN—9217 S CICERO AVE (AT W 92ND ST); 708.499.3810; DAILY 6-12

Fazoli's

"...quick, easy and satisfying Italian food... spacious and comfortable... free breadsticks to keep little minds in check before the meatballs and pasta arrive... a nice step up from the easy fast-food trap... service is quick and the food is good..."

Children's menu .... ✓ $$ .... Prices
Changing station .... ✓ ❹ .... Customer service
Highchairs/boosters .... ✓ ❸ .... Stroller access

WWW.FAZOLIS.COM

JOLIET—2410 W JEFFERSON ST (AT S JOYCE RD); 815.741.1797; SU-TH 10:30-10, F-SA 10:30-11; FREE PARKING

MATTESON—4165 LINCOLN HWY (AT PULASKI RD); 708.283.2465; SU-TH 10:30-10, F-SA 10:30-11; FREE PARKING

Fuddruckers

"...a super burger chain with fresh and tasty food... colorful and noisy with lots of distraction until the food arrives... loads of fresh toppings so that you can make your perfectly cooked burger even better... great kids deals that come with a free treat... noise not a problem in this super casual atmosphere... some locations have video games in the back which will buy you an extra half hour if you need it... low-key and very family friendly..."

Children's menu .... ✓ $$ .... Prices
Changing station .... ✓ ❹ .... Customer service
Highchairs/boosters .... ✓ ❹ .... Stroller access

WWW.FUDDRUCKERS.COM

MATTESON—300 TOWN CTR RD (AT CICERO AVE); 708.747.7763; SU-TH 11-9, F-SA 11-10

Leona's

"...huge portions of tasty salads, pizza and other Italian goodies... thin crust and deep dish pizza... casual setting with awesome staff—the waitresses took turns walking our fussy daughter around while my husband and I finished our dinner... quick, friendly service except on weekends when it's busy... crayons, stickers, toddler cups with straws... good vegetarian (even vegan) items..."

Children's menu .... ✓ $$ .... Prices
Changing station .... ✗ ❹ .... Customer service
Highchairs/boosters .... ✓ ❹ .... Stroller access

WWW.LEONAS.COM

HOMEWOOD—17501 DIXIE HWY (AT 175TH ST); 708.922.9200; SU-TH 11:30-9, F-SA 12-10

OAK LAWN—6616 W 95TH ST (AT CHICAGO RIDGE MALL); 708.430.7070; SU-TH 11-9, F-SA 11-10; MALL PARKING

Olive Garden

"...finally a place that is both kid and adult friendly... tasty Italian chain with lot's of convenient locations... the staff consistently attends to the details of dining with babies and toddlers—minimizing wait time, highchairs offered spontaneously, bread sticks brought immediately... food is served as quickly as possible... happy to create special orders... our waitress even acted as our family photographer..."

Children's menu .... ✓ $$ .... Prices
Changing station.......................... ✓ ❹.......................... Customer service
Highchairs/boosters .... ✓ ❹............................. Stroller access

WWW.OLIVEGARDEN.COM

BURBANK—4801 W 77TH ST (AT LAVERGNE AVE); 708.636.9555; SU-TH 11-10, F-SA 11-11

LANSING—16601 TORRENCE AVE (AT RING RD); 708.895.6110; SU-TH 11-10, F-SA 11-11

MATTESON—5220 LINCOLN HWY (AT CICERO AVE); 708.481.0045; SU-TH 11-10, F-SA 11-11

Original Pancake House

"...consistently the best breakfast around... great flapjacks and appropriately-sized kids meals... food comes quickly... the most amazing apple pancakes ever... service is always friendly, but sometimes it can take a while to actually get the food... the highlight for my daughter is the free balloon when we leave... always a lot of families here with small children on the weekends, so you don't have to worry about being the only one..."

Children's menu .... ✓ $$ .... Prices
Changing station.......................... ✓ ❹.......................... Customer service
Highchairs/boosters .... ✓ ❸............................. Stroller access

WWW.ORIGINALPANCAKEHOUSE.COM

OAK FOREST—5148 W 159TH ST (AT LARAMIE AVE); 708.687.8282; DAILY 6:30-9:30

ORLAND PARK—15256 S LAGRANGE RD (OFF 151ST ST); 708.349.0600; DAILY 6:30-9:30

Snackville Junction

"...grew up going to this restaurant when it was at its original location... the train brings you your food when you sit at the counter (it does derail occasionally)... the atmosphere is fun and kids absolutely love it..."

Children's menu .... ✓ $$ .... Prices
Changing station.......................... ✗ ❸.......................... Customer service
Highchairs/boosters .... ✓ ❸............................. Stroller access

WWW.EVERYTHINGEP.COM

EVERGREEN PARK—9144 S KEDZIE AVE (AT W 92ND ST); 708.423.1313; M-F 11-8, SA 9-8, SU 11-5

TGI Friday's

"...good old American bar food with a reasonable selection for the healthier set as well... I love that the kids meal includes salad... my daughter requests the potato skins on a regular basis (which is good because they are also my favorite)... moderately priced... cheerful servers are used to the mess my kids leave behind... relaxed scene... I'd steer clear on a Friday night unless you don't mind waiting and watching the singles scene..."

Children's menu .... ✓ $$ .... Prices
Changing station.......................... ✓ ❹.......................... Customer service
Highchairs/boosters .... ✓ ❸............................. Stroller access

WWW.TGIFRIDAYS.COM

restaurants

JOLIET—1078 LOUIS JOLIET MALL (AT LOUIS JOLLET MALL); 815.254.1882; DAILY 11:30-1:30; MALL PARKING

ORLAND PARK—15407 S LA GRANGE RD (AT ORLAND PARK PL); 708.460.0269; M-TH 11-11, F-SA 11-12, SU 11-10

doulas & lactation consultants

Editor's Note: Doulas and lactation consultants provide a wide range of services and are very difficult to classify, let alone rate. In fact the terms 'doula' and 'lactation consultant' have very specific industry definitions that are far more complex than we are able to cover in this brief guide. For this reason we have decided to list only those businesses and individuals who received overwhelmingly positive reviews, without listing the reviewers' comments.

Greater Chicago Area

Association of Labor Assistants & Childbirth Educators (ALACE)

Labor doula .... ✓ ✗ .... Postpartum doula
Pre & post natal massage .... ✗ ✗ .... Lactation consultant

WWW.ALACE.ORG

CHICAGO—617.441.2500

Doulas of North America (DONA)

Labor doula .... ✓ ✓ .... Postpartum doula
Pre & post natal massage .... ✗ ✗ .... Lactation consultant

WWW.DONA.ORG

CHICAGO—888.788.3662

La Leche League

Labor doula .... ✗ ✗ .... Postpartum doula
Pre & post natal massage .... ✗ ✓ .... Lactation consultant

WWW.LALECHELEAGUE.ORG

CHICAGO—VARIOUS LOCATIONS; 847.519.7730; CHECK SCHEDULE ONLINE

Lactation Associates

Labor doula .... ✗ ✗ .... Postpartum doula
Pre & post natal massage .... ✗ ✓ .... Lactation consultant

NORTHBROOK—847.509.8302

Northwestern Memorial Hospital (Women & Maternity Classes)

Labor doula .... ✗ ✗ .... Postpartum doula
Pre & post natal massage .... ✗ ✓ .... Lactation consultant

WWW.NMH.ORG

RIVER NORTH/RIVER WEST—251 E HURON ST (AT N FAIRBANKS CT); 312.926.7155; CALL FOR SCHEDULE

Palos Community Hospital (Maternal & Child Education)

Labor doula .... ✗ ✗ .... Postpartum doula
Pre & post natal massage .... ✗ ✓ .... Lactation consultant

WWW.PALOSHOSPITAL.ORG

PALOS HEIGHTS—12251 S 80TH AVE (AT W 129TH ST); 708.923.5758; CALL FOR SCHEDULE

exercise

City of Chicago

"lila picks"

★East Bank Club

★Sweet Peas' Studio

★Walk A Bye Baby

Bloom Yoga Studio

Prenatal ✓ | ✓ Mommy & me
Child care available ✓

WWW.BLOOMYOGASTUDIO.COM

RAVENSWOOD—4663 N ROCKWELL (AT W LELAND AVE); 773.463.9642

Bubbles Academy ★★★★☆

"...prenatal yoga that is both fun and productive... I love that I can do yoga at the same place my daughter can play and also start learning about yoga... friendly and highly competent teachers... I wish they had even more classes for adults..."

Prenatal ✓ | $$$ Prices
Mommy & me ✓ | ❸ Decor
Child care available ✗ | ❸ Customer service

WWW.BUBBLESACADEMY.COM

LINCOLN PARK/DEPAUL/OLD TOWN—1504 N FREMONT ST (AT W NORTH AVE); 312.944.7677; CALL FOR SCHEDULES; FREE PARKING

Bulldog Boot Camp

Prenatal ✗ | ✗ Mommy & me
Child care available ✗

WWW.BULLDOGBOOTCAMP.COM

NORTH CENTER/ST BEN'S—4305 N LINCOLN AVE (AT CULLOM AVE); 708.763.8754; CHECK SCHEDULE ONLINE

East Bank Club ★★★★★

"...complementary prenatal exercise classes with resist-a-ball and water workouts... many personal trainers are certified to work with pre and postnatal clients... beautiful club facilities... pricier than your average gym, but then again the services and offerings at this club are incredible..."

Prenatal ✓ | $$$$ Prices
Mommy & me ✓ | ❺ Decor
Child care available ✓ | ❺ Customer service

WWW.EASTBANKCLUB.COM

RIVER NORTH/RIVER WEST—500 N KINGSBURY ST (AT W HUBBARD ST); 312.527.5800; CHECK SCHEDULE ONLINE

Equinox Fitness Club

"...great prenatal yoga... friendly environment... always clean and well kept... if you book a spa treatment during the week between 8 and 2, or weekends from 8 to 1, they offer free childcare for up to two hours..."

Prenatal.......✓ | $$....... Prices
Mommy & me.......✗ | ❺....... Decor
Child care available.......✓ | ❺....... Customer service

WWW.EQUINOXFITNESS.COM

LINCOLN PARK/DEPAUL/OLD TOWN—1750 N CLARK ST (AT N LA SALLE DR); 312.254.4000; CHECK SCHEDULE ONLINE; PARKING LOT

Global Yoga & Wellness Center

"...fantastic prenatal yoga class... the instructor is the owner, a nurse and a doula—a winning combination... warm, relaxing environment where all expectant moms feel welcome... I feel I was able to avoid a lot of the common ailments associated with pregnancy by incorporating these exercises into my everyday schedule..."

Prenatal.......✓ | $$....... Prices
Mommy & me.......✓ | ❹....... Decor
Child care available.......✗ | ❹....... Customer service

WWW.GLOBALYOGACENTER.COM

BUCKTOWN—1823 W N AVE (AT N HONROE ST); 773.489.1510; CHECK SCHEDULE ONLINE

exercise

Lakeshore Athletic Club

"...state-of-the-art equipment and facilities... lots to do to get you a great workout... great place for moms to exercise—they have childcare that is reasonable, and you can watch them in the childcare room via TVs on the treadmill... their Fit Moms program is a great way to get back in shape after pregnancy... some mommy and me classes..."

Prenatal.......✓ | $$$....... Prices
Mommy & me.......✓ | ❸....... Decor
Child care available.......✓ | ❸....... Customer service

WWW.LSAC.COM

LINCOLN PARK/DEPAUL/OLD TOWN—1320 W FULLERTON AVE (AT N LAKEWOOD AVE); 773.477.9888; CHECK SCHEDULE ONLINE

LOOP—211 N STETSON AVE (AT N COLUMBUS DR); 312.856.9418; CHECK SCHEDULE ONLINE

RIVER NORTH/RIVER WEST—333 E ONTARIO ST (AT N LAKE SHORE DR); 312.944.4546; CHECK SCHEDULE ONLINE; STREET PARKING

RIVER NORTH/RIVER WEST—441 N WABASH AVE (AT E HUBBARD ST); 312.644.4880; CHECK SCHEDULE ONLINE; PARKING LOT

Lincoln Park Athletic Club

"...an amazing facility that includes rock climbing, a pool and group exercise options... the prenatal yoga classes are pretty good as are the aquarobics classes... instructors vary so find one that you like and keep taking his/her classes..."

Prenatal.......✓ | $$$....... Prices
Mommy & me.......✗ | ❹....... Decor
Child care available.......✓ | ❹....... Customer service

WWW.LPACONLINE.COM

CHICAGO—1019 W DIVERSEY PKWY (AT N RACINE AVE); 773.529.2022; CHECK SCHEDULE ONLINE

Moksha Yoga Center

★★★★☆

"...prenatal and mommy and me yoga... scheduled during evening hours... classes are suitable for expectant mothers as well as

moms/dads/caregivers with children under 2... enjoyable class in a relaxed atmosphere... ❞

Prenatal	✓	$$$	Prices
Mommy & me	✓	❸	Decor
Child care available	✗	❸	Customer service

WWW.PRIYAYOGA.COM

EAST/WEST OLD TOWN GOLD COAST/STREETERVILLE—1 E OAK ST (AT N STATE ST); 312.587.7492; CHECK SCHEDULE ONLINE

Stroller Fit ★★★★☆

❝*...a great workout for parents and the kids are entertained the whole time... a great way to ease back into exercise after your baby's birth... the instructor is knowledgeable about fitness and keeping babies happy... motivating, supportive, and fun for kids and moms... sometimes they even set up a play group for after class... not just a good workout, but also a great chance to meet other moms and kids...* ❞

Prenatal	✗	$$$	Prices
Mommy & me	✓	❸	Decor
Child care available	✗	❸	Customer service

WWW.STROLLERFIT.COM

CHICAGO—VARIOUS LOCATIONS; 630.212.5586

Sweet Pea's Studio ★★★★★

❝*...prenatal yoga and baby and me classes... small enough that you feel welcome and comfortable... mix of basic yoga and talking... very informative—geared toward attachment parenting philosophy... easy parking makes this a relaxing and rejuvenating outing...* ❞

Prenatal	✓	$$	Prices
Mommy & me	✓	❹	Decor
Child care available	✗	❺	Customer service

WWW.SWEETPEASSTUDIO.COM

ROSCOE VILLAGE/WEST LAKEVIEW—3717 N RAVENSWOOD (AT W WAVELAND AVE); 773.248.9642; CHECK SCHEDULE ONLINE; STREET PARKING

Three Pillars Wellness Center ★★★☆☆

❝*...currently offering one Mommy and Me class per week.... children's yoga classes also offered...* ❞

Prenatal	✗	$$	Prices
Mommy & me	✓	❸	Decor
Child care available	✗	❸	Customer service

WWW.3PILLARS.ORG

HYDE PARK—1516 E 53RD ST (AT S HARPER AVE); 773.363.7607; CHECK SCHEDULE ONLINE

Walk A Bye Baby ★★★★★

❝*...a stroller exercise class through Lincoln Park... during winter months held inside at the Windy City Field House... met other new moms and got exercise at the same time—a win-win situation... the instructor is fun, knowledgeable and makes working out with a baby easy...* ❞

Prenatal	✓	$$$	Prices
Mommy & me	✓	❺	Decor
Child care available	✓	❺	Customer service

WWW.WALKABYEBABY.COM

CHICAGO—VARIOUS LOCATIONS; 312.829.2229; CHECK SCHEDULE ONLINE

YMCA ★★★★☆

❝*...the variety of fitness programs offered is astounding... class types and quality vary from facility to facility, but it's a must for new moms to* *check out... most facilities offer some kind of kids' activities or childcare so you can time your workouts around the classes... aerobics, yoga, pool—our Y even offers Pilates now... my favorite classes are the mom & baby yoga... the best bang for your buck... they have it all—great programs that meet the needs of a diverse range of families...* ❞

Prenatal..✓ $$$.. Prices
Mommy & me..................................✓ ❸.. Decor
Child care available.........................✓ ❸.......................... Customer service

WWW.YMCA.COM

CHICAGO—501 N CENTRAL AVE (AT W LAKE ST); 773.287.9120; M-F 6-9, SA-SU 7-7; PARKING LOT

CHINATOWN—1608 W 21ST PL (AT S ASHLAND AVE); 312.738.0282; M-F 8-6; STREET PARKING

COLUMET HEIGHTS—3039 E 91ST ST (AT S COMMERCIAL AVE); 773.721.9100; M-F 6-7:30, SA 7-3; PARKING LOT

EAST/WEST OLD TOWN GOLD COAST/STREETERVILLE—30 W CHICAGO AVE (AT N STATE ST); 312.944.6211; CHECK SCHEDULE ONLINE

HUMBOLDT PARK—1834 N LAWNDALE AVE (AT W ARMITAGE AVE); 773.235.2525; M-F 5:30-9, SA 8-3, SU 9-2; PARKING LOT

IRVING PARK/MAYFAIR—4251 W IRVING PARK (AT N KEELER AVE); 773.777.7500; CALL FOR SCHEDULES; FREE PARKING

LINCOLN PARK/DEPAUL/OLD TOWN—1515 N HALSTEAD (AT W CERMAK RD); 312.440.7272; CALL FOR SCHEDULE; STREET PARKING

NEAR SOUTH SIDE—3763 S WABASH AVE (AT E PERSHING RD); 773.285.0020; M-F 8-8:30, SA 9-2; STREET PARKING

ROSCOE VILLAGE/WEST LAKEVIEW—3333 N MARSHFIELD (AT N LINCOLN AVE); 773.248.3333; CALL FOR SCHEDULES; STREET PARKING

ROSELAND—4 E 111TH ST (AT S STATE ST); 773.785.9210; M-F 6-9, SA 9-5, SU 12-5

SAUGANASH—6235 S HOMAN AVE (AT W 63RD ST); 773.434.0300; M-F 9-9, SA 9-2; STREET PARKING

SOUTH LOOP—1001 W ROOSEVELT RD (AT UNIVERSITY OF ILLINOIS AT CHICAGO); 312.421.7800

WEST ROGERS PARK—2424 W TOUHY AVE (AT N WESTERN AVE); 773.262.8300; CALL FOR SCHEDULES; STREET PARKING

WOODLAWN—6330 S STONY ISLAND AVE (AT E 63RD ST); 773.947.0700; M-F 5:30-8:45, SA 6:30-4:15; PARKING LOT

Northwestern Suburbs

"lila picks"

★Lifetime Fitness

Lifetime Fitness

"...top-notch, beautiful, and huge facilities... plenty of equipment, both cardio and weights—never a wait for equipment... the childcare center is incredible—my kids think they're going to an indoor playground... many family and child activities... some locations offer a full service Aveda salon and spa... state-of-the-art and extremely family friendly..."

Prenatal	✗	$$$	Prices
Mommy & me	✗	❺	Decor
Child care available	✓	❹	Customer service

WWW.LIFETIMEFITNESS.COM

SCHAUMBURG—900 E HIGGINS RD (AT N PLUM GROVE RD); 847.843.8500; CHECK SCHEDULE ONLINE; PARKING LOT

YMCA

"...the variety of fitness programs offered is astounding... class types and quality vary from facility to facility, but it's a must for new moms to check out... most facilities offer some kind of kids' activities or childcare so you can time your workouts around the classes... aerobics, yoga, pool—our Y even offers Pilates now... my favorite classes are the mom & baby yoga... the best bang for your buck... they have it all—great programs that meet the needs of a diverse range of families..."

Prenatal	✓	$$$	Prices
Mommy & me	✓	❸	Decor
Child care available	✓	❸	Customer service

WWW.YMCA.COM

LAKE ZURICH—1025 OLD MCHENRY RD (AT RTE 53); 847.438.5300; M-F 5:15-10, SA 5:30-6, SU 8-5; PARKING LOT

PALATINE—1200 W NORTHWEST HWY (AT BALDWIN RD); 847.359.2400; CALL FOR SCHEDULES; FREE PARKING

Northern Suburbs

"lila picks"

★Evanston Athletic Club Yoga

Evanston Athletic Club Yoga

"...prenatal and mommy and me yoga... for moms and babies six weeks to walking... the class is very casual... perfect for beginners... lots of interaction with the babies... a very good bonding experience... the time of the class—9:15 am to 10:30 am—seems to be right at nap time for most babies..."

Prenatal ✓ | $$$ Prices
Mommy & me ✓ | ❸ Decor
Child care available ✗ | ❹ Customer service

WWW.EACONLINE.COM

EVANSTON—1723 BENSON AVE (AT CHURCH ST); 847.866.6190; CHECK SCHEDULE ONLINE; STREET PARKING

Healing Power Yoga

"...great yoga studio with tons of different classes and workshops to choose from... wonderful teachers and I love the poses, support, techniques, and decent price... this place was a lifesaver after my pregnancy—they helped me get my 'normal' body back..."

Prenatal ✓ | $$ Prices
Mommy & me ✗ | ❹ Decor
Child care available ✗ | ❺ Customer service

WWW.HEALINGPOWERYOGA.COM

HIGHLAND PARK—474 CENTRAL AVE (AT SHERIDAN RD); 847.266.9642; CHECK SCHEDULE ONLINE

Jewish Community Center

"...you name it, they've got it... tumbling, mom & tot play groups, arts and crafts, music—even educational programs... an incredibly supportive environment—the staff is so good at what they do... cooking, dress up play, free play which includes lots of running around and giggling... perfect for meeting other moms and finding something to do during the cold months... program costs vary, but we have yet to come across a class that wasn't worth every penny..."

Prenatal ✓ | $$$ Prices
Mommy & me ✓ | ❸ Decor
Child care available ✓ | ❸ Customer service

WWW.JCCOFCHICAGO.ORG

NORTHBROOK—3050 WOODRIDGE LN (OFF LAKE AVE); 847.272.8707; CHECK SCHEDULE ONLINE

YMCA

"...the variety of fitness programs offered is astounding... class types and quality vary from facility to facility, but it's a must for new moms to

check out... most facilities offer some kind of kids' activities or childcare so you can time your workouts around the classes... aerobics, yoga, pool—our Y even offers Pilates now... my favorite classes are the mom & baby yoga... the best bang for your buck... they have it all—great programs that meet the needs of a diverse range of families... ”

Prenatal	✓	$$$	Prices
Mommy & me	✓	❸	Decor
Child care available	✓	❸	Customer service

WWW.YMCACHGO.ORG

NILES—6300 W TOUHY AVE (AT N CALDWELL AVE); 847.647.8222; CALL FOR SCHEDULES; FREE PARKING

Western Suburbs

Delnor Community Health

"...prenatal yoga and water aerobics... I love that I can mix different types of exercise rather than just being stuck at the yoga studio all the time... instructors are wonderful and I've never had a bad workout here..."

Prenatal ✓ — $$ Prices
Mommy & me ✗ — ❸ Decor
Child care available ✓ — ❹ Customer service

WWW.DELNORWELLNESS.COM

GENEVA—296 RANDALL RD (AT WILLIAMSBURG AVE); 630.208.3933; CHECK SCHEDULE ONLINE; PARKING LOT

Universal Spirit Yoga

"...terrific yoga studio with wonderful instructors... I appreciated their pricing policy—you pay for nine classes, but have 12 weeks to use them... handy those weeks when pregnancy or life just got in the way... baby and me yoga is so fun, we look forward to it all week..."

Prenatal ✓ — $$ Prices
Mommy & me ✓ — ❹ Decor
Child care available ✗ — ❸ Customer service

WWW.UNIVERSALSPIRITYOGA.COM

NAPERVILLE—127 W AURORA AVE (AT S WEBSTER AVE); 630.416.7526; CHECK SCHEDULE ONLINE

YMCA

"...the variety of fitness programs offered is astounding... class types and quality vary from facility to facility, but it's a must for new moms to check out... most facilities offer some kind of kids' activities or childcare so you can time your workouts around the classes... aerobics, yoga, pool—our Y even offers Pilates now... my favorite classes are the mom & baby yoga... the best bang for your buck... they have it all—great programs that meet the needs of a diverse range of families..."

Prenatal ✓ — $$$ Prices
Mommy & me ✓ — ❸ Decor
Child care available ✓ — ❸ Customer service

WWW.YMCA.COM

DOWNERS GROVE—711 59TH ST (AT FAIRMOUNT AVE); 630.968.8400; M-F 5-10, SA 5-6, SU 9-5; PARKING LOT

ELMHURST—211 W 1ST ST (AT S YORK ST); 630.834.9200; CALL FOR SCHEDULES; STREET PARKING

Southern Suburbs

Center For Body & Soul ★★★★½

"...pregnancy yoga classes are offered as a new program... consists of 8 one hour sessions on Wednesday afternoons..."

Prenatal .... ✓ $ .... Prices
Mommy & me .... ✗ ❺ .... Decor
Child care available .... ✗ ❸ .... Customer service

WWW.YOUBEWELL.COM

PALOS HEIGHTS—12530 S HARLEM AVE (AT W 125TH ST); 708.448.2221; M-F 11-5:30, SA 11-3; PARKING LOT

YMCA ★★★★☆

"...the variety of fitness programs offered is astounding... class types and quality vary from facility to facility, but it's a must for new moms to check out... most facilities offer some kind of kids' activities or childcare so you can time your workouts around the classes... aerobics, yoga, pool—our Y even offers Pilates now... my favorite classes are the mom & baby yoga... the best bang for your buck... they have it all—great programs that meet the needs of a diverse range of families..."

Prenatal .... ✓ $$$ .... Prices
Mommy & me .... ✓ ❸ .... Decor
Child care available .... ✓ ❸ .... Customer service

WWW.YMCA.COM

HARVEY—178 E 155TH ST (AT PARK AVE); 708.331.6500; M-F 9-8, SA 9-5; PARKING LOT

parent education & support

Greater Chicago Area

"lila picks"

- ★Advocate Good Shepherd Hospital
- ★Condell Medical Center (Childbirth & Family Education)
- ★Evanston Northwestern Healthcare (Maternity Services)
- ★Northwestern Memorial Hospital (Women & Maternity Classes)
- ★Resurrection Medical Center (Family Birthplace)
- ★Silver Cross Hospital

Advocate Good Shepherd Hospital ★★★★★

"...a great selection of classes and extremely helpful and friendly staff—they spent an hour helping me pick classes that fit with my needs and schedule... very well organized... the classes are good and very well presented... the classes tend to fill up quickly so register early..."

Childbirth classes........................ ✓ | $ .... Prices
Parent group/club .... ✓ | ❺ .... Class selection
Breastfeeding support.................. ✓ | ❺ .... Staff knowledge
Child care info .... ✗ | ❺ .... Customer service

WWW.ADVOCATEHEALTH.COM

BARRINGTON—450 W IL RTE 22 (AT N HOUGH ST); 847.381.0123

Advocate Illinois Masonic Medical Center

Childbirth classes........................ ✗ | ✓.................. Breastfeeding support
Parent group/club .... ✓ | ✓............................ Child care info

WWW.ADVOCATEHEALTH.COM/IMMC

LAKEVIEW/WRIGLEYVILLE—836 W WELLINGTON AVE (AT N HALSTED ST); 773.296.5270

Birthways

Childbirth classes........................ ✗ | ✓.................. Breastfeeding support
Parent group/club .... ✗ | ✓............................ Child care info

WWW.BIRTHWAYSINC.COM

EDGEWATER—1484 W FARRAGUT AVE (AT N CLARK ST); 773.506.0607

Bloom Yoga Studio

Childbirth classes........................ ✗ | ✓.................. Breastfeeding support

Parent group/club .... × × .... Child care info

WWW.BLOOMYOGASTUDIO.COM

RAVENSWOOD—4663 N ROCKWELL (AT W LELAND AVE); 773.463.9642

Bradley Method, The ★★★½☆

"...12 week classes that cover all of the basics of giving birth... run by individual instructors nationwide... classes differ based on the quality and experience of the instructor... they cover everything from nutrition and physical conditioning to spousal support and medication... wonderful series that can be very educational... their web site has listings of instructors on a regional basis..."

Childbirth classes	✓	$$$	Prices
Parent group/club	×	❸	Class selection
Breastfeeding support	×	❸	Staff knowledge
Child care info	×	❸	Customer service

WWW.BRADLEYBIRTH.COM

CHICAGO—VARIOUS LOCATIONS; 800.422.4784; CHECK SCHEDULE & LOCATIONS ONLINE

Condell Medical Center (Childbirth & Family Education) ★★★★★

"...a great selection of classes that are reasonably priced... the staff is very knowledgability and presents the facts in a very straightforward manner... supportive and highly informative—we really enjoyed our group and felt well prepared for the birth of my daughter..."

Childbirth classes	✓	$$	Prices
Parent group/club	✓	❺	Class selection
Breastfeeding support	✓	❺	Staff knowledge
Child care info	×	❹	Customer service

WWW.CONDELL.ORG

LIBERTYVILLE—801 S MILWAUKEE AVE (AT CONDELL DR); 847.990.5407; CHECK SCHEDULE ONLINE

Delnor Community Hospital (NewLife Maternity Programs)

Childbirth classes	×	✓	Breastfeeding support
Parent group/club	✓	×	Child care info

WWW.DELNOR.COM

GENEVA—300 RANDALL RD (AT KESLINGER RD); 630.208.3999; CHECK SCHEDULE ONLINE

Edward Hospital (Parent Education Center) ★★★★★

"...Cradle Talk—what a lifesaver for first time moms... best of all, it's free... lots of support and education for parenting... weekly guest speakers include—pediatricians, dentists, children's organization, etc... many other helpful classes, such as—baby care, becoming parents and breastfeeding..."

Childbirth classes	✓	$	Prices
Parent group/club	✓	❺	Class selection
Breastfeeding support	✓	❺	Staff knowledge
Child care info	×	❺	Customer service

WWW.EDWARD.ORG

NAPERVILLE—801 S WASHINGTON ST (AT MARTIN DR); 630.527.7685; CHECK SCHEDULE ONLINE; GARAGE PARKING

Elmhurst Memorial Hospital (Parent Education)

Childbirth classes.......................... ✗ ✓ ....Breastfeeding support
Parent group/club .... ✗ ✗ .... Child care info

WWW.EMHC.ORG

ELMHURST—200 BERTEAU AVE (AT E SCHILLER ST); 630.782.7878; CHECK SCHEDULE ONLINE; GARAGE PARKING

Evanston Northwestern Healthcare (Maternity Services) ★★★★★

"...nothing, but praise for these workshops and classes... Lamaze, breastfeeding, car seat safety, boot camp for new dads—you name it, they're covering it... I especially enjoyed the support group for first time mothers—I made some great friends there... educational and fun..."

Childbirth classes........................ ✓ $$.. Prices
Parent group/club .... ✓ ❺ ....Class selection
Breastfeeding support.................. ✓ ❺ .... Staff knowledge
Child care info .... ✗ ❺ ....Customer service

WWW.ENHFIRST.ORG/CALENDAR

EVANSTON—2650 RIDGE AVE (AT CLINTON PL); 847.570.5020; CHECK SCHEDULE ONLINE

GLENVIEW—2100 PFINGSTEN RD (AT E LAKE AVE); 847.570.5020; CHECK SCHEDULE ONLINE

HIGHLAND PARK—718 GLENVIEW AVE (AT GREEN BAY RD); 847.570.5020; CHECK SCHEDULE ONLINE

Global Yoga & Wellness Center

Childbirth classes.......................... ✗ ✗ ....Breastfeeding support
Parent group/club .... ✓ ✗ .... Child care info

WWW.GLOBALYOGACENTER.COM

BUCKTOWN—1823 W NORTH AVE (AT N HONROE ST); 773.489.1510; CHECK SCHEDULE ONLINE

Hinsdale Hospital (Childbirth & Parenting)

Childbirth classes.......................... ✗ ✓ ....Breastfeeding support
Parent group/club .... ✗ ✗ .... Child care info

WWW.KEEPINGYOUWELL.COM

HINSDALE—120 N OAK ST (AT E WALNUT ST); 630.856.7525; CALL FOR SCHEDULE

La Grange Memorial Hospital

Childbirth classes.......................... ✗ ✓ ....Breastfeeding support
Parent group/club .... ✗ ✗ .... Child care info

WWW.KEEPINGYOUWELL.COM

LA GRANGE—5101 S WILLOW SPRINGS RD (AT GERMAN CHURCH RD); 630.856.7525; CALL FOR SCHEDULE

Lamaze International ★★★★☆

"...thousands of women each year are educated about the birth process by Lamaze educators... their web site offers a list of local instructors... they follow a basic curriculum, but invariably class quality will depend on the individual instructor... in many ways they've set the standard for birth education classes..."

Childbirth classes........................ ✓ $$$...................................... Prices
Parent group/club .... ✗ ❸ ....Class selection
Breastfeeding support................... ✗ ❸ .... Staff knowledge

Child care info	×	❸	Customer service

WWW.LAMAZE.ORG

CHICAGO—VARIOUS LOCATIONS; 800.368.4404; CHECK SCHEDULE AND LOCATIONS ONLINE

Luis A. Weiss Memorial Hospital

Childbirth classes	×	✓	Breastfeeding support
Parent group/club	×	×	Child care info

WWW.WEISSHOSPITAL.ORG

SHERIDAN PARK/UPTOWN—4646 N MARINE DR (AT W WILSON AVE); 800.503.1234

Mocha Moms ★★★★☆

"...a wonderfully supportive group of women—the kind of place you'll make lifelong friends for both mother and child... a comfortable forum for bouncing ideas off of other moms with same-age children... easy to get involved and not too demanding... the annual membership dues seem a small price to pay for the many activities, play groups, field trips, Moms Nights Out and book club meetings... local chapters in cities nationwide..."

Childbirth classes	×	$$$	Prices
Parent group/club	✓	❸	Class selection
Breastfeeding support	×	❸	Staff knowledge
Child care info	×	❸	Customer service

WWW.MOCHAMOMS.ORG

CHICAGO—VARIOUS LOCATIONS

MOMS Club ★★★★☆

"...an international nonprofit with lots of local chapters and literally tens of thousands of members... designed to introduce you to new mothers with same-age kids wherever you live... they organize all sorts of activities and provide support for new mothers with babies... very inexpensive for all the activities you get... book clubs, moms night out, play group connections... generally a very diverse group of women..."

Childbirth classes	×	$$$	Prices
Parent group/club	✓	❸	Class selection
Breastfeeding support	×	❸	Staff knowledge
Child care info	×	❸	Customer service

WWW.MOMSCLUB.ORG

CITY OF CHICAGO—VARIOUS LOCATIONS

Mothers and More ★★★½☆

"...a very neat support system for moms who are deciding to stay at home... a great way to get together with other moms in your area for organized activities... book clubs, play groups, even a 'mom's only' night out... local chapters offer more or less activities depending on the involvement of local moms..."

Childbirth classes	×	$$$	Prices
Parent group/club	✓	❸	Class selection
Breastfeeding support	×	❸	Staff knowledge
Child care info	×	❸	Customer service

WWW.MOTHERSANDMORE.COM

CHICAGO—VARIOUS LOCATIONS; CHECK SCHEDULE & LOCATIONS ONLINE

Mt Sinai Hospital (Women's Health)

Childbirth classes	×	✓	Breastfeeding support
Parent group/club	×	×	Child care info

WWW.SINAI.ORG

LAWNDALE—1500 S CALIFORNIA BLVD (AT 15TH ST); 773.257.5618; CHECK SCHEDULE ONLINE

Northwest Community Hospital (Health Connection)

"...they have a great resource library for new parents—that way you don't have to buy all of those parenting books!.. prenatal classes include the basics and even car seat safety... well run classes... a fun way to get prepared for the 'big day'..."

Childbirth classes	✓	$$	Prices
Parent group/club	✗	❹	Class selection
Breastfeeding support	✓	❺	Staff knowledge
Child care info	✗	❹	Customer service

WWW.NCH.ORG

ARLINGTON HEIGHTS—800 W CENTRAL RD (AT W KIRCHHOFF RD); 847.618.3463; CALL FOR SCHEDULE

Northwestern Memorial Hospital (Women & Maternity Classes)

"...great for my husband who had no clue what to expect... really did answer a ton of my own questions as well... very educational... covered everything from different types of pain medication, to baby's first bath... a lot of info given... you get handouts and other helpful reference materials... we didn't learn about alternative birthing methods, midwifery, or doulas... conservative medical approach... instructors all very personable... a little pricey for expecting parents..."

Childbirth classes	✓	$$	Prices
Parent group/club	✓	❹	Class selection
Breastfeeding support	✓	❺	Staff knowledge
Child care info	✗	❹	Customer service

WWW.NMH.ORG

RIVER NORTH/RIVER WEST—251 E HURON ST (AT N FAIRBANKS CT); 312.926.8400; CALL FOR SCHEDULE

Palos Community Hospital (Maternal & Child Education)

Childbirth classes	✗	✓	Breastfeeding support
Parent group/club	✗	✓	Child care info

WWW.PALOSHOSPITAL.ORG

PALOS HEIGHTS—12251 S 80TH AVE (AT W 129TH ST); 708.226.2300; CALL FOR SCHEDULE

Parent Circle, The

"...an amazing place for people with babies whether you are a traditional family or not... workshops, single parenting group, and baby-sitting co-op... I have found so much support in this group, I don't know what I would have done without this incredible group of parents... a wealth of information..."

Childbirth classes	✗	$	Prices
Parent group/club	✓	❹	Class selection
Breastfeeding support	✗	❹	Staff knowledge
Child care info	✗	❹	Customer service

HTTP://WWW.THEPARENTCIRCLE.COM/

CHICAGO—VARIOUS LOCATIONS; 847.604.0989

Resurrection Medical Center (Family Birthplace)

"...the support and knowledge-base of the midwives (instructors) was extraordinary... their prenatal classes helped my husband and I prepare for the kind of birth we wanted—all natural, no interventions... breastfeeding class was terrific and a big help in getting started nursing... inexpensive and very much worth the time..."

Childbirth classes ✓ | $$$ Prices
Parent group/club ✗ | ❸ Class selection
Breastfeeding support ✓ | ❸ Staff knowledge
Child care info ✗ | ❸ Customer service

WWW.RESHEALTH.ORG

AVONDALE—5645 W ADDISON ST (AT OUR LADY OF THE RESURRECTION MEDICAL CTR); 773.282.7000; CALL FOR SCHEDULE

LAKEVIEW/WRIGLEYVILLE—2900 N LAKE SHORE DR (AT ST JOSEPH HOSPITAL); 773.665.3000; CALL FOR SCHEDULE

WICKER PARK/UKRANIAN VILLAGE—2233 W DIVISION ST (AT SAINT MARY OF NAZARETH HOSPITAL CTR); 312.770.2000; CALL FOR SCHEDULE

EVANSTON—355 RIDGE AVE (AT SAINT FRANCIS HOSPITAL); 847.316.6340; CALL FOR SCHEDULE

MELROSE PARK—1225 W LAKE ST (AT WESTLAKE HOSPITAL); 708.938.7135; CALL FOR SCHEDULE

OAK PARK—3 ERIE CT (AT WEST SUBURBAN MEDICAL CTR); 708.763.6604; CALL FOR SCHEDULE

Rush-Presbyterian (St Luke's Medical Center)

Childbirth classes ✗ | ✓ Breastfeeding support
Parent group/club ✗ | ✓ Child care info

WWW.RUSH.EDU

WEST LOOP—1650 W HARRISON (AT S ASHLAND AVE); 312.942.2336

Sherman Hospital (Childbirth Education)

Childbirth classes ✗ | ✓ Breastfeeding support
Parent group/club ✗ | ✗ Child care info

WWW.SHERMANHEALTH.COM

ELGIN—934 CENTER ST (AT SLADE AVE); 847.429.8996; PARKING AVAILABLE

Silver Cross Hospital (Childbirth Classes)

"...our instructor was fantastic... informative and well presented class... teen pregnancy classes available... breastfeeding, childbirth and sibling classes available, too... I can't say enough about this wonderful program and hospital..."

Childbirth classes ✓ | $ Prices
Parent group/club ✗ | ❺ Class selection
Breastfeeding support ✓ | ❺ Staff knowledge
Child care info ✗ | ❺ Customer service

WWW.SILVERCROSS.ORG

JOLIET—1200 MAPLE RD (AT DRAPER AVE); 815.740.7108; CHECK SCHEDULE ONLINE

St James Hospital (Community Education)

Childbirth classes ✗ | ✓ Breastfeeding support
Parent group/club ✓ | ✗ Child care info

WWW.STJAMESHOSPITAL.ORG

PILSEN—1423 CHICAGO RD (AT E 14TH ST); 708.756.1000; CALL FOR SCHEDULE

St Joseph Hospital

Childbirth classes .... ✗ ✗ .... Breastfeeding support
Parent group/club .... ✗ ✗ .... Child care info

WWW.RESHEALTH.ORG

LINCOLN PARK/DEPAUL/OLD TOWN—2900 N LAKE SHORE DR (AT LINCOLN PARK); 773.665.3000

Turning Point

Childbirth classes .... ✗ ✗ .... Breastfeeding support
Parent group/club .... ✓ ✗ .... Child care info

WWW.SKOKIENET.ORG/EYEARS1/

SKOKIE—8324 SKOKIE BLVD (AT MAIN ST); 847.933.0051; CALL FOR SCHEDULE; PARKING BEHIND BLDG

pediatricians

Editor's Note: Pediatricians provide a tremendous breadth of services and are very difficult to classify and rate in a brief guide. For this reason we list only those practices for which we received overwhelmingly positive reviews. We hope this list of pediatricians will help you in your search.

City of Chicago

Advocate Health Center Sykes

NEAR SOUTH SIDE—2545 S MARTIN LUTHER KING DR (AT E 26TH ST); 312.949.4241; M-TH 8:30-6 F 8:30-5

Children's Memorial Hospital Outpatient Clinic

WWW.CHILDRENSMEMORIAL.ORG

LINCOLN PARK/DEPAUL/OLD TOWN—707 W FULLERTON AVE (AT N ORCHARD ST); 773.880.4649; M-F 8:30-5

Homefirst Family Practice

WWW.HOMEFIRST.COM

PULASKI PARK—550 W WEBSTER #306 (AT N JERSEY AVE); 847.981.1881; M W-TH 9-7, T F 9-4:30

Northwestern Children's Practice, The

WWW.SWEETBABIES.COM

EAST/WEST OLD TOWN GOLD COAST/STREETERVILLE—680 N LAKE SHORE DR (AT E ERIE ST); 312.642.5515; M-F 8-6, SA-SU 10-3

Northwestern Memorial Physicians Group

WWW.NMPG.COM

RIVER NORTH/RIVER WEST—201 E HURON ST (AT N ST CLAIR ST); 312.926.7337; DISCOUNTED GARAGE AT HURON ST

Rush University Medical Center--Pediatric Group

WWW.RUSH.EDU

UNITED CENTER PARK—1645 W JACKSON BLVD (AT S ASHLAND AVE); 312.942.2200; M-F 8:30-5:30

Streeterville Pediatrics

WWW.STREETERVILLEPEDIATRICS.YOURMD.COM

RIVER NORTH/RIVER WEST—233 E ERIE ST (AT N ST CLAIR ST); 312.280.1480; M-F 9:15-4:30, SA 9-1; HOSPITAL PARKING LOTS

Town & Country Pediatrics

WWW.TOWNANDCOUNTRYPEDS.COM

CHICAGO—2073 N CLYBOURN AVE (OFF W CORTLAND); 773.929.2260; M-TH 9-8, F 9-5, SA 9:30-3, SU 10:30-3

Northwestern Suburbs

ABC Dentistry

HOFFMAN ESTATES—1000 GRAND CANYON PKWY (AT W HIGGINS RD); 847.882.3360; CALL FOR APPT

Children & Teens Medical Center

WWW.CHILDRENANDTEENS.COM

BARRINGTON—27401 W RTE 22 (AT N BERTHA LN); 847.382.8900; M TH 9-7:45, T-W F 9-4:45

Pediatric Care Associates

WWW.PEDIATRICCAREASSOCIATES.COM

HOFFMAN ESTATES—2500 W HIGGINS RD (AT BARRINGTON RD); 847.884.7710; M-TH 9-5 F 9-4 SA 9-11; STREET PARKING

Pediatric Care PC

WWW.ADVOCATEHEALTH.COM

BARRINGTON—450 W IL ROUTE 22 (AT RTE 59); 847.382.7337; M-F 9-5 SA 9-12

Vernon Hills Pediatrics

WWW.CONDELL.ORG

VERNON HILLS—10 W PHILLIP RD (AT N DEERPATH DR); 847.367.5400; M-F 9-5

Northern Suburbs

Associates In Pediatric Care

SKOKIE—8707 SKOKIE BLVD (AT DEMPSTER ST); 847.676.5396; M W 9-7, T TH-F 9-5, SA 9-1; PARKING LOT

Elm Street Pediatrics

WINNETKA—716 ELM ST (AT LINCOLN AVE); 847.501.4040; M 8:30-5 T 8:30-7 W 8:30-6 TH 8:30-7 F 8:30-5 SA 9-1

Lake Forest Pediatric Associates

WWW.LAKEFORESTPEDIATRICS.COM

LAKE FOREST—900 N WESTMORELAND RD (AT N WESTMORELAND RD); 847.295.1220; PARKING LOT

Pediatric Health Care

SKOKIE—9669 KENTON AVE (AT GOLF RD); 847.568.9988; M TH 10-7 T-W F 10-5:30, SA 9-3

Western Suburbs

ABC Pediatrics, Ltd

NAPERVILLE—1020 E OGDEN AVE (AT NAPER BLVD); 630.355.0003; M-F 8-7:30 SA 8-12; PARKING LOT

Children's Health Partners

WWW.CHILDRENSHEALTHPARTNERS.COM

NAPERVILLE—2007 95TH ST (AT EDWARD MEDICAL CTR); 630.848.1700; M 8:30-5 T 9:30-8 W 8:30-4 TH 9:30-8 F 8:30-4 SA 8:30-11

Elmhurst Pediatric Association

WWW.EMHC.ORG

ELMHURST—103 N HAVEN RD (AT E PARK AVE); 630.832.3100; M-TH 8:15-5, F 8:15-4:30 , SA 8:15-12

Glen Ellyn Clinic

WHEATON—454 PENNSYLVANIA AVE (AT N MAIN ST); 630.469.7700; M-F 8-8:30 SA-SU 8-1

Lewis & Associates

LA GRANGE—1323 MEMORIAL DR (AT LA GRANGE MEMORIAL HOSPITAL); 708.352.4448; M-F 8:45-4:30

Midwest Pediatrics, Ltd

NAPERVILLE—1020 E OGDEN AVE (AT CASE ST); 630.355.1093; M-T TH 9-9, W F 9-5, SA 9-1; PARKING LOT

Pedios

OAK PARK—260 CHICAGO AVE (AT HARVEY AVE N); 708.383.8070; M 9-5, T 8-7, W 9-5, TH 9-6, F 8-4

River Forest Pediatrics

WWW.LUHS.ORG

RIVER FOREST—7420 CENTRAL AVE (AT WILLIAM ST); 708.366.5800; M-F 9-4:30

River Grove Clinic

RIVER GROVE—8383 BELMONT AVE (AT N CUMBERLAND AVE); 708.452.1200; M 9-5, T, TH 11-8, W 9-3, F, SA 9-3

West Suburban Pediatrics

WWW.WESTSUB.COM

OAKBROOK TERRACE—1S224 SUMMIT AVE (AT 14TH ST BETWEEN ROOSEVELT & BUTTERFIELD); 630.620.6322; M TH 9-7:30, T-W F 9-5, SA 9-12; PARKING LOT

Wheaton Pediatrics

WWW.WHEATONPEDIATRICS.COM

WHEATON—55 E LOOP RD (AT S NAPERVILLE RD); 630.690.7300; M-TH 8-7, F 8-5, SA 8:30-3

Southern Suburbs

Advanced Pediatrics

MATTESON—4440 W LINCOLN HWY (AT LINCOLN MALL); 708.481.6308; M 12-6, T-F 9-1; MALL PARKING

Niazi, Ahsan MD

JOLIET—1721 GLENWOOD AVE (AT MARQUETTE RD); 815.741.8888; M-F 9-5

breast pump sales & rentals

Greater Chicago Area

"lila picks"

★Art of Breastfeeding

★Parkway Drugs

Art Of Breastfeeding

"...great for first-time moms... online and local services... knowledgeable staff and great customer service... lactation support and breast pump sales... they are truly dedicated to making your breastfeeding experience as easy as possible... helpful, knowledgeable, supportive, and friendly..."

Customer Service ....❹ $$$.. Prices

WWW.ARTOFBREASTFEEDING.COM

LOGAN SQUARE—773.745.0992; CALL FOR APPT

Babies R Us

"...Medela pumps, Boppy pillows and lots of other breastfeeding supplies... staff knowledge varies from store to store, but everyone was friendly and helpful... clean and well-stocked... not a huge selection, but what they've got is great and very competitively priced..."

Customer Service ....❸ $$$.. Prices

WWW.BABIESRUS.COM

BURBANK—7750 S CICERO AVE (AT W 78TH ST); 708.424.8755; M-SA 9:30-9:30, SU 11-7 ; PARKING IN FRONT OF BLDG

LANSING—17675 S TORRENCE AVE (AT 177TH ST); 708.474.3222; M-SA 9:30-9:30, SU 11-7 ; PARKING IN FRONT OF BLDG

LOMBARD—481 E ROOSEVELT RD (AT S FAIRFIELD AVE); 630.495.9161; M-SA 9:30-9:30, SU 11-7; PARKING IN FRONT OF BLDG

NAPERVILLE—1955 GLACIER PARK AVE (AT MERIDIAN PKWY); 630.416.2225; M-SA 9:30-9:30, SU 11-7; PARKING IN FRONT OF BLDG

NILES—5660 TOUHY AVE (AT N CENTRAL AVE); 847.588.2081; M-SA 9:30-9:30, SU 11-7; PARKING IN FRONT OF BLDG

ORLAND PARK—15820 94TH AVE (AT ORLAND PARK PL); 708.873.9634; M-SA 9:30-9:30, SU 11-7 ; PARKING IN FRONT OF BLDG

SCHAUMBURG—16 E GOLF RD (AT N ROSELLE RD); 847.781.8889; M-SA 9:30-9:30, SU 11-7; PARKING IN FRONT OF BLDG

VERNON HILLS—295 CENTER DR (AT HAWTHORN SHOPPING CTR); 847.573.1447; M-SA 9:30-8, SU 11-6; PARKING IN FRONT OF BLDG

Ballin Pharmacy

"...a small pharmacy with the greatest staff... personable... large selection of Medela pumps and accessories... buy or rent Medela pumps... the staff is knowledgeable and will help you find the right nursing bras and accessories..."

Customer Service ....❺ $$.. Prices

WWW.BALLINRX.COM

ROSCOE VILLAGE/WEST LAKEVIEW—3330 N LINCOLN AVE (AT W SCHOOL ST); 773.348.0027; M-T TH-F 9-7, W 9-6, SA 9-5

Becker Pharmacy

RAVENSWOOD—4744 N WESTERN AVE (AT W LAWRENCE AVE); 773.561.4486; M-F 9-6, SA 9-4

Breast Pumps Plus

WWW.MYNURSINGSUPPLIES.COM

OAK LAWN—9628 S KOLMAR AVE (AT W 96TH ST); 708.424.9976

Child In You, The

"...sales and rentals... lots of assistance with choosing a breastpump... super friendly and knowledgeable staff... great prices on rentals and they will take the time to show you how everything works... Medela rentals at around $40 per month..."

Customer Service........................ ❸ $$$ .... Prices

WWW.THECHILDINYOU.COM

GENEVA—407 S 3RD ST (AT FULTON ST (INSIDE CRADLES & ALL)); 630.232.4030; M-SA 10-5, SU 12-4; STREET PARKING

Galt Toys & Galt Baby

WWW.GALTTOYSGALTBABY.COM

LINCOLN PARK/DEPAUL/OLD TOWN—900 N MICHIGAN AVE (AT E DELAWARE PL); 312.440.9550; M-SA 10-7, SU 11-6; GARAGE AT E WALTON ST

Parkway Drugs

"...best resource for hospital-grade Medela pumps, for rent or purchase... very reasonable rates—$50 per month and daily rates thereafter... the staff is extraordinarily helpful and goes out of their way to get you set up... they will deliver to some local areas..."

Customer Service........................ ❺ $$$ .... Prices

LINCOLN PARK/DEPAUL/OLD TOWN—2346 N CLARK ST (AT W BELDEN AVE); 773.549.2720; M-F 8-7, SA 9-6, SU 10-4; STREET PARKING

RIVER NORTH/RIVER WEST—680 N LAKE SHORE DR (AT E ERIE ST); 312.943.2224; M-F 8-8, SA 8-6, SU 8-4

GLENCOE—353 PARK AVE (AT VERNON AVE); 847.835.0387; M-TH 8-8, F 8-7, SA 8-6, SU 9-5

WILMETTE—333 RIDGE RD (AT WILMETTE AVE); 847.256.1000; M-TH 7:30-8, F 7:30-7, SA 7:30-5, SU 9-5

Peterson's Pharmacy

WWW.CORNERDRUGSTORE.COM

OAK PARK—715 LAKE ST (AT N EUCLID AVE); 708.848.5020; M-T TH 9-7, W F 9-6, SA 9-3

Right Start, The

"...a small selection of pumps for sale... their prices are on the higher side, and the pump selection is pretty limited... they carry the Medela Pump In Style... they only carry the best... good quality and customer service might make it totally worthwhile..."

Customer Service........................ ❹ $$$$ .... Prices

WWW.RIGHTSTART.COM

LINCOLN PARK—2121 N CLYBOURN AVE (AT N WAYNE AVE); 773.296.4420; M-SA 10-6, SU 11-5; PARKING LOT AT 2121 N CLYBOURN

HIGHLAND PARK—478 CENTRAL AVE (AT ST JOHNS AVE); 847.266.9270; DAILY 11-6

NAPERVILLE—30 W JEFFERSON AVE (AT S WASHINGTON ST); 630.548.2220; M-SA 10-6, SU 11-6

Online

amazon.com

"...I'm always amazed by the amount of stuff Amazon sells—including a pretty good selection of pumps... Medela, Avent, Isis, Ameda... prices range from great to average... pretty easy shopping experience... free shipping on bigger orders..."

babycenter.com

"...they carry all the major brands... prices are competitive, but keep in mind you'll need to pay for shipping too... the comments from parents are incredibly helpful... excellent customer service... easy shopping experience..."

birthexperience.com

"...Medela and Avent products... great deal with the Canadian currency conversion... get free shipping with big orders... easy site to navigate..."

breast-pumps.com

breastmilk.com

ebay.com

★★★★½

"...you can get Medela pumps brand new in packaging with the warranty for $100 less than retail... able to buy immediately instead of having to bid and wait... wide variety... be sure to check for shipping price... great place to find deals, but research the seller before you bid..."

express-yourself.net

healthchecksystems.com

lactationconnection.com

★★★½☆

"...Ameda and Whisper Wear products... nice selection and competitive prices... quick delivery of any nursing or lactation product you can imagine... the selection of mom and baby related items is fantastic..."

medela.com

"...well worth the money... fast, courteous and responsive... great site for a full listing of Medela products and links to purchase online... quality of customer service by phone varies... licensed lactation specialist answers e-mail via email at no charge and with quick turnaround..."

mybreastpump.com

"...a great online one-stop-shop for all things breast feeding... you can purchase hospital grade pumps from them... fast service for all you breastfeeding needs..."

diaper delivery services

Greater Chicago Area

Bottoms Up Diaper Service

"...Bottoms Up provided us with fresh, fluffy diapers every week for the first year after our child's birth... customer service was fast, reliable and easy... no difficulty with adjusting diaper count due to travel... makes an amazing baby shower gift... we found that their diaper covers leaked to the point of being useless... this is the only gig in town and they do a good job with reasonable prices..."

Customer Service ....❸ $$$..Prices

Service AreaLake, Cook, McHeney, & Dupage Counties

WWW.BOTTOMSUPDIAPERS.COM

WAUKEGAN—201 N GREEN BAY RD (AT WESTWAUKEE RD); 847.336.0040; M-TH 8-4, F 8-12

haircuts

Greater Chicago Area

"lila picks"

★Cookie Cutters Haircuts ★Kidsnips

★Kids Hair

Bear With Me

"...Chicago's first children's hair salon offers great haircuts in a playful setting... great fun for the kids..."

Customer Service .... ❷ $$$$ .... Prices

EAST/WEST OLD TOWN GOLD COAST/STREETERVILLE—72 E OAK ST (AT N RUSH ST); 312.664.6170; T TH-F 10-6, SA 9-5; GARAGE PARKING AVAILABLE

Cookie Cutters Haircuts

"...great place for baby's first haircut-even a special first haircut package... a fun salon with an indoor playground in which the kids can play before and after their cuts... very clever concept and well done—it's basically the only way I can get my son's hair cut... the stylists aren't always that consistent, but they do a good enough job... nice and patient staff... this place is perfectly designed for kids who hate having their haircut... my kids refuse to go anywhere else..."

Customer Service .... ❹ $$.. Prices

WWW.HAIRCUTSAREFUN.COM

GENEVA—1540 COMMONS DR (AT WILLIAMSBURG AVE); 630.232.8386; M-F 9-7, SA 9-5, SU 10-4

NAPERVILLE—125 S WASHINGTON ST (AT VAN BUREN AVE); 630.548.4386; M-F 9-7, SA 9-5, SU 10-4

NAPERVILLE—3224 S RTE 59 (AT 111TH ST); 630.904.4386; M-F 9-7, SA 9-5, SU 10-4

Great Clips

"...cheap, decent cuts... not specifically tailored around children so there aren't any horses or cars to sit in... stylists' experience with kids vary, but we generally walk away satisfied... you can't beat the price and you don't have to make an appointment... the balloon at the end makes it all worthwhile..."

Customer Service .... ❺ $$.. Prices

WWW.GREATCLIPS.COM

CAROL STREAM—994 W ARMY TRAIL RD (AT COUNTRY FARM RD); 630.540.9023; M-F 9-9, SA 8-5, SU 9-4

EAST/WEST OLD TOWN GOLD COAST/STREETERVILLE—1235 N CLYBOURN AVE (AT W DIVISION ST); 312.397.1237; M-F 8-8, SA 9-6, SU 10-4; PARKING LOT

LAKEVIEW/WRIGLEYVILLE—3165 N BROADWAY ST (AT W BRIAR PL); 773.871.2699; M-F 9-9, SA 9-6, SU 11-5

LAKEVIEW/WRIGLEYVILLE—539 W DIVERSEY PKWY (AT N CLARK ST); 773.281.2926; M-SA 9-7; FREE PARKING

LINCOLN PARK/DEPAUL/OLD TOWN—2184 N CLYBOURN AVE (AT W SHAKESPEARE AVE); 773.549.4580; M-SA 9-7; FREE PARKING

LAKE ZURICH—716 S RAND RD (AT JUNE TER); 847.550.6270; CALL FOR APPT

LINCOLNWOOD—3333 W TOUHY AVE (AT N MCCORMICK BLVD); 847.677.8865; M-SA 9-7; FREE PARKING

OAK LAWN—8729 RIDGELAND AVE (AT W 87TH ST); 708.598.7973; CALL FOR APPT

Kids Hair

"...one of the best places for kids' haircuts... videos, toys and lollipops... plenty to occupy a kid's attention, the cut is over before they know it... stylists are specially trained in fine-haired, wiggly, screaming clients... you can usually make a last-minute appointment... staff is great, good cuts... lots of turnover so don't get too attached to one stylist... quality varies by stylist... I recommend making an appointment... a little pricey, but a positive experience..."

Customer Service........................ ❸ $$$ .... Prices

WWW.KIDSHAIRINC.COM

DEER PARK—20330 N DEER PARK BLVD; 847.550.6955

Kidsnips

"...easy and stress free kid's cuts... darling decor and they are totally set up for tots... good for fidgety tots with lots of distractions... definitely make an appointment since there isn't much walk-in service... they take a cute picture and put it on a certificate with some hair... the only place my son would get a hair cut without screaming and going bananas..."

Customer Service........................ ❹ $$$ .... Prices

WWW.KIDSNIPS.COM

ARLINGTON HEIGHTS—356 E RAND RD (AT E PALATINE RD); 847.797.9690; M-T F 10-6, W TH 10-8, SA 9-5, SU 11-4

LINCOLN PARK/DEPAUL/OLD TOWN—1953 N CLYBOURN AVE (AT W CORTLAND ST); 773.935.9999; M-TH 10-7, F 10-6, SA 9-5, SU 10-4

DEERFIELD—655 DEERFIELD RD (AT WAUKEGAN RD); 847.374.8000; M W F 10-6, T TH 10-8, SA 9-5, SU 11-4; PARKING LOT

OAK BROOK—513 OAKBROOK CTR (AT 16TH ST); 630.571.1500; M-SA 10-9, SU 11-6; MALL PARKING

VERNON HILLS—128 HAWTHORN CTR (AT RING RD); 847.247.1110; M-SA 10-9, SU 11-6

WHEATON—2007 S NAPERVILLE RD (AT E LOOP RD); 630.653.3300; M-T 10-6, W TH 10-8, F 9-6, SA 9-5, SU 11-5

WILMETTE—3232 LAKE AVE (AT SKOKIE RD); 847.853.0099; M TH 9:30-8, T-W 9:30-7, F 9:30-6, SA 8:30-5:30, SU 10-4

Royal Children's Spa

WWW.ROYALSPA.INFO

BEVERLY—10126 S WESTERN AVE (AT 101ST ST); 773.238.2500; CALL FOR APPT

Snip N' Doodles Kids Salon

WWW.MYSALONONLINE.COM/SNIPNDOODLES

GENEVA—1881 S RANDALL RD (AT FABYAN PKY); 630.845.9820; M-TH 10-7, F 9-6, SA 9-5

Snippet's Mini Cuts

"...they figured it out—the kids are engaged and actually have fun... a great place if your child is afraid of haircuts or especially fidgety... lots of toys to play with and the kids love the car-shaped chairs... over $20 per cut, but it's worth every penny... experienced stylists help make parents and kids feel at ease..."

Customer Service .... ❹ $$$.. Prices

WWW.SNIPKID.COM

LINCOLN PARK/DEPAUL/OLD TOWN—2154 N CLYBOURN AVE (AT SOUTHPORT AVE); 773.755.1000; M-F 10-5:30, SA 9-5, SU 10-4

LOMBARD—YORKTOWN CENTER (AT S HIGHLAND AVE); 630.827.0300; M-F 10-9, SA 10-6, SU 11-6

NORTHBROOK—2240 NORTHBROOK CT (AT LAKE COOK RD); 847.498.4543; M-F 10-9, SA 10-7, SU 11-6

Supercuts

"...results definitely vary from location to location... they did their best to amuse my son and an okay job with his hair... cheap and easy, with decent results... some locations have toys for kids to play with... walk-ins welcome, but make an appointment if you are going on the weekend... ask for the cutter who's best with kids... great cut for the price... fast and easy..."

Customer Service .... ❹ $$.. Prices

WWW.SUPERCUTS.COM

BLOOMINGDALE—142 S GARY AVE (AT STRATFORD SQUARE MALL); 630.582.4746; M-F 9-9, SA 9-5:30, SU 9-5; MALL PARKING

MEDICAL VILLAGE—1651 W ROOSEVELT RD (AT S ASHLAND AVE); 312.829.6035; M-F 9-9, SA 9-6, SU 10-5

SKOKIE—3539 DEMPSTER ST (AT DRAKE AVE); 847.677.8889; CALL FOR APPT

Whipper Snippers Hair Cuts

"...a jungle gym while you wait and race car, barbie jeep, or airplane seats for the haircut... kids get to watch videos... the stylists really listen to what you want... no wait with appointments... we drive 30 minutes to get here and it's worth it... friendly staff..."

Customer Service .... ❹ $$.. Prices

WOODRIDGE—7440 WOODWARD AVE (AT 75TH ST); 630.435.9700; CALL FOR APPT

nanny & babysitter referrals

Greater Chicago Area

"lila picks"

★On The Wings Of An Angel

Nanny On The Net, A ★★★½☆

"...a national agency that places experienced (at least three years) nannies... easy to use and efficient... detailed background checks... all prospects are trained in CPR... legal, financial, and practical help for first-time 'employer' families... about $75 for the application fee and then additional placement fees when you succeed in finding a nanny..."

Baby nurses ✓
Nannies ✓
Au pairs ✗
Babysitters ✗
$$$$ Prices
❷ Candidate selection
❷ Staff knowledge
❷ Customer service
Service Area ..... Greater Chicago Area
WWW.ANANNYONTHENET.COM
CHICAGO—847.578.5000; M-F 9-5

Olive You Nanny Agency

Baby nurses ✓
Au pairs ✓
✓ Nannies
✓ Babysitters
WWW.OLIVEYOUNANNY.COM
CHICAGO—773.208.3370

On the Wings Of an Angel Referral and Support Service ★★★★★

"...wonderful staff and personal attention to all your needs... professional and experienced childcare for part-time and permanent placement... amazing attention to detail... they found me the perfect nanny the first time around!.. reasonable consultancy fees... they offer in-home consultants for families that want an alternative to having a nanny... they provide training for nannies, for example: cooking classes, craft classes, safety first classes and so much more... play groups for both the nannies and parents... you can not go wrong being under the wings of true angels... I would give them a 10 rating!..."

Baby nurses ✓
Nannies ✓
Au pairs ✗
Babysitters ✓
$$ Prices
❺ Candidate selection
❹ Staff knowledge
❺ Customer service
Service AreaAll Chigago land areas; Also located in Florida
WWW.PURPLEMONKEYNETWORK.ORG
HINSDALE—PO BOX 365; 630.915.2241; M-SA 10-7

Online

"lila picks"

★craigslist.org

4nannies.com

Baby nurses .... × | ✓ .... Nannies
Au pairs .... × | × .... Babysitters
Service Area .... nationwide
WWW.4NANNIES.COM

aupaircare.com

Baby nurses .... × | × .... Nannies
Au pairs .... ✓ | × .... Babysitters
Service Area .... International
WWW.AUPAIRCARE.COM

aupairinamerica.com

Baby nurses .... × | × .... Nannies
Au pairs .... ✓ | × .... Babysitters
Service Area .... International
WWW.AUPAIRINAMERICA.COM

babysitters.com

Baby nurses .... × | × .... Nannies
Au pairs .... × | ✓ .... Babysitters
Service Area .... nationwide
WWW.BABYSITTERS.COM

craigslist.org ★★★★★

"...you can find just about anything on craigslist... good starting point, especially if you don't want to spend a lot of money and are willing to do your own screening... we received at least 50 responses to our 'nanny wanted' ad... helped me find very qualified baby-sitters... includes all major cities in the US..."

Baby nurses .... ✓ | ✓ .... Nannies
Au pairs .... × | ✓ .... Babysitters
WWW.CRAIGSLIST.ORG

enannysource.com

Baby nurses .... × | ✓ .... Nannies
Au pairs .... × | × .... Babysitters
Service Area .... nationwide
WWW.ENANNYSOURCE.COM

findcarenow.com

Baby nurses .... × | × .... Nannies
Au pairs .... × | ✓ .... Babysitters
Service Area .... nationwide

WWW.FINDCARENOW.COM

get-a-sitter.com

Baby nurses ✗ ✗ Nannies
Au pairs ✗ ✓ Babysitters
Service Area nationwide
WWW.GET-A-SITTER.COM

householdstaffing.com

Baby nurses ✓ ✓ Nannies
Au pairs ✗ ✗ Babysitters
WWW.HOUSEHOLDSTAFFING.COM

interexchange.org

Baby nurses ✗ ✗ Nannies
Au pairs ✓ ✗ Babysitters
Service Area International
WWW.INTEREXCHANGE.ORG

nannies4hire.com

Baby nurses ✗ ✓ Nannies
Au pairs ✗ ✗ Babysitters
WWW.NANNIES4HIRE.COM

nannylocators.com ★★★½☆

“...many listings of local nannies available... I have found that the listings are not always up to date... $100 subscriber fee to respond and contact nannies that have posted... different regions have varying amounts of listings available...”

Baby nurses ✗ ✓ Nannies
Au pairs ✗ ✗ Babysitters
Service Area Nationwide
WWW.NANNYLOCATORS.COM

sittercity.com ★★★★☆

“...Wonderful online resource... an online baby-sitter database filled with mostly college and graduate students looking for baby-sitting and nanny jobs... candidates are not prescreened so you must check references... Fee to access the database is $35 plus $5 per month... tends to be be more useful for baby-sitters than regular daytime nannies...”

Baby nurses ✗ ✗ Nannies
Au pairs ✗ ✓ Babysitters
Service Area nationwide
WWW.SITTERCITY.COM

student-sitters.com

Baby nurses ✗ ✗ Nannies
Au pairs ✗ ✓ Babysitters
WWW.STUDENT-SITTERS.COM

photographers

Greater Chicago Area

"lila picks"

★Celebrity Kids Portrait Studio

★Classic Kids

★Kiddie Kandids

★Photography by Jacob VanVooren

Art Craft Photographers

WWW.ARTCRAFTPHOTO.COM

BLOOMINGDALE—139 1ST ST (AT W SCHICK RD); 630.529.8400

Celebrity Kids Portrait Studio ★★★★★

"...fast and fabulous kid shots... computerized photos means you get to see and choose your pictures immediately... no negatives so make plenty of copies... they are willing to incorporate your ideas and props to personalize the portrait... the session can feel rushed, but the photos still come out great..."

Customer service........................❹ $$$$....................................Prices

WWW.CELEBRITYKIDS.COM

LINCOLN PARK—2121 N CLYBOURN (AT WEBSTER); 773.281.3686; CALL FOR APPT

GENEVA—1418 COMMONS DR (AT THE PROMENADE AT SAGEMORE); 630.208.5020; CALL FOR APPT

Classic Kids

"...worth every penny... commercial-quality photos... the quality of these archival black and whites and hand-painted photos will not disappoint... my son was a terror throughout the entire shoot and the pictures were still superb... the photographer and assistants are masters of play and distraction... our photos are beautiful, expressive and will be cherished reminders..."

Customer service........................❺ $$$$....................................Prices

Service Area ....in-studio only

WWW.CLASSICKIDS.NET

LINCOLN PARK/DEPAUL/OLD TOWN—917 W ARMITAGE AVE (AT N BISSELL ST); 773.296.2607; CALL FOR APPT

WINNETKA—566 CHESTNUT ST (AT SPRUCE ST); 847.446.2064; CALL FOR APPT

JCPenney Portrait Studio

"...don't expect works of art, but they are great for a quick wallet photo... photographers and staff range from great to not so good... a quick portrait with standard props and backdrops... definitely join the portrait club and use coupons... waits are especially long around the

holidays, so consider taking your Christmas pictures early... the e-picture option is a time saver... wait time for prints can be up to a month... look for coupons and you'll never have to pay full price... ”

Customer service .... ❹ $$ .... Prices

WWW.JCPENNEYPORTRAITS.COM

AURORA—4 FOX VALLEY CTR (AT E NEW YORK ST); 630.851.3833; M-SA 10-7, SU 11-4; MALL PARKING

BLOOMINGDALE—2 STRATFORD SQ (AT W SCHICK RD); 630.307.0358; MALL PARKING

JOLIET—3340 MALL LOOP DR (AT LOUIS JOLIET MALL); 815.439.1441; M-SA 10-6:30, SU 11-3:30; MALL PARKING

LOMBARD—175 YORKTOWN (AT S HIGHLAND AVE); 630.495.3808; M-SA 10-7, SU 11-5

NILES—220 GOLF MILL (AT N WASHINGTON ST); 847.296.6508

NORTH RIVERSIDE—7507 CERMAK RD (AT NORTH RIVERSIDE MALL); 708.442.5446; M-SA 10-7, SU 11-5; MALL PARKING

ORLAND PARK—151ST ST (AT ORLAND SQUARE SHOPPING CTR); 708.349.8999; M-SA 10-6:30, SU 11-4:30

SCHAUMBURG—WOODFIELD MALL (AT GOLF RD); 847.330.2640; MALL PARKING

VERNON HILLS—4 HAWTHORNE (AT E COURTLAND ST); 847.573.1760; M-SA 10-7, SU 11-5

Jessica Tampas Photography

“*...absolutely gorgeous newborn shots... harmonious and luxurious... my kids look completely at ease, totally unaware of the camera and completely in their element... timeless candids—we were thrilled... she is very easy to work with...* ”

Customer service .... ❺ $$$ .... Prices

WWW.JESSICATAMPAS.COM

WICKER PARK/UKRANIAN VILLAGE—312 N MAY ST (AT W FULTON); 312.664.0052; CALL FOR APPT

Kiddie Kandids

“*...good quality photos for all occasions... they made a big effort to get a smile out of my grumpy son... you don't need to make a reservation, just pop in and have the pictures taken... no sitting fee... photographers take the extra time necessary to get a great shot and they have the cutest props... lots of items to buy with your pictures on them—cups, bags, mouse pads... buy the CD of pictures rather than buying the prints... pictures are available right after the sitting...* ”

Customer service .... ❹ $$$ .... Prices

WWW.KIDDIEKANDIDS.COM

BURBANK—7750 S CICERO AVE (AT W 79TH ST); 708.952.4712; M-SA 9:30-8, SU 11-6

LOMBARD—481 E ROOSEVELT RD (AT S FAIRFIELD AVE); 630.916.1163; M-SA 9:30-8, SU 11-6

NAPERVILLE—1955 GLACIER PARK (AT MERIDIAN PKWY); 630.416.1973; M-SA 9:30-8, SU 11-6

NILES—5660 TOUHY AVE (AT N CENTRAL AVE); 847.647.8649; M-SA 9:30-8, SU 11-6

ORLAND PARK—15820 S 94TH AVE (AT SUNRISE LN); 708.873.0421; M-SA 9:30-8, SU 11-6

SCHAUMBURG—16 E GOLF RD (AT N ROSELLE RD); 847.882.4274; M-SA 9:30-8, SU 11-6

VERNON HILLS—295 CENTER DR (AT LAKEVIEW PKWY); 847.918.0452; M-SA 9:30-8, SU 11-6

Marc Harris Photography

Service Area .... will travel

WWW.MARC-HARRIS-PHOTO.COM

BUCKTOWN—1875 N MILWAUKEE (AT N OAKLEY AVE); 773.342.1960; CALL FOR APPT

Modern Madonnas Pregnancy & Family Portraiture

Service Area ..... Greater Chicago area

WWW.MODERNMADONNAS.COM

NAPERVILLE—3S460 BRIGGS AVE (AT BUTTERFIELD RD); 312.543.2265; CALL FOR APPT

Nicole Thomas Photography

"...amazing with kids... will come to your home—very convenient... she even made great suggestions for frames and albums to match my decor... stunning pregnancy shots... an unbelievable photographer with a real talent for capturing children's natural beauty and innocence... well worth every penny... attention to detail is unsurpassed..."

Customer service........................ ❺ $$$..................................... Prices

WWW.NICOLETHOMASPHOTO.COM

CHICAGO—773.764.6778

Photography by Jacob VanVooren

"...Jacob doesn't settle for the obvious... our favorite shot was of our twin's backs... his patience made all the difference—we had so much fun that my kids can't wait for their next session... we brought a bunch of toys just in case, but didn't end up needing them... I loved the black and white shots... unique, simple, fabulous... also reasonably priced..."

Customer service........................ ❺ $$....................................... Prices

WWW.JACOBVANVOOREN.COM

LINCOLN PARK/DEPAUL/OLD TOWN—2640 N HALSTED (AT W WRIGHTWOOD AVE); 773.871.2000; M-W F 10-6

Picture People

"...this well-known photography chain offers good package deals that get even better with coupons... generally friendly staff despite the often 'uncooperative' little customers... they don't produce super fancy, artistic shots, but you get your pictures in under an hour... reasonable quality for a fast portrait... kind of hit-or-miss quality and customer service..."

Customer service........................ ❹ $$$..................................... Prices

WWW.PICTUREPEOPLE.COM

AURORA—1428 FOX VALLEY CTR (AT E NEW YORK ST); 630.585.5400; M-SA 10-9, SU 11-6

BLOOMINGDALE—319 STRATFORD SQUARE MALL C19 (AT W SCHICK RD); 630.582.4120; M-SA 10-9, SU 11-6; MALL PARKING

CHICAGO RIDGE—631 CHICAGO RIDGE (AT W 95TH ST); 708.422.1486; M-SA 10-9, SU 11-6; MALL PARKING

GURNEE—6170 W GRAND AVE (AT GURNEE MILLS MALL); 847.855.1350; M-SA 10-9, SU 11-7; MALL PARKING

JOLIET—3340 MALL LOOP DR (AT LOUIS JOLIET MALL); 815.436.8472; M-SA 10-9, SU 11-6; MALL PARKING

LOMBARD—168 YORKTOWN SHOPPING CTR (AT S HIGHLAND AVE); 630.916.8223; M-F10-9, SA 10-7, SU 11-6

OAK BROOK—89 OAKBROOK CTR (AT KINGERY HWY); 630.575.0207; M-SA 10-9, SU 11-6; MALL PARKING

ORLAND PARK—268 ORLAND SQ DR (AT W 151ST ST); 708.403.0244; M-SA 10-9, SU 11-6

SAINT CHARLES—3800 E MAIN ST (AT CHARLESTOWNE MALL); 630.513.8620; M-SA 10-9, SU 11-6; MALL PARKING

SCHAUMBURG—5 WOODFIELD MALL (AT GOLF RD); 847.995.0081; MALL PARKING

SKOKIE—86 OLD ORCHARD SHOPPING CTR (AT GOLF RD); 847.763.1290; M-SA 10-9, SU 11-6

SOUTH SIDE—444 CHICAGO RIDGE MALL DR (AT 95TH ST); 708.422.1486; M-SA 10-9, SU 11-6; MALL PARKING

VERNON HILLS—716 HAWTHORN CTR (AT E TOWNLINE RD); 847.918.9594; DAILY 10-9, APPTS RECOMMENDED

Sadies

“...a mall-based studio that takes great pictures that are ready in an hour... we have been there twice and will continue to go back... they take a whole roll of pictures to choose from... great staff that is always happy, even when baby isn't... creative photography with props, costumes and funky digital effects... ”

Customer service .... ❹ $$$ .... Prices

WWW.SADIESONLINE.COM

NORTHBROOK—2020 NORTHBROOK CT (AT LAKE COOK RD); 847.559.8960; M-F 10-9, SA 10-7, SU 11-6

Sears Portrait Studio

“...the price is right, but the service and quality are variable... make an appointment to cut down on the wait time... bring your coupons for even better prices... perfect for getting a nice wallet size portrait without spending a fortune... I wish the wait time for prints wasn't so long (2 weeks)... the quality and service-orientation of the photographers really vary a lot—some are great, some aren't... ”

Customer service .... ❸ $$ .... Prices

WWW.SEARSPORTRAIT.COM

ARCHER HEIGHTS/BRIGHTON PARK/GAGE PARK—6153 S WESTERN AVE (AT W 62ND ST); 773.918.4216; M W TH-F 9:30-8, T 9:30-6, SA-SU 9:30-6

AURORA—1951 W GALENA BLVD (AT S EDGELAWN DR); 630.906.1055

BLOOMINGDALE—5 STRATFORD SQ MALL (AT S GARY AVE); 630.924.2792; M-SA 10-8, SU 11-6; MALL PARKING

DOWNERS GROVE—1400A 75TH ST SPC 13 (AT DUNHAM RD); 630.663.1051

IRVING PARK/MAYFAIR—4730 W IRVING PARK RD (AT N CICERO AVE); 773.202.2379; M-F 9:30-8, SA 9-8, SU 10-5

LOOP—2 N STATE ST (AT W MADISON ST); 312.373.6069; M W TH-F 10-8, T SA 10-6, SU 11-6

MCKINLEY PARK—6501 95TH ST (AT CHICAGO RIDGE MALL); 708.346.8069; M-F 10-8, SA 9-8, SU 10-6

NILES—400 GOLF MILL CTR (AT N GREENWOOD AVE); 847.803.7578; M-SA 10-8, SU 11-7

NORTH RIVERSIDE—7503 W CERMAK RD (AT NORTH RIVERSIDE MALL); 708.588.6669; M-; MALL PARKING

OAK BROOK—2 OAKBROOK CTR (AT KINGERY HWY); 630.575.1873; M-SA 10-8, SU 11-6; MALL PARKING

RAVENSWOOD—1900 W LAWRENCE AVE (AT WOLCOTT AVE); 773.769.8324; M W TH-F 10-8, T 10-6, SA 10-6, SU 11-7

SAINT CHARLES—3102 E MAIN ST (AT CHARLESTOWNE MALL); 630.513.3299; M-F 10-8, SA 9-8, SU 11-5

SCHAUMBURG—2 WOODFIELD MALL (AT GOLF RD); 847.330.2366; M-SA 10-7, SU 11-4; MALL PARKING

SOUTH SIDE—1334 E 79TH ST (AT S KENWOOD AVE); 773.933.2090; M-F 9:30-7, T 9:30-5, SA 9:30-5, SU 11-5

SOUTH SIDE—7601 S CICERO AVE (AT FORD CITY SHOPPING CTR); 773.284.4298; M-F 10-8, T SA SU 10-6

VERNON HILLS—2 HAWTHORNE CTR (AT E COURTLAND ST); 847.918.2245; M-SA 10-8, SU 11-6

Sorrells Signature Portraits

WWW.SSPORTRAITS.COM

LA GRANGE—301 W HILLGROVE (AT N CATHERINE AVE); 708.354.0684; M-T-TH-F 10-6, SA 10-5

Tricia Koning Photography

Service Area ..... Greater Chicago area

WWW.TKPHOTOART.COM

SHERIDAN PARK/UPTOWN—1807 W SUNNYSIDE (AT N RAVENSWOOD AVE); 773.561.4178; CALL FOR APPT

Online

clubphoto.com

WWW.CLUBPHOTO.COM

dotphoto.com

WWW.DOTPHOTO.COM

flickr.com

WWW.FLICKR.COM

kodakgallery.com

"...the popular ofoto.com is now under it's wings... very easy to use desktop software to upload your pictures on their site... prints, books, mugs and other photo gifts are reasonably priced and are always shipped promptly... I like that there is no limit to how many pictures and albums you can have their site..."

WWW.KODAKGALLERY.COM

photoworks.com

WWW.PHOTOWORKS.COM

shutterfly.com

"...I've spent hundreds of dollars with them—it's so easy and the quality of the pictures is great... they use really nice quality photo paper... what a lifesaver—since I store all of my pictures with them I didn't lose any when my computer crashed... most special occasions are take care of with a personal photo calendar, book or other item with the cutest pictures of our kids... reasonable prices..."

WWW.SHUTTERFLY.COM

snapfish.com

"...great photo quality and never a problem with storage limits... we love their photo books and flip books—easy to make and fun to give... good service and a good price... we have family that lives all over the country and yet everyone still gets to see and order pictures of our new baby..."

WWW.SNAPFISH.COM

indexes

alphabetical

by city/neighborhood

alphabetical

A J Wright....14, 60
A Pea In The Pod.... 92, 102, 106
ABC Dentistry....225
ABC Pediatrics, Ltd....227
Active Endeavors....14, 45
Active Endeavors Kids....15
Active Kids....15
Adler Planetarium & Astronomy Museum....120
Advanced Pediatrics....228
Advocate Good Shepherd Hospital....216
Advocate Health Center Sykes....224
Advocate Illinois Masonic Medical Center....216
Alamo Shoes....15
Alfie's Inn....191
Alliance Francaise....120
American Girl Place....168
Ann Sather....168
Applebee's Neighborhood Grill. 185, 199
April Cornell.... 35, 45, 60
Archer Park....156
Armour Square Park....156
Art Craft Photographers....244
Art Institute Of Chicago....120
Art Of Breastfeeding....230
Associates In Pediatric Care....226
Association of Labor Assistants & Childbirth Educators (ALACE)....204
Avalon Park....156
Babies N Beds....35
Babies R Us.... 36, 46, 61, 74, 230
Baby, Baby & More....36
Baby Depot At Burlington Coat Factory.... 16, 36, 46, 61, 74, 75, 92, 98, 102, 106, 111
Baby PhD....16, 121
BabyGap/GapKids.... 16, 36, 37, 46, 47, 61, 62, 75
Baja Fresh....185
Ballin Pharmacy....231
Banta Park....163
Barnes & Noble.... 121, 134, 139, 144, 151
Barneys New York....17
Baron's Shoes....17
Beansprout....17
Bear With Me....236
Bearfoot Fun & Fitness Center....144
Becker Pharmacy....231
Beef O'Brady's....191
Belle Plaine Studio....121
Bellini.... 17, 47, 62
Belly Dance Maternity....93, 103
Benihana....169
Bessemer Park....156
Beverly Arts Center, The....121
Big Bowl.... 169, 180
Birthways....216
Bixler Playlot....157
Bloom Yoga Studio....206, 217
Bloomingdale's....18
Bogan Park....157
Bombay Kids.... 18, 37, 62, 75
Borders Books... 121, 122, 134, 135, 139, 140, 145, 151
Bottoms Up Diaper Service....234
Bradley Method, The....217
Bravo Cucina Italiana....185
Breast Pumps Plus....231
Bronzeville Children's Museum....151
Brookfield Zoo....145
Brooks Park....157
Bubbles Academy....122, 206
Buffalo Wild Wings....191
Build-A-Bear Workshop.... 122, 135, 145, 152
Bulldog Boot Camp....206
Buzz Cafe....192
Cafe De Luca....169
Cafe Selmarie....169
Cafe Winberie....192
Caldwell Woods....157
California Pizza Kitchen.... 170, 180, 186, 192
Calumet Park....157
Camera Park....165
Caro Mio....170
Carrara Children's Shoes....18
Carson Pirie Scott....93
Carter's.... 19, 47, 62, 63
Celebrity Kids Portrait Studio....244
Center For Body & Soul....214
Champps Restaurant....186
Cheeburger Cheeburger....186
Cheesecake Factory, The.... 170, 192
Chevys Fresh Mex.... 181, 193
Chicago Beaches....157
Chicago Botanic Garden....140
Chicago Childrens Museum....122
Chicago Cultural Center....123
Chicago Historical Society....123
Chicago River Walk....158
Chicago Water Tower....123
Child In You, The.... 107, 231
Children & Teens Medical Center....225
Children's Health Partners....227
Children's Memorial Hospital Outpatient Clinic....224
Children's Museum In Oak Lawn....152
Children's Museum of Immigration (Swedish American Museum Center)....123
Children's Orchard....75
Children's Place, The.... 19, 47, 63
Chili's Grill & Bar.... 193, 199

participate in our survey at

Chocolate Soup....48
Chopin Park....158
Chuck E Cheese's.... 123, 135, 140, 146, 152
Classic Kids....244
Condell Medical Center (Childbirth & Family Education)....217
Cookie Cutters Haircuts....236
Corner Bakery Cafe.... 170, 171, 181, 186, 187, 193, 199
Corner Playroom....124
Cosley Zoo....146
Costco.... 19, 37, 48, 63
Country Classics....48
Country Kitchen....187
Cradles & All....64
Cut Rate Toys....20
Daydreams....48
Deerfield Farmers Market....140
Delnor Community Health....213
Delnor Community Hospital (NewLife Maternity Programs)....217
Deluxe Diner....171
Denny's.... 193, 200
Disney Store, The....20
Doulas of North America (DONA)....204
DuPage Children's Museum....146
DuSable Museum of African American History....124
Early Notes Music Studio....146
East Bank Club....206
Ed & Annette's Monkeys & More....124
Ed Debevic's Short Orders Deluxe....171, 194
Edward Hospital (Parent Education Center)....217
El Cid 2....171
Eli's Cheescake Factory....124
Elm Street Pediatrics....226
Elmhurst Memorial Hospital (Parent Education)....218
Elmhurst Pediatric Association....227
Emerald City Theater Company....124
Equinox Fitness Club....207
ESPN Zone....172
Euro Bimbi....49
Evanston Athletic Club Yoga....211
Evanston Northwestern Healthcare (Maternity Services)....218
Exploritorium....140
Faded Rose....20
Fantasy Kingdom....125
Fazoli's....200
Feast....172
Fellger Park....158
Fellger Playlot....158
Field Museum, The....125
Firetruck Park (Huntington Estates)....165
Flat Top Grill.... 172, 187, 194
Fleet Feet Sports....93
Forest Grove Athletic Club....135
Francesca's Amici....194
Fuddruckers.... 181, 187, 194, 195, 200
FurnitureKidz....37
Galt Toys & Galt Baby....20, 49, 231
Gap Maternity....93, 98, 111
Garfield Park Conservatory....125
Giggles & Giraffes....49
Gill Park....158
Gino's East Of Chicago....172
Glam To Go....21
Glen Ellyn Clinic....227
Global Yoga & Wellness Center . 207, 218
Goudy Square Playlot Park....158
Grant Park....159
Great Clips....236, 237
Gross Playground....159
Gymboree....21, 38, 49, 64, 76
Gymboree Play & Music.... 125, 135, 141, 146
H & M....21, 38, 50, 64, 76, 93, 94, 99, 103, 107, 112
Hal Tyrell Trailside Museum....147
Hancock Observatory....126
Handlebar Bar & Grill....172
Hands On Children's Art Museum....126
Hanna Andersson....38, 65
Hard Rock Cafe....173
Harold Washington Playlot Park....159
Harvester Park....165
Healing Power Yoga....211
Health World Children's Museum....136
Heller Nature Center.... 141, 164
Helmut Berens Park....165
Hilary's Urban Eatery....173
Hinsdale Hospital (Childbirth & Parenting)....218
Homefirst Family Practice....224
Hummer Park....165
Hunan Beijing....181
Hyde Park Art Center....126
Hyde Park School of Ballet....126
IKEA....39, 182
Ina's....173
Indian Boundary Park....159
Indian Garden....173
Initial Choice....50
Jacadi....22, 50
Jack's Family Restaurant....187
Janie And Jack....39, 51
JCPenney....22, 39, 51, 65, 76, 94, 99, 103, 107, 112
JCPenney Portrait Studio....245
Jeepers....147
Jefferson Playlot Park....159
Jessica Tampas Photography....245
Jewish Community Center.... 126, 136, 141, 152, 211
John's Place....173
Johnny Rockets....174, 188
Jordan Marie....22, 40
Julium Meinl Cafe....174
Jump N Style....51
Juniper Park....159

KB Toys................ 22, 23, 40, 51, 65, 77
Kid's Foot Locker......... 23, 40, 52, 66, 77
Kiddie Kandids..................................245
Kiddieland...147
Kids Hair 237
Kidsnips 237
Kitsch'n...174
Kohl's................ 23, 52, 66, 77, 94, 103, 107, 112
Kohl's Children's Museum of Greater Chicago 141
Krista K Boutique 94
La Grange Memorial Hospital.............218
La Leche League................................204
Lactation Associates 204
Lake Forest Pediatric Associates..........226
Lakeshore Athletic Club......................207
Lala Land...66
Lamaze International..........................219
Lamb's Farm.....................................142
Land of Nod.......................... 23, 52, 66
Lazar's Juvenile Furniture.....................53
Lego Store..24
Leona's 174, 175, 195, 200
Leona's Daughters Restaurant...........175
Lewis & Associates 227
Li'l Deb-N-Heir Children's Furniture 67
Lifeline Theatre..................................127
Lifetime Fitness..................................210
Lillstreet Art Center 127
Lincoln Park.......................................159
Lincoln Park Athletic Club 207
Lincoln Park Conservatory 127
Lincoln Park Zoo................................127
Little Chick Shoe Shop.........................53
Little Gym, The.......... 127, 136, 142, 147
Little Louie's Red Hots 188
Little Munchkins..................................41
Little Soles...24
Little Threads.......................................24
Lollie 53
Lookingglass Theatre.........................128
Lou Malnati's Pizzeria............... 175, 182
Lou Mitchell's Restaurant 175
Loyola Park.......................................160
Luis A. Weiss Memorial Hospital.........219
M & Em's 67
Madison & Friends...............................25
Marc Harris Photography...................246
Margies Candies................................175
Marshall Fields...................................108
Martinelli's Maternity Wear 112
Max & Erma's....................................195
McCormick & Schmicks......................175
McShane's Exchange...........................94
Medici...176
Menomonee Club 128
Mexican Fine Arts Center Museum.....128
Michael's Chicago Style Red Hots.......188
Midwest Pediatrics, Ltd......................227
Millennium Park 160
Mimi Maternity 95, 99, 104, 108, 113
Mocha Moms 219
Modern Madonnas Pregnancy & Family Portraiture 246
Moksha Yoga Center.........................208
MOMS Club 219
Moondance Diner.............................195
Morton Arboretum 147
Motherhood Maternity .95, 99, 104, 108, 109, 113
Mothers and More............................219
Mt Sinai Hospital (Women's Health)...220
Mud Pies 53
Museum Of Science & Industry 128
Music Together.......... 129, 136, 142, 148
Musical Magic 129
My Child's Room 25, 41, 54, 67
My Gym Children's Fitness Center 129, 137, 142, 148, 153
My Own Little Room...........................78
Nanny On The Net, A.........................240
Naper Settlement..............................148
Naperville Riverwalk..........................166
Neiman Marcus 25
Niazi, Ahsan MD...............................228
Nicole Thomas Photography 246
Nordstrom 25, 54, 67
Nordstrom Cafe................................176
North Avenue Beach.........................160
North Park Village Nature Center....... 129
Northwest Community Hospital (Health Connection) 220
Northwestern Children's Practice, The 224
Northwestern Memorial Hospital (Women & Maternity Classes) 204, 220
Northwestern Memorial Physicians Group 224
Oak Park Conservatory 148
Oak Park Farmers Market..................149
Oak Street Beach 160
Odyssey Fun World...................149, 153
Oilily 26, 54
Old Navy.......26, 41, 55, 68, 78, 95, 100, 104, 109, 113
Old Town School Of Folk Music 130
Olive Garden 182, 188, 195, 196, 201
Olive You Nanny Agency 240
On the Wings Of an Angel Domestic Agency Placement..........................240
Once Upon A Bagel 188
Once Upon A Child.................27, 42, 68
Oriental Institute Museum 130
Original Pancake House 176, 182, 189, 196, 201
OshKosh B'Gosh...........................55, 69
Oz Park..160
Palos Community Hospital (Maternal & Child Education) 204, 220
Panang Noodles & Rice 176
Parent Circle, The 220
Parkway Drugs......................27, 55, 231
Payless Shoe Source................27, 42, 69
Pediatric Care Associates 225

Pediatric Care PC ... 225
Pediatric Health Care ... 226
Pedios ... 227
Pelican Harbor Aquatic Park ... 149
Penny's Noodle Shop ... 176, 196
Peterson Park ... 160
Peterson's Pharmacy ... 231
Petit Feet ... 27
Photography by Jacob VanVooren ... 246
Picture People ... 246, 247
Piggy Toes ... 28
Pirate's Cove ... 137
PJ Clarke's ... 177
Portage Park ... 161
Portage Park Center for the Arts ... 130
Portage Park Pool ... 130
Pottery Barn Kids ... 28, 42, 56
Priory Park ... 166
Psychobaby ... 28
Quig's Orchard ... 143
Rainbow Kids ... 29, 69, 78
Red Apple Pancake House ... 196
Red Balloon Company ... 30
Red Robin ... 183, 189, 196
Reel Moms (Loews Theatres) ... 130, 137, 143
Rehm Park ... 166
Resurrection Medical Center (Family Birthplace) ... 221
Ridge Park ... 161
Ridgeland Common Recreation Center ... 149
Right Start, The ... 30, 56, 70, 231
River Forest Pediatrics ... 227
River Grove Clinic ... 227
RJ Grunt's ... 177
Rocking Horse ... 70
Romano's Macaroni Grill ... 183, 189, 197
Room & Board ... 30, 56, 70
Rooms 4 Kids ... 43
Royal Children's Spa ... 237
Ruby Tuesday ... 197
Rush University Medical Center--Pediatric Group ... 224
Rush-Presbyterian (St Luke's Medical Center) ... 221
Sadies ... 247
School of Ballet Chicago, The ... 130
Scoozi ... 177
Sears ... 30, 31, 43, 56, 70, 71, 96, 100, 105, 109
Sears Portrait Studio ... 247, 248
Sears Tower Skydeck ... 131
Seascape Family Aquatic Center ... 138
Second Child ... 31
Shedd Aquarium ... 131
Sherman Hospital (Childbirth Education) ... 221
Sherwood Conservatory Of Music ... 131
Shop Elizabeth Marie ... 31
Silver Cross Hospital (Childbirth Classes) ... 221
Sing 'n Dance ... 131
Six Flags Hurricane Harbor ... 143
Smokey Bones BBQ ... 183, 197
Snackville Junction ... 201
Snip N' Doodles Kids Salon ... 237
Snippet's Mini Cuts ... 238
Sorrells Signature Portraits ... 248
Souplantation/Sweet Tomatoes. 183, 190, 197
Special Delivery ... 71
Spring Valley Nature Center & Heritage Farm ... 138
St James Hospital (Community Education) ... 222
St Joseph Hospital ... 222
Stella's Diner ... 177
Strasburg Children ... 31, 57
Streeterville Pediatrics ... 224
Stride Rite Shoes ... 57, 71
Stroller Fit ... 208
Sunshine Playlot ... 161
Supercuts ... 238
SuperDawg ... 177
Suzuki-Orff School for Young Musicians ... 132
Sweet Occasions ... 177
Sweet Pea's Studio ... 208
Swell Maternity ... 96
T-Shirt Deli, The ... 32
Talbots Kids ... 32, 57, 71
Target ... 32, 33, 43, 58, 72, 79, 97, 100, 101, 105, 110, 114
TGI Friday's ... 178, 184, 190, 197, 198, 202
Three Pillars Wellness Center ... 208
Tiddlywinks & Scallywags ... 72
Toast Two ... 178
Tommy-Terri Shop ... 43
Town & Country Pediatrics ... 224
Toys Et Cetera ... 33, 58
Toys R Us ... 33, 44, 58, 72, 73, 79
Tricia Koning Photography ... 248
Turning Point ... 222
Ty Warner Park ... 166
Ukrainian Village Children's Center ... 132
Uncommon Ground ... 178
Unique So Chique ... 33
Universal Spirit Yoga ... 213
Value City ... 34
Vernon Hills Pediatrics ... 225
Village Green Park ... 164
Village Tavern & Grill ... 184, 198
Von Maur ... 59, 73
Vose-Sanders Bootery ... 59
Walk A Bye Baby ... 208
Walker Brothers Original Pancake House ... 190
Walsh Playground Park ... 161
Washington Square Park ... 161
Waterworks ... 138
Welles Park ... 161
Wesley Shoe Corral ... 34

West Suburban Pediatrics....................227
Wheaton Pediatrics 227
Whipper Snippers Hair Cuts 238
Wicker Park...162
Wild Child..59
Wilder Park 166
Wishbone Restaurant..........................178
Wonder Works....................................149
World Folk Music Company 132
Wrigley Field 132
YMCA.............. 132, 133, 138, 143, 150, 153, 209, 210, 212, 213, 214
Yoshi's Cafe.......................................179

by city/neighborhood

Addison

Fuddruckers....194

Algonquin

Borders Books....134
FurnitureKidz....37
Red Robin....183

Archer Heights/Brighton Park/Gage Park

Chuck E Cheese's....123
Rainbow Kids....29
Sears Portrait Studio....247
Target....32, 97

Arlington Heights

Baby Depot At Burlington Coat Factory....36, 98
BabyGap/GapKids....36
Banta Park....163
Barnes & Noble....134
California Pizza Kitchen....180
Corner Bakery Cafe....181
Kidsnips....237
Motherhood Maternity....99
My Child's Room....41
My Gym Children's Fitness Center....137
Northwest Community Hospital (Health Connection)....220
Olive Garden....182
Original Pancake House....182
Rooms 4 Kids....43
Target....43, 100
Toys R Us....44

Ashburn

Rainbow Kids....29

Aurora

BabyGap/GapKids....61
Carter's....62
Fuddruckers....194
H & M....64, 107
JCPenney....65, 107
JCPenney Portrait Studio....245
KB Toys....65
Marshall Fields....108
Motherhood Maternity....108
My Child's Room....67
My Gym Children's Fitness Center....148
Oshkosh B'gosh....69
Picture People....246
Sears Portrait Studio....247
Smokey Bones BBQ....197
TGI Friday's....197
Toys R Us....72

Avondale

Leona's....174
Resurrection Medical Center (Family Birthplace)....221
Target....32, 97

Back of the Yards

Value City....34

Barrington

Advocate Good Shepherd Hospital....216
Children & Teens Medical Center....225
Health World Children's Museum....136
Little Munchkins....41
Music Together....136
Pediatric Care PC....225
Tommy-Terri Shop....43

Belmont Central

Kid's Foot Locker....23

Beverly

Borders Books....121
Royal Children's Spa....237

Big Oaks

Eli's Cheescake Factory....124

Bloomingdale

Art Craft Photographers....244
Baby Depot At Burlington Coat Factory....61, 106
BabyGap/GapKids....61
Barnes & Noble....144
Children's Place, The....63
Chili's Grill & Bar....193
Costco....63
Gymboree....64
JCPenney Portrait Studio....245
KB Toys....65
Motherhood Maternity....108
Old Navy....68
Olive Garden....195
Payless Shoe Source....69
Picture People....246
Sears....70, 109
Sears Portrait Studio....247
Supercuts....238
TGI Friday's....198
Toys R Us....72

Bolingbrook

Borders Books....145
Carter's....63
Music Together....148
Olive Garden....195
Pelican Harbor Aquatic Park....149
TGI Friday's....198

Bridgeport

Armour Square Park 156

Brookfield

Brookfield Zoo 145

Bucktown

Belly Dance Maternity 93
Cafe De Luca 169
Global Yoga & Wellness Center207, 218
Handlebar Bar & Grill 172
Kohl's 23, 94
Marc Harris Photography 246
My Gym Children's Fitness Center 129
Penny's Noodle Shop 176
Psychobaby 28
Red Balloon Company 30
T-Shirt Deli, The 32
Toast Two 178
Walsh Playground Park 161

Buffalo Grove

Jewish Community Center 136
Music Together 136
My Gym Children's Fitness Center 137

Burbank

Babies R Us 74, 230
Kiddie Kandids 245
Kohl's 77, 112
Olive Garden 201
Toys R Us 79

Burr Ridge

Harvester Park 165
Max & Erma's 195
Moondance Diner 195

Canaryville/Fuller Park

Rainbow Kids 29

Carol Stream

Great Clips 236
Red Apple Pancake House 196
Village Tavern & Grill 198

Chicago

Active Endeavors 14
Alliance Francaise 120
Association of Labor Assistants & Childbirth Educators (ALACE) 204
Barneys New York 17
Belle Plaine Studio 121
Bradley Method, The 217
Brooks Park 157
Chicago Beaches 157
Chicago Historical Society 123
Chicago River Walk 158
Chicago Water Tower 123
Corner Bakery Cafe 170
Disney Store, The 20
Doulas of North America (DONA) ... 204
Field Museum, The 125
Gross Playground 159
Jewish Community Center 126
La Leche League 204
Lamaze International 219
Lego Store 24
Lifeline Theatre 127
Lillstreet Art Center 127
Lincoln Park Athletic Club 207
Margies Candies 175
Menomonee Club 128
Mexican Fine Arts Center Museum . 128
Mocha Moms 219
Mothers and More 219
Music Together 129
Nanny On The Net, A 240
Nicole Thomas Photography 246
Olive You Nanny Agency 240
Oriental Institute Museum 130
Original Pancake House 176
Parent Circle, The 220
Rainbow Kids 29
Room & Board 30
Sears 30, 96
Strasburg Children 31
Stroller Fit 208
Sweet Occasions 177
Talbots Kids 32
Town & Country Pediatrics 224
Walk A Bye Baby 208
Wrigley Field 132
YMCA 132, 209

Chicago Ridge

KB Toys 77
Motherhood Maternity 113
Old Navy 78
Picture People 246

Chinatown

YMCA 132, 209

Columet Heights

A J Wright 14
Rainbow Kids 29
YMCA 133, 209
Kohl's 77, 112

Countryside

Baby Depot At Burlington Coat Factory 61, 106

Crystal Lake

Barnes & Noble 134
Borders Books 134
Corner Bakery Cafe 181
Gymboree Play & Music 135
TGI Friday's 184

participate in our survey at

Deer Park
April Cornell 35
BabyGap/GapKids 36
Barnes & Noble 134
California Pizza Kitchen 180
Gap Maternity 98
Gymboree 38
Kids Hair 237
Mimi Maternity 99
Pottery Barn Kids 42

Deerfield
Baja Fresh 185
Barnes & Noble 139
Borders Books 139
Carter's 47
Children's Place, The 47
Deerfield Farmers Market 140
Kidsnips 237

Downers Grove
Barnes & Noble 144
Fuddruckers 194, 195
Hummer Park 165
Music Together 148
Old Navy 68
Olive Garden 195
Once Upon A Child 68
Ruby Tuesday 197
Sears Portrait Studio 247
Toys R Us 72
YMCA 150, 213

East/West Old Town
A Pea In The Pod 92
Bear With Me 236
Children's Place, The 19
Great Clips 236
Hard Rock Cafe 173
Johnny Rockets 174
Madison & Friends 25
McCormick & Schmicks 175
Moksha Yoga Center 208
Panang Noodles & Rice 176
Scoozi 177
Washington Square Park 161
YMCA 133, 209

Edgebrook
Cut Rate Toys 20
SuperDawg 177

Edgewater
Alamo Shoes 15
Ann Sather 168
Birthways 216
Borders Books 121
Children's Museum of Immigration (Swedish American Museum Center) 123
Deluxe Diner 171
Leona's 174
Rainbow Kids 29

Elgin
Sherman Hospital (Childbirth Education) 221
Target 43, 100

Elk Grove Village
Payless Shoe Source 42
Pirate's Cove 137

Elmhurst
Bearfoot Fun & Fitness Center 144
Buffalo Wild Wings 191
Elmhurst Memorial Hospital (Parent Education) 218
Elmhurst Pediatric Association 227
Francesca's Amici 194
Helmut Berens Park 165
Kohl's 66, 107
Lala Land 66
Music Together 148
Wilder Park 166
YMCA 150, 213

Englewood
Sears 31, 96

Evanston
Active Endeavors 45
Barnes & Noble 139
Borders Books 139
Evanston Athletic Club Yoga 211
Evanston Northwestern Healthcare (Maternity Services) 218
Flat Top Grill 187
Little Chick Shoe Shop 53
Lollie 53
Mud Pies 53
Music Together 142
Resurrection Medical Center (Family Birthplace) 221
Target 58, 105
Toys Et Cetera 58
Vose-Sanders Bootery 59
Wild Child 59

Evergreen Park
Bronzeville Children's Museum 151
Martinelli's Maternity Wear 112
Rainbow Kids 78
Snackville Junction 201

Flossmoor
Jewish Community Center 152

Ford City
Bogan Park 157
KB Toys 22
Kid's Foot Locker 23
Rainbow Kids 29
Sears 31, 96

Garfield Park

Garfield Park Conservatory 125
Kid's Foot Locker 23
Rainbow Kids 29

Geneva

April Cornell 60
Barnes & Noble 144
Borders Books 145
California Pizza Kitchen 192
Carter's 63
Celebrity Kids Portrait Studio 244
Child In You, The 107, 231
Cookie Cutters Haircuts 236
Corner Bakery Cafe 193
Cradles & All 64
Delnor Community Health 213
Delnor Community Hospital (NewLife Maternity Programs) 217
Gymboree Play & Music 146
Mimi Maternity 108
Old Navy 68
Snip N' Doodles Kids Salon 237
Special Delivery 71

Glen Ellyn

Alfie's Inn 191
Beef O'Brady's 191
M & Em's 67
Music Together 148
Tiddlywinks & Scallywags 72

Glencoe

Active Endeavors 45
Chicago Botanic Garden 140
Parkway Drugs 55, 231

Glendale Heights

Camera Park 165
Jeepers 147
Target 72, 110

Glenview

Bravo Cucina Italiana 185
Cheeburger Cheeburger 186
Corner Bakery Cafe 186
Costco 48
Country Classics 48
Evanston Northwestern Healthcare (Maternity Services) 218
Jump N Style 51
Kohl's 52, 103
Kohl's Children's Museum of Greater Chicago 141
Little Gym, The 142
Music Together 142
Original Pancake House 189
Souplantation/Sweet Tomatoes 190
Strasburg Children 57
Target 58, 105
TGI Friday's 190
Von Maur 59

Gold Coast/Streeterville

BabyGap/GapKids 16
Barnes & Noble 121
Benihana 169
Big Bowl 169
Bloomingdale's 18
Borders Books 121
California Pizza Kitchen 170
Cheesecake Factory, The 170
Corner Bakery Cafe 170
Goudy Square Playlot Park 158
Gymboree 21
H & M 21, 93
Hancock Observatory 126
Jacadi 22
Mimi Maternity 95
Northwestern Children's Practice, The 224
Oak Street Beach 160
PJ Clarke's 177

Grand Crossing

Sears 31, 96

Gresham

Rainbow Kids 29

Gurnee

Applebee's Neighborhood Grill 185
Baby Depot At Burlington Coat Factory 46, 102
BabyGap/GapKids 46
Borders Books 139
H & M 50, 103
KB Toys 51
Little Gym, The 142
Motherhood Maternity 104
Old Navy 55
OshKosh B'Gosh 55
Picture People 246
Six Flags Hurricane Harbor 143
Target 58, 105
TGI Friday's 190

Hamilton Park

Rainbow Kids 29

Harvey

YMCA 153, 214

Highland Park

A Pea In The Pod 102
BabyGap/GapKids 46
Bellini 47
Belly Dance Maternity 103
Borders Books 140
Corner Bakery Cafe 186
Country Kitchen 187
Daydreams 48
Euro Bimbi 49
Evanston Northwestern Healthcare

(Maternity Services)..........................218
Fuddruckers..187
Healing Power Yoga 211
Heller Nature Center.............. 141, 164
Michael's Chicago Style Red Hots ...188
Once Upon A Bagel 188
Right Start, The..........................56, 231
Toys R Us..58
Walker Brothers Original Pancake House..190

Hillside

Leona's...195

Hinsdale

Corner Bakery Cafe 193
Hinsdale Hospital (Childbirth & Parenting)..218
On the Wings Of an Angel Domestic Agency Placement...........240

Hoffman Estates

ABC Dentistry...................................225
Hunan Beijing...................................181
My Child's Room 41
Payless Shoe Source............................42
Pediatric Care Associates 225
Romano's Macaroni Grill.................183
Seascape Family Aquatic Center......138
TGI Friday's.......................................184

Homewood

Leona's..200

Humboldt Park

Children's Place, The..........................19
Old Navy.....................................26, 95
Rainbow Kids.......................................29
YMCA 133, 209

Hyde Park

Harold Washington Playlot Park 159
Hyde Park Art Center.......................126
Jewish Community Center 126
Leona's..174
Medici 176
Museum Of Science & Industry 128
Three Pillars Wellness Center 208
Toys Et Cetera 33

Irving Park/Mayfair

Ed & Annette's Monkeys & More 124
Once Upon A Child.............................27
Portage Park 161
Portage Park Pool 130
Sears Portrait Studio 247
YMCA 133, 209

Joliet

Applebee's Neighborhood Grill 199
Barnes & Noble.................................151
Chuck E Cheese's 152
Fazoli's 200
JCPenney 76, 112
JCPenney Portrait Studio 245
KB Toys 77
Motherhood Maternity...................113
Niazi, Ahsan MD 228
Old Navy 78
Picture People 246
Silver Cross Hospital (Childbirth Classes)..221
TGI Friday's 202
Toys R Us 79

Kilbourn Park/Kelvyn Park/Hermosa

Archer Park 156

Kildeer

Old Navy 41, 100

La Grange

Corner Bakery Cafe..........................193
La Grange Memorial Hospital 218
Lewis & Associates 227
Sorrells Signature Portraits..............248

La Grange Park

Original Pancake House..................196

Lake Forest

Initial Choice 50
Lake Forest Pediatric Associates......226

Lake Zurich

Costco 37
Great Clips..237
Original Pancake House..................182
TGI Friday's 184
YMCA.................................... 138, 210

Lakeview/Wrigleyville

Advocate Illinois Masonic Medical Center..216
Ann Sather..168
BabyGap/GapKids 16
Barnes & Noble 121
Beansprout...17
Borders Books 121
Emerald City Theater Company 124
Flat Top Grill.....................................172
Gill Park 158
Gino's East Of Chicago....................172
Great Clips...............................236, 237
Gymboree Play & Music..................125
Jewish Community Center 126
Julium Meinl Cafe 174
Krista K Boutique 94
Leona's 174
Penny's Noodle Shop.......................176
Petit Feet..27
Resurrection Medical Center (Family Birthplace)..221

Shop Elizabeth Marie 31
Stella's Diner 177
Uncommon Ground 178
Yoshi's Cafe 179

Lansing

Babies R Us 74, 230
Baby Depot At Burlington Coat Factory 74, 111
Olive Garden 201
Toys R Us 79

Lawndale

Mt Sinai Hospital (Women's Health) 220

Libertyville

BabyGap/GapKids 46
Condell Medical Center (Childbirth & Family Education) 217
Lamb's Farm 142

Lincoln Park/DePaul/Old Town

Active Endeavors Kids 15
Active Kids 15
BabyGap/GapKids 16
Barnes & Noble 121
Bellini 17
Bombay Kids 18
Borders Books 122
Bubbles Academy 122, 206
Carrara Children's Shoes 18
Carter's 19
Celebrity Kids Portrait Studio 244
Children's Memorial Hospital Outpatient Clinic 224
Classic Kids 244
Corner Playroom 124
Equinox Fitness Club 207
Faded Rose 20
Flat Top Grill 172
Fleet Feet Sports 93
Galt Toys & Galt Baby 20, 231
Great Clips 237
Gymboree 21
Gymboree Play & Music 125
John's Place 173
Kidsnips 237
Lakeshore Athletic Club 207
Land of Nod 23
Lincoln Park 159
Lincoln Park Conservatory 127
Lincoln Park Zoo 127
Little Soles 24
Lookingglass Theatre 128
McShane's Exchange 94
Menomonee Club 128
North Avenue Beach 160
Old Town School Of Folk Music 130
Original Pancake House 176
Oz Park 160
Parkway Drugs 27, 231
Penny's Noodle Shop 176
Photography by Jacob VanVooren .. 246
Piggy Toes 28
Pottery Barn Kids 28
Right Start, The 30, 231
RJ Grunt's 177
Second Child 31
Sing 'n Dance 131
Snippet's Mini Cuts 238
St Joseph Hospital 222
Sunshine Playlot 161
Suzuki-Orff School for Young Musicians 132
Swell Maternity 96
Toys Et Cetera 33
YMCA 133, 209

Lincoln Square

Cafe Selmarie 169

Lincolnshire

Original Pancake House 189
Red Robin 189

Lincolnwood

Great Clips 237
KB Toys 51
Kohl's 52, 103
Lazar's Juvenile Furniture 53
Motherhood Maternity 104
Old Navy 55, 104
Olive Garden 188

Lisle

Morton Arboretum 147

Little Village

Rainbow Kids 29

Logan Square

Art Of Breastfeeding 230
El Cid 2 171
Jewish Community Center 126

Lombard

Babies R Us 61, 230
BabyGap/GapKids 62
Bombay Kids 62
Ed Debevic's Short Orders Deluxe ... 194
Gymboree 64
JCPenney 65, 107
JCPenney Portrait Studio 245
KB Toys 65
Kid's Foot Locker 66
Kiddie Kandids 245
Motherhood Maternity 108
My Child's Room 67
Picture People 246
Snippet's Mini Cuts 238
TGI Friday's 198

Von Maur 73

Long Grove

Baby, Baby & More 36

Loop

Art Institute Of Chicago..................120
Borders Books.................................122
Carson Pirie Scott 93
Chicago Cultural Center 123
Corner Bakery Cafe 170, 171
Grant Park 159
H & M 21, 94
Kid's Foot Locker 23
Lakeshore Athletic Club 207
Lou Mitchell's Restaurant................175
Millennium Park..............................160
Mimi Maternity.................................95
Motherhood Maternity 95
Old Navy......................................26, 95
Payless Shoe Source.........................27
School of Ballet Chicago, The 130
Sears Portrait Studio 247
Sears Tower Skydeck 131

Marquette Park

Hyde Park School of Ballet 126
Rainbow Kids....................................29

Matteson

Advanced Pediatrics........................228
Baby Depot At Burlington Coat
Factory 75
Borders Books.................................151
Chuck E Cheese's 152
Fazoli's 200
Fuddruckers....................................200
Kid's Foot Locker 77
Old Navy..78
Olive Garden 201
Target......................................79, 114
Toys R Us...79

McKinley Park

Sears Portrait Studio 247

Medical Village

Leona's...174
Supercuts 238

Melrose Park

Denny's 193
Kiddieland 147
Resurrection Medical Center
(Family Birthplace)..........................221
Target......................................72, 110
Toys R Us...72
Toys R Us...33

Morgan Park

Baron's Shoes 17
Beverly Arts Center, The 121

Mundelein

Baby Depot At Burlington Coat
Factory 46, 102
Gymboree Play & Music.................141
My Child's Room.............................54
Quig's Orchard...............................143

Naperville

ABC Pediatrics, Ltd 227
Babies R Us 61, 230
Baby Depot At Burlington Coat
Factory 61, 106
Barnes & Noble 144
Borders Books 145
Chevys Fresh Mex..........................193
Children's Health Partners 227
Chuck E Cheese's..........................146
Cookie Cutters Haircuts.................236
Corner Bakery Cafe 193
Costco 63
DuPage Children's Museum 146
Early Notes Music Studio 146
Edward Hospital (Parent Education
Center)...217
Firetruck Park (Huntington Estates). 165
Kiddie Kandids 245
Li'l Deb-N-Heir Children's Furniture .. 67
Little Gym, The..............................147
Midwest Pediatrics, Ltd..................227
Modern Madonnas Pregnancy &
Family Portraiture 246
Motherhood Maternity...................108
Music Together 148
Naper Settlement 148
Naperville Riverwalk 166
Odyssey Fun World........................149
Old Navy 68
Olive Garden 195
Once Upon A Child 68
Right Start, The 70, 231
TGI Friday's 198
Universal Spirit Yoga 213

Near North

American Girl Place 168

Near South Side

Advocate Health Center Sykes........224
Target 97
YMCA..................................133, 209

Niles

Babies R Us 46, 230
Costco 48
JCPenney 51, 103
JCPenney Portrait Studio 245
KB Toys 51
Kid's Foot Locker.............................52
Kiddie Kandids 245
Kohl's......................................52, 103
Motherhood Maternity...................104
My Child's Room.............................54

Sears 56, 105
Sears Portrait Studio 247
Stride Rite Shoes 57
Target....................................58, 105
Toys R Us...58
YMCA 143, 212

North Center/St Ben's

Bulldog Boot Camp 206
Juniper Park 159
Little Threads 24

North Ravenswood

North Park Village Nature Center....129
Peterson Park..................................160

North Riverside

Baby Depot At Burlington Coat Factory 61, 106
JCPenney..................................65, 107
JCPenney Portrait Studio.................245
KB Toys 65
Kohl's.......................................66, 107
Motherhood Maternity 108
Old Navy..68
Olive Garden 195
Rainbow Kids....................................69
Sears 70, 109
Sears Portrait Studio 247
Stride Rite Shoes 71
Toys R Us...73

Northbrook

April Cornell 45
BabyGap/GapKids 47
Corner Bakery Cafe 186
Galt Toys & Galt Baby 49
Gymboree 49
Gymboree Play & Music 141
Jacadi 50
Janie And Jack 51
Jewish Community Center..... 141, 211
Johnny Rockets...............................188
Lactation Associates........................204
Land of Nod 52
Little Louie's Red Hots.....................188
Mimi Maternity...............................104
Oilily 54
Sadies...247
Snippet's Mini Cuts.........................238
Stride Rite Shoes 57
Village Green Park 164

Oak Brook

A Pea In The Pod 106
BabyGap/GapKids 62
Borders Books.................................145
Build-A-Bear Workshop 145
Cheesecake Factory, The.................192
Corner Bakery Cafe 193
Costco..63
Gymboree 64
Hanna Andersson 65
Kidsnips 237
Land of Nod 66
Motherhood Maternity...................108
Music Together 148
Nordstrom..67
Old Navy 68, 109
Picture People 247
Room & Board..................................70
Sears 70, 109
Sears Portrait Studio.......................247
Talbots Kids......................................71

Oak Forest

Original Pancake House..................201

Oak Lawn

Breast Pumps Plus 231
Children's Museum In Oak Lawn.... 152
Denny's..200
Great Clips 237
Leona's 200

Oak Park

BabyGap/GapKids 62
Borders Books 145
Buzz Cafe.......................................192
Cafe Winberie 192
Denny's..193
Flat Top Grill...................................194
Leona's 195
Music Together 148
Oak Park Conservatory...................148
Oak Park Farmers Market 149
Old Navy 68
Original Pancake House..................196
Pedios 227
Penny's Noodle Shop......................196
Peterson's Pharmacy.......................231
Rehm Park......................................166
Resurrection Medical Center (Family Birthplace)......................................221
Ridgeland Common Recreation Center..149
Rocking Horse 70
TGI Friday's 198
Wonder Works...............................149

Oakbrook Terrace

Barnes & Noble 144
Bellini 62
Denny's..193
West Suburban Pediatrics...............227

Oakland/Kenwood

Baby PhD 16, 121
Borders Books 122
Wesley Shoe Corral 34

Orland Park

Babies R Us 74, 230

BabyGap/GapKids....75
Barnes & Noble....151
Bombay Kids....75
Borders Books....151
Build-A-Bear Workshop....152
Children's Orchard....75
Chili's Grill & Bar....199
Corner Bakery Cafe....199
Gap Maternity....111
Gymboree....76
H & M....76, 112
JCPenney....76, 112
JCPenney Portrait Studio....245
KB Toys....77
Kiddie Kandids....245
Mimi Maternity....113
Motherhood Maternity....113
My Gym Children's Fitness Center....153
My Own Little Room....78
Old Navy....78, 113
Original Pancake House....201
Picture People....247
TGI Friday's....202
Toys R Us....79

Palatine

Forest Grove Athletic Club....135
Fuddruckers....181
Music Together....136
Sears....43, 100
Target....43, 100
YMCA....138, 210

Palos Heights

Center For Body & Soul....214
Palos Community Hospital (Maternal & Child Education)....204, 220

Pilsen

St James Hospital (Community Education)....222

Portage Park

Caldwell Woods....157
Chopin Park....158
KB Toys....23
Portage Park Center for the Arts....130
Sears....31, 96

Pulaski Park

Homefirst Family Practice....224

Ravenswood

Becker Pharmacy....231
Bloom Yoga Studio....206, 217
Caro Mio....170
Old Town School Of Folk Music....130
Sears Portrait Studio....247
Welles Park....161

River Forest

Children's Place, The....63
Hal Tyrell Trailside Museum....147
Motherhood Maternity....108
My Gym Children's Fitness Center....148
Priory Park....166
River Forest Pediatrics....227

River Grove

A J Wright....60
River Grove Clinic....227

River North/River West

BabyGap/GapKids....16
Big Bowl....169
Bloomingdale's....18
Build-A-Bear Workshop....122
California Pizza Kitchen....170
Cheesecake Factory, The....170
Chicago Childrens Museum....122
Children's Place, The....19
Corner Bakery Cafe....171
East Bank Club....206
Ed Debevic's Short Orders Deluxe....171
Gap Maternity....93
Gino's East Of Chicago....172
Indian Garden....173
Jordan Marie....22
Lakeshore Athletic Club....207
Leona's....175
Lou Malnati's Pizzeria....175
My Child's Room....25
Neiman Marcus....25
Nordstrom....25
Nordstrom Cafe....176
Northwestern Memorial Hospital (Women & Maternity Classes)....204, 220
Northwestern Memorial Physicians Group....224
Oilily....26
Parkway Drugs....27, 231
Payless Shoe Source....27
Reel Moms (Loews Theatres)....130
Sears....31, 96
Streeterville Pediatrics....224
TGI Friday's....178

Riverside

Kid's Foot Locker....66

Roscoe Village/West Lakeview

Ballin Pharmacy....231
Costco....19
Fellger Park....158
Fellger Playlot....158
Glam To Go....21
Kitsch'n....174
Little Gym, The....127
Motherhood Maternity....95
Musical Magic....129

Old Navy....26
Sweet Pea's Studio....208
Target....32, 97
Toys R Us....33
Wishbone Restaurant....178
YMCA....133, 209

Roseland

Rainbow Kids....29
YMCA....133, 209

Saint Charles

Borders Books....145
Gymboree....64
Olive Garden....196
Picture People....247
Sears....71, 109
Sears Portrait Studio....247
Souplantation/Sweet Tomatoes....197
TGI Friday's....198
Toys R Us....73
Von Maur....73

Sauganash

YMCA....133, 209

Schaumburg

Babies R Us....36, 230
BabyGap/GapKids....37
Barnes & Noble....134
Big Bowl....180
Bombay Kids....37
Borders Books....135
Build-A-Bear Workshop....135
California Pizza Kitchen....180
Chevys Fresh Mex....181
Corner Bakery Cafe....181
Costco....37
Fuddruckers....181
Gymboree....38
H & M....38, 99
Hanna Andersson....38
IKEA....39, 182
Janie And Jack....39
JCPenney....39, 99
JCPenney Portrait Studio....245
Jordan Marie....40
KB Toys....40
Kiddie Kandids....245
Lifetime Fitness....210
Little Gym, The....136
Lou Malnati's Pizzeria....182
Mimi Maternity....99
Motherhood Maternity....99
My Gym Children's Fitness Center....137
Old Navy....41
Olive Garden....182
Once Upon A Child....42
Payless Shoe Source....42
Picture People....247
Red Robin....183
Reel Moms (Loews Theatres)....137
Sears....43, 100
Sears Portrait Studio....248
Smokey Bones BBQ....183
Souplantation/Sweet Tomatoes....183
Spring Valley Nature Center & Heritage Farm....138
Target....43, 101
TGI Friday's....184
Toys R Us....44
Village Tavern & Grill....184
Waterworks....138

Sheridan Park/Uptown

Borders Books....122
Leona's Daughters Restaurant....175
Loyola Park....160
Luis A. Weiss Memorial Hospital....219
Rainbow Kids....29
Sears....31, 96
Tricia Koning Photography....248
Unique So Chique....33

Skokie

Associates In Pediatric Care....226
BabyGap/GapKids....47
Barnes & Noble....139
California Pizza Kitchen....186
Champps Restaurant....186
Chuck E Cheese's....140
Corner Bakery Cafe....186, 187
Exploritorium....140
Gymboree....49
Gymboree Play & Music....141
Jack's Family Restaurant....187
Janie And Jack....51
Jewish Community Center....141
Johnny Rockets....188
Mimi Maternity....104
Motherhood Maternity....104
My Gym Children's Fitness Center....142
Nordstrom....54
Old Navy....55, 104
Pediatric Health Care....226
Picture People....247
Pottery Barn Kids....56
Reel Moms (Loews Theatres)....143
Romano's Macaroni Grill....189
Room & Board....56
Supercuts....238
Talbots Kids....57
Turning Point....222

South Loop

Adler Planetarium & Astronomy Museum....120
Jefferson Playlot Park....159
Shedd Aquarium....131
Sherwood Conservatory Of Music....131
YMCA....133, 209

South Side

Avalon Park 156
Baby Depot At Burlington Coat Factory 16, 92
Bessemer Park 156
Bixler Playlot 157
Calumet Park 157
Children's Place, The 19
Gymboree 21
Hands On Children's Art Museum 126
JCPenney 22, 94
Leona's 175
Motherhood Maternity 95
Old Navy 26, 95
Original Pancake House 176
Picture People 247
Ridge Park 161
Sears Portrait Studio 248
Target 33, 97
Toys R Us 33
World Folk Music Company 132

Stoney Island

Rainbow Kids 29

Streamwood

Babies N Beds 35
Chuck E Cheese's 135

Tinley Park

Baby Depot At Burlington Coat Factory 75, 111
Chuck E Cheese's 152
Odyssey Fun World 153

United Center Park

Rush University Medical Center--Pediatric Group 224

Vernon Hills

Babies R Us 36, 230
BabyGap/GapKids 37
Barnes & Noble 134
Build-A-Bear Workshop 135
Gymboree 38
JCPenney 39, 99
JCPenney Portrait Studio 245
KB Toys 40
Kid's Foot Locker 40
Kiddie Kandids 245
Kidsnips 237
Motherhood Maternity 99
Olive Garden 182
Picture People 247
Sears Portrait Studio 248
Target 43, 101
TGI Friday's 184
Toys R Us 44
Vernon Hills Pediatrics 225

Villa Park

Baby Depot At Burlington Coat Factory 61, 106
Chuck E Cheese's 146
Once Upon A Child 68
Target 72, 110

Warrenville

Red Robin 196

Washington Park

DuSable Museum of African American History 124

Waukegan

Bottoms Up Diaper Service 234

West Loop

Corner Bakery Cafe 171
Flat Top Grill 172
Rush-Presbyterian (St Luke's Medical Center) 221
Wishbone Restaurant 178
Ina's 173

West Rogers Park

Indian Boundary Park 159
Indian Garden 173
YMCA 133, 209

Westmont

Gymboree Play & Music 146
Ty Warner Park 166

Wheaton

Barnes & Noble 144
Borders Books 145
Cosley Zoo 146
Glen Ellyn Clinic 227
Gymboree Play & Music 146
Kidsnips 237
Mimi Maternity 108
Music Together 148
Old Navy 68
Red Robin 196
Romano's Macaroni Grill 197
Talbots Kids 71
Wheaton Pediatrics 227

Wicker Park/Ukranian Village

Active Endeavors 14
Ann Sather 168
California Pizza Kitchen 170
Fantasy Kingdom 125
Feast 172
Hilary's Urban Eatery 173
Jessica Tampas Photography 245
Leona's 175
Old Navy 26
Payless Shoe Source 27
Rainbow Kids 29

Resurrection Medical Center (Family Birthplace)....................221
Ukrainian Village Children's Center....................132
Wicker Park....................162

Wilmette

Borders Books....................140
Giggles & Giraffes....................49
Kidsnips....................237
Music Together....................142
Parkway Drugs....................55, 231
Walker Brothers Original Pancake House....................190

Winnetka

Chocolate Soup....................48
Classic Kids....................244
Elm Street Pediatrics....................226
Vose-Sanders Bootery....................59

Woodlawn

Rainbow Kids....................29
YMCA....................133, 209

Woodridge

Motherhood Maternity....................109
Music Together....................148
Whipper Snippers Hair Cuts....................238

Notes

YOUR RECOMMENDATIONS MAKE THE LILAGUIDE BETTER!
PLEASE SHARE YOUR NOTES WITH US AT WWW.LILAGUIDE.COM

Notes

YOUR RECOMMENDATIONS MAKE THE LILAGUIDE BETTER!
PLEASE SHARE YOUR NOTES WITH US AT WWW.LILAGUIDE.COM

Notes

YOUR RECOMMENDATIONS MAKE THE LILAGUIDE BETTER!
PLEASE SHARE YOUR NOTES WITH US AT WWW.LILAGUIDE.COM

Notes

YOUR RECOMMENDATIONS MAKE THE LILAGUIDE BETTER!
PLEASE SHARE YOUR NOTES WITH US AT WWW.LILAGUIDE.COM